SCHAUM'S OUTLINE OF

THEORY AND PROBLEMS

of

COLLEGE BUSINESS LAW

•

by

R. ROBERT ROSENBERG, Ed.D., C.P.A.
Educational Consultant
Former President of Jersey City Junior College

and

WILLIAM G. OTT, LL.B.
President and Director of Law
Goldey Beacom College

SCHAUM'S OUTLINE SERIES
McGRAW-HILL BOOK COMPANY

New York St. Louis San Francisco Auckland Bogotá Düsseldorf Johannesburg London Madrid Mexico Montreal New Delhi Panama Paris São Paulo Singapore Sydney Tokyo Toronto

0-07-053805-0

5 6 7 8 9 10 11 12 13 14 15 16 17 18 19 20 SH SH 8 7 6

Library of Congress Cataloging in Publication Data

Rosenberg, Reuben Robert, 1900-

Schaum's outline of theory and problems of college business law.
(Schaum's outline series)
Includes index.

1. Commercial law—United States. I. Ott, William G., joint author. II. Title. III. Title: Theory and problems of college business law.
KF889.R67 346'.73'07 77-940

ISBN 0-07-053805-0

Preface

Law can be defined as the rules of conduct governing people in their relations to one another. The law prescribes what is right and prohibits what is wrong. It has often been said that the United States is a nation governed by law. This means that our society is not simply ruled by those who happen to have the most power or the greatest influence. Instead, it means that *all* people in our society, regardless of their social status or economic position, have certain rights and certain obligations. Likewise, businesses and other organizations, including our government itself, must abide by the rights and obligations that the law has established.

As a citizen, as a seller or consumer, as a tenant or homeowner, and as an employer or employee, you have and will continue to have certain rights and obligations. Some of these rights and obligations are outlined in the United States Constitution and the various state constitutions. Others are contained in federal, state, county, and local statutes—laws duly enacted by legislative bodies. Still other rights and obligations depend on judicial precedents—court decisions that may modify and interpret any given law. Finally, the common law—the legal tradition passed down to us from our Founding Fathers and the English legal system—contributes the basic beliefs on which our entire legal system is built.

Business law, as a field of study, takes its principles from all of these sources—constitutions, statutes, judicial decisions, and the common law. Thus, business law is a complex and ever-changing field, responding to constitutional amendments, new statutes, judicial decisions, and the constantly changing environment of modern business. To further complicate matters, the laws of one state or locality do not necessarily agree with those of another.

The Uniform Commercial Code (U.C.C.) has done much to standardize business law in this country. The Code was formulated in 1952 by the National Conference of Commissioners on Uniform State Laws. The Code was offered to the state legislatures, and all states except Louisiana adopted it.

As you study this Outline, you will notice many references to the Code. You should always keep in mind, however, that laws do still differ from state to state and from locality to locality. In any real-life situation, it is always best to check local laws and ordinances and, if necessary, to seek professional legal advice.

Schaum's Outline of College Business Law presents to the reader a concise statement of the basic principles of American business law. The Outline may be used as a self-teaching tool, in and of itself. It may also be used in conjunction with a standard textbook and classroom instruction.

Each chapter begins with a discussion of *legal theory*. Almost every principle set forth is illustrated with a hypothetical case from everyday life.

Following the statement of legal theory in each chapter is a group of *Solved Problems*. In each problem, a case is described, and the probable outcome is explained. These problems contain specific examples of the principles covered at the beginning of the chapter, including exceptions to and refinements of these principles.

Review Problems, which appear near the end of each chapter, are questions about the theories and principles discussed. They will provide a helpful self-test of your grasp of legal theory.

Finally, each chapter contains a list of important *Legal Terms*. Like all disciplines, the law has a specialized vocabulary, and familiarity with it is essential.

In addition, four quarterly examinations and a comprehensive examination, with solutions, are provided in the Outline. By taking each examination, you should be able to measure how well you have mastered the legal theory and its practical applications.

R. ROBERT ROSENBERG
WILLIAM G. OTT

CONTENTS

PART I: Contracts

Chapter 1

Formation of Contracts

A contract is an agreement between two competent parties. The agreement is based on mutual promises to do or to refrain from doing some particular thing that is neither illegal nor impossible. A contract serves as a form of personal law, willingly agreed to, permitting parties to bind themselves to legally enforceable obligations not required under either federal, state, or the common law. Once made, a contract obligates the parties, and courts will enforce it with the dignity given the enforcement of all laws governing persons, businesses, and governments.

Parties obligate themselves to one another by many types of contracts. Sometimes an agreement is made between only two persons. In other cases, two or more parties may join together for the purpose of contracting with other parties. In this chapter we will review the essentials of law related to the formation of valid, enforceable agreements. Succeeding chapters will deal with the actual operation and final discharge of contracts.

THE CONTRACT AGREEMENT

1.1 Requisites of a Contract

To be enforceable as a contract, an agreement must contain four essentials:

1. Mutual Assent (See Sections 1.2 – 1.17.)
2. Competent Parties (See Sections 1.18 – 1.25.)
3. Consideration (See Sections 1.26 – 1.31.)
4. Valid Subject Matter (See Sections 1.32 – 1.40.)

Many *social agreements* also contain these four essentials, but only in rare cases are social agreements enforceable as contracts.

EXAMPLE 1. Torbert accepted Jordan's proposal that they go to the Fall Cotillion together. In return for Jordan's willingness to purchase tickets and pay all expenses, Torbert set aside the time and restricted herself from doing anything else on the evening of the dance. Although the agreement contained mutual consent, competent parties, consideration, and was lawful, the courts would be very reluctant to define the arrangement between Jordan and Torbert as a contract. It was merely a social agreement.

MUTUAL ASSENT

1.2 Communication, Intent, and Clarity

Mutual assent consists of an offer made by an *offeror* to an *offeree* and the offeree's unconditional acceptance of that offer. To be valid, the offer must have been communicated, seriously intended, and in terms that are clear and understandable.

EXAMPLE 2. Hastings advertised a reward of $50 to anyone who would return his lost luggage. MacDonald found the luggage with its name-tags attached and he returned it to Hastings. MacDonald had not, however, seen Hastings' advertisement. Although there was a strong moral obligation to give MacDonald the $50 reward, there was no legal obligation because there was no contract between them. (Some states now have statutes that make reward payments mandatory even when the finder has not seen the owner's advertisement.)

EXAMPLE 3. In a moment of great emotional distress, the owner of a stolen car shouted out, "I'll give $1,000 to anyone who will find the thief and return my car to me." The offer, while communicated to everyone within earshot and clear in its terms, was not seriously intended. People who are intoxicated, mentally ill, emotionally upset, or acting in a spirit of frolic and fun are not held responsible for what might otherwise be a seriously intended offer. The owner of the stolen car would not be obligated to pay the $1,000 reward.

1.3 Requests for Bids Are Not Offers

A proposal seeking bids or estimates is not an offer. The parties submitting bids are usually defined as the offerors. Bids for large undertakings must often be submitted along with a bond that assures the bidder's performance if the bid is accepted.

EXAMPLE 4. The city of Dover proposed the construction of a modern jail by submitting specifications and engineering drawings to three building contractors. DeMasi, one of the contractors, submitted the lowest bid. DeMasi incorrectly claimed that he had a contract with the city of Dover. To create a contract with DeMasi, the city of Dover would have had to accept his bid, and it had not done so. The party receiving bids is not obligated to accept the lowest bid. Qualifications of ability, reputation, financial stability, and other matters may be considered in the final acceptance of any bid.

1.4 Invitations to Trade

An offer is made to one person or a collective group, not to several people. An announcement seeking potential offers and made in a newspaper or other public medium is called an *invitation to trade*. An invitation to trade is not an offer. Invitations to trade seek to interest many persons, with the intent that one or all will respond with offers to purchase the merchandise or services advertised.

EXAMPLE 5. Cottman's General Store advertised a special sale of women's stockings for 79¢ a pair. The advertisement had been incorrectly printed; it should have read 99¢ rather than 79¢. Many shoppers demanded the stockings for 79¢, the advertised price. The advertisement was an invitation to trade, not an offer. Customers going to the store made offers, which could be accepted or rejected by the store. (Consumer-protection laws often contradict the law of contracts in such matters. Such laws may require that the store sell merchandise as advertised, even when the advertisement contains an honest mistake. Under such circumstances, the store would have to seek reimbursement from the advertising medium for damages resulting from the mistake.)

1.5 Disposition of an Offer

Offers may be (1) accepted, (2) rejected, or (3) revoked. Acceptance of an offer requires communication to the offeror and must be made in terms the same as those contained in the offer.

EXAMPLE 6. Heald Truck Company wrote Lincoln Van Lines, offering to sell four available vans for $18,000 each if all four were purchased in one deal. Lincoln answered, stating that they would buy only two of the vans for $15,000 each if the seller would paint and letter the vans according to specifications supplied by Lincoln. Acceptance had been *communicated,* but the conditions and changes made by the offeree terminated the offer. Offers made between merchants, however, are not summarily terminated by changes or additions made by the offeree.

1.6 Duration of an Offer

Communication of an offer by telegram implies the necessity of expressing acceptance without delay. Excessive delay serves to invalidate the offer.

EXAMPLE 7. Burchnall received a telegram from the Rockville Realty Company. In the telegram, Rockville offered Burchnall a vacation home on Lake Michigan for $38,000. Burchnall took several days to discuss the matter with his family. Eight days after receiving the offer, Burchnall wrote a letter of acceptance. The long delay in replying to the telegram may have invalidated the offer.

1.7 Silence as Acceptance

Silence or the failure to act may indicate acceptance of an offer only when such has been agreed to by both the offeror and the offeree.

EXAMPLE 8. Carrington agreed to have his television set connected to the local cable system on a trial basis. Carrington stated that if he decided to keep the connection and be billed, he would *not* contact the company. If he did not want to continue the service beyond the trial period, he would call and cancel. Carrington and the company agreed that silence would indicate acceptance.

1.8 Rejection of an Offer

An offeree may *reject* an offer either by communicating with the offeror or by not reacting in any way to the offer. Rejection terminates an offer. Rejection may also result from an offeree's *counteroffer*.

EXAMPLE 9. Stanley received a message from Martin Home Decorators in which they offered to paint the interior of his house for $1,900. Stanley informed Martin that the price was too high and contacted other painters. Comparison of other offers proved that Martin Home Decorators had given the best price. Stanley would have no assurance that Martin would be willing to reopen negotiations at the $1,900 price originally quoted.

1.9 Revocation of an Offer before Acceptance

The offeror may revoke an offer any time before it has been accepted. Revocation by the offeror may be done through communication to the offeree; it may be automatic because of the terms of the offer; it may be caused by the passing of more than a reasonable length of time; or it may occur because of the death or insanity of the offeror.

EXAMPLE 10. Accurate Machine Sales offered five stenography machines to Sanderson. The machines were in almost-new condition and were offered at less than one-half the average wholesale price. Sanderson was given six days in which to make up his mind. Without waiting for Sanderson's reply, Accurate sold the machines only two days after making the offer. Sanderson was informed at once of the sale. An offeror may withdraw, or revoke, an offer *any time up until the time it is accepted.* (This rule does not apply when offers are made *between merchants.*)

1.10 Automatic Revocation through Delay

If no time period for acceptance is specified in an offer, it remains valid for a "reasonable period of time" unless it is revoked by the offeror. A "reasonable period of time" is determined by the *custom of the market place*—what others in the same trade would deem to be reasonable under the circumstances.

EXAMPLE 11. Heavy Equipment, Inc., offered the city of Centerville a road grader for $18,500. No time limit was indicated in the written offer. The town board delayed decision on the purchase for three months. They then sent a letter of acceptance. The price of heavy construction equipment fluctuates with the market and with inflationary trends. Waiting three months was too long in this case. The offer would have revoked itself after the passing of a reasonable length of time—an uncertain length of time, but obviously less than three months.

1.11 Options

By mutual agreement and contract, an offeror and offeree may enter into an *option agreement.* An option agreement is a contract obligating the offeror to keep an offer open—at a stated price and for a set period—in return for a payment of *earnest money* by the offeree. An option removes the offeror's right to revoke the offer.

EXAMPLE 12. Murray offered to sell a 3.5-hp gasoline engine to Casper for $57. Casper asked for a week to consider the deal and gave Murray $5 earnest money to hold the offer open. Murray and Casper had a contract called an option. Murray would be held guilty of a breach of contract if he withdrew the offer or sold the engine to another buyer during the one-week option period. If Casper decided to exercise his option and buy the mower, he would owe Murray only $52, since he had already paid $5 as earnest money. If, however, he decided not to buy the mower, he would forfeit the earnest money. (Murray could, of course, return the earnest money as a goodwill gesture, but he is under no obligation to do so.)

1.12 Void and Voidable Contracts

Contracts are voidable by a wronged party when the other party is guilty of having used fraud, deception, misrepresentation, duress, or undue influence in securing the other's acceptance. Mutual mistakes, those made innocently by both parties, also void an existing agreement. Using threats against a person or a person's family or property is known as *duress*. Agreements arrived at under duress are also voidable.

EXAMPLE 13. Shorter Real Estate Developers offered MacLary $8,000 an acre for his farm. MacLary knew the land was worth twice that amount as a potential housing project. Shorter threatened to build an undesirable industrial plant on acres adjoining the farm if MacLary would not accept the $8,000 offer. Any agreement based on these facts would be voidable by MacLary because of the threats (duress) used by Shorter.

1.13 Fraud

To void a contract by a claim of *fraud,* the wronged party must prove that the agreement was created through the other's false statements or deception, knowingly made by one party with intent that the other party rely on such false statements or deceptions.

EXAMPLE 14. Riley was solicited by a salesman who offered to coat Riley's blacktop driveway with a sealer preparation. Riley agreed, but when the work was finished he discovered that old crankcase drainings, rather than the promised sealer, had been used. The salesman's proven statements amounted to fraud, and Riley would not be obligated to pay for the work. He may also seek damages for what was done to his driveway.

1.14 Misrepresentation

An action of *misrepresentation* may be brought against one who has made a false statement innocently, with no intent to deceive. The statements in misrepresentation are made in good faith. In actions of misrepresentation, the parties are both released from the contract, each returning to the other any goods or consideration already delivered under the contract.

EXAMPLE 15. Burton Used Cars sold Kirk a five-year-old Plymouth for $600. Kirk showed his new buy to a friend who worked in a Plymouth agency. The friend showed Kirk that the car's motor was from an earlier model and was more than seven years old. If Burton was not aware of the older motor, only an action of misrepresentation would be brought against him. Burton would then return the $600 and Kirk would return the car.

1.15 *Caveat Emptor*

Contracting parties are subject to the principle of *caveat emptor,* which means "Let the buyer beware." Most buyers have an opportunity to examine the goods being sold to them. Buyers who do not take advantage of this opportunity may find out later that what they've bought is damaged or unacceptable in some way. Under the principle of *caveat emptor,* buyers may not return the goods or claim damages, especially if the goods have obvious defects that would have been discovered on ordinary examination. (The principle of *caveat emptor* is not as strictly interpreted today as it once was. New federal, state, and local laws make it easier for consumers to claim damages on merchandise or to return merchandise that they find unacceptable in some way.)

EXAMPLE 16. Hitch bought a welding torch and two gauges from Dale for $75. Dale invited Hitch to examine his purchases before paying, but Hitch did not want to bother. Later, however, Hitch discovered that both gauges were exactly alike, and not the pair he needed for gas welding. Hitch complained about this, but Dale defended himself with a proper claim of *caveat emptor.*

1.16 Undue Influence

Undue influence is the use of one's superior position to achieve another party's acceptance of an unsatisfactory agreement. Undue influence is an acceptable reason for voiding an otherwise enforceable agreement.

EXAMPLE 17. A salesman at Midland Motors attempted to sell a new car to one of his coworkers, the shop foreman. The salesman said that if the foreman did not accept the deal, he would see to it that the foreman would lose his job. (The salesman had great influence with the management of Midland Motors.) If the foreman signed the deal, he could later have it rescinded on grounds of undue influence.

1.17 Mistake

A mistake of fact made by both parties to an agreement renders the agreement voidable. A mistake by one party alone, however, does not automatically void the agreement.

EXAMPLE 18. Sanders bought a lawnmower, thinking it had a four-cycle engine. Later, when he read the instructions, he discovered that he had purchased a lawnmower with a two-cycle engine, which requires a special oil-gasoline mixture. The salesperson did not misrepresent the lawnmower to Sanders. Rather, Sanders alone was careless and made a mistake. Sanders therefore had no legal justification for demanding the return of his money.

COMPETENT PARTIES

1.18 Incapacity to Contract

Contract law protects parties from most agreements that they make when they are minors, mentally ill, or in any way incapable of understanding and comprehending the obligations of a binding agreement. This protection is regarded as a *shield* for incompetent parties, and not as a *sword* giving them advantages over others.

EXAMPLE 19. Faulkner, nineteen years old, realized that his contracts were not enforceable because of his age. He bought an expensive television set for which he agreed to pay $47.50 per month for twelve months. The seller did not know that Faulkner was a minor. After using the set for two months, Faulkner refused to make any additional payments and demanded the return of all money paid. Faulkner had used his incompetence as an advantage; a court of law would probably rescind the agreement and charge Faulkner a reasonable amount for his use of the television.

1.19 Contracts for Necessaries

Most contracts with minors are voidable, but some are not. Contracts for *necessaries*—goods or services relating to health, safety, welfare, or education—are enforceable against minors. Minors who enter into contracts for necessaries are personally liable for the costs of their purchases unless what they have purchased has already been provided to them by their parents or other guardians.

EXAMPLE 20. Reynolds, a minor, purchased a winter coat at a reasonable price. (She lived in a northern state and had no other winter coat.) After wearing the coat for more than four months, she returned it to the store and demanded her money back. Reynolds would not be entitled to the return of the money because the coat was a necessary—she had no other coat and none was supplied by her parents.

1.20 Affirmance of Contract when Minor Reaches Majority

A minor's contract becomes fully enforceable if by act or promise the minor *affirms* the contract after reaching his or her *majority* (legal adulthood). At that time, the minor may either affirm or disaffirm the agreements, with certain restrictions as above (Section 1.19).

EXAMPLE 21. Umbrecht bought a diamond ring on the installment plan when she was within six months of reaching her majority. When, seven months later, she visited the store and made another installment payment on the ring, she *affirmed* the contract. The contract was then treated as if it had been made after Umbrecht reached legal adulthood.

1.21 Emancipation and Abandonment

Minors are *emancipated* when parents cease to assert parental responsibility over them. At that time, the protection given minors is withdrawn, and the minors may freely enter into enforceable agreements of all kinds. *Abandonment* occurs when a minor no longer receives the protection and support of his or her parents' household. Abandonment also removes the restrictions placed on minors in entering into enforceable contracts.

EXAMPLE 22. Stenger and Robinson, both minors, married with the consent of their parents and left home. They set up their own household and supported themselves with jobs. As husband and wife, they contracted to buy furniture on an installment plan, payable over a one-year period. The married couple would have no rights in trying to avoid the responsibilities of their contract for furniture. Although they were both still minors, they had been emancipated and had lost their rights as minors when they married and left their parental homes.

1.22 Minor's Torts and Crimes

The *law of torts* pertains to civil wrongs for which an individual may be held liable in a civil action. A civil wrong, or a *tortious act,* is the commission or omission by one person, without right, of an act which results in injury to the person, property, or reputation of another party. The *law of crimes* pertains to offenses against the state. An offense may be a tort as well as a crime.

The parents of minors less that seven years of age are responsible for their childrens' torts and crimes. Minors older than seven years are responsible for their own torts, unless their parents instruct or condone the torts.

EXAMPLE 23. Wesley, fifteen years old, hit a small girl while riding his bicycle along the sidewalk. At the time, Wesley was not on an errand for his parents nor was he following their expressed wishes. He was riding "on his own." Only Wesley, the minor, would be held responsible for any injuries or damages resulting from his own negligence.

1.23 Mental Incapacity

Persons declared mentally incompetent (*non compos mentis*) by a state agency are not liable for any contracts. Anyone dealing with such persons does so at his or her own risk. It is the responsibility of all people to determine the mental competence of those with whom they deal. Furthermore, it is especially difficult to enforce agreements with any mentally incompetent person when that person's condition is obvious to the other contracting party. (Persons mentally incompetent but not declared so by the state are treated much the same as minors; only agreements for necessaries are enforceable against them.)

EXAMPLE 24. Stephens was under psychiatric care because of mental illness. He was not irrational and posed no threat to those with whom he lived and associated. To a stranger, Stephens gave every evidence of being normal. He had never been declared insane. Only those contracts made for necessaries could be enforceable against Stephens. (Age is not a factor in these cases.)

1.24 Intoxication and Drugs

Persons with a temporary loss of reason (caused by intoxicants, by prescription or nonprescription drugs, or by recurring mental illness) are not obligated on the contracts they make while in an irresponsible condition. To claim incompetence as a defense against contract obligations, it must be shown that the party was unaware of what he or she was doing.

EXAMPLE 25. Swanson attended a party at which he became intoxicated. While in this condition he sold his $225 watch to a more sober guest for $30. The following day, he demanded the return of the watch, offering to give back the $30 the other guest had paid him. Swanson did not know what he was doing when he sold the expensive timepiece for only $30, so the contract could be rescinded and both parties returned to their original positions.

1.25 Enemy Aliens

Contracts made with a person owing allegiance to a country with which the United States is at war are void when such contracts give aid or comfort to the enemy or involve the security of the United States. Persons owing allegiance to a country with which the United States is at war are defined as *enemy aliens*.

EXAMPLE 26. A physicist was employed by a research-and-development corporation engaged in work on new types of nuclear submarines. The man was not an American citizen, although he had resided in this country for fifteen years. War broke out between the country in which he still held citizenship and the United States. Even though the physicist's employment contract had not yet run out, it would be voided due to his professed allegiance to the other country.

CONSIDERATION

1.26 Benefit and Sacrifice

Consideration in contracts consists of elements of *benefit* and *sacrifice* to the contracting parties. *Consideration* may be money or anything else of value given in return for the other's act or promise. Unless there is a benefit and sacrifice *to each party,* the agreement lacks the requisite of consideration.

EXAMPLE 27. Haggerty offered an antique bench to Jones and demanded nothing in return. The offer was accepted, but when Jones arrived to take possession of the bench, Haggerty refused to give it up. Although there had been communication, mutual assent, and competent parties, there had been no benefit to Haggerty. The promise was not enforceable.

1.27 An Act or a Promise May Constitute Consideration

Consideration may consist of an act or promise to do that which the law does not require one to do or a promise to refrain from doing that which the law permits one to do.

EXAMPLE 28. Cleveland promised his son $500 if he would refrain from using nonprescription hallucinatory drugs while living in his parents' home. Cleveland also promised the young man a new car if he would continue his studies and graduate from college. The first promise would not be enforceable because Cleveland's son had to promise nothing more than what the law required. The promise of a new car, however, would be enforceable because the law does not require people to graduate from college.

1.28 Legality of Consideration

To support a contract's enforceability, the consideration must be legal. Promises to make or sell goods prohibited by law or to render illegal services do not satisfy the requirement of consideration.

EXAMPLE 29. O'Sullivan agreed to drive Reuther's truck to Orlando, a city in another state. O'Sullivan was on probation for a crime he had committed three months before and was restricted from driving any motor vehicle. He was also prohibited from leaving the state. The contract was void due to illegality. O'Sullivan would fail in any action brought against Reuther if Reuther failed to pay the amount promised.

1.29 Barren Promise

A *barren promise* is a promise which obligates someone to do that which she or he is already obligated to do either by law or by a previous contract. A promise which obligates someone *not* to do that which is already prohibited, either by law or by a previous contract, is also a barren promise. Barren promises are not valid as consideration.

EXAMPLE 30. Orson, an agent of the FBI, tracked down and arrested an escaped felon. A $2,500 reward had been posted for the person who discovered the criminal and brought him to justice. Orson had no legal right to seek this reward. Because he was employed by a law-enforcement agency, he had a previous obligation to do exactly what he did in this situation. To Orson, the consideration offered constituted a *barren promise*.

EXAMPLE 31. Tingle owed Style Shoppe $325 for a tailored suit and other articles she had purchased a year before. The credit manager proposed that if Tingle would pay the store $250, he would not ask for any further payment. Tingle did nothing more than she was already obligated to do, and the store received less than it was owed. *No consideration* was given by Tingle in return for the reduction of the amount she owed. The law would support Style Shoppe's suit for the balance of $75 still owed.

1.30 Modification of Contracts

The Uniform Commercial Code permits a modification of an executory sales agreement without the need of additional consideration.

EXAMPLE 32. Cycle Shop sold Dunbar a trail bike for $1,350. After the agreement had been written up and signed, Dunbar asked if Cycle Shop would include a visible gas gauge in the purchase. Cycle Shop added this condition to the written agreement even though Dunbar gave no additional consideration. The gas gauge would be considered as a part of the agreement based on the original consideration of $1,350.

1.31 Past Consideration

A promise to pay for something that had been done without expectation of payment is *past consideration*. A promise of past consideration is not enforceable. The intent of consideration must exist at the time a contract or agreement is initially made.

EXAMPLE 33. As a friendly gesture, O'Brien helped Johnson lay the foundations for a new garage Johnson was building next to his house. The work required an entire Saturday. When it was completed, Johnson said to O'Brien, "You were such a great help, I'm going to give you $50 for all you have done." O'Brien entered the job with no expectation of payment. Johnson's promise was *past consideration* and would not support any action by O'Brien to enforce payment of the $50.

VALID SUBJECT MATTER

1.32 Legality of Subject Matter

When the subject matter of an agreement is in conflict with the common law, constitutional law, statutes, or local ordinances, or when the subject matter is contrary to the welfare and security of the public, the agreement is not enforceable.

EXAMPLE 34. Johnson Motor Company offered to install an exhaust system in Higgins's car. The system was one that had been ruled illegal by federal law. The agreement was therefore invalid and not enforceable. Both parties were engaged in an agreement that was prohibited by law.

1.33 "Dirty Hands" Doctrine

The plaintiff in a civil action "may not go into court with dirty hands." This means that one who performs an illegal act for another may not expect the court to support any claim for work done or materials used in the performance of the act.

EXAMPLE 35. Fredericks & Sons installed a septic tank and cesspool to be connected to a new home being built in Sea Crest. Local laws prohibited the installation of sewage systems of this type. Fredericks & Sons would be unsuccessful in seeking payment for work and materials should a civil suit develop. They, along with the homeowner who contracted for the work, were equally wrong. Both parties to the agreement are said to be *in pari delicto* ("in equal fault").

1.34 Divisible Contracts

Illegality confined to one part of a *divisible contract* does not render the other parts of the contract invalid. If the illegality is obviously criminal in nature or is a threat to persons and property, a court decision could, however, void the entire agreement.

EXAMPLE 36. Saunders & Company, Inc., was chartered under the laws of the State of Delaware to operate a chain of auto-accessory stores in three states. The company's management decided to install lunch counters in all stores, a right not provided for in the corporate charter. The lunch counters were operated illegally and could be shut down by a court order, but this would not render the entire corporate charter void. Had the company been engaged, for example, in the importation and sale of illegal merchandise, the corporate charter could be withdrawn because the intent to do wrong would have affected the entire operation.

1.35 Contracts Made on Sundays and Legal Holidays

Agreements made on Sundays and legal holidays are usually regulated by state laws. It is safe to say that contracts made on a Sunday for work to be performed on another business day are usually enforceable. Local law may prohibit enforcement of agreements made at any time for work to be performed on Sundays, with the exception of contracts for work or the sale of goods necessary to the health, welfare, or safety of a party to the contract.

EXAMPLE 37. Harkness contracted with the Heubner Earth Moving Company to have them dig a cellar for a home to be built in upstate Minnesota. The county in which the new home was to be built was one with strict laws regulating construction operations on Sunday. The Harkness job was scheduled to start on August 17, a Sunday. Heubner Construction would not be liable for damages if it postponed the work until August 18, a Monday.

1.36 Gambling and Wagering Contracts

Gambling and wagering agreements are not enforceable in states that prohibit gambling. Insurance contracts, claimed by some to be a type of wager, are enforceable in consideration of the good that comes from spreading a risk of loss to property or life over a great number of contributors to a common fund.

EXAMPLE 38. In a state in which gambling was a crime, Derrickson bet Holliday $50 that he would produce more tons of tomatoes per acre than Holliday would. Both men were excellent farmers, but at the end of the season Holliday's production per acre exceeded Derrickson's. Holliday would fail in any action brought against Derrickson to collect on the wager.

1.37 Usury

Charging more interest than is permitted by state law is called *usury*. Usury is considered a criminal act and may void a loan contract, depending on specific state statutes. Some states void the promise of repayment of both principal and interest; some states excuse the debtor from payment of any interest; other states require the debtor to pay interest according to the rate set by law, not the rate indicated in the contract.

EXAMPLE 39. The Charlestown Finance Company loaned Spencer $500 and accepted Spencer's promissory note to repay the loan in sixty days with interest of $50. The interest charged far exceeded the rate permitted by statute. The note would be unenforceable and penalties would be imposed on the lender according to the laws of the state.

1.38 Licensing Regulations

Contracts made with professional persons and businesses are invalid when such persons or businesses have not complied with the licensing regulations of the state or local government.

EXAMPLE 40. Dr. Jofsky treated patients in City Hospital, where he was a staff physician. Jofsky carried on a practice outside of the city and had secured a license to practice from the state medical board. He had not, however, paid the license fees required of physicians practicing within the city limits. Within the city, the doctor was carrying on an illegal practice because he had failed to comply with the license requirements. Any legal action he brought for the collection of fees for services rendered within the city would be invalid.

1.39 Agreements against Public Policy

Agreements against public policy may be declared void if they in any way affect and/or disregard the best interests of the citizens and the community. Judicial decision and precedent are as important as legislation in determining what agreements come within this definition of illegality.

EXAMPLE 41. The owners of four service stations on a five-mile stretch of highway agreed to increase the price of gasoline by 3¢ per gallon in all four stations. They also agreed that there would be no price reduction unless all four owners met and agreed. This agreement would be invalid and unenforceable because it eliminates competition and harms the rights of consumers in a free market.

EXAMPLE 42. Jones, a certified public accountant, sold his practice to a newly licensed C.P.A. for $38,000. Included in the agreement was the seller's promise not to re-enter the profession for a period of ten years at any location within the same state. This agreement was considered *in restraint of trade* because it was so inclusive as to remove Jones's right to make a living. It would also be unenforceable because it was against the public's interest. Had the agreement been more reasonable, permitting Jones to open a practice beyond a 25-mile radius of his old office and within one or two years, it might have been enforceable.

1.40 Monopolies

Monopolies are generally considered illegal. Exceptions are *legal monopolies,* which provide protection to authors, musicians, painters, and sculptors, and to businesses that operate utilities under the regulations of a state's public-service commission. These monopolies provide protection for the large investment of time and money in the creation and development of individual projects and businesses that serve the public interest.

EXAMPLE 43. Pennsylvania Light & Power was granted a franchise by the state to provide electric energy to industries and other consumers throughout the state. The investment of millions of dollars was necessary to give the services required. The franchise protected the corporation from any invasion of the market by competitors, who might wreck the company's financial investment. The state utility commission would oversee all services and the rates charged customers, making sure that they would be fair and equitable.

EXAMPLE 44. Jefferson spent ten years in researching and writing her historical novel about the exploration of lands west of the Ohio River. When published, the novel was copyrighted in her name. This created a legal monopoly for Jefferson, prohibiting others from copying and selling her writings.

Solved Problems

1.1 Lodge placed an advertisement in the *Evening Journal* seeking a person who might have found his lost dog. The advertisement offered a reward of $25 to the person who would find and return the dog. Haberstadt found the dog and responded to the advertisement, claiming the $25 reward. Lodge refused to give the reward, stating that the advertisement was merely an *invitation to trade.* Must Lodge pay the reward?

An advertisement that seeks out one person is defined as a public offer, not an invitation to trade. The advertisement was directed to the finder, whoever the finder might be. Haberstadt *accepted the offer* by responding to the advertisement that had been communicated through the newspaper. Lodge must pay the $25.

1.2 Tolson signed a contract with a publishing company to purchase a set of books on an installment plan. Tolson alleged that the company's salesman said that the contract would obligate Tolson to twelve payments of $15.95 each. The confirmation Tolson received from the publishing company stated that the installment payments would be $22.95 each. Tolson refused to make the payments, stating in court that there had never been a communication of that information to him. Was Tolson correct in his defense?

There is always a presumption of communication of terms and conditions contained in an agreement signed by the offeree. Some courts may consider a defense that states that an offeree did not have an opportunity to read a contract that was signed. However, Tolson's oral denial of obligation did not overcome the presence of his signature, which acknowledged that he understood what the agreement stated.

1.3 A dairy farmer agreed to sell his farm's daily production to Hurlock Wholesale Milk Producers Association. The agreement was complete in all respects except for the price to be paid per pound for milk delivered to the Association. Is the agreement valid in spite of the lack of clarity in its terms?

An agreement that does not contain a specific price is enforceable if the price may be determined by market conditions or some other measure acceptable to a court. Milk has a daily market price that is determined by supply and demand in the wholesale market and by prices set by state marketing agencies. Thus the agreement made between the farmer and the Association is enforceable.

1.4 The Household Supply Company sent a set of stainless-steel cooking utensils to Harrigan, who had never ordered the cookware. Shortly after receiving the shipment, Harrigan received a letter that instructed her either to begin making a series of twelve monthly payments or to return the utensils to the seller. Harrigan delayed making any decision and subsequently received other letters threatening legal action if the money or utensils were not sent immediately. What were Harrigan's rights and obligations?

The receipt of the merchandise was nothing more than an offer. Harrigan may either accept or reject Household's offer. She is not legally obligated to return the merchandise. Using the cookware would be no different from accepting the seller's offer, thus making her liable for payments. However, Harrigan may store the merchandise in a safe place, keep it for a reasonable time, and then assume that the seller has abandoned any interest in it. At that point she may claim it as her own. Postal regulations permit the recipients of unordered goods delivered by parcel post to treat these goods as a gift, with no obligations whatsoever.

1.5 Warner wrote to King, offering to sell his farm for $135,000. King, anxious to secure the property, wrote back, stating that he accepted the offer. Before King's acceptance reached him, Warner called King and revoked his offer. King brought an action against Warner, charging breach of contract. Did Warner have a contract with King?

If an acceptance is transmitted by the same agent used to transmit the offer, the acceptance is complete as soon as it is given to the agent. The contract between Warner and King was complete as soon as King *mailed* the acceptance. Warner's revocation came too late because one may not revoke an offer that has already been accepted. If, however, the offeree changes the agent's means of transmittal, the acceptance is not complete until it reaches the offeror. If King had replied by letter to a telegram offer from Warner, acceptance would not have been effective until King's letter reached Warner.

1.6 Walker left a suit and spring coat at Smith's for dry-cleaning. When she returned to get her things, two buttons were missing from the coat. Smith pointed out that on the reverse side of the redemption ticket were the words "Not responsible for buttons, bows, discoloration, and defects in materials resulting from cleaning process." Could Walker recover her loss?

Disclaimers included in an agreement are valid only when they are sufficiently conspicuous to get the party's attention. When a disclaimer is printed on the reverse side of a contract or a claim check or in very small type, it will not be accepted as an enforceable condition to the agreement. Terms that reduce the offeror's obligations are valid only when they are clearly included within the body of the agreement. Walker's rights against the cleaner are not reduced by the disclaimer.

1.7 Chapman offered to sell a surfboard to Young for $85. Young inspected the board but said nothing. A day later Young returned and told Chapman that he was accepting the offer. In the meantime, Chapman had sold the board to another party, who took it as soon as it was offered. Was Chapman obligated to Young?

Young implied a rejection when he walked away without making any comment about Chapman's offer. The rejection was not expressed, but it was clearly implied. Chapman was free to sell the board to anyone else.

1.8 Insley called Huber and offered him $15 to wash and wax his (Insley's) car. Huber gave no immediate reply, saying only "I'll think about it." Two weeks later Huber, without Insley's knowledge, washed and waxed the car during Insley's absence. Was Insley obligated to pay Huber for the work done?

Insley made an offer that could have created a *unilateral contract,* a contract in which a promise is made in return for another's act. However, Huber waited more than a reasonable time to accept the offer by acting on Insley's request. Two weeks is too long a time to consider such an offer still actionable.

1.9 Standard Motor Parts offered Limestone Shell ten dozen sets of socket wrenches at a bargain price of $21 per set. (The usual price was $53 a set.) Limestone did not make an immediate reply but prepared advertising to promote the sets it intended to buy. Four weeks later, without warning, Standard Motor Parts withdrew its offer. May Limestone Shell demand delivery of the wrenches at the quoted price?

No. Offers made *between merchants* are irrevocable during a "reasonable length of time." A merchant who plans a promotional campaign or sale of goods offered should be able to depend on delivery of those goods. This does not mean, however, that the offer must remain open for an indefinite period of time.

1.10 Wilson Camera Shop demonstrated a projector to Jackson. The salesman said, "This projector will beat anything on the market today. Find me a better one at the same price and I'll give you all your money back. Your friends will love the color that you get from this machine." The projector proved no better than others on the market, and Jackson demanded the return of his money. Did he succeed?

The salesman did no more than express an *opinion.* His exaggerated statements would be interpreted as "puffing." The court will act only on proof that there has been a *misstatement* of fact. Wilson Camera has no obligation to return Jackson's money.

1.11 Hickman, a minor, purchased an expensive watch on March 16. He planned to celebrate his birthday the next day, March 17, when he would reach his majority. A few hours after buying the watch, Hickman changed his mind and returned to the store. He demanded his money back on the grounds that his agreement with the store was voidable. Could Hickman enforce his rights as a minor in this case?

No. A person's *legal birthday* comes at 12:01 A.M. of the day *prior* to the day on which one would celebrate his or her birthday. Hickman's legal birthday arrived at 12:01 A.M. March 16, the day he *completed* his current year. Hickman, then, had reached his majority on March 16 and was legally an adult, not a minor, when he made the purchase.

1.12 A minor entered into an agreement with a sales clerk for the purchase of a formal suit that cost $175. Delivery and payment were to be made at the end of the week, as provided in the agreement signed by both the minor and the clerk. The store manager learned that the buyer was a minor and voided the agreement. Was the store permitted to rescind the minor's contract?

Only the minor is permitted to rescind an agreement made with a capable party. This right does not extend to the other party. The store manager would be obligated to respect the agreement made by the clerk. If, in the agreement, the minor had signed his name below a condition that stated "I have reached my majority and have full capacity to contract," the store would be permitted to dispute the buyer's right because the buyer would have been deceitful.

1.13 A representative of Larkin Frozen Foods sold a 21-cubic-foot freezer and fifty-two weekly deliveries of frozen foods to McCartney, who was a widow with four children and a small income ($325 per month) from insurance and social security. She had agreed to pay $150 per month for twelve months for the freezer and food. When McCartney missed two payments, Larkin sued her for the remaining balance of the contract. Did the widow have any defense in this action?

The Uniform Commercial Code now gives persons a defense against agreements that are unconscionable. *Unconscionable agreements* are those in which an offeror knowingly takes advantage of an offeree's ignorance or unfamiliarity with legal language and persuades the offeree to enter into agreements that are unreasonable because of the offeree's financial weakness. McCartney could defend herself in this action by seeking rescission of the contract on grounds of unconscionability.

1.14 Francine, a minor who was sixteen years of age, ran over a small boy while she was riding her bicycle on the sidewalk. Francine had paid no attention to pedestrians and was negligent in every sense. The parents of the injured child threatened suit against Francine's parents. Are Francine's parents liable?

No. Parents are not responsible for the torts of minor children who have reached the age of seven. Children less than seven years old are considered to be "in their tender years," and parents are in such cases held liable for their children's torts. (An exception that is now included in many statutes makes parents responsible for the *malicious* torts of all children, but only up to an amount of $300 or some other limit set by state law.)

1.15 Juell entered into a contract with Parisienne Modeling School for a nine-week course of instruction for her daughter. Juell agreed to pay $390 for tuition and other fees. When billed for the $390, Juell refused to pay, claiming, under the principle of consideration, that she received no benefit. Was she correct in this statement?

No. A party to a contract may be held responsible for debts arising from benefits that will be bestowed on a third party. Juell's benefit, supporting her obligation to pay the $390, is the education promised for her daughter. (A third-party beneficiary must be intended, not *incidental*. Thus, if a house painter agreed to paint a house with Sherwin-Williams paint, the paint manufacturer becomes an *incidental beneficiary* only. If the house painter used another brand of paint, Sherwin-Williams would have no right of action against the painter.)

1.16 Sturgiss contracted to buy a snowmobile from Dale for $425. The machine was one year old and in good running condition. Sturgiss later learned that he could have bought the same model from other dealers for $300. Sturgiss sought to rescind the agreement on grounds that the price charged was unreasonable. Was this a good defense?

No. The courts are not interested in the *adequacy of consideration*. Parties are left to their own devices in negotiating a contract. Unless there has been fraud or deception resulting in the payment of an unreasonable price for goods or services, the courts will not interfere.

1.17 Dr. Hinkson submitted a bill of $700 to Jonathan for setting his broken bone. Jonathan refused to pay the bill. Instead, he mailed Hinkson a check for $500 with the notation "in full payment of all medical services and treatment." Dr. Hinkson accepted the check and then sued Jonathan for the $200 difference. Will the doctor be successful in her suit?

In cases where there is a dispute over the amount owed and where the parties had not named a price when making their agreement, the payment of a lesser amount, if accepted, liquidates the debtor's obligation. This is true only when the amount charged is *in dispute*. Hinkson's acceptance of the $500 check with the conditions noted discharged Jonathan from any further payment to her.

1.18 Andover Trucking Company employed Roberts as a driver. Interstate Commerce rules provide that no driver is permitted to drive continuously for more than eight hours. Roberts was assigned a trip that required fifteen hours straight driving. Andover later refused to pay Roberts, claiming that their agreement with Roberts was illegal. Will Roberts be permitted to collect for the work he did?

The courts do not favor an employer who uses illegality as a defense for not paying an employee who was following instructions. Although both parties were involved in a wrongdoing, Andover would not be permitted to use Roberts's wrongdoing as a defense against payment. Roberts had not committed an intentional criminal act. (Had Roberts agreed to transport illegal drugs, the decision would be different.)

1.19 In a state where gambling was illegal, Hopkins agreed to act as a "bookie." His job was to accept bets from persons known to him and his employer. Hopkins's employer refused to pay him for work done in the "bookie" establishment. May Hopkins recover these lost wages?

Agreements to commit crimes are not valid or enforceable. Hopkins had knowingly agreed to commit an illegal act—working in a "bookie" shop. The courts would not accept Hopkins's claim for consideration.

1.20 Concord Bank & Trust Company loaned Vandegrift $5,000, payable three months after the date on Vandegrift's note. The note carried 7 percent interest and was dated April 4. The note came due on July 4, a Friday. When would Vandegrift have to make his payment?

Agreements to be performed on a legal holiday will be delayed to the next business day following. Because July 4 is a legal holiday, and Saturday and Sunday are also exempt as business days, Vandegrift would not be obliged to make payment on the note until the following Monday, July 7.

1.21 New England Dye Corporation hired Dr. Hinds as a chemist in its research-and-development center. He was hired for a period of five years. The contract prohibited Hinds from accepting similar employment with competing companies for a two-year period after his contract with New England Dye terminated. Hinds complained that this condition was invalid because of the restraint placed upon him in his chosen profession. Was Hinds correct?

Probably not. Terms restricting an employee from working for a competing firm that might pirate the initial employer's trade secrets, ideas, and research findings have been held enforceable *when reasonable*. What is reasonable will be determined by all circumstances surrounding any particular employment situation.

1.22 Emrich agreed to remain single from age 21 to age 31 on her father's promise that he would then pay her $25,000 in consideration of having given up her right to marry during this period. At the end of the ten years, Mr. Emrich refused to pay his daughter the $25,000. Would she be successful in a suit brought to enforce payment?

No. The courts do not look with favor on agreements that take away a person's fundamental rights. The right to marry is one of these. Contracts in restraint of marriage are unenforceable because they are considered against public policy. An agreement to refrain from marrying one particular individual would be enforceable. The law looks only on the *institution* of marriage as a guaranteed right to all persons.

1.23 Research & Development Corporation perfected a new drug effective in the treatment of certain types of cancer. The cost of research was more than $3,500,000. The company patented the new drug and created new facilities for its production and marketing. Some groups contested the company's right to withhold the production and distribution of the drug from other manufacturers and sales organizations that might wish to handle it. Does Research & Development Corporation have a legal right to this monopoly?

Yes. United States law gives individuals and private industries the right to claim ownership through patent. Of course, Research & Development has a moral obligation to distribute the drug quickly and widely, and it would probably license other companies to use the patented formula. Thus, the populace would be served and Research & Development would gain back its $3,500,000 investment, plus a profit.

1.24 Tasty Chicken, Inc., did extensive advertising and promotion of its product throughout the United States. The company sold franchises to persons in all fifty states. The franchises were roadside consumer outlets for the company's products. Kirshner, a dietician, opened her own roadside market. She constructed a building that matched those of the franchise and used the same name, competing with persons who had purchased Tasty Chicken franchises. Did Kirshner have this right?

A party who purchases a franchise is protected from infringement by others. Kirshner would be stopped from using the copyrighted name "Tasty Chicken" as well as trademarks, patented recipes, and other property rights of the parent company.

1.25 Cartwright was the manager of a chain store. At the end of one working day, he took the store's receipts out of the register and, instead of taking them to a bank, pocketed them and headed for a race track. There he lost all the money. If Cartwright had intended to return the money, could he be charged with the commission of a crime?

Yes. Cartwright was guilty of *embezzlement*. If he had come into possession of the money through unlawful means, he would have been guilty of *larceny*. In this case, however, he had come into possession of the money through the normal course of his business duties. By appropriating it for his own use, he embezzled it.

Review Problems

1.26 Name the four requisites of every enforceable contract.

1.27 In what situation may it be said that communication of an offer is presumed?

1.28 What three things may happen to an offer?

1.29 How does an *offer* differ from an *invitation to trade?*

1.30 When is one's legal birthday?

1.31 Under what condition may one claim incompetence through intoxication?

1.32 Explain the basic requisites of consideration.

1.33 What is a *public offer?*

1.34 Name two or more examples of *legal monopolies.*

1.35 What is a *barren promise?*

1.36 What are the three requisites of a valid offer?

1.37 Is an *option* a contract?

1.38 What is the effect of a counteroffer?

1.39 What options does one have in respect to *unordered merchandise?*

1.40 When is an acceptance complete, if the offeree communicates it through the same agent as that used by the offeror?

1.41 Are parents responsible for the torts of their minor children?

1.42 May a person who has been declared insane by the courts be held responsible for contracts for necessaries?

1.43 Explain *past consideration.*

1.44 May sales agreements be modified without additional consideration?

1.45 What is the meaning of *earnest money?*

1.46 What is *usury?*

1.47 Explain the difference between *fraud* and *misrepresentation.*

1.48 How much time does an offeree have to accept a telegraphed offer?

1.49 Explain the meaning of *undue influence.*

Answers to Review Problems

1.26 (1) mutual assent, (2) competent parties, (3) consideration, (4) valid subject matter

1.27 A person who signs a written contract is presumed to have read what he or she signed; thus, communication is presumed.

1.28 An offer may be (1) accepted, (2) rejected, or (3) revoked.

1.29 An offer is a proposal made to one person or a collective group. An invitation to trade is an announcement made to many people with the intention of receiving offers from those to whom the invitation was communicated.

1.30 It is at 12.01 A.M. of the day prior to the day on which one celebrates a birthday.

1.31 Intoxication is a defense to contract obligation when the defendant is able to prove that she or he had reached a point of not understanding what she or he was doing.

1.32 There must be a benefit and a sacrifice to each of the contracting parties.

1.33 It is an offer made through a public announcement when the identity or location of the offeree is not known; differs from an invitation to trade in that the proposal is meant for only one specific person.

1.34 patents, copyrights, trademarks, trade names, franchises.

1.35 It is a promise to do that which one is already obligated to do either by previous contract or by law.

1.36 communication, serious intent, clarity

1.37 Yes. An option contains the four requisites of a valid contract.

1.38 A counteroffer acts as a rejection of an original offer.

1.39 The recipient may send it back, pay for it, or do nothing.

1.40 Acceptance is complete when it is delivered to the offeror's agent, as when a letter of acceptance is placed in the mailbox. (The mails, in this case, are the agent.) If another agent is used, acceptance is not complete until it actually reaches the offeror.

1.41 They are not if their children have reached the age of seven, unless the parents instructed performance of the tort or condoned it.

1.42 No. Persons *declared* insane are incapable of making any kind of enforceable contract.

1.43 Past consideration consists of a promise of reward for services that have already been performed without expectation of reward.

1.44 Yes.

1.45 It is money given an offeror to hold an offer open or as a downpayment for the purchase of goods or services.

1.46 It is interest in excess of the maximum rate established by state statute.

1.47 Fraud results from an intentional false statement or the concealment of a fact. Misrepresentation is based on an unintentional false statement of fact that was made innocently.

1.48 Very little; the use of a telegram in making an offer implies the need for an immediate reply.

1.49 It is the use of one's position of superiority as a means of securing the acceptance of an offer.

Legal Terms

Abandonment. When a minor no longer receives the protection and support of his or her parents' household; removes the restrictions placed on minors in entering into enforceable agreements.

Acceptance. Agreeing to the terms of an offer.

Barren promise. A promise which obligates someone to do that which he or she is already obligated to do, either by previous agreement or by law. Not acceptable as valid consideration in support of a contract.

Bilateral contract. A contract in which something is required to be completed by both parties.

Communication. The transmission of an offeror's proposal to an offeree. Communication may be made in any way selected by the offeror or may be implied by obvious acts of the offeror recognized as an offer by the offeree.

Consideration. An element of all contracts, it requires that there be a benefit and a sacrifice to each party to a contract. The benefit may be money or anything else of value given in return for the acts or promises of the other contracting party.

Duress. The use of force or the threat of force against a person or a person's property or family. Agreements arrived at under duress are voidable.

Earnest money. Payment of part of the purchase price in order to bind a sale or hold open an offer.

Emancipation. When parents cease to assert their responsibilities as guardians over minors; removes the restrictions placed on minors in entering into enforceable agreements.

Embezzlement. The fraudulent appropriation of money or goods by one to whom they have been entrusted.

Fraud. Intentional false statements or concealments made by one party in dealing with another in matters pertaining to the subject matter of a contract. Proof of fraud may invalidate a contract and permit a demand for damages by the injured party.

Incidental beneficiary. A party who indirectly benefits from an agreement made between two others who did not intend to benefit the party.

In pari delicto. Equal in fault or guilt. Persons will not be assisted by the courts to carry out illegal objectives nor will they be awarded damages when they are *in pari delicto.*

Invitation to trade. An announcement, not directed to a specific individual or collective group, seeking potential offerors for goods or services advertised. Radio, television, newspaper, and magazine advertisements are often invitations to trade.

Legal birthday. 12:01 A.M. of the day prior to the date on which one ordinarily would celebrate his or her birthday.

Legal monopolies. Exclusive rights granted public-service ventures, inventors, authors, artists, and others; protects their rights from invasion by other parties.

Misrepresentation. An incorrect statement innocently made by a party to a contract. Misrepresentation permits rescission of an otherwise valid agreement but not damages to the complaining party.

Mutual assent. The agreement between an offeror and offeree, comprising the obligations accepted by and the promises granted to each party to the contract.

Necessaries. Goods or services necessary for maintaining a person's health, safety, education, or welfare. Minors and some others whose contracts are not ordinarily enforceable are held to contracts for necessaries.

Non compos mentis. Not of sound mind; insane.

Option agreement. A contract obligating the offeror to keep an offer open at a stated price and for a set period in return for a payment by the offeree.

Past consideration. A promise of reward for acts that have already been performed without expectation of payment of any kind. Such promises are not enforceable in claims for consideration.

Public offer. An offer to the general public by means of an advertisement in which all the terms are set out.

Rejection. The termination of an offer by act, expression, or counteroffer on the part of an offeree.

Revocation. The withdrawal of an offer through one of the many courses that directly or by implication result in the termination of the offer.

Undue influence. The use of one's position of superiority over another party to induce that party to enter into a contract.

Unilateral contract. An agreement by which, though a legal obligation is created, one party receives as consideration for his or her promise the performance or forbearance of some act.

Usury. Interest in excess of that permitted by law.

Chapter 2

Operation of Contracts

A successful contract depends upon the clear understanding expressed by the contracting parties. The successful outcome of the parties' intentions depends on the manner in which they respect and carry out their obligations.

Contract performance will meet the standards of expectation only if the parties are willing and able to give satisfaction. Satisfaction depends on what the parties intended during the formative stage of an agreement and on whether or not their words meant the same to each other. When misinterpretation leads to a dispute, the parties must interpret the contract according to the *custom of the market place*. In other words, what would the same contract convey to other persons engaged in the same type of business?

Millions of agreements are made daily. The parties carry out their obligations responsibly, and nothing more is heard of the agreements. Thousands of dollars change hands between satisfied contracting parties with no complaints. Disputes in contract operation usually arise from careless performance, fraudulent and deceptive schemes, or financial difficulties not anticipated by either party.

At times, parties make their own rules to be followed in the event that the contract is not carried out as expected. Agreements may contain set figures for damages to be awarded in the event of dissatisfaction or failure to carry out an agreement. Sometimes a contract may name a third party whose sole function is to determine whether or not each other party has done what was promised. Payment schedules based on performance may also be included in a contract.

2.1 Oral Agreements

Most agreements are oral. Oral agreements are enforceable if they are not of a type *required* to be in writing and if they contain the four requisites of a contract.

EXAMPLE 1. The O'Malley Roofing Company verbally agreed to replace the roof on Johnson Brother's warehouse for $57,000. Construction was to begin at once, and completion was guaranteed in sixty days. The law would support this agreement as valid if the parties were successful in proving the agreement's obligations and conditions. Oral agreements of a greater dollar value than this one are common between trusting parties. If a dispute is anticipated, however, the terms should be set down in a written contract.

2.2 Written Agreements

Written contracts may take any form desired, except in the case of formal contracts. (Formal contracts must be signed and under seal.) Written agreements need only express the rights and obligations of each party, together with signatures obligating each to the terms contained in the agreement. Written agreements are preferred when performance is delayed to a much later date or when the agreement contains many conditions and terms that might be confusing or easily forgotten.

EXAMPLE 2. John's Body Shop agreed to repaint Turner's Mustang for $290. Turner promised to deliver the car to the shop at 8 A.M., April 14, one month subsequent to making the agreement. The color to be used was a patented *Smoke Blue*, shown in John's color charts. Although not required, the agreement should be written and signed to prevent any possible dispute about the terms the parties had accepted.

2.3 Implied Agreements

Implied agreements are obligations created through the actions of the parties. A bus that is marked for a specific destination implies that the carrier will take a passenger to that destination in consideration of the money the passenger drops into the fare box. Millions of transactions are performed each day through implied agreements, in which parties express themselves neither orally nor in writing.

EXAMPLE 3. The Horrid Heet Fuel Oil Company delivered 250 gallons of fuel oil to Hazard's home. Hazard had not ordered the delivery, but he watched the driver pump the oil into his basement tank. Hazard denied any liability and would not pay for the oil. A court held that there was an implied agreement because Hazard was aware of the driver's mistake but stood by and permitted him to deliver the 250 gallons. Hazard implied that he agreed to have the oil delivered, and he would be obligated to pay.

2.4 Quasi Contracts

In emergency cases, a party may be held responsible for benefits bestowed upon him or her at the expense of another. Obligations of this kind are based on the doctrine of *quasi contracts*. (*Quasi* means "*like*" or "*similar to*.")

EXAMPLE 4. Colby was unconscious as a result of a hit-and-run accident. He was taken to the hospital, where he underwent emergency treatment and surgery. After regaining consciousness, Colby denied any responsibility for the hospital charges, stating that he had been incompetent to contract while in an unconscious state. Colby could be made to pay under the precedents established by quasi contracts. The care was necessary to save his life, and it would be unfair to permit him to deny his obligation to pay for the services on grounds of incompetency.

EXAMPLE 5. A minor purchased a ticket to travel from San Francisco to New York on a commercial airline flight. After arriving in New York, he demanded the return of his money. He claimed that because he was a minor the contract was voidable. (The ticket was not within the definition of a necessary.) On grounds of a quasi contract, the carrier could refuse reimbursement. The minor had taken advantage of the carrier by claiming incompetence to contract. The minor tried to use the law as a *sword*, and not as a *shield* as it was meant to be used.

2.5 Formal Contracts

Formal contracts are required in some transactions, such as the sale and transfer of real property rights. In some states, formal contracts must be under seal to be enforceable.

EXAMPLE 6. Robino sold a house to Sullens. Written agreements not under seal were signed, and a down payment was made. Sullens changed her mind about buying the house and demanded the return of money already paid. In a state requiring that a formal contract be under seal, the sales agreement would be invalid and unenforceable. Sullens would have no obligation to Robino, who would be required to return the down payment.

2.6 Void, Voidable, Valid

Contracts are either valid, void, or voidable. When *valid*, they are enforceable by either party. A *voidable* contract contains defects that permit only the wronged party to claim the contract to be either valid or void. *Void* agreements are those that are invalid or illegal, regardless of the wishes of either party.

EXAMPLE 7. DeLuca, a minor, signed a contract and made a partial payment on a fur-trimmed winter coat. The coat was expensive and did not represent a necessary to DeLuca. The agreement was voidable. DeLuca had the option to carry out her promise to pay for the coat or to return it and demand back her money.

2.7 Statute of Frauds

The *statute of frauds* requires certain types of agreements to be evidenced by written contracts if they are to be legally enforceable. Agreements under the statute include: (1) contracts by an executor or administrator to answer for the debts of the deceased out of her or his own pocket; (2) contracts guaranteeing the debts, defaults, or wrongdoings of another; (3) contracts that cannot be carried out within one year of the date appearing on the contract; (4) contracts in consideration of marriage; (5) contracts for the sale of any interest in real property except for leases of less than one year; and (6) contracts for the sale of personal property valued at $500 or more.

EXAMPLE 8. Engineering Research, Ltd., hired Jacobs to work on a research project that would require at least three years to complete. The offer of employment and salary was oral, and Jacobs accepted it. The agreement, in its oral form, would not be enforceable by either Jacobs or the employer because its terms could not be carried out within one year of the date when the agreement was made.

2.8 Substantial Performance

Anything less than complete performance is considered either *substantial performance* or a *breach* of an agreement. When one party's performance is complete with the exception of minor details, there has been substantial performance. The other party is obligated to pay the contract price less an amount covering that which was left undone.

EXAMPLE 9. Custom Builders built a house and garage for Simpkins. When the work was finished, Simpkins discovered that Custom had failed to install two electrical outlets in the recreation room. Simpkins refused to pay the $38,500 due Custom Builders because of this omission. Simpkins will be required to pay the $38,500, after deducting an amount sufficient to install the two missing outlets, because there had been substantial performance.

2.9 Third-Party Referees

Contracting parties may appoint third-party referees, who agree to rule on the performance of existing contracts. Architects, engineers, and other specialists often judge the performance of contracts.

EXAMPLE 10. Carter Boat Company agreed to build a thirty-eight-foot sailing yacht for Hamilton. Plans and specifications were provided by Hamilton. Steuber, a marine architect, was appointed by the parties to pass judgment on the satisfactory completion of the project. *Only Steuber's evaluation* would be acceptable in determining satisfactory performance and Hamilton's obligation to honor the boat company's demand for payment.

2.10 When "Time Is of the Essence"

When time is a matter of importance in performance, a wronged party may declare the agreement breached when goods are not delivered or services are not performed according to schedule. In such agreements, "time is of the essence."

EXAMPLE 11. Colonial Motors agreed to deliver a new Ford to Grahm on August 15, two days before Grahm planned to leave on a trip to Canada. On August 13, Colonial called Grahm and informed him that the car would not be ready until August 20. Colonial was aware of Grahm's need for the car on August 15. Delivery on August 20 would not be satisfactory. Time was of the essence, and Grahm may treat the agreement as breached.

2.11 Third-Party Beneficiaries

A third party (not the offeror or the offeree) may bring action against a defaulting party when a contract is created for the purpose of benefiting that third party. The third party must be able to prove that one of the contracting parties owed him or her an obligation at the time the contract was made. Otherwise, the third party is known as an *incidental beneficiary* and cannot bring action against the breaching party.

EXAMPLE 12. Lauder filed an application for admission of his daughter Julia to the Arnold School of Figure Skating. The application was accepted. When Julia reported for classes, she was refused admission without cause. Julia, a third-party beneficiary, may bring an action in her own name against the school.

2.12 Assignment of Contract Rights

Contract rights are property rights and as such may be sold and transferred to others. Unless restricted from doing so by a provision in the contract, the owner of a contract right may *assign* that right to a third party without permission of the other contracting party. The party that assigns rights is known as the *assignor*; the party to whom rights are assigned is known as the *assignee*.

EXAMPLE 13. Thomas owed $75 to King, who lived in a city several miles away. King wrote to an acquaintance in Thomas's area, assigning to him the right to the $75. King had legally transferred his right to the $75 to an assignee.

2.13 Equal-Dignities Rule

The *equal-dignities rule* requires that an assignment be made in the same form as the contract through which the original obligation was created. Oral agreements may be assigned orally; written ones by writing; contracts under seal only through an assignment under seal.

EXAMPLE 14. Arundel Properties, Inc., appointed Jefferson as broker for the sale of houses and lots in its three developments. Jefferson assigned the agreement to the Stevens Company. The assignment must have been in writing and under seal, the same formality required in Arundel's agreement with Jefferson.

2.14 Nonassignable Contracts

Three types of agreements may not be assigned: (1) contracts that state within their terms that they are not assignable; (2) contracts for personal services of a professional nature or those requiring a special talent; and (3) agreements not assignable by law.

EXAMPLE 15. The Selectrons contracted to play for a spring dance held at the Jackson Institute. Another job, bigger and better-paying, came up for the Selectrons, so the leader incorrectly assigned the Jackson job to another capable group. The contract with the Jackson Institute was not assignable because of the distinctive type of music played by the Selectrons.

2.15 Conforming Assignee's Rights to Assignment

The party who owes money or has the duty to perform is entitled to notice of assignment. Communication of the notice must be made by the assignee, the party to whom the assignment has been made. A contracting party has the right to check out the validity of an assignment before complying with the demands of the assignee. Because an oral contract need not be evidenced by a written agreement, the party to whom notice of assignment is given is permitted a reasonable length of time to verify the assignment by contacting the assignor.

EXAMPLE 16. Higby entered into an agreement with City Painters. They were to paint his house. City Painters, due to the pressure of other jobs, assigned the contract to the Home Painting Company, which informed Higby of the assignment. Higby may take a reasonable time to determine the validity of the Home Painting Company's notice of the assignment.

2.16 Assignee's Rights and Obligations

The assignee "steps into the shoes of the assignor." Whatever rights and obligations were carried by the assignor are now carried by the assignee. The assignor remains as a *guarantor* of the assignee's performance. The assignor also guarantees that the assignee will be paid by the other party.

EXAMPLE 17. Roebling Plumbing Contractors assigned to Hertzel its contract to install new copper lines and bathroom fixtures in Leach's house. (Hertzel was another reputable plumbing contractor in the same community.) Roebling would be responsible to Leach if Hertzel performed less than satisfactory work. Furthermore, Roebling would be similarly liable to Hertzel if Leach failed to pay for the work.

2.17 Executor as Assignee

Death has the effect of automatically assigning all contract rights of the deceased to the executor or administrator of the deceased's estate. All rights to collect money, to demand performance of executory agreements, and to sell or purchase real estate or personal property are, at death, assigned by law.

EXAMPLE 18. Ladd & Company agreed to sell five acres of pasture land to Harper for $12,000. After executing all sales agreements but before any transfer of ownership, Harper died. Harper's rights would be assigned to Harper's executor or administrator by law. Ladd & Company would be obligated to respect the executor's rights under the automatically assigned agreements.

2.18 Novation

By mutual agreement, contracting parties may change the terms, the conditions, or the parties of an agreement. Any such change is called a *novation*. Novations differ from assignments in four ways: (1) Novations must have the assent of all contracting parties; assignments do not. (2) Novations may transfer all rights *and* obligations; assignments release assignors from rights but not from obligations. (3) In a novation, a new party does not necessarily carry out all the obligations previously in force; in an assignment, the assignee "steps into the shoes of the assignor." (4) In a novation, a former party can be made free and clear of all obligations of the original agreement; an assignor is never fully released from a contract until it has been executed.

EXAMPLE 19. Charleton agreed to act as the pilot of an aircraft owned by the Harvestor Products Corporation. He was under contract to continue the job for two years. If a more profitable position became available to Charleton, he might suggest a replacement to his present employer. If Harvestor Products agreed, a novation would take place, removing Charleton from the existing agreement and replacing him with the new pilot.

2.19 Joint Liability

Joint liability in contracts exists when either the offeror or the offeree consists of two or more persons. Their promises are preceded by the words "We promise to . . ." Joint parties are usually sued together, although some courts permit a wronged party to sue only one of the joint parties.

EXAMPLE 20. Holden and Castle jointly bought a boat and outboard motor. In a contract they signed, they agreed to make a full payment of $1,185 within sixty days of delivery of the boat and motor. Their failure to pay resulted in an action against Holden alone. The seller found that Holden had sufficient funds to pay the $1,185, whereas Castle had no assets to cover a possible judgment in the seller's favor. Holden would have a right of action for *contribution* against Castle in an amount equal to one-half of the judgment.

2.20 Joint and Several Liability

Parties are in *joint and several liability* on agreements that state "We jointly and severally agree and promise . . ." Such liability always permits a wronged party to sue them individually or together.

EXAMPLE 21. Arnold and Brown agreed jointly and severally to be obligated on an agreement to purchase a new television. If Arnold and Brown do not make payment in accordance with the terms of the sales contract, the seller may sue either one or both. (The seller's decision to sue one or the other would probably depend on his knowledge of the financial condition of each of the purchasers and their ability to satisfy a court judgment in favor of the plaintiff.)

Solved Problems

2.1 Jarmon Brothers Garage agreed to renew the piston rings, rebuild the carburetor, and tune the motor of Steelman's MG. Steelman called for the car at the agreed time. He was told that the garage had had time only to work on the carburetor and to tune the motor. The garage had not replaced the piston rings as agreed. The garage demanded payment for the work done. Steelman refused to pay, claiming that the most important part of the agreement had been disregarded. Was Steelman correct?

In this case, Jarmon Brothers did not make a substantial performance. The most important condition of the agreement was the work required in replacing the rings. The other work was almost incidental. Jarmon Brothers breached its agreement. If he were sued, this would be Steelman's defense. Some courts might allow a token payment to Jarmon for work done. Others would release Steelman of any liability whatsoever.

2.2 Computer Programs, Inc., experienced serious financial difficulties. Creditors started proceedings of involuntary bankruptcy against the firm. A trustee was appointed, and she took over all of the bankrupt's assets. Two creditors questioned the trustee's right to this action. Were the two creditors justified in their complaint?

The Federal Bankruptcy Act provides that when an individual, partnership, or corporation is declared bankrupt, a trustee should be appointed to take over all of the bankrupt's assets. For the equitable distribution of Computer Program's assets, the law requires that its assets be assigned. The complaints were without justification.

2.3 Cheriton owed $250 to Hugh Barclay. The Standard Machine Company, in return for work Cheriton did for them, agreed to assume Cheriton's $250 debt. Was this a valid assignment?

No. One may assign rights, but not obligations. Cheriton's creditors had depended on Cheriton's credit history and ability to pay, not on anyone else's. Cheriton could enter into an agreement with Standard Machine whereby the company might agree to satisfy the $250 debt. He may not, however, *assign* this obligation.

2.4 Zabinsky, an artist, was commissioned to do a portrait of Governor Simms. When Zabinsky was called to Europe to do paintings of seven members of a wealthy family, he assigned the governor's portrait project to a famous artist who had taught him in his youth. Was this assignment valid and enforceable?

No. One may not assign contracts that require the performance of personal services. The agreement with Zabinsky could not be assigned to even the most talented artist. Only Zabinsky could do Zabinsky's work.

2.5 Sergeant Reilly purchased a 16-mm movie camera, projector, and sound recording system for $1,876. Instead of paying cash, he signed papers that assigned $100 per month from his army pay to the camera shop that sold him the equipment. The assignee was refused any rights under the assignment. Was Reilly's assignment valid?

Certain types of agreements are not assignable by law. Although Reilly has a contract with the army for payment of regular income, federal law prohibits the assignment of all or any part of that income. The seller will have to look to Reilly personally for payment.

2.6 Juell owed $125 to Archino for books sold to Juell by Archino. Archino assigned the right of collection of the $125 to Milton Bilkson, to whom Archino owed a large sum of money. Juell, who had not been informed of the assignment, sent a check for $125 to

Archino. Archino deposited the check to his account. Bilkson also demanded payment from Juell, claiming that the account had been assigned to him. Does Juell have to pay Bilkson?

The assignee has the responsibility of giving notice of assignment. Bilkson, the assignee, had not communicated notice of the assignment to Juell soon enough. Archino was wrong in accepting payment after the $125 had been assigned. Juell, however, had done nothing wrong and is free of liability to either Archino or Bilkson.

2.7 Grimshaw contracted to work as a pharmacist for three years for the McHenry Drug Store, which was solely owned by Robert Hilton. Hilton sold the business to Carney. A part of the sales agreement included an assignment of the Grimshaw contract to Carney. Must Grimshaw continue to work for Carney for the duration of the three-year agreement?

The owner of a business may not assign personal-service contracts to another who buys the business. Grimshaw's contract is not assignable through the purchase of the McHenry Drug Store.

2.8 Holmbark agreed to pay Custom Builders $2,760 for the construction of a one-car garage. Custom Builders assigned its contract to the Home Construction Company. (Custom had found that it would not be able to complete the project on time.) Home Construction did a poor job, and Holmbark brought an action to recover damages. Against whom would Holmbark bring his claim?

The assignee "steps into the shoes of the assignor." Any rights of recovery that a contracting party has against the assignor it also has against the assignee. Holmbark, thus, could sue Home (the assignee) for proven damages. Furthermore, because the assignor remains as guarantor of work done by the assignee, Holmbark could also sue Custom. The action should be brought against the party whose financial condition would best assure recovery of any judgment awarded in a civil suit.

Review Problems

2.9 Explain *joint and several liability.*

2.10 May a contracting party assign duties?

2.11 What is a *novation*? How does it differ from an *assignment?*

2.12 What is *substantial performance?* Does an injured party have the right to rescind a contract when there has been only substantial performance?

2.13 Does death create assignment of the deceased's contract rights? Explain.

2.14 What three types of agreements may not be assigned?

2.15 What is an *incidental beneficiary*? May incidental beneficiaries seek legal action in enforcing agreements in which they are named?

2.16 Give an example of a *voidable* agreement.

2.17 What is meant by the expression *under seal?*

2.18 Give an example of a *quasi contract*.

2.19 May enforceable contract obligations be created without the expressed intentions of both parties?

2.20 Under what two conditions are written agreements preferred over oral agreements?

2.21 What types of contracts must be evidenced by written agreements under the statute of frauds?

2.22 When may a party treat a contract as breached for want of performance?

2.23 What types of personal-service agreements may not be assigned?

Answers to Review Problems

2.9 Joint and several liability means that the members of one party to an agreement are held both collectively and individually responsible for their promises in the agreement. Persons seeking recovery of damages from such a party may proceed against either one member or all of them at once.

2.10 Duties may not be assigned; only rights (or property) may be.

2.11 A *novation* is the creation of a new contract through the substitution of a new party, new consideration, or some other new condition. To create a novation, both parties must mutually assent to the changes. *Assignment*, on the other hand, does not change the contents of the original agreement; it merely transfers the contract to another party. Assignment is accomplished by only one party, without the requirement of mutual assent.

2.12 Incomplete contract performance is called substantial performance only if those things left incomplete or undone are not at the very heart of the intent of the parties. Unimportant details that do not materially affect the main purpose of the agreement will not defeat enforcement of the contract obligations. Contracts cannot be rescinded because there has been only substantial performance.

2.13 Yes, it does, except in the case of a contract right that depends on the deceased's personal services.

2.14 (1) Contracts that contain terms prohibiting assignment; (2) agreements for personal services of a professional or artistic nature; (3) agreements not assignable by law.

2.15 An *incidental beneficiary* is one who benefits from the terms and conditions of an agreement drawn up specifically to benefit another. The incidental beneficiary has no right of action against a breaching party.

2.16 A contract for things other than necessaries by either a minor or an incompetent person who is not declared insane.

2.17 This means that one signing the agreement must accompany his or her signature with a seal, which is important in formal agreements and in the transfer of real property.

2.18 An unconscious person receiving medical treatment is not a party to an express agreement but would be held responsible for certain benefits granted her or him.

2.19 Yes. Implied contracts, created through the *acts* of parties, are enforceable.

2.20 Written agreements are preferable when performance is scheduled for a much later date or when the agreement contains numerous terms and conditions, which may be forgotten or be confusing.

2.21 (1) Agreements by executors or administrators who answer for the debts of a deceased person out of their own pockets; (2) agreements guaranteeing the debts, defaults, or wrongdoing of another; (3) agreements that cannot be completed within one year of the date of the contract; (4) agreements in consideration of marriage; (5) agreements for the sale of any interest in real property except for leases of less than one year; and (6) agreements for the sale of personal proeprty valued at $500 or more.

2.22 When performance has been less than substantial performance. (That is, when the failure to perform reaches into the very heart of the agreement.)

2.23 Contracts that require performance by professional people or contracts that require performance of an artistic and unique nature.

Legal Terms

Assign. To transfer or to make over to another the property or the rights of an agreement.

Assignee. The person to whom property or rights have been assigned.

Assignor. The person who assigns property or rights to another.

Equal-dignities rule. The assignment of rights of an agreement must be made in the same form in which the original agreement was made.

Implied agreement. Agreements created through the actions of the parties, rather than through their oral or written statements.

Joint and several liability. The contract obligations of persons who hold themselves both collectively and individually to the terms of an agreement.

Novation. A new contract resulting from the substitution of new terms, new parties, or some other new factor not contained in the original agreement; requires the mutual assent of all parties to the original contract.

Quasi contract. An obligation resulting from the benefit of one party at the innocent expense, under unusual circumstances, of another.

Voidable contract. A defective agreement, but one that remains valid unless the *wronged party* chooses to declare it void.

Chapter 3

Discharge of Contracts

No contract is meant to continue forever. Contracts may be discharged through either cancellation or termination. (See Section 3.1.)

Carefully written agreements usually contain conditions of discharge. Strikes, mob violence, accidental fires, and many other hurdles to performance may be included as releases for both parties, if they so wish.

Many of the disputes and weaknesses described in this chapter could have been avoided if the parties had given greater attention to details of the formation and operation of contracts.

3.1 Termination and Cancellation of Contracts

Contracts are most often terminated by mutual agreement and by the satisfactory performance of the parties' promises. *Termination* implies an amicable discharge of contract obligations. *Cancellation* implies a *breach* of agreement, either by a party's failure to perform or by a disregard of certain conditions of the agreement.

EXAMPLE 1. The Charles Printing Company engaged two certified public accountants to audit its books and prepare financial statements for the annual stockholders' meeting. The accountants performed their work in a satisfactory manner, and the printing company willingly paid the fee charged. The contract was terminated—completely and satisfactorily discharged—through the performance of all obligations by both contracting parties.

3.2 Termination by Mutual Assent

Contracts may be terminated prior to complete performance by mutual agreement of both parties.

EXAMPLE 2. Derrickson Brothers hired Ralston as a security guard at its Portland plant. He was measured for a uniform, given full training in police and security practices, and hired on a three-year contract. Seven months later, Ralston was appointed to the State Police. Derrickson Brothers agreed to release Ralston on his promise that he would pay Derrickson for the uniform they had provided. Through amicable mutual agreement, the contract was terminated.

3.3 Satisfactory Performance

The satisfactory performance of a contract for personal services of a professional or artistic nature will be determined only by the party for whom the services are performed. Satisfactory performance in other types of agreements will be determined by the ordinary expectations and judgment of experts engaged in the same type of business.

EXAMPLE 3. Moderne Studios agreed to provide photographs of The Keys, a group of musical entertainers. The studio promised that no bill would be submitted if the group was not satisfied with the proofs. Twenty proofs were examined, and the group expressed dissatisfaction with all of them. Even though the photos were excellent according to the judgment of other photographers, the decision as to whether or not the photographs were satisfactory rested with The Keys alone.

EXAMPLE 4. Stabler contracted with Electrical Heating Contractors for installation of an electric heating system in her residence. The contractor assured Stabler that she would be delighted with electric heat. He said, "If it is not satisfactory, you won't have to pay us a cent." Stabler did claim dissatisfaction, and she refused to pay for the installation. Satisfactory performance in agreements of this type will be determined by the judgment of experts in the field, rather than by the personal decision of an individual. If the job had been done well according to the standards of the market place, Stabler would have to pay.

3.4 Tender of Payment

To *tender* means to offer. Tenders may be offers of goods, services, or money. Cash is defined as *legal tender*. One party's obligation to another party implies payment in cash unless the parties have mutually agreed that payment may be made by check or may be delayed through some form of credit.

EXAMPLE 5. Truman ordered five tons of topsoil to be delivered to his home. The terms were c.o.d. ("cash on delivery"). When the dump-truck arrived at his home, Truman wrote out a check for $75, the agreed-on price. The seller refused to accept the check and would not dump the topsoil. Truman claimed that the seller had breached the agreement. In fact, Truman himself had breached the agreement by not offering a cash payment and not making any previous arrangements to pay by check.

3.5 Tender of Performance

A *tender of performance* is any act by a contracting party that shows the party's willingness and ability to carry out contractual obligations. Contracting parties must be able to show that they have tendered performance when they seek damages against parties they are charging with breach of contract.

EXAMPLE 6. Landscape Contractors contracted to plant trees and bushes on the grounds of the Wrigley Retirement Home. When crews arrived at the home according to the prearranged schedule, Wrigley refused to allow them to proceed with the work. Landscape had tendered performance, and later successfully sued for all damages resulting from Wrigley Retirement's refusal.

3.6 Impossibility of Performance

An agreement is terminated if, before it is signed, circumstances known about by neither party and beyond their control have already made performance impossible. If the circumstances making performance impossible arise only *after* a contract is signed, the contract is not necessarily terminated.

EXAMPLE 7. Sunrise Aircraft Company of Detroit sold a Piper Cub to Samworth for $4,300. The aircraft was in a hangar in upper Michigan. Samworth paid Sunrise for the plane on March 10, the day he signed the sales agreement. It was later learned that the hangar housing the aircraft had been destroyed by heavy winds on March 8. As a result, the plane had been completely ruined. Because neither party knew about these circumstances when they signed the agreement, performance was impossible. Samworth may demand the return of the $4,300 paid, but he cannot sue Sunrise for breach of contract.

3.7 Acts of God

In contracts, an *act of God* is any natural phenomenon that prevents performance. Contracting parties are not automatically released when acts of God make performance impossible. Except in very special situations, parties must specify in their agreements that acts of God release a party from its obligation of performance.

EXAMPLE 8. Concrete Products Company contracted to manufacture concrete pipes and deliver them to Falls City for use in a sewage system. A fire caused by lightning destroyed the pipe plant, and deliveries stopped. Falls City sued Concrete Products for its failure to deliver. The manufacturer, not protected by an act-of-God clause, remained responsible for the agreement. Delivery could be made by having the pipes manufactured by another company in the same business. (The pipes were not so unique that they could not be procured elsewhere in fulfillment of the Falls City agreement.)

3.8 Material Alteration

Contract obligations may be discharged when one party intentionally makes a *material alteration* in a written agreement without the consent of the other party. Material alterations made with the intent to defraud may result in a criminal complaint as well as a civil suit.

EXAMPLE 9. The Sanford Tailoring Company agreed to deliver five dozen spring coats to My Lady's Sport Shoppes. The parties had neglected to fill in the date of delivery when signing the agreement. Later, Sanford's sales manager inserted the agreed-on date. My Lady's buyer objected, claiming a material alteration. Inserting the date did not in any way change the intent of the agreement; this was not an objectionable material alteration.

3.9 Termination through Death, Disability, or Illness

Personal-service agreements are terminated through death, disability, or illness if the service contracted for is of such a personal nature that it cannot be performed by another.

EXAMPLE 10. Wendel, an Olympic skater, turned professional and signed an agreement with Ice Shows, Inc. After four weeks of practicing intricate skating routines with other members of the cast, Wendel suffered a broken ankle during a rehearsal. Wendel and Ice Shows would be excused from all obligations due to impossibility of performance. Wendel would not be required to provide a replacement.

3.10 Illegality of Performance

Contracts are automatically terminated when legislation makes performance illegal, even if such legislation comes into effect after the contract is created. Both parties are discharged of any liability.

EXAMPLE 11. Robertson Brothers contracted to install a septic tank and sewage drainage system for Harkness's suburban residence. Before Robertson started the work, county commissioners passed a new regulation requiring all homes in Harkness's area to connect with a newly constructed sewer system. The contract with Robertson Brothers would be terminated because the construction and use of a septic tank on Harkness's lands had been made illegal.

3.11 Right to Cancel Contract

A wronged party may consider a contract discharged by cancellation when the other party is guilty of either nonperformance or careless performance. Only the wronged party has the right of cancellation because of the other's breach.

EXAMPLE 12. Dawson put down a deposit and contracted for the rental of a trailer that he would pick up on March 27, at 8 A.M. When Dawson went to pick up the trailer, the service station manager informed him that it was not available. The contract could be canceled by Dawson and he could demand the return of his deposit. Or, Dawson might refuse to accept the return of the deposit and sue the service station for damages resulting from the breach.

3.12 Breach of Contract

Once a contract has been breached, the wronged party must do whatever is possible to minimize damages that could otherwise be claimed as a result of the breach. Contracts partially executed must be halted, not continued to completion. Processes that cannot be halted may be finished and charged to the party who has breached the agreement.

EXAMPLE 13. Continental Steel Company agreed to supply American Arms Company with a special high-grade steel used in the manufacture of handguns. American Arms gave notice that it intended to cancel the agreement during the "cooking" process that Continental was performing on the first lot of steel. Continental would be permitted to continue processing this first lot of steel, but further processing must be halted.

EXAMPLE 14. Hallway Milling Company accepted an order for the manufacture of 125 roof trusses to be shipped to King Homes, in Montgomery, Alabama. King telephoned Hallway to cancel its order after 63 of the trusses had been finished. Hallway would be restricted from continuing with production of the rest of the order. It could make a claim for damages for all units completed plus any other losses experienced through King's breach.

3.13 Abandonment of Performance

Deliberate abandonment of performance, when a contract has been only partly executed, gives the wronged party the right to treat the contract as canceled. In some cases, the breaching party may demand payment for the work already done and the parts used. Other situations disallow any recovery for work and materials already used.

EXAMPLE 15. Century Plumbing Manufacturing Company prepared a new catalog for publication and distribution to the trade. Industrial Printing was given the manuscript for composition and printing. When only ten pages of the catalog had been set in type, the job was shelved for other jobs in the shop. Century Plumbing's demands for the catalogs went unheeded, so they notified Industrial that they were canceling the contract. It is doubtful that any court would award damages to Industrial for work already done.

3.14 Discharge of Contract through Bankruptcy

Bankruptcy acts as a discharge for contracts that require performance by the bankrupt. Legal actions against a bankrupt for unfulfilled agreements are barred. The receiver in bankruptcy may elect, for the better protection of creditors, to carry out a contract that will increase the bankrupt's assets.

EXAMPLE 16. Raleigh Manufacturing Company, declared bankrupt, had contracted to manufacture 25,000 hardened steel mower shafts for Harley Mower Company. The work had just been started when the receiver took over the firm's assets. Harley Mower Company would be powerless in attempting to seek damages for breach of agreement.

3.15 Proving Money Damages in a Court of Law

In all claims against one who has breached a contract, the complaining party has the burden of proving all damages sought. A party suing on a contract *in a court of law* can seek an award of money damages only, not an order of performance of the agreement.

EXAMPLE 17. Stanbro contracted to buy a CB radio from Dougherty Radio Shop. Dougherty breached the agreement by not delivering the radio. A court of law could not order Dougherty to deliver the radio, but it could award damages to Stanbro. The damages would be the proven difference between the amount stipulated in the contract and the larger amount that Stanbro would have to pay another dealer for the same radio.

3.16 Speculative Damages

Damages are certain amounts of money a party can recover, by court action, as compensation for an injury, detriment, or loss caused by another. *Actual damages* compensate a party for whatever was lost or injured. *Incidental damages* compensate a party for expenses directly related to the loss. *Speculative damages,* which are those based on hopeful expectations, are not admissible in court and do not result in compensation.

EXAMPLE 18. City Cab Company ordered four new taxis from Checker Cab Sales Company. The taxis were not delivered, and Checker's contract was considered breached. City Cab sought damages of $2,875, representing the added cost of securing the taxis from another source. City also claimed $900 damages based on passenger fares they expected to collect over the time during which they did not have the use of the four new cabs. The $2,875 represented actual damages and would be a proper claim. The $900 expected from passenger fares was not based on any real evidence of loss, but only on the optimistic expectations of the cab company. This $900 in speculative damages would not be allowed.

3.17 Nominal Damages

When no real damage is proven, the court may award *nominal damages* to the successful litigant in an action on a breached contract. Nominal damages, as derived from the traditions of English courts, usually amount to 6¢. (The amount awarded in many other courts is $1.)

EXAMPLE 19. Stark brought a trespass action against a neighbor who walked over Stark's front lawn each day. The court found the neighbor had truly trespassed on Stark's property. However, the court could not establish any actual damage to Stark's lawn. Nominal damages of $1 were therefore awarded to Stark by the court.

3.18 Specific Performance

Courts of equity attempt to correct wrongs that cannot be righted by the award of money damages. They usually require parties to perform as they agreed to in a contract. A party's failure or refusal to deliver unique goods or to transfer promised real property gives the wronged party the right to petition a court of equity for a decree of *specific performance*. Such a decree, demanding performance, is not allowed in cases where it may be proven that money damages would suffice.

EXAMPLE 20. Stolts agreed to buy an eighteenth-century chest from Empire Antiques for $4,700. When Stolts went to pick up the chest, Empire refused delivery, stating that the chest was going to be given to a museum. Stolts, knowing that it would be impossible to purchase the identical chest elsewhere, brought action in a court of equity, seeking specific performance of the contract. The court would order performance—delivery of the chest to the buyer on tender of the $4,700.

EXAMPLE 21. Urie bought standard bathroom fixtures at General Plumbing Supply and signed an order for their delivery in two weeks. General Plumbing breached the agreement, delaying Urie's installation of the units in a house under construction. A court of equity would not accept this matter under a petition for specific performance. The same fixtures could be purchased elsewhere. The goods were not in themselves unique. Urie should have sought money damages in a court of law.

3.19 Acts of God as a Condition in a Contract

Impossibility of performance resulting from an act of God will not excuse a promissor (the party promising to perform) when performance might be possible in other ways, even at additional expense. Impossibility through an act of God will excuse the promissor only if such a condition is contained in the contract.

EXAMPLE 22. Purity Flour Company contracted to delivery 1,000 ten-pound sacks of white flour to Retail Grocery Exchange. A fire resulting from lightning destroyed Purity's mills, and the flour was not delivered. In a suit by Retail Grocery, Purity claimed impossibility of performance through an act of God. This defense was not acceptable to the court because Purity had not shown that it could not have purchased white flour from another mill and made the delivery. Although the cost might have been greater, Purity Flour still had an obligation to discharge the contract.

Solved Problems

3.1 DeSalvo, a professional baseball player, signed with an American League team. In the middle of the season, DeSalvo had difficulties with the team's manager and left the ballpark. He refused to play for the remainder of the season. May the team's owner seek a decree of specific performance against DeSalvo?

Courts of equity will not issue decrees of specific performance in personal-service contracts. The courts may, however, issue an *injunction* that will enjoin (prohibit) a person from the use of his or her specific skills for anyone other than the one with whom a contract is then in force. DeSalvo cannot be made to play ball, but he may be enjoined from playing ball with any other team for the duration of his contract. He may also be sued by the team for damages.

3.2 Soltow Foundry Company contracted to do iron castings for Superior Motor Company. The agreement involved production of more than 1 million dollars worth of castings. Both parties agreed that if Soltow failed to make deliveries as promised there would be *liquidated damages*—damages owed to Superior Motor—in the amount of $250,000. Is this agreement legal and enforceable?

Liquidated damages are legal, but they are not enforceable if they are greatly in excess of the actual damages caused by the breach of contract. If a court believes that the liquidated damages specified in a contract are unrealistic or unreasonable, it will disregard the contract and set damages itself. Whether $250,000 damages is reasonable in this case depends on the actual damages that Superior Motors might suffer through Soltow's breach.

3.3 Rainbow Decorators did work for DuVall, a wealthy client, at a cost of $37,900. DuVall suffered financial reverses and refused to pay his debt to Rainbow. Rainbow, through a civil suit for breach of agreement, recovered a judgment for the amount of the bill, plus interest and expenses of litigation. The judgment went unpaid, and Rainbow again sought recovery. Will Rainbow ever recover its loss from DuVall?

When a judgment is not satisfied by the defendant in a civil suit, the clerk of the court will issue a *writ of execution* or a *writ of garnishment* to the sheriff for execution. The judgment will then be satisfied by taking possession of the defendant's property and disposing of it at public sale (writ of execution) or by securing possession of the defendant's assets held by other persons (writ of garnishment). DuVall obviously owns furniture, cars, real estate, bank accounts, stocks, bonds, and other securities. These assets will be taken and sold to recover the amount of the judgment owed Rainbow Decorators.

3.4 Dolbow had his car repainted by IXL Body Shop. He agreed to pay $285 for the job. When the car was ready, Dolbow inspected it and found several unpainted spots. Dolbow believed the paint job did not come up to reasonable expectations. He discussed the matter with IXL but paid the $285. He later decided to sue for a return of part of the payment due to the poor work done. Will Dolbow recover?

No. Parties voluntarily give up (*waive*) their rights of complaint on a breach of agreement when they accept incomplete or defective performance. Dolbow's payment of the full amount was a *waiver*. Only if payment is made *under protest* and the promissor refuses to complete or correct the matters complained of may the wronged party seek reimbursement or damages. Dolbow did not protect himself in accepting and paying for the poor workmanship. He thereby waived his rights against IXL Body Shop.

3.5 Darlington Brothers did extensive landscape work at Pioneer Farms and billed the owners for $8,675. The bill was not paid over an extended period of time. During this period, Darlington continued to *dun* (to harass with repeated and insistent requests for payment) their client. Four years after the first bill was submitted, Darlington brought suit for payment of the amount owed, with interest. Will Pioneer Farms be held responsible for this debt?

Executory contracts and the contract liability of a party may be discharged through the passing of a period of time longer than that allowed by the statute of limitations. The time during which actions may be taken on contracts varies from state to state. In most cases, oral contracts must be acted upon within three to six years. Written agreements usually give a party from six to ten years to begin action. Darlington Brothers, in a state requiring action within three years, would not be successful in any attempt to recover the $8,675.

3.6 Shockley damaged April's new Cadillac in an accident for which Shockley accepted all blame. Repairs would cost $1,350. Due to Shockley's financial difficulties, April was willing to settle the matter by Shockley's payment of $900. Without giving additional consideration, Shockley received a waiver, signed and delivered by April, covering any other claims he might have as a result of the accident. Does the waiver discharge Schockley from further claims by April?

By common law, an aggrieved party's claims cannot be discharged unless consideration is given by the offending party. However, the Uniform Commercial Code states that "any claim or right arising out of an alleged breach can be discharged in whole or in part without consideration by a written waiver or renunciation signed and delivered by the aggrieved party." Thus, Shockley would be discharged from liability to April even for damages not covered by Shockley's $900 payment.

3.7 Robinson applied for admission to Grant College and was accepted. He was required to post a performance bond that would assure payment of tuition even if he did not register in the September term. Robinson planned a trip to Europe during July and August. The bond contained a condition that stated that the bonding company would be responsible for Robinson's tuition payment only if he returned to the United States by September 1. Was this agreement enforceable?

Yes. If Robinson returned from Europe by September and did not register, the bonding company's agreement would be enforceable. If he did not return to the United States, the bonding company would be discharged from any liability, and the contract would be terminated.

3.8 Security Storage Company contracted with Dunmon Roofing Company to replace the roof on its warehouse. Work was to begin on July 15; the completion date was set at September 1. On July 10, the warehouse was destroyed by a fire that was not due to the negligence of Security or its employees. May Dunmon demand damages equal to the profit it would have realized had it been able to carry out the contract?

The proof of impossibility of performance is that *it cannot be done*, not *I cannot do it*. In this case, the work clearly *could not be done*. Both Security Storage Company and Dunmon Roofing Company were discharged from any liability on the agreement. The decision would have been different had the fire been the result of intentional or grossly negligent acts on the part of Security.

3.9 Interstate Truck Company entered into a one-year agreement with Huntley Products Company to haul its goods from plants in Kansas to a distribution center in St. Louis. Three months after commencing operations, Interstate was forced to pay new licensing fees and insurance rates for its trucks. The new expenses made it impossible for Interstate to continue performance without losing a large sum over the remaining months of the agreement. Interstate informed Huntley of its intention to discontinue hauling the goods. May Interstate declare the agreement rescinded because of the new regulations that made a loss inevitable?

When new legislation makes the subject matter of an agreement illegal, both parties are excused from performance and the contract is rescinded. However, if new laws, regulations, or fees make performance more difficult or more expensive, the promissor is *not* released from the terms of the agreement. Interstate is not involved in an illegal agreement; it has only been subjected to added operating costs. Only if a condition in the agreement protected Interstate from such losses would it be excused from performance.

3.10 Specialty Assemblers, Inc., accepted an offer to assemble automatic transmissions for Transmission Manufacturing Company. The terms of the agreement included the price, the length of time the contract was to run, and other pertinent conditions and agreements. Both parties agreed to the appointment of Podolsky as an inspector. His decisions, in

the form of performance certificates, would be accepted as final judgments of Specialty's work. After 300 transmissions had been assembled from parts supplied by Transmission Manufacturing, Podolsky refused to certify the work as satisfactory. He was not, however, able to point to any specific defect in the work done. What are Specialty's rights?

When a performance certificate is arbitrarily withheld, there may be fraud or collusion between the appointed inspector and one of the contracting parties. If such is the case, the wronged party may sue for the contract price even without the performance certificate. In this case, the inspector showed bias and possible collusion with Transmission Manufacturing Company. Inspection of the work done by other experts in the field could prove Specialty's right to full payment.

3.11 **Stark rented an apartment from Ocean Arms, signing a lease that would give him possession on April 1. On April 1, and for two days previous to that date, Stark had requested keys to the apartment. The manager would not turn them over, so Stark rented another apartment. He was later sued by Ocean Arms for breach of his lease agreement. Is Stark liable to Ocean Arms?**

The right to seek damages on breach of agreement requires the party suing to show proof of ability and willingness to perform as promised. In other words, there must be a *tender of performance*. Stark had made tender by obligating himself to the lease and by requesting the keys. Ocean Arms, on the other hand, made no tender. By failing to provide Stark with keys, Ocean Arms had breached the agreement.

3.12 **Ableman Construction Company signed a contract with Grant's TV and Appliance Company to install partitions, build shelves and counters, and decorate the interior of a new store. A week before starting work, Ableman received a letter from Grant's that canceled the contract. May Ableman begin legal action against Grant's immediately?**

Grant's has been guilty of an *anticipatory breach*. While performance was not required until the passing of another week, Grant's already showed intent to rescind the agreement. Today, most courts would permit the wronged party to begin action on breach of contract at once. Options permitted the wronged party in cases of anticipatory breach are: (1) to await performance for a reasonable time before bringing suit; or (2) to bring an action at once, even if the breaching party has been assured of the wronged party's decision to wait. In either case, the wronged party will have no obligation to the agreement once notice of anticipatory breach has been communicated.

3.13 **Dukes signed an agreement in which she contracted to sell her car to Clark Auto Sales for \$3,300. Dukes died of a sudden illness before carrying out the agreement. The executor of the estate declared the agreement terminated through the death of the promissor. May Clark Auto Sales enforce this contract?**

Contracts requiring personal service of a professional or artistic nature are not enforceable against the estate of a deceased. The sale of Dukes's car, however, did *not* require any personal services on her part. The agreement remains enforceable against Dukes's estate through Dukes's executor or an appointed administrator.

Review Problems

3.14 Explain the difference between *substantial performance* and *breach of contract.*

3.15 Does death or insanity always excuse contracting parties from their obligation of performance?

3.16 What is an anticipatory breach?

3.17 May contracts be terminated by the parties before performance is commenced?

3.18 What determines whether a personal-service contract will be terminated through impossibility of performance?

3.19 Is a contract terminated when one party is not able to perform because of the destruction of the contract's subject matter?

3.20 What is the definition of *legal tender?* How does *tender* differ from *legal tender?*

3.21 Does an act of God that makes performance impossible relieve promissors of their obligations under contracts?

3.22 What is the general rule related to minimizing (mitigating) damages?

3.23 What are *nominal damages?*

3.24 When may a wronged party seek redress through a court of equity?

3.25 What two types of damages may a wronged party seek against the party who has breached a contract? What type of damages may not be sought?

Answers to Review Problems

3.14 Substantial performance is complete performance except for minor details that do not affect the real intent of the contract. A breach is a failure of performance which reaches into the very heart and intent of an agreement.

3.15 No. Only in personal-service contracts of a professional or artistic type does death or insanity excuse a contracting party from performance.

3.16 A promissor's communication, before the required performance date, of his or her intention to cancel.

3.17 Yes, by mutual agreement of both contracting parties.

3.18 Agreements requiring services of a professional or artistic nature may be terminated through death, insanity, accident, or illness.

3.19 Not if performance is possible in other ways.

3.20 Legal tender is coin and currency declared to be legal in payment of all debts, public and private. Tender is offering to do, without qualification, what one is bound to do under a contract.

3.21 No, unless this release from performance is specified in the agreement.

3.22 A wronged party must do all that is reasonably possible to minimize any damages resulting from another's breach.

3.23 Nominal damages are damages awarded to a successful litigant who has not proven any actual damages. They are usually 6¢ or $1.

3.24 When money damages do not satisfy; for example, when goods to be delivered are of a unique type that cannot be secured elsewhere.

3.25 Actual damages and incidental damages may be sought; speculative damages may not.

Legal Terms

Act of God. In contracts, interference with performance resulting from wind, storm, floods, lightning, and other natural phenomena that a contracting party did not anticipate; acts of God do not release parties from their contractual obligations unless such a condition is contained in the contract.

Actual damages. Damages proven to have resulted from the other party's breach of contract.

Breach. The breaking or violation of a law; in contracts, the failure to fulfill the terms of an agreement.

Cancellation. The discharge of an otherwise enforceable agreement due to the breach of one of the parties.

Decree. The judgment of a court of equity.

Equity. A branch of law that grants relief where common law offers no adequate remedy.

Incidental damages. In addition to actual damages, other proved expenses incurred by a wronged party in a breach of contract.

Injunction. An order, issued by a court of equity, that forbids the performance of a certain act.

Liquidated damages. An amount that the parties to a contract agree will be paid as damages in case of breach.

Material alteration. An intentional alteration of the terms of a written agreement, made without the consent of both parties and resulting in changes in the rights and obligations of the parties.

Nominal damages. A small amount (usually 6¢ or $1) awarded to a person whose rights have been violated but who has not sustained any actual loss.

Rescind. To cancel or annul a contract by an act of one of the parties.

Satisfactory performance. Performance that meets the customary standards of the market place; when applied to the performance of artistic or professional obligations, satisfactory performance is determined solely by the party for whom the services are rendered.

Specific performance. A court of equity may demand such performance in cases where money damages would not be satisfactory (where the subject matter of the breached agreement is unique).

Speculative damages. Damages claimed on the basis of the hopeful expectations of the complaining party, not on factual proof of loss; speculative damages are not permitted in determining the other party's obligation to the complaining party.

Tender of performance. The act of a contracting party that shows the willingness and ability of that party to carry out an agreed-on promise.

Termination. The amicable discharge of a contract by mutual agreement.

PART II: Sales

Chapter 4

The Law of Sales

No branch of the law affects the lives of as many people as does the law of sales. Sales law provides rules that help to determine at what moment a buyer assumes title—becoming the owner of the seller's property.

What does the law do to protect a buyer of a defective television set? Who pays for the tire that blows out after only fifty miles of use? Must sales contracts always be in writing to be enforceable? No, but when may they be oral? May the seller demand the return of goods if the buyer fails to pay for them? And what may the buyer do when the seller refuses to deliver the car he agreed to sell?

All disputes over questions of ownership like these can be settled by a careful application of the principles of sales law.

CONTRACTS FOR THE SALE OF GOODS

4.1. Contracts of Sale

An agreement to sell goods is a *contract of sale* if the goods exist and are ready for delivery at the time of the sale.

EXAMPLE 1. Rodney offered to buy a motorcycle displayed at Avenue Cycle Sales. The machine was ready for delivery, and nothing had to be done to put it into operating condition. Thus, when Avenue Sales accepted Rodney's offer, a contract of sale resulted.

4.2. Contracts to Sell

Contracts to sell goods at some future time or to sell those things known as *future goods* are *contracts to sell*. The sale is not complete at the time the parties make their agreement, but at some later date. A contract to sell creates definite rights and obligations for buyer and seller but it does not make an immediate transfer of title of goods.

EXAMPLE 2. Home Products Company agreed to sell Turner a dining room set for $800. Only a floor sample, which Turner did not want, was available at the time he made the agreement. The store promised that a new set would be available in one month. Turner and the store made a contract to sell. Future delivery and payment would result in a contract of sale.

4.3 Future Goods

Goods not yet manufactured, goods not available for sale, minerals not yet mined, and wild animals in their wild state are all *future goods*. Future goods may not be transferred under a contract of sale because they are not yet owned.

EXAMPLE 3. Pacific Canneries contracted for the purchase of twenty tons of fresh tuna from a local fishing company. The fish were netted three days later and delivered to Pacific Canneries at its coastal dock. The tuna were future goods, and the contract with the fishing company was a contract to sell. Delivery of the tuna resulted in a contract of sale.

4.4 Tangible and Intangible Property

Tangible property is property that can be perceived with the senses. Tangible property has physical dimension, and its value is in the property itself. *Intangible property* consists of rights rather than goods. The value of intangible property lies in the rights assured its owner rather than in the trifling value of the document that gives proof of those rights.

EXAMPLE 4. Albert received a title certificate to a new car he recently purchased. The car had been moved from the dealer's showroom to Albert's garage. The car itself was tangible property; the title certificate was intangible property.

4.5 Things Growing

Things growing that are intended to remain in the ground are *real property*. Those things planted for the purpose of harvesting after one crop are *personal property*. (Perennials are real property. Annuals are personal property.)

EXAMPLE 5. Rogers sold his farm to Anderson Realty. He had planted a crop of wheat that was not yet harvested. He also had fields of asparagus, alfalfa, rhubarb, and other perennial crops. Rogers would be allowed to remove the wheat, his personal property. The other crops belonged to Anderson Realty, purchasers of the real property.

4.6 The Sales Agreement

An enforceable sales agreement must contain the contract requisites of (1) mutual assent, (2) competent parties, (3) consideration, and (4) valid subject matter.

EXAMPLE 6. Arthur's Men's Shop sold Rudolph four shirts and three neckties. The parties mutually agreed to the contract, they were competent to contract, each received a benefit in return for some sacrifice, and the agreement was lawful. The agreement was therefore valid and enforceable.

4.7 Express and Implied Agreements

Sales contracts may be expressed by oral or written agreements. Sales contracts may also be implied by the parties' acts.

EXAMPLE 7. Saunders offered the Lake Marina $550 if they would sand and paint his boat. The marina did what Saunders had requested without saying yes or no to his proposition. In this case, Saunders expressed his offer; the marina's acceptance was implied by their actions—doing the work.

4.8 Statute of Frauds

The statute of frauds requires a written agreement in all executory contracts for the sale of goods valued at $500 or more. Parts of agreements already carried out are valid when there has been partial delivery or partial payment.

EXAMPLE 8. Miller Furniture Mart sold Hart furniture that was valued at $1,900. There was no written agreement. Miller delivered $450 worth of the furniture, which was accepted by Hart. Hart is obligated to pay the $450, but neither party could enforce the uncompleted delivery or payment in absence of a written agreement.

4.9 Sales with Right to Return Goods

In a *sale on approval*, ownership of goods does not pass until the buyer registers approval of goods delivered. In a *sale or return* agreement, title passes at the time of delivery, but the buyer has the right to return goods if they are not satisfactory.

EXAMPLE 9. Mitchell agreed to try out a new tractor sold by Hewett Farm Supply. It was agreed that Mitchell had one week to decide whether he would buy the machine or return it. This was a sale on approval. Had Mitchell bought the tractor under terms that he could return it if it was unsatisfactory, the contract would have been a sale or return agreement.

4.10 Conditional Sales

Sales that contain conditions that must be fulfilled before or after title passes are *conditional sales*. The conditions may be written, oral, or implied.

EXAMPLE 10. O'Rourke bought a used motorcycle from Cycle Service. The seller agreed to renew the points, replace the spark plugs, and adjust the brake cables before delivery. Until the work was finished, title would not pass to O'Rourke. These were *conditions precedent*. A condition that would give O'Rourke the right to return possession and ownership to the seller "if not satisfied" would be a *condition subsequent*.

4.11 Right to Transfer Title

Only the owner or the owner's agent has the right to transfer title. Title may not be transferred by one who has possession of goods that are lost, stolen, or left for servicing or repair. The owner, however, may not deny title of an *innocent purchaser*—one who has innocently purchased goods from an unauthorized seller.

EXAMPLE 11. Turner bought a diamond ring from Poland Jewelers. He signed a conditional sales agreement that stated that title would *not* pass until twelve installment payments had been made. The jeweler's right of ownership was expressed clearly in the agreement, but Turner sold the ring to an innocent purchaser. Title to the ring would pass to this third party unless Poland Jewelers had filed a copy of the conditional sales agreement in a public office. If they had not done so, their only recourse for recovery of the balance of the sales price would be to sue Turner and obtain a judgment against him. Poland could not sue the innocent purchaser.

EXAMPLE 12. Ahern left a new bag at a shop to have her initials put on it. By mistake, the shop sold the bag to another customer, receiving full payment. Ahern would be barred from recovering the bag from the innocent purchaser. She could, however, recover money damages from the shop.

4.12 When Does Title Pass?

Title passes to a buyer when there has been an *unconditional contract* of sale of *specific goods* in a *deliverable state*.

EXAMPLE 13. Retail Outlet Stores sold Nelson two sweaters from a lot of one-hundred that were displayed. The sweaters were boxed and ready for delivery, with no conditions to be fulfilled by either party prior to passing of ownership. Thus there was a contract of sale for two specific sweaters. Title therefore passed.

4.13 Passing Title to Fungible Goods

Fungible goods are those sold by weight or measure. Identification of a buyer's specific lot is not required in passing title to fungible goods. Damage to fungible goods owned by two or more parties and stored together are proportionally shared.

EXAMPLE 14. Forman purchased 10,000 gallons of number one fuel oil held in storage tank Number 231, which contained 100,000 gallons. The rest of the fuel oil in the tank was held by the seller and others. Title to the oil was passed to each owner without the necessity of separating or identifying each owner's specific lot. A leak in the tank resulted in the loss of 5,000 gallons of the oil. Each owner would be required to accept a loss proportional to the number of gallons he or she owned. Forman would have to accept a loss of 500 gallons.

4.14 Ownership of Goods in Transit

Goods may be sold with the condition that delivery will be by the seller's carrier; in that case, title will not pass until delivery is complete. When goods are shipped by a common carrier, ownership passes according to the shipping terms. If the terms are "f.o.b. shipping point," title passes when the goods are delivered to the carrier. If the terms are "f.o.b. destination," title passes when the goods reach the destination stated in the bill of lading. (The letters *f.o.b.* mean "free on board.")

EXAMPLE 15. A front-end loader was shipped to Corrado Contractors, of Chicago, by Road Machines, Inc., of Seattle. The terms were f.o.b. Seattle. The loader was damaged during shipment by rail. By the terms of shipment, title passed when the loader was delivered *to* the railroad in Seattle. Recovery for damages must be sought by Corrado Contractors.

4.15 Express Warranties

Seller and buyer may agree on any warranties to be included in the agreement. *Warranties* are factual statements or representations by the seller made through advertising or made during negotiation of an agreement. Warranties may be either written or oral.

EXAMPLE 16. Acme Radio Corporation advertised a new radio that would pick up police calls, aircraft messages, and amateur communications. Palone purchased one of the sets. He could not, however, pick up any police broadcasts. The advertisement represented the manufacturer's and the seller's warranty. Palone could seek damages or demand reimbursement on his return of the radio.

4.16 Implied Warranties

The law implies warranties of quality and warranties of title. A seller implies that she or he is the owner with the right to sell (*implied warranty of title*). A seller also implies that goods will fit the description the seller has made and that the goods will be suited to the purpose for which they are sold (*implied warranty of quality*).

EXAMPLE 17. Harrington bought a typewriter from Simpson for $95. It was later discovered that Simpson had stolen the machine. Harrington had to give the typewriter to detectives who were investigating the robbery. Harrington could demand reimbursement and damages from Simpson because of the implied warranty of title.

4.17 *Caveat Emptor*

The principle of *caveat emptor* ("let the buyer beware") holds that there is no warranty against defects that would have been obvious to the buyer on her or his ordinary examination of the goods. Of course the buyer must have the opportunity to examine the goods, and the seller must not be guilty of concealing any defects.

EXAMPLE 18. Zebley bought a new outboard motor from Whitbread's Marina. When the seller demonstrated the motor, Zebley failed to notice an oil emission coming from the exhaust. (This emission signalled the motor's excessive use of oil.) *Caveat emptor* would bar Zebley from recovery of damages because she had not taken advantage of the opportunity to examine the motor closely.

4.18 Seller's Rights in Breached Contract

A buyer's refusal to accept delivery of or to pay the price for ordered goods gives the seller the right: (1) to store the goods and sue the buyer for the price; (2) to sell goods of a perishable nature and sue the buyer for any loss due to the breach; or (3) to keep the goods and sue the buyer for the difference between the contract price and the present market price.

EXAMPLE 19. Harper, a farmer, contracted to deliver 1,000 baskets of ripe tomatoes to Webber Cannery. When the tomatoes were delivered, the cannery manager refused to accept them because of a glut on the market. Harper sold the tomatoes to another cannery, but at a price that was 10¢ per bushel less than the price on the contract with Webber. Harper would be right in demanding $100 and other related damages from Webber Cannery.

4.19 Right of Stoppage in Transit

Discovery of a buyer's insolvency after goods have been shipped gives the seller the right to instruct a carrier to interrupt delivery. This may be done even in shipments that are f.o.b. shipping point. The seller must give a bond to the carrier to cover any damage the carrier might suffer should the buyer turn out to be solvent.

EXAMPLE 20. One-hundred television sets were shipped by All-State Electronics to Hendley Stores. The terms were f.o.b. shipping point. Financial writers reported that Hendley was bankrupt. To protect its company from an almost certain loss, All-State instituted proceedings of *stoppage in transit*, even though title had already passed to Hendley.

4.20 Buyer's Remedies in Seller's Breach

Delivery of the wrong quantity, delivery of unsatisfactory goods, or complete failure to deliver gives the buyer the right to demand damages. Before title has passed, the buyer may seek damages based on the contract. If the seller fails to deliver goods after title has already passed, the buyer may also seek recovery under a tort action of *conversion*, a claim that the seller who has given up title to certain goods still treats the goods as his or her own.

EXAMPLE 21. Avenue Jewelers sold a pocket watch to Roberts for $225, which Roberts paid in full. There were no conditions attached to the sale. Roberts arranged to pick up the watch the next day. When he arrived at the store, the jeweler would not give it to him, saying that the salesman had mistakenly shown him a $525 watch. The jeweler is guilty of a breach of a contract of sale, and Roberts may seek damages. Roberts may also sue the jeweler in tort for conversion because in withholding the watch the jeweler was acting as if he still owned it.

4.21 Actions in Equity Against Seller

When goods are unique (not available generally in the market place), a buyer may demand delivery, against the seller's wishes, by petitioning a court of equity for a decree of *specific performance*. This procedure is not permitted in a breach of a sale of goods that are generally available. (If the goods are generally available, money damages may be sought in a court of law.)

EXAMPLE 22. Sobocinski bought a Stradivarius violin from Salter. A written agreement specified that the violin would be delivered the following day, on receipt of Sobocinski's certified check for $15,000. When the check was tendered, Salter refused to deliver the violin. Sobocinski's interest in the instrument would not be satisfied in an action for damages. His interest was in securing the instrument. The violin in question was unique; it could not be duplicated by going into the market place. A decree of specific performance would demand delivery of the instrument to the buyer.

4.22 Credit Sales Agreement

Goods sold under an ordinary thirty-day *charge account* imply passing of title at the time of the sale. *Installment sales* usually provide for the passing of title only after all payments have been made. A *bailment lease* agreement provides for the rental of goods for a period of months, after which title passes on payment of a token sum, such as $1. To be valid and enforceable, interest charged must be within the amounts permitted by state law.

EXAMPLE 23. Durstein bought four new tires at the Auto Accessories Shop, charging them with his credit card. Payment was due at the end of thirty days. Durstein failed to make payment as agreed. Auto Accessories attempted to take back the tires. Under the regular charge account agreement, title to the tires had already passed to Durstein. The seller's only remedy would be an action brought for collection of money owed.

4.23 Credit and the Truth-in-Lending Law

Regulation *Z* of the Truth-in-Lending Law (a federal law) requires sellers and lenders to disclose all pertinent information related to any credit transaction. The cash price, the cost of financing in dollars, and financing charges shown as an annual percentage rate must be communicated to the buyer or debtor. If credit terms are included in advertising, all of the above information must be shown.

EXAMPLE 24. Arundel Appliance Center advertised air conditioners at "$21 each month, payments not to start until sixty days after installation." The appliance store did not include the cash price, interest, and other information required by the Truth-in-Lending Law. Thus, the store was liable to criminal action and fine.

Solved Problems

4.1 Central Coin Shop contracted to sell Wilson six one-dollar bills that were more than one-hundred years old. (The bills were no longer accepted as legal tender.) Central breached its agreement, and Wilson brought suit on the sales contract. Central responded by arguing that the money was intangible property and thus did not come within the requirements of sales law. Was Central's argument valid?

No. Old currency is not valued for its intangible quality—what it assures a buyer in the market place. The value is in the paper currency itself, for its collector's value. The money was tangible property, and Wilson's action against Central was correctly brought.

4.2 South Atlantic Importers contracted to deliver 1,000 songbirds to Eastern Department Stores on or before October 15. A federal agency discovered that the type of bird being sold carried an infectious disease. The agency ruled against any importation of the birds into the United States. May Eastern Department Stores recover damages for breach of this agreement?

No. A requisite of all enforceable sales agreements is that they conform with federal, state, and local laws. Sales agreements are also regulated by decisions of agencies created for the protection of the health, safety, and welfare of the citizens of the United States. The agreement between Eastern and South Atlantic is therefore voided. At the time it was created, the contract was valid; however, the subsequent regulation made the agreement invalid and unenforceable.

4.3 Reuther orally agreed to the delivery of a chain hoist for $238, a small air compressor and tank for $285, and a pneumatic shop jack for $187. When the goods arrived, Reuther refused to accept them. In the seller's action on breach, Reuther defended himself by citing the statute of frauds, which requires that sales agreements of $500 or more be in writing. Was Reuther's argument valid?

No. Reuther's agreement was for three separate items, each of which was priced below $500. No one of the tools he agreed to purchase was an integral part of the other two. Reuther's defense may be set aside, and damages may be assessed in favor of the seller.

4.4 Hanlaw's Paper Supply entrusted a bill of lading to one of its employees, who was instructed to go to the local freight station and pick up a shipment of lighting fixtures. The employee, for value received, transferred the bill of lading to an innocent purchaser, who then took delivery of the fixtures from the carrier. Hanlaw's attempted to recover title and possession of the shipment from the innocent purchaser. Does Hanlaw's have sufficient title rights to succeed in this action?

No. Hanlaw's permitted its employee to have evidence of title. The innocent purchaser believed that his transaction with the employee was authorized. Hanlaw's may not recover the goods from the third party. Their only action is against the employee.

4.5 Alberts purchased clothing on a lay-away plan. (The store would keep possession of the clothes until Alberts returned and paid for them.) Alberts had picked out the items in question, and the clerk had marked them for her. Before Alberts returned, the clothes were sold to another buyer. What action may Alberts take against the store?

This was a sale *with a lien reserved*. The goods were specific, in a deliverable state, and there were no conditions to be carried out. Title had already passed to Alberts. The store retained possession only as security of payment. The store had sold goods belonging to Alberts, who could sue for damages on grounds of breach of contract. Alberts could also bring a suit on grounds of a tort of conversion because the store treated Alberts's goods "as their own."

4.6 Hershey made the successful bid on an eighteenth-century highboy at the Gap Auction. Her bid was $2,750. At the close of the sale, Hershey refused to make payment of the $2,750, claiming that the agreement should have been in writing because the price exceeded $500. May Gap Auction enforce the sale?

Yes. Agreements made at auction need not be in writing to satisfy the statute of frauds. The entry in the auction clerk's record is sufficient. Hershey is liable on the bid that she made and that was accepted by the auctioneer.

4.7 Midwest Wheat Company sold 100,000 bushels of harvested wheat to the Maryland Baking Company. The agreement did not indicate which of Midwest's ten grain elevators held the grain sold. Fire destroyed all of the elevators and their contents. Is Maryland Baking Company obligated to pay Midwest for the wheat on the grounds that title had passed?

No. Title to fungible goods passes at the time of the sale without the usual requisite of identifying the goods. However, when the seller has similar goods stored in more than one tank, elevator, or other depository, there must be an identification of the depository in which the sold goods are held. Midwest had not identified the elevator in which Maryland's wheat was stored. Therefore title did not pass, and the buyer had no liability in the loss of the wheat.

4.8 Harley agreed to sell an acquaintance a one-half interest in a power boat stored at Lake Placid. Disputes later arose about the boat, and Harley threatened to remove the engine and other parts of the craft that he claimed as his one-half share in ownership. Was Harley's claim correct?

No. Co-owners of *indivisible property* have a proportional title interest in the *entire* property, not in any separate, identifiable part. Harley did not have full title to the motor and the other parts he selected. Both Harley and the other party had equal title rights to the *entire* boat. (This is known as an *undivided interest*.)

4.9 Four boxes of books were shipped to the Community Book Store by Books, Inc. The terms were f.o.b., c.o.d. Community demanded immediate delivery from the common carrier, who refused on the grounds that Community had not yet paid for the books. Community claimed that title to the books had passed when the boxes were delivered to the carrier at the point of shipment. Was the carrier correct in retaining possession until payment was made?

Yes. F.o.b., without further designation, implies that title passes at the shipping point. The added term c.o.d. implies that the carrier is the seller's agent for collection of money due. This is a *sale with a lien reserved,* where title passes to the buyer but possession is retained until payment is made. The carrier would have been in error if it had given up possession before receiving payment.

4.10 Ulmstead bought a used car from General Car Sales. He thoroughly inspected the car before signing a sales agreement. The agreement contained terms of guaranty that stated, "Seller warrants that it will replace defective parts within a period of thirty days of purchase date. Buyer will be charged 50 percent of the cost of parts and labor needed for replacement. No other warranties, express or implied, are made with this sale." The car turned out to be generally unsatisfactory, and Ulmstead attempted to enforce the implied warranty of fitness. Will he succeed in an action against General Sales?

No. A seller's disclaimer is valid if it is conspicuous enough so that the buyer can see it in the agreement. General's disclaimer was contained in the body of the agreement, along with the express warranty.

4.11 TV and Radio Sales sold a color television set to Blackstone. The salesman told Blackstone that the set was superior to any other on the market, that the price could not be equalled elsewhere, and that the set would out-perform any set sold by any other manufacturer. Blackstone bought the set and found it to be somewhat inferior to another set, which was owned by a friend. Blackstone attempted to rescind the sale on grounds of breach of warranty. Would he succeed?

No. Courts recognize "puffing" and opinion as separate and different from *statements of fact*. Factual statements that influence a person's decision to buy are accepted as warranties, even when the words *warranty and guarantee* are not used in making such statements. All of the claims made by the salesman, however, were opinion and "puffing." Although they influenced Blackstone's actions, they were not actionable.

4.12 Shoppers' Hardware Store sold five gallons of "outside white" paint to Eastburn. Eastburn was seeking paint suitable for use on an oceanside property, but he did not mention this fact to anyone at the store. Several months after it was applied, the paint greyed and showed serious erosion from salt spray. Eastburn asked for damages on a breach of the implied warranty of fitness. Is the seller or manufacturer liable?

No. An implied warranty of fitness exists when the seller is informed by the buyer of some special use intended for a product. A warranty also exists when statements on the label or in advertising express or imply that the product may be used with success in specific applications. Eastburn did not consult the seller about how he intended to use the paint. This was a case of *buyer's choice*. Had the seller recommended the paint for oceanside use, this would have been a case of *seller's choice*, and an implied warranty of fitness could have been inferred. As it was, Eastburn had no actionable complaint.

4.13 Ralston purchased a new automobile from Avenue Auto Sales. The agreement carried the usual new-car warranties and exclusions. Three months after taking delivery, Ralston, his wife, and a family guest were seriously injured when the right front wheel collapsed while the car was traveling at 52 m.p.h. The injured parties began an action against Avenue Auto Sales and the manufacturer for all damages resulting from the accident. Will they win this suit?

Yes. Manufacturers are now liable to parties injured as a result of defects in the design, manufacture, or assembly of their products. This is known as *product liability*. The obligation is to the buyer, to family members or guests, and, under *strict liability*, to other parties who might be injured from the manufacturer's or seller's failure to provide a safe consumer product.

4.14 Brass Fittings, Inc., contracted to sell Central Plumbing Supply merchandise amounting to $4,245. Contracts and confirmations were executed, and shipment was made. Central Plumbing refused delivery, so Brass Fittings commenced action for damages resulting from the breach. How will damages be determined in this case?

The seller may sell to another the goods refused by Central. If the market price has dipped, the seller may sue for the difference between the contract price and the market price available on resale. If there has been a market-price increase, there will be no damages related to price. However, if Brass Fittings, Inc., experienced any other damages through the buyer's breach, it may seek recovery for them.

4.15 One week before the contracted delivery date of a new car, Granby called the dealer and said to her that he had changed his mind and was going to buy his new car from another dealer. "Just forget the whole thing," were his words. Must the dealer await the date of delivery or may she immediately treat the agreement as breached?

Granby's statement was an *anticipatory breach* because the date of delivery had not yet arrived. Some courts will not even consider a complaint of breach until the agreed-on date of performance. Other courts will allow the seller to declare the agreement rescinded before the date of performance. In either case, the party guilty of the breach (the buyer) may be billed for damages. Furthermore, any down payment previously paid to the dealer would not be returnable unless the down payment was unreasonably high in view of the damages suffered by the seller.

4.16 Echrich was guaranteed satisfaction when she purchased a new raincoat from Hanby's. Shortly after buying the coat, she returned it, saying only that she was not satisfied and wanted her money returned. Does Echrich have the right to make an arbitrary decision of dissatisfaction in this case?

Probably not. The buyer of manufactured goods is not the sole, arbitrary judge of satisfaction. (By contrast, the buyer of a personal service, such as having a portrait painted, *is* the only judge of satisfaction.) Whether or not the raincoat was satisfactory depends on more than Echrich's judgment; it would depend also on the judgment of people who were familiar with the market place of women's clothes and women's raincoats in particular.

4.17 Cycle Shop sold a new 250-cc motorcycle to Trainer. The terms of sale included Cycle Shop's agreement to tune up the engine and have the cycle road-ready. When Trainer returned to take delivery of the machine, Cycle Shop informed him that they had decided to keep it as a demonstration model. Trainer sought delivery through a decree of specific performance in a court of equity. Will Trainer succeed?

No. A decree of specific performance will not be permitted when money damages satisfy. Trainer might be set on getting delivery of that specific motorcycle, but a court would probably rule that the cycle was not unique. Other machines of the same make, model, style, and color would be available elsewhere. Trainer's only remedy would be in an action for damages he sustained because of the dealer's breach.

4.18 Doughten purchased living-room and dining-room furniture for her new home. The sale was financed and secured by a *chattel mortgage* on all personal property owned by Doughten. When she failed to meet scheduled payments, the seller sought a court order giving him the right to sell Doughten's car and other property to recover money owed. Doughten countered the action, claiming that the seller had a right only to the furniture bought. Was she correct?

No. Installment sales, like other debts, may be secured by a chattel mortgage, which gives the creditor a right to recover by selling any or all of the debtor's property, excluding certain things barred by law.

4.19 Baldt signed an agreement with Broadway Sales for the purchase of lawn furniture. The agreement included financing arrangements with Citywide Loans. Baldt agreed to make twelve monthly payments of $50 each for the furniture. In effect, this meant that he was paying 24 percent interest. The contract did not state the cash price of the furniture, the cost of financing in dollars, or the rate of interest expressed as an annual percent rate. Was the financing agreement valid?

No, for several reasons. The seller and financing agent were guilty of not having followed the requirements of the Truth-in-Lending Act, making them both liable to a criminal complaint from Baldt. Furthermore, it is not likely that any state would accept 24 percent *per annum* as a rate of interest. For both reasons, Baldt's agreement with Broadway Sales would be invalid.

Review Problems

4.20 Distinguish between *contracts of sale* and *contracts to sell.*

4.21 What are *future goods?*

4.22 How do sales agreements compare with other contracts?

4.23 Are sales contracts regulated by any provision of the statute of frauds?

4.24 Compare the title rights of a seller in a *sale on approval* and in a *sale or return agreement.*

4.25 Who has the right to pass title to a buyer in the sale of personal property?

4.26 When does title pass?

4.27 Enumerate the implied warranties associated with the sale of goods.

4.28 Explain *caveat emptor* as it applies to a sale of personal property.

4.29 Under what conditions may a buyer enter a complaint in a court of equity?

4.30 When does title pass to the buyer under the usual terms of a thirty-day charge account?

4.31 How does the Truth-in-Lending Law protect a credit customer?

Answers to Review Problems

4.20 In a contract of sale, title to goods passes at the time of the sale. In contracts to sell, title does not pass until some later time.

4.21 Future goods are those not in existence at the time a contract is made. They include minerals not yet mined, fish still in the sea, wild animals in the field, and goods not yet manufactured.

4.22 There is no difference. A sales agreement is a contract that contains the same contract requisites that are required of any other enforceable agreement.

4.23 Yes. All contracts for sales of personal property must be written when the price is $500 or more.

4.24 In a sale on approval, title does not pass to the buyer until approval has been expressed. In a sale or return agreement, the buyer receives title at the time of the sale, with a right to return the goods to the seller if not satisfied.

4.25 Only the owner or the owner's authorized agent has this right.

4.26 Title passes when the parties intend it to pass.

4.27 *The implied warranties of title:* that the seller is the owner, has the right to sell, and that the buyer will not be interrupted in title rights to the goods. *Implied warranties of quality:* that the goods will fit their description, will be no different from a sample, and will be fit for the purpose for which they were sold.

4.28 A buyer, when given the opportunity to examine goods being sold, has an obligation to make a reasonable examination of them. The buyer may not complain, after the sale is completed, of defects or damages that would have been discovered on a reasonable examination of the goods.

4.29 In cases where money damages will not satisfy.

4.30 Title passes at the time of the sale, not when payment is finally made.

4.31 All details concerning the credit agreement must be disclosed at the time of the sale and in any advertising which contains mention of credit as a feature of a sale.

Legal Terms

Caveat emptor. "Let the buyer beware." The obligation of the buyer to examine goods purchased when such a right is given before the sale is completed; *caveat emptor* waives the buyer's right of complaint when goods received do not meet specifications or the seller's description.

Conversion. The unlawful assumption and exercise of ownership over property belonging to another.

Fungible goods. Goods, each unit of which is substantially the same as every other; may be sold, estimated, and replaced according to weight, measure, or number.

Future goods. Goods not yet manufactured or made ready for the market place; includes minerals not yet mined and wild animals in their wild state.

Intangible property. Ownership rights or documents giving proof of these rights, rather than property itself; deeds, currency, title certificates, and commercial paper are all classified as intangible property.

Sale on approval. A sale of personal property with the condition that title does not pass to the buyer until the buyer's approval is stated or is implied by action.

Sale or return. A sale containing a condition that gives the buyer the right to return both title and possession of goods to the seller in the event of dissatisfaction or other agreed-to circumstance.

Stoppage in transit. A seller's statutory right to interrupt delivery of goods shipped by common carrier when buyer's insolvency becomes apparent after shipment has been made; applicable to both shipping-point and destination shipments.

Tangible property. Goods that have value in and of themselves, that are discernible to the senses, and that have physical dimension.

Warranty. A seller's statement of fact about the goods she or he is selling.

Examination I

Contracts, Sales

1. Goldstein found a watch. There was no identification that permitted him to locate its owner. An advertisement appearing in the local newspaper two days later identified the watch and offered a $25 reward to the finder if he or she would return it. Goldstein responded to the advertisement and returned the watch. The owner refused to pay the reward, stating that the advertisement was merely an invitation to trade, not a binding offer. May Goldstein recover the $25 reward?

Yes. The advertisement was not directed to the general public, but to one person—the finder of the watch. Goldstein, alone, could accept the offer, which he did while the offer was still in force. The owner's reasoning was incorrect.

2. A CB radio was sold to Downie by a salesman working in Central Radio Stores. The salesman stated that the set had twenty-three channels. Downie later discovered that the set had only eleven channels. Downie sued Central Radio in an action of fraud. The salesman, denying any intent to defraud Downie, claimed that he had made a mistake. Will Downie recover damages in his action of fraud?

No. Fraud requires proof that the defendant knowingly misrepresented goods or services with the intent to defraud the other party. Unless he could prove that the salesman had intentionally cheated him, Downie would not succeed in his complaint. Downie's claim should have been based on misrepresentation, which requires no proof of wrongful intent. Such a claim would return Downie and Central Radio to their original positions: Central Radio would take back the CB radio, and Downie would have his money returned.

3. While intoxicated, Hill bought an expensive fur jacket from Harvey's Fur Shop, paying with her check for $1,390. Several hours later, realizing what she had done, she stopped payment on the check. Harvey's sued Hill for the $1,390 and refused to accept the return of the jacket. Will Harvey's succeed in its action against Hill?

No. Hill was intoxicated and was therefore not competent to enter into a contract with Harvey's. Harvey's could force payment only if they could prove that Hill's intoxication did *not* deprive her of her mental abilities and awareness of her actions.

4. Gumpert, an auto mechanic, agreed to adjust the timing and tune the engine of Reynolds's Cadillac for $190. Delivery was promised for the next day at 4 P.M. Gumpert called Reynolds the next morning and said that he could promise delivery only if Reynolds would pay him an additional $25. Reynolds went along with the mechanic's proposition, but when he went to pick up the car he would pay only the $190 originally agreed on. Was Reynolds legally justified in refusing to pay the additional $25?

The promise to pay the additional $25 was made without additional consideration to Reynolds. He was to receive no benefit over and above what Gumpert had agreed to do for $190 when the contract was made. The promise to pay the $25 was a barren promise, not supported by consideration and therefore not enforceable.

5. Murray Builders agreed to construct a two-car garage next to Corrozi's house. Murray assured Corrozi, "If you are not absolutely satisfied, you won't have to pay a cent!" Murray Builders did a flawless job, but Corrozi expressed dissatisfaction and held Murray to his "absolute satisfaction" statement. May Murray Builders force Corrozi to pay the contract price for the new garage?

Satisfaction in contracts of this kind does not depend solely on the buyer's personal judgment. Satisfaction is determined by standards of the market place: what would ordinarily be accepted as satisfactory by those engaged in the same trade in the same geographic area.

6. Price Associates orally agreed to hire Minsky, an engineer, for five years. Minsky was to work as a project leader. Her main responsibilities were to supervise and evaluate a team of experts who were trying to reduce water pollution in a coal-mining operation. After six months Minsky was fired, with no reason given, with no separation pay, and with an immediate cutoff of salary. May Minsky recover damages for breach of the employment agreement?

No. The statute of frauds and the Uniform Commercial Code require that contracts must be evidenced by *written* promises when they cannot be completed within one year of the date on which the contract is made. Minsky, without knowledge of these requirements, entered into an oral agreement that was to run for five years. Price Associates acted legally.

7. Shirley Frozen Foods, Inc., contracted to buy sugar corn grown by Hindsley Farms. Shirley was to harvest the corn and transport it to its local freezing plant. Two weeks before the corn was ready for harvesting, Hindsley permitted others to go into his fields and gather several bushels of corn. Shirley threatened to bring an action against these other parties, claiming that they had taken Shirley's corn. Would this action succeed?

No. The contract with Hindsley Farms was for future goods. Title would not pass until the corn was ready for harvesting, as judged by inspectors from Shirley Frozen Foods, Inc. The decision to harvest had not been made at the time the others were allowed to take the corn. Title to the corn had not passed to Shirley and Shirley had no title rights on which to base an action. However, Shirley could have sued Hindsley for damages on the contract.

8. The owner of Hobby Craft designed and built a small biplane, which was displayed for sale on a mall adjacent to Hobby Craft's store. Dale contracted to buy the plane for the asking price, $3,900. He was to take delivery on July 18. On that date, Hobby Craft refused to part with the aircraft when Dale tendered the $3,900. Dale sought to enforce delivery through an action in a court of law. Did he succeed?

No. A court of law could do no more than order money damages for breach of contract. Dale's action should have been through a court of equity because he was seeking a decree of specific performance in the sale of unique goods (goods not available elsewhere). Money damages would not satisfy in this case.

9. Standard Supply, Inc., called Butler Office Furniture and placed the following order: (1) One secretary's desk, $350; (2) one electric water cooler, $185; (3) three oak office chairs, $127 each. Standard Supply refused delivery when the order arrived, claiming that the agreement was not enforceable under the provisions of the statute of frauds. May Butler Furniture enforce its agreement with Standard?

Yes. The statute of frauds and the Uniform Commercial Code require that sales agreements be evidenced by written contracts when the sales price of the articles sold exceeds $500. Standard's contract was for specific, unrelated items, not one of which was priced above the $500 statutory limit. This was a *divisible contract,* not an *entire contract.* The agreement was enforceable.

10. Chapman sold a used car to Young, claiming that it was an excellent buy at the price, that Young could do no better elsewhere, that the appearance of the car always brought compliments from those who saw it, and that no better selection could be made in seeking economical transportation. Young became unhappy with the car after buying it and sued Chapman on grounds of fraud, claiming that all of his statements were false. Will Young succeed in this action against Chapman?

No. Statements made by a seller are actionable in fraud only when they are made as statements of fact. Everything stated by Chapman came within the definitions of "puffing" or opinion. Lacking proof of any intentionally false statements of fact, Young would fail in this action.

PART III: Commercial Paper

Chapter 5

Types of Commercial Paper

Try to imagine an economic system in which consumers and businesses would use only cash for *all* of their purchases. Trade and commerce over long distances would be practically impossible. The problems of loss and theft would surely increase. And all large financial transactions would be cumbersome and time-consuming. The situation would be chaotic.

Commercial paper, in its many forms, takes the place of cash in our modern economy. Today, as much as 90 percent of all the business transacted in the United States makes use of commercial paper. Currency alone could not even begin to meet the needs of our economic system.

With commercial paper, people and institutions can either *promise* to pay money or *order* that money be paid to some other person or institution. Such a promise or order is written on a document called an *instrument*. Everyday examples of such instruments are checks, bonds, and certificates of deposit. Some instruments are negotiable—ownership of them can be *transferred* (or *negotiated*) from one party to another, almost as if they were cash. Other instruments are *nonnegotiable*—they may not be transferred. Regulations covering negotiability are discussed in this and the two following chapters.

In many ways, instruments are like contracts that promise payment or that order payment. But there are important differences between ordinary contracts and the instruments of commercial paper. Contract rights may be assigned, but commercial paper can be transferred only through negotiation. The assignee of a contract never has rights superior to those of the assignor, whereas the person to whom a negotiable instrument is transferred may have rights superior to those of the previous holder of the instrument.

Laws relating to commercial paper came first from the common law; later, they were incorporated in the statutes of most states. As interstate commerce developed, most states adopted the Uniform Negotiable Instrument Law (N.I.L.). And finally, in 1952, regulations concerning commercial paper were standardized in the Uniform Commercial Code (U.C.C.).

PROMISE INSTRUMENTS

Commercial paper may be classified into two general types, one of which is the *promise instrument*. A promise instrument contains the words "I [we] promise to pay . . ." or words to that effect. Promise instruments involve two parties, a maker and a payee. The *maker*, who makes and signs the instrument, is responsible for paying the *payee*, the person to whom the instrument is payable. Promise instruments may or may not bear interest, and they may or may not be negotiable.

EXAMPLE 1. Jensen promised to give his daughter $200 on June 25, when she would graduate from college. As a contract, this promise would not be enforceable because no consideration was given to Jensen. Suppose, however, that Jensen (as maker) gave his daughter (as payee) a negotiable promise instrument for $200, payable on June 25. If she negotiated (transferred) this note to a new holder, such as a merchant from whom she had purchased a $200 coat, her father would have to pay the holder $200 on June 25.

5.1 Negotiable Promissory Notes

A *negotiable promissory note* is one of the most common promise instruments. It is an unconditional written promise, signed by the maker, to pay on demand or at a definite time in the future a sum certain in money. The payee may be either a specific person or the bearer of the note.

EXAMPLE 2. Curley borrowed $1,500 from the Hartford Finance Company. He signed a negotiable promissory note for the amount, payable in ninety days with 4½ percent interest. Hartford Finance then discounted the note at the National Bank of Springfield. In other words, Curley's note was transferred, during the ninety-day period, from one holder to another. When the note came due, National Bank presented it to Curley for payment.

5.2 Bonds

A *bond* is a promissory note signed by the maker and under seal. The makers of bonds are usually corporations or political entities like cities, state commissions, or even nations. The makers usually issue interest-bearing bonds for sale to investors. Bonds may be either negotiable or nonnegotiable.

EXAMPLE 3. To secure new funds, the Cleaver Corporation offered a series of interest-bearing bonds to investors. The bonds matured at the end of twenty years from the date of issue. At that time, the holders of bonds could collect from Cleaver the original purchase price plus the agreed-on interest.

ORDER INSTRUMENTS

The second type of commercial paper is the *order instrument*, in which the person making the instrument orders another to make payment to a third party. Order instruments involve at least three parties; promise instruments require only two parties. The parties involved in all order instruments are: the *drawer*, who makes and signs the instrument; the *drawee*, on whom the instrument is drawn and who makes the payment; and the *payee*, the party to whom payment is made. The most common order instruments are checks.

EXAMPLE 4. Carmello (the drawer) deposited money in his checking account in the Home Bank & Trust Company (the drawee). He then issued checks to various people (the payees). In effect, Carmello was *ordering* Home Bank & Trust to pay out definite amounts of money. Checks differ from other order instruments in that they are *always* made payable by a named bank. The drawee in other order instruments is not necessarily a bank.

5.3 Drafts

A *draft,* or *bill of exchange,* is an unconditional written order in which one person (the drawer) requests another (the drawee) to pay a certain sum of money to a third person or the bearer (the payee). A *sight draft* requires a drawee to pay the payee on demand—as soon as the draft is presented. A *time draft* gives the drawee a certain amount of time to pay: the draft may be payable a definite number of days after it is presented ("payable after sight") or a certain number of days after the date on the instrument ("payable after date"). If the draft, or bill of exchange, is drawn in one state or country and payable in another state or country it is considered to be a *foreign bill of exchange*.

EXAMPLE 5. Stanley, of Baltimore, owed $300 to Jefferson, who lived in Kansas City. Jefferson, in turn, owed $300 to Holden, who lived in Baltimore. Jefferson (the drawer) signed a draft ordering Stanley (the drawee) to pay Holden (the payee) at sight. Jefferson issued a sight draft to Holden, who then presented it to Stanley for immediate payment of the $300.

5.4 Traveler's Checks

Traveler's checks that are not drawn on banks are not, strictly speaking, checks. They are, instead, drafts. If drawn on a reputable financial institution, traveler's checks are very useful: they are accepted almost as legal tender in most places and they can be replaced if they are stolen or lost.

5.5 Certificates of Deposit

A *certificate of deposit* is a negotiable order instrument issued by a bank to a depositor. With it, the bank acknowledges receipt of the depositor's money and promises to pay the money, at a definite future date, to the depositor or some other party named in the instrument. Corporations often deposit money with banks and receive interest-bearing certificates of deposit in return. They do this because in most states corporations are prohibited from having interest-bearing savings accounts.

EXAMPLE 6. Chandler, Inc., received a $25,000 cash payment for merchandise it sold. Chandler's managers did not think the company would need this cash for some time, so they deposited the money with the Hamilton Trust Company. Chandler received, in return, a certificate of deposit, payable in ninety days with 5½ percent interest. (This interest-bearing commercial paper could be converted into cash at any time before it matured, but with a loss of interest income to the depositor.)

USES OF COMMERCIAL PAPER

5.6 Uses of Promissory Notes

Promissory notes are commonly used: (1) in borrowing money; (2) as an acknowledgement of debt in the purchase of goods or services; and (3) as evidence of an already existing debt. A creditor, in agreeing to accept a note *in lieu* of cash, may demand that the debtor secure a cosigner or that the note be secured by collateral.

EXAMPLE 7. Dugan Brothers owed $800 to Plumbing Supply Company for materials delivered over a three-week period. Plumbing Supply refused to honor further orders until the $800 debt was included in a promissory note signed by Dugan Brothers and another responsible party (a cosigner). The purpose of the cosigner was to guarantee payment of the note. Once Plumbing Supply had this guarantee of payment for goods already delivered, it reopened Dugan Brothers' account.

5.7 Use of Drafts

Either a sight draft or a time draft may be used in the collection of funds, in the transfer of owed funds from one party to another, and in financing the movement of goods by common carrier between a seller and buyer who are in different parts of the country. As a legally enforceable instrument, the draft has *no real value* until it has either been paid or accepted by the drawee as a future obligation.

EXAMPLE 8. Illinois Trading Corporation of Chicago sold $3,500 worth of goods to the Starling Company of Mississippi. The account went unpaid for three months. Illinois Trading (the drawer) drew a draft on Starling Company (the drawee) for $3,500, naming its Chicago bank as payee. The payee bank forwarded the draft to a correspondent bank in Mississippi for collection. The Mississippi bank presented the draft to Starling Company for payment or for acceptance. Although not required to pay or even accept the draft, the Starling Company will be under pressure to preserve a good credit reputation with its home bank. Thus, a draft may be effective in securing collection of an overdue account.

5.8 Uses of Certificates of Deposit

Certificates of deposit are a form of short-term interest-bearing savings facility used principally by businesses, not individuals. They do not share the importance of other forms of commercial paper because of their limited application. They are readily acceptable by creditors as a form of security.

EXAMPLE 9. Drury Corporation applied to a bank for a $20,000 loan. The loan was to be used to bolster Drury's payroll account until other funds, currently due from customers, were received. As security for the loan, Drury posted certificates of deposits that they held. (Drury preferred to borrow funds rather than disturb the interest income accruing on the certificates.)

5.9 Use of Checks

The most common of all types of commercial checks is the bank check. Its use by businesses and individuals has been almost universal. More than anything else, the check has replaced the need for cash in commercial transactions.

REQUISITES OF NEGOTIABILITY

Section 3–104 (1) of the Uniform Commercial Code sets forth the requisites of negotiable commercial paper. The following is quoted from the U.C.C.:

"Any writing to be a negotiable instrument within this Article must:

"(a) be signed by the maker or drawer; and

"(b) contain an unconditional promise or order to pay a sum certain in money and no other promise, order, obligation or power given by the maker or drawer except as authorized by this Article; and

"(c) be payable on demand or at a definite time; and

"(d) be payable to order or the bearer."

The seven basic requirements of negotiability are outlined, section by section, in the next few pages.

5.10 A Negotiable Instrument Must Be in Writing

Only written instruments are accepted as negotiable. The instrument may be handwritten in ink or pencil, typewritten, engraved, or printed in any other way, just as long as it is durable and clear enough to contain and preserve the obligations and intentions of the parties. For practical purposes and ease of transfer, commercial paper is usually printed, with spaces to be filled in as desired by the maker or drawer.

EXAMPLE 10. Danby had $2,000 on deposit in a checking account with the Bank of New England. During a trip to a nearby town, Danby decided to pay a local merchant for an overdue account. Danby had no checks with him. On a blank sheet of typing paper, he wrote a proper check, signed it, and presented it in payment of the account. A check like this is valid and negotiable if it satisfies all of the requisites contained in the Uniform Commercial Code.

5.11 A Negotiable Instrument Must Be Signed by the Maker or Drawer

An instrument is not enforceable unless it is signed. The law does not restrict the manner of signing. Usually, signatures are in longhand and ink. Signing in any other way is acceptable, however, if the signer adopts the signature as a binding sign. If desired, signatures may be nothing more than symbols, initials, and the like. However, it is up to the holder of an instrument to prove the validity of any signatures when the instrument is presented for payment.

EXAMPLE 11. Henley borrowed $500 from a business associate, giving in return a negotiable promissory note in the same amount. Rather than signing the note by his name, "George A. Henley," he signed it "Henley A. George." Although this is a poor practice and it could cause problems to the holder of the instrument, the law would have no complaint against the signature.

5.12 A Negotiable Instrument Must Contain an Unconditional Promise or Order to Pay

The order or promise to pay must *not* be contingent on any conditions that are made a part of the instrument. Placing conditions of payment in the instrument creates a simple contract instead of a negotiable instrument.

EXAMPLE 12. Hobart purchased a fur jacket. She made a cash deposit of $50 and gave the store her sixty-day note for $250. The note contained the following: "I promise to pay to the order of Griffith Furriers $250 upon their delivery of a new fur jacket, which must meet my satisfaction." Both conditions—of delivery and of satisfaction—prevent the note from being negotiable. However, the note remains enforceable as a simple contract, which may be assigned rather than negotiated.

5.13 A Negotiable Instrument Must Be Payable in a Definite Sum of Money

To be negotiable, an instrument must express payment in terms of money. The Uniform Commercial Code defines this as a "sum certain in money." It may be payable in United States currency or the legal currency of another nation that may easily be converted to U.S. dollars and cents. A promissory note made payable in currency *or* goods is negotiable if the method of payment is "at the option of the holder." The note would *not* be negotiable if the method of payment is "at the option of the maker."

EXAMPLE 13. Holmquist borrowed $1,500 from the U.S. Grain Corporation, the firm to which he sold his wheat crop each year. The note read: "I promise to pay to order of U.S. Grain Corp. $1,500 or wheat of equivalent value at option of maker. Signed, Holmquist." The note is an enforceable contract between the two parties but is not a negotiable instrument because the method of payment is at the option of the maker.

5.14 A Negotiable Instrument Must Be Payable at a Definite Time

Negotiable instruments must be payable on demand or at a definite time expressed in the body of the instrument. When payment is to be made on or after the occurrence of a specified event, the instrument is not negotiable.

EXAMPLE 14. Albers, for consideration received, delivered his promissory note to Berry. The note stated, "Thirty days after sale of Berry's merchandise, I promise to pay to the order of Berry $485. Signed, Albers." This instrument is merely a contract between Albers and Berry.

EXAMPLE 15. Henry owed the Macklin Finance Company $800, for which he gave the following note: "Ninety days after date, or earlier, I promise to pay to order of Macklin Finance Company $800, with interest at 7½ percent. Signed, Henry." This note is fully negotiable. It is legally payable and collectible ninety days after the date, a definite time. Henry, however, has reserved the right to pay sooner if that should suit his purposes.

5.15 The Instrument Must Be Payable "To the Order of" or "To Bearer"

The words of negotiability are *to the order of* or *to bearer*. Instruments made payable *to the order of* a specific payee are negotiable to third parties only by the named payee. When it is made payable to bearer, an instrument may be negotiated by anyone possessing it.

EXAMPLE 16. Knapp gave Hollingsworth his promissory note in return for delivery of building supplies. The note stated "I promise to pay Hollingsworth $395, thirty days after date of this note. Signed, Knapp." The note is evidence of Knapp's debt, but it may *not* be negotiated by Hollingsworth to a third party. It may, however, be assigned as a contract right.

5.16 A Draft Must Name the Drawee with Reasonable Certainty

A draft, or bill of exchange, is a three-party instrument, and must therefore indicate the name of the person on whom it is drawn (the drawee) with reasonable and sufficient certainty. (Only in this way does the holder have knowledge of the party to whom the instrument may be presented for payment.)

EXAMPLE 17. Clark owed Thornton $1,200, which was past due. Thornton prepared a draft, naming his bank as the payee of the $1,200. Thornton had written in only the name "John Clark" as the drawee. There were at least eight "John Clarks" living in the same town. This draft failed to be negotiable due to its uncertainty.

NONESSENTIALS IN COMMERCIAL PAPER

5.17 Recital of Consideration

Phrases such as "value received" are often included in instruments as acknowledgement of consideration. Such phrases are not required. In commercial paper, there is a presumption of consideration.

5.18 Omitting Date

The omission of the date in making an instrument does not rob it of negotiability. It is presumed that the date on which the payee receives the instrument is the date of the instrument. A date written in by the holder does not alter the negotiability of the instrument.

5.19 Place of Making and Place of Payment

Omission of the place of making or the place of payment does not affect the negotiable quality of commercial paper. In both cases, it is presumed to be the maker's home or place of business.

5.20 Sum Payable Expressed in Figures

Although it is customary and a good practice, it is not required by the U.C.C. that the sum payable be expressed both in words *and* figures. Figures are used to confirm the amount written in words. When the two do not agree, the amount shown in words is the amount accepted as correct.

5.21 Numbering the Instrument

It is customary and good business practice to number checks to correspond with check stubs. Other types of commercial paper may also be numbered to facilitate record-keeping. Failing to number them, however, does not affect their negotiability.

Solved Problems

5.1 Jarmitz gave Little the following note: "I promise to pay to the order of Albert Little, $350 on demand when Little delivers selected dining-room furniture to my home. Signed, Jarmitz." Is it negotiable?

No. This note contains a condition and is therefore nonnegotiable. It is, in the present form, evidence of an agreement between Jarmitz and Little.

5.2 A note given by Stevens to Pritchard read: "I owe Pritchard $250, which I will pay him on demand. Signed, Stevens." Is the note negotiable?

No. Stevens has not made a promise. He has merely acknowledged that he owes Pritchard $250, which he agrees to pay. Without a *promise* or *order,* commercial paper is not negotiable.

5.3 A check given by Hayes to Wesco Electric was complete in all respects but one: Hayes had neglected to fill in the date. Was the check negotiable?

Yes. The date of the making of an instrument is not one of the requisites of negotiability. The payee may fill in the date without destroying the validity of the instrument. The date of the instrument will be presumed to be the date on which it was delivered to the payee.

5.4 Stewart Brothers gave the following note to Roberts: "We promise to pay to the order of Roberts, on demand, $175, to be paid out of income from the sale of merchandise consigned to us by Roberts. Signed, Stewart Brothers." Was this note negotiable?

No. The instrument contains a condition of payment. A negotiable instrument must be an unconditional promise.

5.5 Is the following note negotiable? "We promise to pay Bradford, or order, $800 on demand. Payment is to be made from our Account Number 12. Signed, Levin Company."

Designation of which account an instrument will be charged to is not a condition affecting payment. The notation is merely of importance to the maker for internal administrative purposes. The note is negotiable.

5.6 Is the following note negotiable? "I promise to pay Julliard Institute $100, thirty days after date. Signed, Zurko."

No. The instrument does not contain words of negotiability ("*to bearer*" or "*to order of*") and is therefore not negotiable. It may, however, be assigned.

5.7 Is the following check negotiable?

"Pay to order of J. R. Swartz & Co., ... $________.

Fifty & no/100 .... Dollars.

Signed, L. M. Higgins"

Yes. Although the amount is expressed only in words, the instrument is negotiable. Banks, however, may require a depositor to show the amount both in words and figures before accepting the check.

5.8 Must a bank or other financial institution accept an instrument on the proof that it is negotiable?

No. A payee or transferee is not required to accept commercial paper. As in Problem 5.7, a payee or transferee may have to follow rules and regulations that have nothing to do with the instrument's negotiability.

5.9 Stern plans to attend an advertised auction of personal property at a public sale in Corning, New York. Stern is not known in that area and realizes that his checks might not be accepted by the auctioneer. What type of paper should Stern take to the auction?

Stern could use traveler's checks from a reputable company. He could also use a certificate of deposit from a reputable bank in his own state. The certificate of deposit may be negotiated to the auctioneer. Any difference between the purchase price and the amount of the certificate can be made up with cash or with traveler's checks.

5.10 Bringhurst purchased $5,000 in traveler's checks issued by the National Finance and Security Corporation. Were these *checks* in the strict sense of the word?

Although negotiable and issued in check form, they were not checks. They were issued by a dependable financial institution, but not by a bank. Only if they were issued by a bank would they be classified as checks.

5.11 Crew, a university student in her senior year, gave a note to the university for her final tuition payment. The note included this statement. "to be paid out of my first month's income after graduation." The university had difficulty in negotiating the note to its bank. Why?

The Crew note was not negotiable. It did not contain a *definite* date of payment. In effect, it contained a condition. Either one of these deficiencies would defeat the note's qualities of negotiability. As is, it is a simple contract between Crew and the university.

5.12 Salmons was two months overdue in payments he owed to the Badencroft Company for merchandise purchased. Badencroft drew a draft on Salmons for the amount owed, naming its bank as the payee. Payment was to be made to the order of the bank on demand. What is the value in money of this instrument?

Until the draft is accepted by Salmons, it has no money value. Salmons is under no legal obligation to accept the draft when it is presented by the bank. The draft may be of *psychological* value in the collection process, but it is not enforceable until it has been accepted either through payment or by the drawee's signature.

5.13 Walter made out a $1,350 check to Johnson Brothers Contractors for work done on his home. Walter made out the check, while sitting in his truck, by using a pencil. Johnson Brothers hesitated to accept the check, doubting its validity in that form. Is Walter's check valid and negotiable?

Yes. The requisite that an instrument must be in writing does not specify how it must be written. Writing an instrument in pencil is not a good idea; a dishonest person might make alterations in the instrument. However, writing in pencil does not affect an instrument's negotiability.

5.14 First National Bank received a note made payable to American Imports, Inc., in English pounds. The note clerk in the bank questioned the note's negotiability, stating that the law required that the amount payable be expressed in *currency of the realm* (in this case, U.S. dollars and cents). Was the note negotiable?

Early decisions required that the "sum certain in money" in negotiable commercial paper be expressed in currency of the realm. This is no longer the rule. The sum may be expressed in another nation's currency as long as that nation exchanges its currency with U.S. currency. The value of the note, in U.S. dollars and cents, can be calculated by First National.

Review Problems

5.15 Name the two general types of commercial paper.

5.16 What are the so-called *words of negotiability?*

5.17 How does *negotiability* differ from *assignment?*

5.18 Recite the requisites of negotiability.

5.19 Is it essential to show the amount of an instrument both in figures and words?

5.20 In what set of laws does one find the laws relating to commercial paper?

5.21 What is a *certificate of deposit?*

5.22 How do *checks* compare to *drafts?*

5.23 What money value does a draft have prior to its acceptance by the drawee?

5.24 How do corporations use certificates of deposit?

5.25 What is meant by *writing* as a requisite of negotiable instruments?

5.26 Does a draft that is used to collect a debt force the drawee to pay?

Answers to Review Problems

5.15 (1) promise instruments and (2) order instruments

5.16 (1) "to the order of" and (2) "to bearer"

5.17 An assignee acquires no better rights than those of the assignor of the contract. One who receives commercial paper by negotiation from a payee often acquires a better right against the maker than the payee ever had.

5.18 To be negotiable, an instrument: (1) must be in writing; (2) must be signed by the maker or drawer; (3) must contain an unconditional promise or order to pay; (4) must be payable in a "sum certain in money"; (5) must be payable at a definite time; (6) must be payable "to the order of" or "to bearer"; and (7) must name or indicate the drawee with reasonable certainty if it is a draft.

5.19 No, words are sufficient.

5.20 the Uniform Commercial Code

5.21 A certificate of deposit is a negotiable instrument issued by a bank. It shows that a specified amount has been deposited in the bank and is being held by the bank for payment at a definite future date.

5.22 Checks are a form of draft in which a bank is named as the drawee; other drafts need not name a bank as the drawee.

5.23 It has no value whatsoever until it is accepted.

5.24 In many states, corporations are not permitted to deposit their surplus funds in interest-bearing savings accounts. Thus, in order to earn interest on their surplus funds, they deposit money with banks and receive in return interest-bearing certificates of deposit.

5.25 A negotiable instrument may be written by hand with a pencil or pen; it may be written with a typewriter; or it may be printed on a press, mimeograph machine, or with any other convenient method.

5.26 No. It has only psychological value in collecting from debtors who do not wish to harm their credit reputation. Refusal to accept a draft will not, except in special cases, harm the drawee's credit rating.

Legal Terms

Bond. A kind of promissory note that is signed by the maker and under seal; corporations or other makers usually issue interest-bearing bonds for sale to investors.

Check. The most common kind of order instrument; its drawee is always a bank.

Draft. An unconditional written order instrument.

Foreign bill of exchange. A draft drawn in one state or country and payable in another state or country.

Negotiability. The quality of some commercial paper that permits it to be transferred, or negotiated, from one holder to another.

Order instrument. A form of commercial paper in which one party (the drawer) orders another party (the drawee) to pay a certain sum of money to a third party (the payee).

Promise instrument. A form of commercial paper in which one party (the maker) promises to pay another party (the payee) a certain sum of money.

Promissory note. An unconditional written promise instrument.

Sight draft. A draft that requires the drawee to pay the payee on demand—as soon as the draft is presented.

Time draft. A draft that requires the drawee to pay the payee a certain number of days after the draft is presented or a certain number of days after the date of the instrument.

Traveler's check. A kind of draft that is usually drawn on a financial institution rather than on a bank; strictly speaking, it is not a check.

Words of negotiability. The phrases "to the order of" and "to bearer"; failure to include one or the other of these phrases on an instrument will prevent it from being negotiable.

Chapter 6

Delivery and Endorsement of Commercial Paper

Commercial paper has no value in the market place until it has been issued by delivery to a payee. Thereafter, the instrument maintains its value as it continues on its way around, through delivery to other holders, who accept the instrument in much the same way they would accept money.

Title to some instruments may be passed from one holder to another by delivery alone. Title to other instruments passes only if the instruments have been delivered *and endorsed*. A party who endorses a piece of commercial paper indicates, by placing his or her name on the instrument, the intention to transfer title to the instrument.

Most individuals are unaware of the various types of endorsements available to them. Consequently, they often use the most unsafe of all endorsements, the blank endorsement. Knowledge of all types of endorsements would help these people choose the kind that best suits their purposes.

This chapter outlines the basic types of endorsements, the responsibilities of endorsers, and the conditions under which an endorser may either be held responsible or discharged from any future liability for his or her endorsement.

DELIVERY

6.1 Negotiation by Delivery

Commercial paper made payable to the bearer may be negotiated (transferred) by *delivery alone*. The use of words like "cash" or "to holder" creates a *bearer instrument*. Instruments in which a payee other than the bearer is named become bearer instruments when endorsed in blank by the payee. (See Section 6.3 for a discussion of endorsement in blank.)

EXAMPLE 1. Jordan purchased an antique barometer at a flea market for $15. Not knowing the seller's name, Jordan made the check payable to "Cash." This created a bearer instrument. The seller could transfer the check to other parties by mere delivery, without endorsing it.

6.2 Negotiation by Endorsement and Delivery

Commercial paper made payable to a named payee is transferred by *endorsement and delivery*. If the payee endorses the instrument in blank, it becomes a bearer instrument in the hands of subsequent parties.

EXAMPLE 2. Suppose that in Example 1 Jordan had known the seller to be Henry Marsh and made the check out to the order of Henry Marsh. Marsh now would be required to endorse the instrument, by writing his name on the check, before transferring it to another party.

ENDORSEMENTS

6.3 Blank Endorsement

In a *blank endorsement*, or *endorsement in blank*, a payee signs his or her name, usually on the back of the instrument, exactly as it appears on the face of the instrument. (It is only customary, and not required, that the endorsement appear on the *back* of the instrument.) A blank endorsement does not specify a particular *endorsee* (the party to whom the endorser is transferring the instrument).

6.4 Full, or Special, Endorsement

A *full*, or *special, endorsement* is one in which the payee or subsequent holder indicates the name of the person to whom or firm to which the instrument is being transferred. Transfer of an instrument in such a case may be accomplished only by endorsement and delivery, not by delivery alone. Blank and full endorsements are called unqualified endorsements. There are no restrictions on their negotiation and transfer by subsequent holders.

EXAMPLE 3. Durkes was the payee on a check that she transferred to Simon and Company. She endorsed the check in the following manner: "Pay to order of Simon and Company, Signed Durkes." This full endorsement would not permit transfer by delivery alone. Simon and Company would have to endorse the instrument in order to transfer it to another party. Without Simon and Company's endorsement, the check could not be collected or negotiated by any subsequent holder.

6.5 Restrictive Endorsement

A *restrictive endorsement* designates the endorsee as the only party to whom payment may be made. Such an endorsement may prohibit any further transfer of the instrument. The party holding an instrument with a restrictive endorsement must do with the instrument what the endorsement directs.

EXAMPLE 4. Jersey Outfitters, Inc., received numerous checks each day in payment of mail-order merchandise it had shipped. Each check was endorsed with a rubber stamp that read, "For Deposit Only in Fairfield Bank & Trust Co., Jersey Outfitters, Inc." Anyone who might get possession of the checks could do nothing with them other than deposit them to the endorser's account in the Fairfield Bank.

6.6 Qualified Endorsement

A *qualified endorsement* is one in which the endorser transfers title to the instrument, accepting no obligation as a guarantor if the instrument is not honored when presented for payment. One to whom an instrument is negotiated by qualified endorsement is given notice of the endorser's intentions by the endorsement itself. To effect such an endorsement, the endorser writes the words "without recourse" above his or her endorsement.

EXAMPLE 5. Chambers accepted a check from Roland in payment of an overdue account. Chambers knew that payment by check was final payment only if the instrument would be honored on presentment for payment. Chambers endorsed the check "without recourse" when he transferred it to one of his own creditors. Should the check "bounce" when presented to the bank, Chambers would be free of obligation. (A qualified endorsement does not relieve the endorser of all warranties; this will be discussed in Section 6.9.)

6.7 Conditional Endorsement

A *conditional endorsement* contains conditions that relate to the endorsee. The condition does not *restrict* further negotiation, but it does qualify the rights and obligation of the party receiving the instrument.

EXAMPLE 6. Mrs. Whann questioned a bill she received from Dr. Handy. She felt that $100 was fair payment for services for which the doctor had charged her $175. On the back of her $100 check to Dr. Handy, she wrote the following condition: "In full payment of all professional services." The doctor added his blank endorsement to the check, below the condition, and transferred it to another holder. The *doctor* is bound by the conditional endorsement, but it has no reference to the rights of subsequent holders.

6.8 Accommodation Endorsement

One endorsing an instrument merely for the purpose of securing payment of the instrument is an *accommodation,* or *irregular, endorser.* Such endorsements, added to those of regular endorsers, are usually blank endorsements. The endorser is liable to all parties other than the one who was accommodated and at whose request the endorsement was added.

EXAMPLE 7. Young, a student away from home, wished to cash a personal check at a bank near his college. A member of the faculty who had an account in the bank endorsed the check as an accommodation to Young, assuring Young that the check would be paid by the bank. The bank would thus accept the responsible faculty member as a guarantor of the instrument. Obviously, an accommodation endorser may not use a qualified endorsement.

OBLIGATIONS OF ENDORSERS AND HOLDERS

6.9 The Endorser's Guarantee and Warranties

Endorsers are liable to the subsequent holders of instruments they have signed if the instruments are *dishonored*—not paid when presented to the maker or drawee. (Endorsers who use a qualified endorsement are the exception to this rule.)

In addition to guaranteeing payment, all endorsers, including qualified endorsers, are bound by the following *implied warranties* to all subsequent holders: (1) The instrument is genuine and in all respects what it is represented to be: the signature is genuine and not a forgery, there has been no material alteration, and the instrument is valid. (2) The endorser further warrants that all prior parties had the legal capacity to contract: the maker, drawee, and all other endorsers were not minors nor were they otherwise incompetent. (3) The endorser further warrants that he or she has good title to the instrument, and did not merely find it or secure it by theft or through deception. (4) The endorser further warrants that the instrument is legally valid and is an existing obligation. The endorser is legally liable if payment is refused because of forgery, material alteration, or usury or any other illegal promise or act.

EXAMPLE 8. Harding endorsed in blank a $500 check that he had received from the previous holder as payment for the delivery of goods. When the check was presented for payment, the endorsee was told by the bank that the maker did not have and had never had a checking account. Because of his implied warranties as an endorser, Harding is liable to the holder of the check. Likewise, Harding may proceed against the party from whom he received the dishonored check.

6.10 Limiting Warranties When Negotiation Is by Delivery Only

A party who achieves negotiation of an instrument by delivery alone gives warranties only to the person to whom the instrument is delivered. Subsequent holders are *not* protected by the first party's warranties. When transfer is accomplished by endorsement *and* delivery, the endorser's warranties protect *all* subsequent holders.

EXAMPLE 9. Dowling received a check from Hershey, who had written the word "Cash" in the space designated for payee. Dowling negotiated this check to Smith by delivery alone. (Dowling did not need to endorse the check because it was a bearer instrument.) Subsequent holders transferred the check by delivery and endorsement until it was presented for payment. The check was not honored by the bank because of insufficient funds. Dowling need not fear prosecution from any subsequent holder other than Smith, to whom he had transferred the check by delivery alone.

6.11 Endorser's Obligations Conditioned by Holder's Obligations

Endorsers are free of liability under their warranties unless the holder of a dishonored instrument can present evidence of not having neglected to fulfill the following responsibilities: (1) that the holder did present the instrument, as required, to the maker or acceptor for payment; (2) that the holder did present the instrument to the drawee for acceptance, if payable *after sight*; (3) that the holder gave notice to prior holders-endorsers of the dishonor of the instrument; (4) that the holder, if the dishonored instrument is a foreign bill, has protested as required. (See Section 5.3 for a discussion of foreign bills.)

EXAMPLE 10. Alton's Grocery Store accepted a check in payment of groceries from Mrs. Kauffman, who had endorsed it. The check also contained endorsements of three prior holders. When presented at the bank for payment, the check was dishonored for lack of sufficient funds. Alton's Grocery delayed informing all the endorsers of the check, and instead spent valuable time in trying to obtain payment from the maker. Failure to inform the prior endorsers-holders released them of any obligation related to their endorsements.

6.12 Discharge of Endorser's Liability

Endorsers and any others who might be secondarily or conditionally liable to a holder or previous holders are excused from liability by: (1) any acts that might discharge the instrument; (2) the discharge of a prior holder or the release of the principal party or debtor; (3) the intentional cancellation of the endorser's signature by the holder; (4) refusal of valid tender of payment by a prior party; (5) an agreement to extend the time of payment of the instrument or to delay the holder's right to enforce the instrument.

EXAMPLE 11. Hathaway was an endorser of a note dated February 8, payable in sixty days. Atkinson, a subsequent holder, agreed with the maker of the note that the time of payment be extended thirty days beyond the due date. Hathaway and other holders prior to Atkinson are relieved of *all* liability on the instrument. Atkinson should have presented the note and requested payment on the date contained in the note.

EXAMPLE 12. Reynolds held a note endorsed by Stern, Thomas, Higgins, and Stevens. Reynolds, for reasons unknown, obliterated Higgins's signature from the note. This would relieve all the other endorsers, who had a right to depend on Higgins as one whose endorsement guaranteed payment of the note.

Solved Problems

6.1 Crimshaw held a check made out to his order by Soloway. Crinshaw used the check to pay his electric bill by transferring it to City Electric Company without endorsing it. Does City Electric have any rights in collecting the instrument?

Yes. Crimshaw did not negotiate the check to City Electric because he did not endorse it; however, Crimshaw did assign his *rights* in the instrument to City Electric. City Electric's rights are no better and no worse than those previously held by Crimshaw. City Electric, an assignee, has "stepped into the shoes of the assignor."

6.2 Suppose that in Problem 6.1 City Electric Company refused to accept the check without Crimshaw's endorsement. Is Crimshaw *obligated* to endorse the instrument?

Yes. The assignee of an *order* instrument given for value has the right to demand that the assignor endorse the instrument.

6.3 Urie transferred a check made to his order to Sugarman. He used a restrictive endorsement that read "Pay to Sugarman Only." Sugarman endorsed the check over to Klingman, using a blank endorsement. Did Urie's endorsement prohibit Sugarman's negotiation of the instrument?

The Uniform Commercial Code (Sec. 3-206-1) provides that a restrictive endorsement will not prevent further transfer or negotiation of a negotiable instrument. Klingman, then, has all of the rights of a transferee on this check.

6.4 Sanders held Roger's negotiable note for $5,000. Sanders endorsed the note in the following manner: "Pay to Canby $2,000 of this note." Did this constitute a legal negotiation of the instrument?

No. A negotiable instrument may not be negotiated except in full. However, a holder may make an *assignment* of less than the full amount of the instrument. Sanders, then, merely assigned to Canby the right to collect a part of the note. Canby does not have all of the rights of an endorsee.

6.5 Barrows endorsed Heald's $3,000 note in the following manner: "I hereby assign all of my rights in this note to Hawthorne. Signed, Barrows." Barrows later denied his obligation under an endorser's warranty, claiming that his endorsement created an assignment, not a negotiation. Was this assumption correct?

No. Barrows had transferred the instrument to Hawthorne and would be liable as an endorser. He satisfied the requirements of negotiation by adding an endorsement to the instrument and delivering it to Hawthorne.

6.6 Cleaver made out a check to "Harley and Quick" in the amount of $1,000, a gift. He delivered the check to Quick, who endorsed it with both his own and Harley's name. Quick presented the check for paymnet. Was this a valid endorsement, transferring title to the bank?

No. Both signatures were required to effect a valid endorsement. Quick did not sign as Harley's agent. He actually perpetrated a forgery, thus invalidating the endorsement.

6.7 Suppose that in Problem 6.6 the check had read: "Pay to the order of Harley or Quick . . . $1,000." Quick endorsed it, using only his signature. Would this have been a valid and complete endorsement?

Yes. Commercial paper made payable to either one of two or more named payees may be transferred by only one of those named. Quick's endorsement would have been proper and sufficient.

6.8 Taylor endorsed a check that he had received from Williams, another holder. The names of four persons were listed as endorsers of the instrument when it was finally presented to the bank. The bank declared the check a forgery and would not make payment. Williams denied all responsibility, pointing out that he had used the words "without recourse" above his name when signing. Was Williams relieved of liability?

No. A qualified endorsement does not relieve the endorser of the implied warranties that guarantee the instrument to be genuine and all that it purports to be. Williams would have been relieved if payment had been refused because of insufficient funds; but he is not relieved in the case of forgery. Williams is liable, along with the other endorsers, to Taylor.

6.9 Arnold held a check given to him by Vary. It was a bearer instrument, and he transferred it to Samson for value. Transfer was by delivery alone. The check was dishonored for insufficient funds when Samson presented it to the bank for payment. Arnold denied liability, stating that he had not endorsed the instrument. Is Arnold liable to Samson?

Yes. One transferring a bearer instrument by delivery alone is fully liable to the next holder. Lack of endorsement does not relieve Arnold of his guarantee and warranties to Samson.

6.10 D'Angelo was executor of Bland's estate. Among Bland's assets were three negotiable notes. D'Angelo claimed to be the transferee of the notes by operation of law. As executor of the estate, is D'Angelo considered a transferee?

No. D'Angelo is considered an assignee, not a transferee. He is not a holder of the notes; he did not receive them through endorsement and delivery. Any defenses that had been available to the makers against Bland would now be available to them against the estate.

6.11 Zebley, treasurer of Motor Sales Corporation, endorsed a note that his firm transferred to its bank for discount. Zebley's endorsement stated: "Pay to order of Merchant's Bank. Signed, Zebley, treasurer." Would Zebley or Motor Sales Corporation be charged, if necessary, as the endorser of this note?

Zebley. The endorsement, as made, was merely descriptive of Zebley. While circumstances would indicate that he was acting as an agent of the Motor Sales Corporation, the endorsement did not say so. The endorsement should have read: "Motor Sales Corporation, by Zebley, treasurer."

6.12 Zebley issued a promissory note to Autoparts Company for $2,500. The note was signed: "Zebley, agent." Who is liable on the note?

Zebley alone is liable. If the note were imprinted with the name "Motor Sales Corporation" on its face, anyone receiving the note would recognize it as Motor Sales Corporation's note. Otherwise, it would be Zebley's own note.

6.13 Bringhurst held a check that had been made to his order. He endorsed the instrument in full, as follows: "Pay to order of Baldt and Trimmer, signed Bringhurst." May Baldt alone negotiate this instrument?

No. Any further negotiation would require the signatures of both persons named in Bringhurst's endorsement.

Review Problems

6.14 When may commercial paper be transferred by delivery alone?

6.15 What effect does a blank endorsement have on an instrument in addition to passing title to the instrument to a new holder?

6.16 What are the obligations of parties who use qualified endorsements?

6.17 Are accommodation endorsers responsible to all holders?

6.18 To what extent are warranties enforceable against one who negotiates a bearer instrument by delivery alone?

6.19 Under what conditions is the endorser relieved of warranties on the instrument?

6.20 What are an endorser's warranties?

6.21 What are the holder's obligations in presenting an instrument for payment and in giving notice to previous holders of the dishonor of the instrument?

6.22 How does an assignee differ from an endorsee in rights of collection of the instrument?

6.23 Is the executor or administrator of an estate an assignee or transferee of commercial paper possessed by the deceased?

Answers to Review Problems

6.14 When the instrument is a bearer instrument it may be negotiated by delivery alone.

6.15 It converts the instrument to a bearer instrument.

6.16 Qualified endorsers are obligated by the implied warranties of all endorsers. They are, however, relieved of the guarantee that there are funds available for payment and honor of the instrument.

6.17 They are responsible to all holders except the one accommodated.

6.18 Such a person's liability extends only to the one to whom he or she delivered and negotiated the instrument.

6.19 Endorsers are relieved of obligation when the holder: (1) did not present the instrument to the maker or acceptor for payment; (2) did not present the instrument for acceptance, if it was payble after sight; (3) did not give notice to prior holders of the dishonor of the instrument; and (4) has not protested dishonor of a foreign bill.

6.20 (1) The instrument is genuine and in all respects what it is purported to be; (2) all prior parties had the legal capacity to contract; (3) the endorser has good title to the instrument; and (4) the instrument is legally valid and is an existing obligation.

6.21 The holder must present the instrument for payment on its due date. If dishonored, prior parties must be informed of the dishonor.

6.22 An assignee has no better rights of collection than those the assignor had. One who receives commercial paper by negotiation may be in a stronger position to collect than was the one from whom the instrument was transferred.

6.23 The executor or administrator is an assignee.

Legal Terms

Accommodation endorser. A party who endorses an instrument, without consideration, solely for the purpose of securing another's payment.

Bearer instrument. A piece of commercial paper made payable to the bearer; may be negotiated by delivery alone.

Blank endorsement. An endorsement that specifies no particular endorsee; may consist of a mere signature; a blank endorsement makes any instrument a bearer instrument.

Delivery. The holder's actual transfer of the instrument itself to the party to whom title is passed; endorsement without delivery negates the intention to transfer title.

Endorsement. The act of a holder of commercial paper in placing her or his name on the instrument as an indication of the intention to transfer title to a new holder, known as the endorsee.

Endorser's warranties. Warranties, implied by law, that guarantee the rights of subsequent holders and that assure payment by the party initially liable on the instrument.

Full, or special, endorsement. Endorsement that specifies the person to whom, or to whose order, it makes the instrument payable.

Qualified endorsement. An endorsement in which the endorser accepts no obligation as a guarantor should the instrument not be honored.

Restrictive endorsement. An endorsement which is conditional, or purports to prohibit further transfer of the instrument; may include the words "for collection," "for deposit," "pay any bank," or similar terms signifying a purpose of deposit or collection; may otherwise state that the instrument is for the benefit or use of the endorser or another person.

Chapter 7

Negotiating Commercial Paper

The quality of commercial paper that permits it to take the place of money is its ease of transfer and acceptance in the market place. The acceptance of checks, notes, and other types of commercial paper is almost universal. Without them, business in this country would grind to a sudden halt.

This chapter outlines the important aspects of negotiability, the rights of different types of holders, certain defenses against payment, and steps taken when an instrument is dishonored on presentment.

Distinct differences are noted between the rights of *immediate parties* and those parties called *holders in due course*. Likewise, the defenses that may be used by one from whom payment is sought differ according to the legal qualifications of the holder. Equally important are the warranties of endorsers that give relief to the holder when an instrument presented for payment is dishonored by the maker or drawee.

The law of negotiable instruments is today strictly defined in the Uniform Commercial Code. State laws, however, prescribe limits to the amount of interest parties may agree to pay before the instrument is deemed invalid through usury.

Special mention has been made of the rights of the holder in due course. There is also a discussion of new regulations of the Federal Trade Commission that protect consumers from forced payment.

The outline concludes with a discussion of the discharge of commercial paper and the manner and time within which notice of dishonor must be given to prior endorsers.

HOLDER IN DUE COURSE

7.1 Remote Parties

Anyone named on the face of an instrument of commercial paper is known as an *immediate party*; all others who have rights and liabilities relating to the instrument are known as *remote parties*. Unless qualified as a holder in due course (see Section 7.2) a remote party has no better rights than the payee or the one from whom the instrument was transferred.

EXAMPLE 1. Schmidt held a promissory note given to him as a gift by a minor. He transferred the note to Gunther for value. In discussing the note, Schmidt told Gunther that it was signed by a minor and that he had received it as a gift. Gunther, with knowledge of the maker's incapacity and the fact that no consideration was given for the note, is a remote party. Gunther's powers of collection are no better than those previously held by Schmidt. (Gunther is much like the assignee of an unenforceable agreement.)

7.2 Holders in Due Course

A *holder in due course* is a remote party who takes an instrument (1) in good faith, (2) for value, (3) prior to maturity, and (4) without knowledge of any defects in the instrument or its creation.

EXAMPLE 2. Suppose that in Example 1 Gunther had purchased the note from Schmidt in good faith, not knowing that it had been a gift from a minor, who had the right to void the agreement. Gunther would then qualify as a holder in due course. Although his rights would not be superior to the minor's right to disavow any obligations on the instrument, Gunther would have the assurance of an endorser's warranty that the instrument had been created by a capable party.

7.3 Acquiring Title from a Holder in Due Course

A party (the transferee) receiving an instrument from a holder in due course is vested with the rights of the transferor. The transferee, of course, must also qualify personally as a holder in due course.

EXAMPLE 3. Thornton sold a CB radio to Honeywell, who gave Thornton a note for $250. Thornton had used deception and fraud in his dealings with Honeywell, facts that would have defeated Thornton's right to collect on the note. Thornton transferred the note to his brother, who knew nothing of the fraud and who acquired the note in good faith. Thornton's brother would be a holder in due course, with full rights to demand payment from Honeywell, the defrauded maker.

7.4 Reacquirer of Commercial Paper

The holder of an instrument may negotiate the instrument and then at a later date *reacquire* it. In reacquiring the instrument, the holder does not change his or her legal position. A party who was a holder in due course of an instrument is a holder in due course on reacquiring the same instrument. A party who was not a holder in due course cannot become one by negotiating an instrument to and then reacquiring it from a holder in due course.

EXAMPLE 4. Suppose that in Example 3 Thornton reacquired the note from his brother, who was a holder in due course. Thornton's previous experience with the Honeywell note would prevent him from now becoming a holder in due course.

PERSONAL DEFENSES AGAINST PAYMENT

7.5 Personal Defenses Are Limited

The makers of notes and the drawees of drafts may defend themselves against the claims of immediate parties or third parties *who are not holders in due course* by using one of the so-called *personal defenses*. Personal defenses against payment of commercial paper include fraud, duress, and undue influence, and are similar to the defenses available to a person who seeks to invalidate mutual assent in an executory contract.

7.6 Lack of Consideration

A maker or drawee can use lack of consideration as a defense against the claims of an immediate party or a remote party who is not a holder in due course.

EXAMPLE 5. Mahler gave Peltz his promissory negotiable note, payable on demand, for $2,500. The note was given as a birthday gift. If the note was presented for payment by Peltz or a subsequent holder who was not a holder in due course, Mahler would not be required to honor it. In the hands of a holder in due course, however, it would be an enforceable claim against Mahler.

7.7 Fraud, Duress, and Undue Influence

Commercial paper obtained through the payee's use of fraud, duress, or undue influence may not be enforced between the payee and the maker. Persons taking such instruments as holders in due course would, however, have a right of collection against the maker.

EXAMPLE 6. Conway agreed to join the Employees' Protective Association after being threatened by his foreman. Conway signed a promissory note, agreeing to pay the $50 membership fee at the end of his first month's employment. Conway had been coerced into signing the note and could defend any claim of payment on grounds of undue influence. Had the note been transferred for value to a holder in due course, Conway would be obliged to honor it.

7.8 Nondelivery of Complete Instrument

An immediate party has no right of collection from the maker when possession of a complete instrument was secured by other than lawful means. When such an instrument has reached a holder in due course, however, the maker or drawee has no defense.

EXAMPLE 7. Smolko carelessly left a note for $50, made out to the order of Kadis, on his own desk. Kadis entered the office during Smolko's absence, saw the note, and took it. He later presented it to Smolko for payment. Payment may be denied to Kadis, although Smolko still owed him the $50. Had Kadis negotiated the note to a holder in due course, that holder could have demanded payment from Smolko.

7.9 Payment of Unsurrendered Instrument

The maker of a note or the acceptor of a time draft need not honor an immediate party's demand for payment of an instrument if payment has already been made. (This situation arises when the immediate party, for some reason, has not surrendered the paid note or draft.) However, such a note in the hands of a holder in due course must be honored.

EXAMPLE 8. Fehr mailed Broadway Motors her check for $300, in satisfaction of a promissory negotiable note due in five days. Unknown to Fehr, her note had been transferred to Price for value. Price, a holder in due course, presented the note for payment on the due date. Fehr would have no defense against paying Price.

7.10 Offset by Counterclaim

An immediate party responsible on an instrument may reduce the amount claimed by an amount owed him or her by the other immediate party. This, again, is a defense permitted only against those who are not holders in due course.

EXAMPLE 9. Jules presented for payment a note for $750 that evidenced a debt owed him by Murray, the maker. Murray tendered $600 in payment, claiming that Jules had owed him $150 on another deal that they had made several months before. If proven, the $150 counterclaim would offset that amount of the $750 note.

REAL DEFENSES AGAINST PAYMENT

7.11 Defenses against Holders in Due Course

Certain defenses are available against both immediate parties *and* those parties claiming to be holders in due course. These defenses, unlike the personal defenses, often result from illegality or from incapacity in the creation of the instrument. They are known as *real defenses*, or *absolute defenses*.

7.12 Incapacity to Contract

Neither immediate parties nor remote parties, including holders in due course, can enforce their claims against persons who did not have the capacity to contract when they created a negotiable instrument. Incapacity must have existed at the time the instrument was created, and not just at the time the instrument is presented for payment.

EXAMPLE 10. Foley gave her note for $100 to Dobson Jewelers in payment of a gold ring. The note was discounted at the bank, which later presented it to Foley for payment. Foley, only 17 years of age, disclaimed liability on grounds of incapacity. Although Foley is not responsible, Dobson Jewelers will be liable to the bank on its warranties as an endorser.

7.13 Illegality

Instruments issued in connection with illegal acts or promises between the immediate parties create a real defense against *all* subsequent holders.

EXAMPLE 11. Harbison gave his demand note for $25,000 to Reynault, a state representative, in return for Reynault's vote in favor of a bill before the state legislature. The bill was adopted, and Reynault presented the note to Harbison and demanded payment of the $25,000. This note would not be collectible, even by an innocent purchaser who had no knowledge of the illegal transaction between Reynault and Harbison.

7.14 Fraud in Creation of the Instrument

Fraud or deception used to induce an innocent party to make and issue commercial paper creates a real defense. This is not to be confused with fraud as a personal defense. Fraud as a real defense relates to the *making* of the instrument, whereas fraud as a personal defense relates to the agreement made between the two contracting parties. Thus, a person who is in no way negligent and who signs a paper that is apparently not a negotiable instrument but which is later fraudulently converted into a promissory note cannot be held liable even by a holder in due course. This was fraud in the *execution* of an instrument, and thus an *absolute defense*. If, however, the person signs and delivers a note in payment of goods that were not as represented by the merchant, he or she may refuse payment on the grounds of fraud in the *inducement* of the contract. This would be a *personal defense*, good against anyone except a holder in due course.

EXAMPLE 12. Henderson, a public figure, was asked to sign his autograph on a paper given to him by one of his "admirers." At a later time, a negotiable demand note for $1,000 was written above Henderson's signature. The note was sold to an innocent purchaser, who later presented it for payment. Henderson could deny any liability on the note, even to this holder in due course, because fraud and trickery had been used in its *creation*.

7.15 Forgery

An instrument to which another's signature has been affixed without that person's knowledge or authority is a *forgery*. The one charged with liability on a forged instrument may refuse payment to anyone holding the instrument.

EXAMPLE 13. A dishonest employee stole blank checks from the Harvester Trucking Company. She made the checks out to herself and signed the names of two company officers at the bottom, as required by the firm. The checks were transferred to other parties, holders in due course, and ultimately honored by Harvester Trucking Company's bank. The bank is liable to Harvester Trucking Company for the amount paid out of its checking account.

EXAMPLE 14. Suppose that in Example 13 it had been a practice of both officers to sign a number of blank checks that might then be available as needed during their absence. Had these checks been stolen and negotiated, Harvester Trucking Company, not the bank, would have been at fault.

7.16 Material Alterations

A *material alteration* is an alteration that in some way changes the rights of the parties to the instrument. Alteration of the date of payment or the amount of money ordered or promised are examples of material alterations. Writing in a date when no date was included is not a material alteration. Neither is writing in the amount in figures when the figures agree with the amount shown in words. The maker may be held liable for the originally intended amount of the note even if there has been a material alteration.

EXAMPLE 15. Jefferson signed a negotiable demand note for $700, made payable to Hamilton. A subsequent holder changed the amount from $700 to $750. A later holder in due course presented the note to Jefferson for payment. Jefferson was still liable for the original amount, $700. The last holder may hold previous endorsers liable on the warranty that the instrument was genuine and all that it was purported to be.

EXAMPLE 16. Suppose that in Example 15 Jefferson had written the note in pencil or had carelessly left space on the note, making it easy for a dishonest person to make the alteration. Because Jefferson's own negligence had invited the dishonest act, he could be held liable for the entire amount shown on the note.

7.17 Special Statutes

Real defenses are sometimes embodied in state statutes. The statutes may declare instruments illegal because they include usurious interest rates or for other reasons specifically stated. Local laws must be consulted in determining grounds for these defenses.

EXAMPLE 17. Green borrowed $500 from a loan shark, signing a promissory note in which he agreed to pay 10 percent interest each week on any unpaid portion of the note. State law specified that usurious loan agreements relieved the maker of a note from all interest payments *and* from payment of the principal. This defense would be allowed against both immediate parties and those claiming to be holders in due course.

7.18 Bankruptcy

Bankrupts are relieved of all obligations evidenced by commercial paper. The holder of such paper receives no preference over other creditors, unless the debt was included among those given preference under bankruptcy law. (See Chapter 20.)

EXAMPLE 18. Holcomb Corporation was declared an involuntary bankrupt. The firm had liabilities of $875,680 and assets of only $132,000. Peoples Bank & Trust Company filed a claim, introducing a ninety-day negotiable note secured by a mortgage on the firm's office building in New York. Preference would be allowed on such a note. Had the note not been secured by the mortgage or some other recorded lien, Peoples Bank & Trust would have received payment in line with payments received by other general creditors.

7.19 Consumer Legislation and the Holder in Due Course

Until recently, the sellers of "big-ticket" merchandise sold the notes they held to banks and finance companies, who took the paper as holders in due course. Regardless of the buyer's dissatisfaction with merchandise, the new holders were fully protected in demanding payment.

As of May 14, 1976, the Federal Trade Commission (F.T.C.) issued regulations that would protect consumers in contracts for goods and services in which notes are signed and negotiated to holders in due course. To meet the new requirements, contracts should now contain the following statement. "Any holder of this consumer credit contract is subject to all claims and defenses which the debtor could assert against the seller of goods or services obtained pursuant hereto or with the proceeds hereof. Recovery hereunder by the creditor shall not exceed amounts paid by the debtor."

Most contracts for "big-ticket" items once contained waivers of defenses or other clauses that restricted the rights of the debtor. Contracts containing such clauses should now be avoided because their waivers are in conflict with the rights assured consumers by the F.T.C.

EXAMPLE 19. Hornsby contracted to have a fire-alarm system installed in his home by a firm that did door-to-door selling. When the work was finished, Hornsby signed a negotiable note for $2,800. This note was then sold by the payee to an out-of-town bank. The alarm system, when tested by Hornsby, would not work, and he refused to make installment payments to the bank according to the note's terms. The bank, as a holder in due course, sued on the note and collected.

EXAMPLE 20. Suppose that in Example 19 Hornsby's agreement with the fire-alarm firm had contained the new F.T.C. statement. Without any waiver of defenses, Hornsby would be permitted to use the same personal defenses against the bank that he might have used against the alarm company.

PRESENTMENT FOR PAYMENT OR ACCEPTANCE

7.20 Acts of Presentment

Presentment is the act of submitting commercial paper to the person or persons primarily liable on the instrument. It consists either of exhibiting a note to the maker and at the same time demanding payment or showing a draft or bill of exchange to the drawee and at the same time requesting payment or acceptance.

7.21 Fixing Liability of Endorsers and Subsequent Holders

One holding an instrument is required to present the instrument for payment or acceptance at the proper time, stated on the face of the instrument. Failure to do so relieves all endorsers of liability if the instrument is not honored when it finally is presented.

7.22 Time of Presentment

Presentment must be made during business hours on the day designated in the instrument. When the due date falls on a Saturday, Sunday, or legal holiday, the instrument must be presented for payment or acceptance on the very next business day. Demand instruments must be presented within a "reasonable" time after the date of the instrument.

EXAMPLE 21. Higgins was the holder of a note due September 10. He arrived at the maker's place of business late in the evening on that date. Seeing lights on, he rang a doorbell and demanded entrance. The maker had no obligation to open the office and allow Higgins to present the instrument.

7.23 Presentment of Uncertified Check

The Uniform Commercial Code states that an uncertified check must be presented within thirty days of the date on the check. Failure to do so relieves the drawee of liability on the instrument should the bank fail, thus making payment impossible.

7.24 Place of Presentment

When a place of presentment is specified on the face of the instrument, presentment must be made there. If a place is not designated, the instrument should be presented at the maker's place of business (in commercial transactions) or at the maker's home (in personal transactions). Presentment may be made at the maker's last-known place of business or residence if the maker cannot be found. Presentment may be made face-to-face, by mail, or, in the case of checks, through a bank clearing house.

EXAMPLE 22. Savage held a note signed by Leonard. The note was due, but there was no place of presentment on it, and Leonard was not listed in the city telephone directory. Savage did locate a rooming house where Leonard had lived most recently. He attempted to locate Leonard and present the note at that place, but without success. The endorsers of the note would be bound by Savage's attempted presentment.

7.25 To Whom Presentment Is Made

The holder of a note or draft must make presentment to the maker or acceptor or to that person's agent. Presentment may also be made to anyone else available at the designated place of payment. If the instrument was issued by a partnership, it is sufficient to make presentment to any one of the partners. Presentment of an instrument to one deceased must be made to the executor or administrator of the estate. If they have not been appointed, presentment is temporarily waived.

7.26 Excused Delay in Presentment

When presentment has been made impossible by an act of God or by other circumstances acceptable to the court, the delay will be excused. In such an event, the endorsers are not relieved of liability should the instrument be dishonored when presented.

EXAMPLE 23. Cleming Brothers held a note signed by Matthew. The note was due on October 18. The note specified that presentment was to be made at Matthew's home, in a town five miles upriver from Cleming and on the opposite bank. A severe flood washed out all the bridges over the river. This caused a delay in the presentment of the note until October 20. Failure to present the note on the due date would be excused by most courts in this case. Endorsers could not successfully claim their release from liability because of the delay.

7.27 Waiver of Necessity of Presentment

By special endorsement, endorsers may waive the holder's responsibility of presentment as outlined above. In such cases, presentment may be dispensed with.

DISHONOR OF COMMERCIAL PAPER

7.28 Dishonored Instruments

The failure of a drawee to accept or pay an instrument when it is presented constitutes *dishonor*. The failure to pay the holder of a note when it is presented and due also constitutes dishonor. An instrument for which presentment has been excused or waived is dishonored when it becomes past due and remains unpaid.

EXAMPLE 24. Fulmer presented the Haas Company's check for payment at the company's bank. The teller compared signatures with those on file with the bank. He informed Fulmer that the check was a forgery and that the bank would not pay it. Thus, the check had been dishonored. Prior endorsers would be responsible to Fulmer on their endorsers' implied warranties. (Insufficient funds in the drawer's account would also render the instrument dishonored.)

7.29 Communicating Notice of Dishonor

Notice of dishonor is given by the holder of the dishonored instrument, by the holder's agent, or by a certifying public officer. The notice may be oral, written, by telephone, by messenger, by telegraph, or by any other means, just as long as it is communicated. When notice is given by mail, the time of notice is assumed to be when it is mailed, not when it is received.

EXAMPLE 25. Clancy presented a note to Stevenson on the due date. Stevenson, the maker, did not accept the note for payment, so Clancy mailed notices of dishonor to all endorsers of the note. One endorser did not receive notice until five days after the mailing and thus claimed release from obligation due to the delay. This endorser remains liable. Clancy fulfilled his obligation by mailing the notice soon after the dishonor.

7.30 When Notice Must Be Given

Notice of dishonor must be communicated to the prior endorser before midnight of the third business day after dishonor; a notice that is to be mailed should be in the mails on the business day after dishonor. All that a holder is required to do is to give notice of dishonor to the endorser immediately prior to his or her endorsement. In turn, each other endorser is required to notify only the immediate prior endorser, following the same time requirements outlined above. To assure that all prior endorsers will be held liable, however, the last holder may give notice to all prior endorsers at once.

7.31 Protest

Notice of dishonor may be a certification of dishonor over the signature or seal of the United States consul, vice-consul, notary public, or any other with the authority to certify dishonor according to the law of the place where the instrument was dishonored.

Solved Problems

7.1 Johnson issued a valid check to Armstrong in payment of work done by Armstrong. Armstrong subsequently endorsed the check in blank and gave it to a local Boy Scout troop as a gift. Was the Boy Scout troop a holder in due course?

The Boy Scout troop was *not* a holder in due course. To be a holder in due course, a party must take an instrument *for value*. No consideration passed between Armstrong and the troop in return for Armstrong's transfer of the check.

7.2 On June 15, Leonard endorsed and transferred a note to Turner. The note was payable on June 2. When Turner presented it for payment, the maker refused on grounds of a personal defense. Turner held that he was a holder in due course, not to be reached by personal defenses. Was he correct?

No. To qualify as a holder in due course, one must receive an instrument prior to its maturity. Turner accepted the note thirteen days after the date of maturity. He is not a holder in due course and may be refused payment on grounds of both personal and real defenses.

7.3 Albright Motors sold a used car to Stewart for $2,500. Stewart gave Albright a check for $1,500 as a partial payment. Albright then endorsed the check and gave it to Art's Brake Service for work that had been done on Albright's used cars. Stewart stopped payment on the check, claiming that Albright Motors had perpetrated a fraud when selling him the car. Does Art's Brake Service qualify as a holder in due course?

Art's took the check for value, in good faith, and with no knowledge of the fraudulent transaction between Albright and Stewart. Art's is a holder in due course, with full rights to demand payment from Stewart.

7.4 Ripley signed an installment note, making Western Electronics the payee. A short time later, Ripley missed several payments on the note. Western then endorsed the note and sold it to Harvey. Ripley contended that Harvey was not a holder in due course because of Ripley's own failure to make further payments. Was Ripley correct?

No. Harvey is a holder in due course. Delay in making payments on an installment note does not mean that Harvey accepted the note after maturity. The due date is still in the future. Ripley has neither a personal nor a real defense against the present holder of his note.

7.5 Kristy sold goods to Marvin on November 1, 1976. Marvin paid for the goods with his $1,800 check, dated November 1, 1976. Kristy held the check until February, at which time he endorsed it over to Zellinsky for value. Marvin disclaimed liability on the instrument, claiming that the goods received from Kristy were defective and not as described when sold. Zellinsky pursued his claim, stating that he was a holder in due course, against whom personal defenses may not be used. Was this contention correct?

Zellinsky accepted the check more than thirty days after its due date. This is more than the reasonable time during which it should have been presented. The Uniform Commercial Code specifies thirty days as the time during which checks are to be presented for payment. Zellinsky is not a holder in due course, and Marvin may defend his dishonor of the check with personal defenses.

7.6 Chambers sold goods to Darby on March 17. Darby gave Chambers her check, postdated to March 22. On March 19, Chambers endorsed the check and delivered it to Robbins for value. Was Robbins a holder in due course?

When not related to a fraudulent transaction, there are no restrictions against giving a postdated check. The date of the check was written on the face of the instrument, and Robbins was aware of the date when he accepted the check. Robbins, then, is a holder in due course of the check and may present it for payment on March 22.

7.7 Jegers bought a television from Urie, giving in payment his negotiable note for $200, payable on demand. When Urie presented the note for payment, Jegers refused it. Jegers claimed that Urie had misrepresented the type of television and that he was therefore guilty of fraud. Urie then negotiated the note to Bowers for value, without recounting the difficulty he had encountered with Jegers. Jegers again refused to pay the note when

Bowers presented it. Urie claimed that Bowers was not a holder in due course. May Bowers enforce payment?

Bowers was a holder in due course. He had no knowledge of the fraud, nor was he aware of Urie's failure to enforce the note. Bowers has every right of collection on the note.

7.8 On December 15, Searles presented Stauffer's check for payment at Stauffer's bank. The bank had received notice of Stauffer's death on December 6. The bank cashed the check. Stauffer's executor sought reimbursement by the bank, claiming that it had no right to cash the check. Was the executor correct?

No. The Uniform Commercial Code prohibits the cashing of a check by a bank when the bank is informed of the depositor's death and when the executor has notified the bank, by means of a stop order, not to honor any outstanding checks issued by the deceased. Otherwise, the bank may continue to honor and pay instruments presented within ten days of the date of the depositor's death. Stauffer's bank had done nothing wrong in honoring Stauffer's check only nine days after his death.

7.9 Freed presented to Charles, for payment on the due date, Charles's note for $500. Charles dishonored the note, claiming that he did not have funds sufficient to make payment. Three days later, Freed sent letters to all prior endorsers, giving them notice of dishonor. They disclaimed liability, saying that notice was not received until five days after dishonor. Are the endorsers still liable on the note?

Yes. Notice of dishonor must be given before the end of the third business day following dishonor. Notice is presumed to have been complete when the notice of dishonor, or protest, has been deposited in the mail. Freed had met both of these requirements of giving notice, and the endorsers are still liable on the note.

7.10 Suppose that in Problem 7.9 notice of dishonor had been given by a telephone call to each endorser. Would Freed, in this case, have the right to seek payment from them in view of Charles's dishonor?

It is up to the holder to *prove* that notice of dishonor has been made. Oral communication is sufficient, but proof may be difficult. It is customary to confirm an oral notice with a written notice, also made within the time allowed by the Uniform Commercial Code. Unless Freed could prove that prior endorsers had been given notice, he would have no right of action against them.

7.11 Dalton Electrical Company had accepted by endorsement a note made by Severance. It was generally known that a few days prior to the due date of the note Severance had become insolvent and would not be able to honor any demands for money. Dalton Electrical deemed it useless to present the note for payment under these circumstances. Within the time allowed, Dalton Electrical mailed notices of dishonor to all prior holders-endorsers. Are the endorsers liable on the note?

No. Dalton Electrical should have presented the note to the maker for payment. In fact, the note had never actually been dishonored. Dalton Electrical may not *assume* dishonor because of circumstances or information coming from outside sources.

7.12 Kelly sold a motorcycle to Flock, fraudulently representing the machine as being in excellent condition and free of any mechanical defects. Flock gave his $750 note in payment, making it payable on May 15. A subsequent holder took the note for value and presented it on the due date. Flock refused payment, claiming that fraud was his valid defense against all parties, including holders in due course. Was Flock correct?

No. Fraud related to the subject matter of a transaction in which a negotiable instrument is given is a personal defense only. The note was presented by a holder in due course, against whom personal defenses may not be used. Fraud as a real defense must relate to the *creation* of the instrument itself.

7.13 Benson loaned money to Riley, accepting Riley's thirty-day negotiable note as security. Benson then endorsed the note and transferred it to Sharp for value. The note was dishonored when Sharp presented it to Riley. Sharp immediately demanded payment from Benson, who had endorsed and delivered the note to him. Is Benson liable?

Yes. An endorser's liability is created when presentment has been made and notice of dishonor is given. Sharp did present the note when due, and it was dishonored. Sharp combined the notice of dishonor and demand for payment from Benson in one proper act. Benson is liable.

7.14 Suppose, in Problem 7.13, that Benson had held the note himself and that on the due date Riley failed to make payment. Without giving Riley notice, Benson immediately started suit for payment. May Benson, the payee, start suit without making a demand for payment?

The maker of a note has an obligation to pay its holder promptly on the due date if the holder is the original payee of the instrument. Riley failed to meet his obligation on the note on the due date, thus giving Benson, the payee, the right to commence action against him.

7.15 Taylor borrowed money from Davis. Taylor gave his promissory note, payable in sixty days to Davis. Davis asked Taylor to secure another person's signature to guarantee the note. Taylor asked Green to write a letter to Davis to the effect that he would guarantee the note, which Green did. Davis transferred the note to Ralph, who presented it for payment on the due date. It was dishonored. Does the guarantee in the letter to Davis give Ralph rights against Green?

No. The letter is not a part of the note, so Green would not be considered an accommodation endorser, with liability to all subsequent holders. To be an accommodation endorser, Green would have had to sign the actual note.

7.16 Drummond gave a note to Harcum Company, a wholesale firm supplying Drummond's service center. No place of presentment was indicated on the note. Stevens, a later holder in due course, presented the note for payment at Drummond's home address. Drummond refused payment, claiming that he ran a business and that the note was not properly presented when brought to his residence. Was Drummond correct?

No. A note may be presented at either the maker's place of business or home, when no place of presentment has been indicated on the face of the instrument. The holder made a valid presentment of Drummond's note.

7.17 Powers, Anderson, and Roberts cosigned a promissory note, payable on June 6, in return for a loan of $800 made by Harvey. On the due date, a holder in due course presented the note to Anderson for payment. Anderson refused to pay, stating that only Roberts had the authority and responsibility to honor the note. Had Anderson, by his action, dishonored the instrument?

Yes. Comakers are equally responsible when presentment is made at the proper place and on the due date. The holder may make presentment to any party listed as a comaker of the note. Anderson, therefore, dishonored the note.

7.18 Kaplan, as a holder in due course, held a note that had been signed by Curley and was payable on October 3. Kaplan delayed presentment of the note until October 20. Curley refused to pay the note, claiming that it should have been presented on October 3 or within three business days of that date. Was Curley right in this refusal?

No. Curley was primarily liable on the note and may not complain of late presentment, as might a previous holder who was called upon to guarantee a dishonored instrument. Curley may not deny his obligation due to late presentment.

7.19 Vance was a holder in due course of a $2,500 note signed by Flaherty. Flaherty refused payment when Vance presented the note on the due date. Early the next morning, Vance instituted a suit against Cope, a previous holder from whom Vance had purchased the note. Was Vance's action appropriate?

No. Before demand may be made upon an endorser, the endorser must be given notice of dishonor. Vance did not give Cope the notice to which he was entitled.

7.20 Harper held a note payable by Olsen on August 10. The note was presented for payment on Friday, August 10, and dishonored by Olsen because of lack of funds. Harper gave notice to the payee, from whom he had received the instrument, on Wednesday, August 15. The payee denied liability, claiming that there had been too great a delay in Harper's notice of dishonor. Was notice given in time?

Yes. Notice of dishonor must be given within the next three business days following dishonor. Saturday and Sunday are not counted as business days.

7.21 General Finance Associates held Robinson's 6 percent note for $5,000, payable March 30. Robinson tendered full payment of the note with accrued interest on March 1. Payment at that time was refused by General Finance. Payment was demanded by General Finance on March 30. Robinson refused, claiming that the payee's refusal of tender at the earlier date had erased his obligation. Was Robinson correct?

No. By mutual agreement when the note was initiated, the instrument was a contract to repay the loan with interest for a period ending March 30. The payee's refusal to accept payment at an earlier date did not release the maker.

7.22 Suppose that in Problem 7.21 Robinson had made tender of payment and interest on the due date, but it was refused by General Finance. What obligation would Robinson have if payment were demanded on April 30, one month after the due date?

Robinson would not be released from his original obligation. Robinson is liable to the payee for the $5,000 plus 6 percent interest up to the due date. He may not, however, be charged interest for the days following his tender of payment. In addition, Robinson is no longer obligated to make an effort to pay. After the refusal, it is General's obligation to go to Robinson for collection.

7.23 Norcross was indebted to Talley for $4,000, as evidenced by a note payable on November 12 and issued by Norcross. Talley's office was destroyed by fire on the night of November 9, and the note was destroyed along with all the other contents of the office. Will Talley succeed in an attempt to collect the $4,000 from Norcross?

Yes, if he can prove to the satisfaction of the court that there had been a $4,000 note as described. In the event that the note was not destroyed and had instead been transferred to a holder in due course, Norcross would face the possibility of a second claim. She could protect herself from this by demanding, through the courts, that Talley post a bond in the amount of $4,000. Thus, if Talley had been mistaken and the note was in fact in the hands of a holder in due course, Norcross would be protected from paying twice on the same $4,000 note.

7.24 Hurlock held a note signed by Bailey, with interest set at 15 percent. When the note came due, it was presented to Bailey for payment. Bailey refused payment, claiming the interest was usurious and therefore the note was illegal. Was Bailey's contention correct?

The decision would depend to some extent on the law of the state in which the note was presented. State laws differ on what constitutes a usurious instrument or a usurious contract. If the rate was in fact usurious, Bailey might, depending on the state, do one of three things: (1) repay the principal with no interest; (2) repay the principal with interest at the maximum rate allowed by the state; or (3) repay neither the interest nor the principal and be discharged of liability.

Review Problems

7.25 What are the qualifications of a holder in due course?

7.26 Against whom may personal defenses be used by one who issues an instrument?

7.27 Against whom may the real defenses be used?

7.28 How does fraud as a personal defense differ from fraud as a real defense?

7.29 When must presentment be made if endorsers' warranties are to be enforced?

7.30 Does the law ever excuse a delay of presentment?

7.31 Is notice of dishonor, or protest, considered complete at the time it is mailed or at the time it is received by the endorsers?

7.32 How may a holder communicate notice of dishonor?

7.33 When may presentment be made either at the maker's residence *or* place of business?

7.34 May the former owner of an unintentionally destroyed negotiable instrument collect what was due on the instrument?

7.35 How long does a holder have to present an uncertified check for payment without fear of loss?

7.36 What protection has the Federal Trade Commission provided consumers against the collection of a note given for defective merchandise and then presented by a holder in due course?

Answers to Review Problems

7.25 A holder in due course is one who accepts an instrument prior to maturity, for value, in good faith, and with no knowledge of any defect.

7.26 Personal defenses may be used against immediate parties and any third parties who are not holders in due course.

7.27 Real defenses may be used against any holders of a negotiable instrument, including holders in due course.

7.28 Fraud as a personal defense is no different from fraud as a defense against contract obligations. As a real defense, fraud relates to deception in the creation of the instrument itself. Thus, a person who is in no way negligent and who signs a paper that is apparently not a negotiable instrument but which is later fraudulently converted into a promissory note cannot be held liable even by a holder in due course. This was fraud in the *execution* of an instrument and is therefore an *absolute defense*. If, however, a buyer signs and delivers a note in payment of goods that were not as represented by the merchant, he or she may refuse payment on the grounds of fraud in the *inducement* of the contract. This would be a personal defense, which is good against anyone except a holder in due course.

7.29 On or before the due date; presentment of a demand instrument must be made within a "reasonable time" of the date of the instrument.

7.30 Yes, when presentment has been made impossible for reasons such as an act of God.

7.31 Notice of dishonor is accepted as completed at the time of mailing.

7.32 Communication may be by any means selected by the holder: face-to-face or by telephone, telegram, letter, etc.

7.33 When the instrument does not designate the place of presentment.

7.34 Yes, but the one seeking collection will have the burden of proof in establishing the maker's or drawee's obligation.

7.35 The Uniform Commercial Code establishes the time as thirty days from the date of the check.

7.36 The addition to a consumer's contract and to the note of a condition that gives prospective holders notice that any defenses allowable against the payee of the instrument may also be used against subsequent holders of the instrument.

Legal Terms

Acceptance of draft. A drawee's act of paying, or promising in writing to pay, a draft.

Default. Omission or neglect of duty; failure to meet a legal obligation.

Dishonored instruments. Instruments which are not accepted or paid when presentment is made by the holder at the proper time and place.

Forgery. Affixing another's signature to an instrument without that person's knowledge or authority.

Holder in due course. A remote party who takes an instrument in good faith, for value, prior to maturity, and with no notice of any defect in the instrument or its creation.

Honor. To accept or pay a bill of exchange, note, or check.

Maturity. The date on which a negotiable instrument falls due.

Personal defenses. Defenses available to the maker of an instrument or a drawee; they are effective defenses when the instrument is presented for payment by an immediate party or by a remote party who is *not* a holder in due course.

Presentment. The act of (1) submitting commercial paper to the person or persons primarily liable on the instrument and (2) demanding acceptance or payment.

Protest. A statement by a notary public or other authority that an instrument has been dishonored.

Real defenses. Defenses available against the claims of *all* parties, both immediate and remote, including holders in due course..

Remote parties. Holders of commercial paper other than those named on the face of the instrument; those named on the face of the commercial paper are known as *immediate parties*.

Chapter 8

The Law of Bailments, Hotelkeepers, and Common Carriers

Almost every type of business and almost all people have, at one time or another, borrowed or rented someone else's property. American law has recognized the rights and obligations of a person who has temporary possession of the property of another. The law also gives rights and responsibilities to those who lend or rent their own property to others. The laws covering these kinds of situations are known collectively as the *law of bailments*.

A *bailor* is a party who temporarily gives possession of property to another. A *bailee* is the party to whom property is temporarily entrusted. Both bailors' and bailees' rights and obligations are reviewed in this chapter.

Hotelkeepers and common carriers are also reviewed in this chapter because the nature of their services requires that they accept the personal property of those they serve. The laws regulating hotelkeepers and common carriers are in many ways similar to the law of bailments.

BAILMENTS OF PERSONAL PROPERTY

8.1 Transfer of Possession

A bailment is created when one party, the *bailor,* transfers possession of tangible personal property to another, the *bailee*. *Possession* means that the bailee has physical control coupled with the right of judgment in the care or use of the other's property.

EXAMPLE 1. Kincaid offered to take care of his neighbor's dog while the neighbor was on an extended vacation. The dog was delivered to Kincaid and accepted by him when the neighbor departed from home. Thus, through the transfer of possession of the dog, a bailment relationship was created. Although this act may seem like nothing more than a favor, both Kincaid and his neighbor were responsible to one another under long-established bailment law.

8.2 Obligation to Return Property

The bailee has a primary obligation to return to the bailor the same property he or she received, either in its original form or in an altered form. Failure to return the very same property is a breach of the bailment agreement.

EXAMPLE 2. Bicycle Rentals rented a ten-speed English racer to Broadbent for $8 a day. Due to Broadbent's carelessness, the bicycle was stolen from his home. Broadbent bought another used bicycle and returned it to Bicycle Rentals. Broadbent breached his bailment contract. Bicycle Rentals may refuse the replacement and sue Broadbent for the value of the stolen bike, plus damages if any.

8.3 The Bailment Contract

Bailment agreements are contracts. To be enforceable, they must contain the four requisites of a valid contract: (1) mutual assent, (2) capable parties, (3) consideration, and (4) valid subject matter. Bailments that are created to benefit only one of the parties may be terminated at any time due to the absence of consideration.

EXAMPLE 3. Harrison loaned a tent to his friend Brown, charging nothing for the favor. After four days, Harrison needed the tent himself and requested its return. Even though Harrison had agreed to let Brown use the tent for an entire week, he may demand its return at any time because no consideration had been given by Brown.

8.4 Gratuitous Bailments

Gratuitous bailments are those that benefit only the bailor or only the bailee. In a gratuitous bailment for the *sole benefit of the bailor,* the bailee must use *slight care* and will be responsible for damage resulting from gross negligence. In a bailment for the *sole benefit of the bailee, great care* must be exercised, and the bailee is responsible for damages due to even slight negligence.

EXAMPLE 4. Campbell asked his neighbor for permission to leave his car in the neighbor's garage during a period of stormy weather. The neighbor took Campbell's car, put it into his garage, and locked the doors. The agreement benefitted only the bailor, Campbell. If the car were stolen, the bailee could say that by locking the garage he had given the car necessary care, and this was all that was required of him.

EXAMPLE 5. Wilson borrowed Miller's snowblower to clean his driveway. He had forgotten that his son had left roller skates and other toys on the driveway before the snowstorm. The machine was wrecked when one of the roller skates bent its blade and motor shaft. Wilson had not exercised the great care required in this type of bailment. The damage was due to his negligence in not clearing the driveway of his son's toys. Wilson would be obligated to pay for all damage and repairs.

8.5 Condition of Chattel

A bailor must deliver *safe chattel* to the bailee. (*Chattel* means personal property.) Damage to the bailee or the bailee's property caused by an unsafe chattel becomes a liability of the bailor.

EXAMPLE 6. Without charge, McCarthy loaned an electric drill to Rawlins. While using the drill, Rawlins received a shock that paralyzed his right arm. Investigation disclosed that the shock came from an exposed wire touching the metal casing of the drill. McCarthy could be held responsible to Rawlins for having given the bailee a drill that on examination would have proven to be unsafe.

8.6 Using Bailed Property

The bailee is restricted to using the bailor's property in the manner agreed to in the bailment agreement. Extended or unpermitted use makes the bailee fully responsible in the event of any loss or damage to the property. A bailee who makes unauthorized use of someone else's property becomes an *insurer* of that property, liable for it regardless of the care taken in its use.

EXAMPLE 7. Polsky loaned his power saw to Robinson, who said he was going to use it to cross-cut 12-foot 2×4s into 4-foot lengths. After finishing the job, Robinson used Polsky's saw to rip several 3×12 boards lengthwise. In doing so, Robinson burned out the saw's motor. Even though Robinson used extreme care, he was responsible for the damage. He had exceeded the rights given him by the bailor.

8.7 Bailment-Related Expenses

The bailor must reimburse the bailee for all *necessary expenses* related to the bailment if it is for the sole benefit of the bailor. Bailees, in bailments for solely their benefit, must be reimbursed only for unusual and unexpected expenses related to the care of the bailor's property.

EXAMPLE 8. Henson agreed to take care of Arvin's truck during Arvin's absence. The weather became unseasonably cold, so Henson added antifreeze to the truck radiator. The antifreeze cost Henson $3.39. Henson, as a bailee, had an obligation to protect Arvin's truck. Adding antifreeze was a necessary expense, for which Arvin must give Henson $3.39.

EXAMPLE 9. Archino borrowed Jewell's power lawnmower. While Archino was carefully operating the mower, its drive belt, which was three years old, broke. Archino purchased a new belt, costing $1.53, to replace the old one. Archino may demand $1.53 from Jewell.

8.8 Lost Property

One who finds and takes possession of lost property becomes a bailee for the sole benefit of the bailor. The finder has possession only, not title. The finder must exercise slight care and is responsible for damages resulting from gross negligence. The finder must also make a reasonable effort to locate the real owner.

EXAMPLE 10. Dugan spotted a wallet on the sidewalk and reached over and picked it up. It contained credit cards, $107 in cash, and an identification card. Dugan would be legally responsible to return the wallet and its contents to the owner. He may not demand a reward, but he may demand reimbursement for any expenses he incurred in trying to locate the owner or in caring for and delivering the owner's property.

8.9 Mutual-Benefit Bailments

Business bailments in which both the bailor and bailee are to be benefitted are *mutual-benefit bailments*. The bailor must deliver a safe chattel; the bailee must exercise *ordinary care*. Right to use is limited and restricted in the same way as other types of bailments are restricted. Mutual-benefit bailments may be contracts for: (1) the use of chattels; (2) the custody of chattels; (3) work or service on chattels; or (4) security of the bailor's promise of performance.

EXAMPLE 11. Rembaldt borrowed $50 from the owner of a pawnshop. As security for repayment of the $50 with interest, Rembaldt left an expensive pocket watch with the owner. The watch was to be returned to him when the debt was paid. The pawnshop owner has no right to use the watch. He must exercise ordinary care in its protection, and if the watch is lost or stolen through negligence, Rembaldt may demand damages.

EXAMPLE 12. Southby left his CB radio with Higgins Radio for repairs. The night guard left the shop to go for coffee. He did not lock the door. Southby's radio was stolen. The employee's negligence in not locking the shop door was the cause of the loss. Ordinary care had not been taken. Higgins Radio would be obligated to reimburse Southby for the loss.

8.10 Parking Lots and Garages

Parking lots and garages usually give to a car owner a claim check that states that the agreement is a lessor-lessee agreement, not a bailment. However, if the management takes possession of the car, retains the key, and requires the return of the claim check before giving up possession of the car, courts will usually consider the arrangement to be a bailment.

EXAMPLE 13. Talbot drove her car into a public parking lot, stopping to get a claim check as she drove in. She selected her own parking place without direction or assistance, kept the car keys, and was able to go directly to her car when she returned, without reporting to an attendant. This was not a bailment because the parking lot had not taken possession of the car. The lot owner had merely permitted Talbot to park for a fee.

8.11 Tortious Bailees

Persons who refuse to give up possession of a bailor's property when they do not have rightful possession are *tortious bailees*. An action of *replevin* is proper in demanding the return of the property. The owner may elect to use an action of *trover* if the value of the property is desired rather than the property itself. A *trespass* action is used to recover the property or its value and any profits gained from its unauthorized use.

EXAMPLE 14. Reybold rented a car from Rent-Al. The rental was for three days. Reybold refused to return the car at the end of the third day. An action of replevin would get the car back. An action of trover would recover the value of the car. An action of trespass would recover the car or its value, plus any profits Reybold may have realized from the extended and unpermitted use of the automobile.

HOTELKEEPERS

8.12 Hotels *versus* Lodginghouses

Hotels are facilities offering shelter and food to the public; they do not have the right to select their own guests and they must, if they have room, accept all persons seeking accommodations. Hotels differ from lodginghouses, dormitories, and boarding houses in that owners of these facilities may select their guests. Both hotels and lodginghouses are governed by the Civil Rights Act of 1964: they may not discriminate against persons because of race, color, creed, or national origin.

EXAMPLE 15. Keystone Hotel accepted transients for rooms. Lee, an Oriental, attempted to register for a room but was turned away. The management gave no reason for their refusal, and there were rooms available. The hotel would be liable for damages and may be subject to criminal complaint by Lee.

8.13 The Right to Refuse Guests

A hotelkeeper may refuse persons whose presence might imperil the health, welfare, or safety of other guests. A hotel may also refuse guests after all of its accommodations have been filled or reserved.

EXAMPLE 16. A boisterous and intoxicated person demanded a room in the Hotel Sanderson. The manager would not permit him to register, although several rooms were available. The manager was well within his rights because the would-be guest might have been a threat to the safety of the other guests.

8.14 Hotelkeeper's Degree of Care

A hotelkeeper must exercise *reasonable care* in protecting the guests from injury while they are on the hotel premises. The hotel is not an insurer, but it will be liable for injuries resulting from negligence and lack of care.

EXAMPLE 17. An elevator in the Hotel Gloriana lost power and was caught between floors, where it remained for three hours. The cause of the accident was the hotel's failure to inspect and correct defects in the elevator system. Passengers in the elevator and any other inconvenienced guests have rightful claims against the management.

8.15 Hotelkeeper's Liability for Guest's Property

A hotelkeeper is an insurer of the guest's property up to an amount set by state statute. The hotelkeeper is not liable, however, when damage is caused by (1) the guest's contributory negligence, (2) acts of God, (3) acts of a public enemy, (4) accidental fire, or (5) the inherent nature of the goods damaged.

EXAMPLE 18. Andrews, a guest at the Charlotte Hall Hotel, left her room without locking the door. On her return, she discovered that her suitcase had been taken from the room. Her negligence in failing to lock the door would prevent Andrews from making a successful claim against the hotel management.

EXAMPLE 19. A malfunction of the Newton Hotel's sprinkler system caused water damage to rooms throughout the eighteenth floor. Clothing and other property of guests was damaged or destroyed by the water that gushed into the rooms. The hotel was responsible as an *insurer* for losses claimed and proven by guests, even though no negligence was shown.

8.16 Hotelkeeper's Right of Lien

A hotelkeeper may take possession of a guest's property when the guest refuses or is not able to pay the bill for accommodations supplied. This is the hotelkeeper's *right of lien*. The right is terminated when payment is made.

EXAMPLE 20. Cavendish ran up a bill of $362 during a stay at the Hotel Espresso. When he checked out, he was not able to pay the bill. The manager took possession of Cavendish's luggage, holding it until he returned later with funds to pay his debt to the hotel.

COMMON CARRIERS

8.17 Common Carriers and Private Carriers

Private carriers may be compared with common carriers in the same way that lodginghouses are compared with hotels. Private carriers engage in hauling goods and passengers by contract; they have the right to select their customers. Common carriers, on the other hand, operate under federal and state franchises; they serve consumers as a quasi-public institution, and must accept business without discrimination.

EXAMPLE 21. Ohio Limousine Service provided cars for funeral directors in the Cleveland area. The firm worked by appointment and under individual contract. A call was received from Cornwall, who requested a limousine to take him to a wedding. Ohio Limousine Service was not franchised as a common carrier. It had no obligation to serve Cornwall. Had the company operated under a public-service franchise, it would have been required to act on Cornwall's, or anyone else's, request for service.

8.18 Obligations to Carry Freight Indiscriminately

Common carriers of freight must accept all goods tendered for shipment. The carrier is relieved of this obligation only when: (1) the carrier is not equipped to carry the type of goods submitted; (2) when goods are inherently dangerous and could create hazards beyond the carrier's usual safety facilities; (3) when the goods are different from those the carrier represents itself as carrying; and (4) when the goods are improperly or insecurely packed.

EXAMPLE 22. Airways Express operated out of Chicago and carried frozen beef products to all parts of the continental United States. Illinois Chemical Company was refused a request to fly an emergency consignment of nitric acid to Atlanta, Georgia. Airways did not breach its obligation as a common carrier. Its aircraft were not designed to carry any goods other than frozen beef, nor had the carrier held itself out to the trade as one that carried chemicals.

8.19 Rights of Common Carriers

Common carriers have two essential rights against shippers: (1) the right to payment for the shipment of goods and (2) the right of lien on goods shipped, up to the amount of any unpaid shipping charges. The right of lien is lost when the carrier loses possession of the goods or when all due charges have been paid.

EXAMPLE 23. A crate of furniture was shipped to Ginsworth in Albany, New York. Ginsworth was to pay shipping fees before receiving delivery in Albany. The carrier's freight agent gave the crate to Ginsworth, forgetting to collect the money due. Thus the carrier lost the right of lien on the goods. By the terms of the shipment, the carrier could have held the goods until all charges were paid.

8.20 Carrier as Insurer of Freight

A carrier of freight is a bailee of goods carried. It is also an *insurer* of the goods. The carrier's responsibility stems from its own negligence or a lack of care. (The obligation is analogous to that of a hotelkeeper to the guest's property.) The carrier is relieved of liability for loss when damages result from: (1) acts of public authorities; (2) acts of God; (3) acts of a public enemy; (4) acts of the shipper; or (5) the inherent nature of the goods.

EXAMPLE 24. A new "miracle" drug was shipped from St. Louis to Denver by Continental Truck Service, a common carrier. The Food and Drug Administration learned that the shipment had been released before the drug had been properly tested and certified for public use. The F.D.A. confiscated the shipment before it reached Denver. Continental Truck Service would not be liable to either the shipper or consignee for their losses in the shipment.

8.21 The Bill of Lading

The written contract between a shipper and a carrier is contained in a printed document known as the *bill of lading*. The bill of lading in interstate shipments must be acceptable in form and content to the Interstate Commerce Commission. Bills used in intrastate shipment must be of a type approved by the state's public-service commission.

EXAMPLE 25. Charlestown Press shipped two boxes of printed forms to Heubner Brothers. The freight agent signed Charlestown's bill of lading when he accepted the goods. The shipment was f.o.b. Charlestown. The bill of lading would serve as a document of title to the goods during transit. If an *order bill of lading* had been used, the consignee, Heubner Brothers, could transfer title to the goods to other parties merely by endorsing and delivering the bill of lading to such parties. A so-called *straight bill of lading* may not be negotiated. As with contracts, however, it may be assigned.

8.22 Liability of Carriers

Carriers may limit their liability as insurers through terms included in the bill of lading and within the restrictions imposed by law. Shippers, by paying higher fees, may increase the amount of coverage accepted by the carrier. However, carriers are never excused from damages that result from their own negligence.

EXAMPLE 26. Peninsula Express Trucking Company accepted a shipment of aluminum cans, in a truckload lot, to be delivered to a factory in Virginia. The bill of lading limited Peninsula's obligation as insurer to $500. Enroute, the driver fell asleep, the truck crashed, and the entire load of cans was destroyed. The carrier would be liable for the entire loss through the negligence of the driver, its employee.

8.23 Termination of Carrier's Liability

The carrier's liability as insurer commences when the goods are accepted from the shipper. The liability is terminated when the goods arrive at their destination, the consignee has been informed of their arrival, and forty-eight hours have passed. At that time, the carrier's liability is that of a mutual-benefit bailee. The carrier is reduced from the status of an insurer to that of one who must give only ordinary care.

EXAMPLE 27. Holloway Motor Freight accepted a shipment of shag carpeting from Randolph Carpet Company. The carpeting was consigned to Miller Furniture, f.o.b. shipping point. The carpet reached Holloway's depot in the buyer's city, and Miller Furniture received an arrival notice on March 8. The goods remained in the depot until the night of March 14, at which time they were destroyed by accidental fire. Holloway Motor Freight was no longer an insurer at the time of the fire. Failure to prove Holloway's lack of ordinary care relieved the carrier of any responsibility to Miller Furniture. Had the fire taken place on March 9, Holloway would have been liable as an insurer of Miller's goods.

COMMON CARRIERS OF PASSENGERS

8.24 When a Person Becomes a Passenger

A *passenger* is anyone entering the premises of a common carrier with the intention to purchase a ticket for transportation at that time. (Purchase of reservations for a *later* trip does not give the purchaser status as a passenger.) Passenger status continues until a person reaches the destination shown on her or his ticket and then leaves the carrier's premises.

EXAMPLE 28. Daugherty purchased a ticket for Miami on Eastern Airlines. The flight reservation was on a plane that would leave in forty minutes. While waiting to board the aircraft, Daugherty was injured. He demanded damages under his rights as a passenger. Daugherty had the same rights as one who had already boarded the carrier's aircraft.

8.25 Obligations of Carriers to Accept All Persons

A common carrier must accept all persons seeking passage, with a few exceptions. (The exceptions to this obligation are similar to the hotelkeeper's right to refuse guests.) Would-be passengers may be rejected when: (1) no reservations or seats are available; or (2) the applicant is intoxicated, disorderly, under the influence of nonprescription drugs, insane, or infected with a contagious disease.

EXAMPLE 29. Koviac requested a reservation on Flight 73, from San Francisco to Honolulu. The reservations clerk noted Koviac's intoxicated condition and refused to issue a ticket to him. Koviac later entered a complaint with the Interstate Commerce Commission on his rights as a passenger. The clerk was within his rights in refusing to sell a ticket to Koviac. However, the clerk would be required to give proof of Koviac's condition if an inquiry were conducted.

8.26 Degree of Care to Be Used

Common carriers must exercise reasonable care in protecting passengers from injury. Reasonable care is always a question of fact, determined by what would ordinarily be expected of other carriers under the same conditions.

EXAMPLE 30. Urey was a passenger in a taxi when the driver negligently ran into the back of a truck that was stopped for a red light. Urey was thrown to the floor, receiving injuries. Urey will recover damages on proof of the driver's failure to give reasonable care to the safety of the cab company's passenger. (Taxi businesses are in almost all cases common carriers regulated by public-service commissions.)

8.27 Carrier as Insurer of Passenger's Luggage

Common carriers are obligated as insurers of the luggage to which the carrier has been given possession. Luggage retained by the passenger during the journey continues to be the passenger's responsibility, except in cases of negligent operation by the carrier. As with hotelkeepers, the law limits the amount of money recoverable against the carrier for loss of goods in its possession.

EXAMPLE 31. Ebright checked her two suitcases with the counter clerk before receiving her boarding pass for a flight to New Orleans. Careless handling resulted in the loss of Ebright's luggage. The carrier, as an insurer, would be required to reimburse Ebright for the amount of proven loss within the limit set by law.

8.28 I.C.C. Control over Common Carriers

Without notice to and permission from the Interstate Commerce Commission (I.C.C.) or a state public-service commission, common carriers are not permitted to change schedules, raise rates, or reduce the quality of service provided under the carrier's franchise.

EXAMPLE 32. Richey commuted regularly between New York City and Stamford, Connecticut. When Richey purchased his regular monthly commuter ticket, the clerk informed him that there had been a price increase of 25 percent. Richey discovered that the carrier had introduced the increase without petitioning the Interstate Commerce Commission for permission to do so. The carrier would be required to reimburse all who paid for tickets at the higher price.

Solved Problems

8.1 Harvey loaned Jordan, his neighbor, a chain hoist that Jordan used in removing the motor from his Jeep. In the middle of the operation, Harvey demanded the return of the hoist. Must Jordan interrupt the procedure and return the hoist at once?

Bailments for the sole benefit of the bailee are created without consideration. They may be terminated at any time at the decision of either party. The bailor, however, may not demand possession at a time that might cause injury or damage to the bailee. Jordan may continue to use the chain hoist until the motor has been removed and is safely locked up.

8.2 Pawlson asked Harbeson to drive his car to a service station. Harbeson agreed. Before commencing the trip, Harbeson tried the car's brakes and commented that they were in very poor condition and needed attention. Harbeson was injured on the way to the service station because the brakes failed. Will Harbeson recover damages from Pawlson?

No. Bailors are obligated to deliver safe chattels to their bailees. However, if a bailee is aware of a defect, there will be no grounds for a recovery on a claim of unsafe chattel. Harbeson discovered the defect in the brakes, announced his discovery, but proceeded anyway. Therefore Harbeson will not recover against Pawlson.

8.3 Winchester Stables agreed to board Richardson's mare for several months, during Richardson's vacation abroad. When Richardson returned, he learned that the mare had given birth to a prize colt. Winchester Stables claimed the colt as their own. May Richardson demand possession of the colt?

Yes. The owner of an animal bailed to another has title to any natural increase by the animal. There is no intention to pass title to progeny born during a bailee's possession. Richardson has complete title rights to the colt and may acquire possession of it from Winchester Stables through an action of replevin.

8.4 During a severe windstorm, property of Highland Amusement Park blew over onto Klair's farmland. Klair promptly gathered up the goods and delivered them to a dump, where they were burned. Highland's manager sued Klair for the loss resulting from his act. Will Highland recover damages from Klair?

Yes. When goods are delivered by forces beyond the control of a bailor and bailee, an *involuntary bailment* is created. The involuntary bailee is required to give slight care to the other's property. Likewise, the bailee is responsible for damages resulting from gross negligence or wanton misconduct. Klair had failed to fulfill his duty as an involuntary bailee and is therefore liable for damages claimed by Highland Amusement Park.

8.5 Danvers rented a car from Hanover Car Rental. Certain conditions were printed in the agreement, one of which restricted bailees from taking rented cars out of the state. Danvers drove the car ten miles into an adjoining state. Did Danvers's act affect the bailment contract?

Yes. Danvers had violated the bailment agreement and had become a tortious bailee. When he crossed into another state, he had wrongful possession of the car. At that point, the bailment agreement was terminated by his breach. Danvers immediately became an insurer of the car, rather than a bailee having only an obligation to give ordinary care.

8.6 Woodrow reserved a room in the All-State Hotel. He rented the room for a period of two weeks at a special rate advertised by the hotel. During his stay, his suit was taken from the room. (The room had been locked, and all precautions against anyone entering the room had been taken.) Woodrow demanded damages from All-State on grounds that the hotel was the insurer of all guests' property. Will Woodrow be reimbursed for this loss?

No. Woodrow was not a *guest* of the All-State Hotel. Hotel guests are defined as *transients,* who take rooms for an indefinite period of time. Woodrow was a *lodger,* renting the room for an extended period of time at a weekly rate. The hotelkeeper is not an insurer of property belonging to a lodger. The hotel is obligated to give only ordinary care to a lodger's property. Unless it can be proven that the hotel had failed to give *ordinary care* or had been negligent, Woodrow will not be reimbursed for the loss.

8.7 Challenger entered a hotel and went to the desk, where he bought a newspaper and a bus ticket to the next town. While awaiting the arrival of the bus, Challenger sat in the hotel lobby. An employee who was carrying a box of tools stumbled and fell over Challenger, injuring him. The hotel denied any obligation to Challenger, claiming that he was not a guest of the hotel. Was the hotel liable to Challenger?

Yes. Persons entering a hotel for the purpose of doing business are *business guests.* To such persons, the hotelkeeper owes a duty of care equal to that owed to one who is a hotel guest. (The duty is restricted to the person, and does not cover the person's property.) Challenger was a business guest. His injuries resulted from the negligent act of a hotel employee. Reasonable care had not been given. Challenger may demand reimbursement for damages resulting from the injuries he received.

8.8 Cooper was a guest in the Hotel Starling. His room door was opened by another guest, who had been mistakenly assigned to the same room. (The desk clerk had given this second guest a key and directed him to Cooper's room.) Cooper demanded damages from the hotel for this disregard of his rights. Will Cooper recover?

Yes. The hotelkeeper is obligated to guard a guest's right of privacy. Invasion of privacy, resulting either from the hotelkeeper's negligence or through intentional acts, provides grounds for a tort action for damages. Cooper, in this case, could recover damages against the Starling Hotel.

8.9 Sharpley Company shipped ten crates of waste to Henderson Mills, f.o.b. the buyer's location. In the interstate shipment, the crates had to be carried the final eighteen miles on another carrier, which served the Henderson Mills area. The goods were damaged during transit on this connecting carrier. Is the initial or connecting carrier liable for the loss incurred?

In *interstate shipments,* damages resulting to goods in possession of a connecting carrier are the responsibility of the initial carrier. In *intrastate shipments,* the initial carrier is relieved, making the connecting carrier fully responsible to anyone making a claim. Sharpley Company, under the terms of the shipment, was the owner of the goods when they were damaged. Sharpley will make its claim against the initial carrier.

8.10 Carmody had reservations for the 6:47 A.M. flight from Minneapolis to Atlanta. One hour before flight time, Carmody checked in at the airline counter. The reservations clerk informed him that his seat had been given up in favor of another party, who had an emergency appointment in Atlanta. Carmody demanded reinstatement as a passenger on the 6:47 flight. Will Carmody be successful in this demand?

Yes. A carrier is not permitted to "bump" one passenger from a reservation in favor of another. The passenger receiving such treatment may appeal to federal agencies and recover damages. In all likelihood, the carrier would agree to Carmody's demands, realizing that he understood his legal rights in the matter.

8.11 Kerlish, Compton, and Ilyas organized a car pool for commuting to and from their daily jobs in the city. No money exchanged hands, but they alternated in providing cars for the trip. In an accident in which Kerlish and Ilyas were injured, Compton's insurance company refused payment, claiming that the car pool was an illegal venture because it had not received a state franchise for carrying passengers. Was the insurer correct?

No. Persons grouped together in organized car pools are not recognized as carriers for hire. They do not require a franchise under a state commission.

8.12 Rocky Mount Explosives Company delivered five boxes of dynamite to Southeastern Trucking Services, a common carrier, for shipment to Baltimore. Southeastern's agent refused to accept the shipment, so Rocky Mount made a formal complaint to the Interstate Commerce Commission. Was Rocky Mount justified in this complaint?

No. A carrier is not required to accept goods that are inherently dangerous or goods for which the carrier has insufficient facilities to give safe transit. Southeastern's agent was correct in refusing to accept the shipment. Acceptance would create hazards to the property of others, for which Southeastern Trucking might have been liable.

8.13 Western Railroad accepted a carload of fertilizer for shipment to Albuquerque, New Mexico. While the car was on a siding awaiting pickup by a scheduled freight, a warning was issued about water rapidly rising in a river adjacent to the freight yard. No efforts were made to move the car to higher ground. Later, water caused extensive damage to the shipment. The carrier disclaimed any liability, giving an act of God as its defense. Was the carrier justified in this defense?

No. A carrier forewarned of an impending hazard caused by an act of God must take care to remove a shipper's goods to a safe place. Western Railroad made no effort to protect the shipper's goods. The damage resulted not from an act of God but from the carrier's failure to react to the warning given. The carrier, then, remains an insurer of the shipment and is liable for damages.

8.14 MowPower shipped lawn tractors to Everson & Company, Elsmere. The terms of shipment were f.o.b. shipping point. An order bill of lading was mailed to Everson & Company after the goods had been delivered to the carrier. An officer of Everson & Company transferred the bill of lading to Harrington Hardware for Harrington's payment of $17,890 to Everson. Everson's officer had no authority to make this transfer. The tractors were delivered to Harrington by the railroad on presentation of the bill of lading. May Everson reclaim the tractors?

No. An *order* bill of lading is negotiable and may be used as a means of transferring title to one who is an innocent purchaser for value. Harrington had no reason to distrust the officer of the company to which the bill was originally made. The carrier acted properly, and Harrington Hardware has rightful title to and possession of the tractors.

8.15 Blatchford met one of her friends in the lobby of the Hotel Canfield. A sign there warned persons to be careful in walking over a recently waxed floor. Blatchford did not heed the sign; she walked across the floor, fell, and was injured. She sought damages on grounds that the hotel had not provided her with reasonable care. Will she recover?

No. Blatchford was not a guest or a business guest. She was a *licensee*. Licensees are persons permitted to enter the hotel's premises without having business with the hotel, its services, or its guests. To a licensee, a hotel owes no duty other than that of pointing out existing hazards. The hotel had met its obligations to Blatchford, and she may not recover against the hotel.

8.16 Tursky rented a floor sander from U-Rent-It. He was proficient in operating such equipment and was experienced in refinishing hardwood floors. The floor he worked on was ruined because of a serious fault in the sander's wheel housing. Does Tursky have legal grounds on which to demand damages?

Yes. In a bailment for use of chattels, the bailor must deliver not only a safe chattel, but a chattel that is fit for the purpose for which it was rented. Breach of this implied warranty caused damage to Tursky's floors, and damages may be sought.

8.17 The Iowa Trust and Deposit Bank rented a safe-deposit box to Klund. She deposited $7,850 worth of silver jewelry and gems in the box. Thieves broke into the bank, blew open the safe, and removed, among other valuables, Klund's jewelry. Klund sought damages from the bank on the grounds that it failed to provide reasonable care, as required in all mutual-benefit bailments. Will she recover on these grounds?

No. One who rents a safe-deposit box signs an agreement similar to that which covers the rental of an apartment. The bank is a lessor, the renter of the box is a lessee. There is no bailment relationship. The lessee does not give the bank possession of the goods stored in the box. The owner locks the contents in the box with a key available only to her or him. Klund's arguments will not provide her with recovery of the loss.

8.18 Harmon ate lunch at Jimmy's Country Corner, a "fast-food" establishment. He hung his coat on a hook near the counter. When ready to depart, he discovered that the coat had been stolen. Harmon brought action for damages against the lunchroom on grounds that the coat was hung in a place provided, implying that the manager had taken possession. Was Harmon correct?

It is sometimes necessary for an owner to give up possession of personal property in order to transact business. The law calls such a situation a *bailment by necessity* if it can be shown that the management encourages and is aware of the owner's transfer of possession. Harmon was not eating lunch in a type of restaurant where custom and manners demanded that customers remove their coats and hats. The hooks were available only as a convenience, not because of a necessity. Had Harmon been a guest in a hotel dining room, the situation would have been different. Guests in such surroundings are expected to remove their outer clothing when dining; a bailment by necessity could exist under such conditions. In any case, the proprietor or the proprietor's agent must be aware of the guest's transfer of possession.

8.19 Talbot drove her car to a repair shop for inspection and repair. She accompanied the shop foreman on a trial run, pointing out the difficulties she had experienced with her car. The foreman damaged Talbot's car when he failed to see a patch of ice, skidded, and collided with a tree. Talbot demanded damages on grounds of a bailor's rights in a bailment for mutual benefit. Was the repair shop a bailee at the time of the accident?

No. Talbot had not given up *possession* of her car to the foreman. Although the foreman had physical control of the car, Talbot was still in command because she was riding at the foreman's side. The foreman had *custody,* but not possession. The basic requirement of a bailment agreement is possession by the bailee.

8.20 Greenbank Mill received ten bushels of wheat from Palmer. The mill agreed to give Palmer a barrel of white flour the next day. During the night, the wheat was stolen from the mill. There was no proof of negligence or lack of care by the mill. The miller refused to give the promised flour to Palmer, claiming that they had created a bailment and he had fulfilled his obligation of care. Was the miller correct?

No. When goods are delivered to a party in *exchange* for a promise to deliver other goods, the transaction is an exchange, not a bailment. Palmer had not specified that the flour he was to receive would come from the wheat he gave the mill. The wheat, at the time of loss, belonged to the mill, not to Palmer. Palmer is correct in demanding delivery of the barrel of flour promised.

8.21 Washington Appliance Repair Shop accepted Slocomb's automatic washer for overhaul. When repairs had been made but the machine had been only partly reassembled, Washington Appliance put the job aside to do other work. Demands over a period of two months brought no results. What are Slocomb's rights in this bailment dispute?

Slocomb had a bailment for work and service with the repair shop. The shop had *abandoned* its obligation to complete the job. Without cause, the machine had been set aside and nothing further was done. The shop had become a tortious bailee and no longer had the right of possession. Slocomb may start an action of replevin for recovery of his property. He is not liable for work or parts already billed to the job by the breaching bailee.

8.22 Armstrong was a guest at the Hotel Bellehaven. A sign posted in Armstrong's room stated that guests were required to deliver all jewelry, cash, and other valuables to the main desk for safekeeping in the hotel vault during the night or when a guest was away from the room. When Armstrong retired for the night, she kept her watch and earrings with her in the room. They were stolen during the night. The hotel denied any responsibility as an insurer, stating that Armstrong did not comply with instructions contained in the notice posted in the room. Is the hotel liable to Armstrong?

A hotel may protect itself from loss by requiring guests to deposit valuables in the hotel safe or vault. Exceptions to the rule include those items that one would ordinarily keep possession of at all times. It is customary that a guest would keep a watch while occupying a hotel room. Earrings are a matter of dispute. If the earrings were of an ordinary sort, Armstrong could have kept them with her in the room. If, however, they were extremely valuable and tempting to a thief, the answer could be otherwise. The hotel, then, would be liable for the value of the watch; reimbursement for the earrings would depend on a court's decision.

8.23 Eastburn borrowed $50 from Whann, promising to return the money the next morning when they met at work. Whann had given Eastburn 5 five-dollar bills, 2 tens, and 5 ones. Eastburn gave 5 tens back to Whann. Was Whann's act of kindness a bailment for the sole benefit of the bailee? Was Eastburn correct in returning currency in denominations different from those she had received?

No bailment was intended. Whann did not loan Eastburn the money with expectation of getting back the very same money. This was a credit-debit transaction only. Title to the money, as well as possession, passed to Eastburn. Eastburn was not required to return money in the same denominations that she had received.

8.24 Stanton Cycle Shop made repairs on Nicholson's Honda. When the cycle was ready, the shop refused to give it back to Nicholson until she paid the $38.50 due for labor and parts. She had no money and demanded possession, claiming that the cycle shop had no legal right to retain her property against her will. Was Nicholson right?

No. A bailee in contracts for work and service has a right of lien for money owed in connection with the contract. Only if some credit agreement has been made at the time of contracting is this right of lien given up. Nicholson has no right of possession until she has paid the charges for labor and parts.

8.25 Lester's Money Office loaned Sylvester $25 and accepted Sylvester's electric guitar as security. Lester took the guitar home one evening and played it. It was stolen from his home the same night. Sylvester demanded the return of the guitar, which was worth $150, when he tendered the $25 borrowed plus charges. What are Sylvester's rights in this bailment arrangement?

Sylvester and Lester's Money Office had created a mutual-benefit bailment. Lester, the bailee, had no right to use the guitar. Converting it to his own use made him responsible for any and all damages, regardless of the cause and regardless of the amount of care given. Sylvester's demand for the value of the guitar will be met if appealed in court.

Review Problems

8.26 How does a *bailment* differ from a *sale?*

8.27 What is the difference between *possession* of goods and *custody* of goods? Give an example of each.

8.28 Explain the obligation of the initial carrier when goods are damaged while in possession of a connecting carrier in (1) interstate shipments and (2) intrastate shipments.

8.29 In what way is a common carrier of passengers similar to a hotelkeeper in the matter of accepting customers and guests?

8.30 Why may the bailor, in a gratuitous bailment, terminate the bailment agreement at any time?

8.31 Does leaving one's car in a privately owned parking lot create a bailment agreement?

8.32 What is a *tortious bailee?*

8.33 At what point does a person become a passenger? When does a person's passenger status end?

8.34 Under what conditions would an owner decide to bring an action of: (1) trover, (2) replevin, and (3) trespass?

8.35 How does a common carrier differ from a private carrier? Which type of carrier operates under a public franchise?

8.36 What is a *safe chattel?* How is this term interpreted in the law of bailments?

8.37 Explain how the following terms relate to the law of common carriers: (1) *right of lien;* (2) *order bill of lading*; (3) *insurer*; (4) *reasonable care*; and (5) *licensee*.

8.38 How much care must a bailee give to the bailor's property in: (1) a bailment for the sole benefit of bailor; (2) a bailment for the sole benefit of bailee; and (3) a mutual-benefit bailment?

Answers to Review Problems

8.26 In a bailment, only possession is transferred. In a sale, both possession and title are transferred.

8.27 With possession, one has both physical control over and the power of judgment over property, as when one borrows another's car and drives it in the absence of the owner. With custody, one has only physical control, as when someone drives another's car with the owner sitting at his or her side.

8.28 In interstate shipments, the initial carrier continues as an insurer of goods in possession of the connecting carrier. In intrastate shipments, the initial carrier is relieved of liability when goods are given to the connecting carrier, who then assumes the role of insurer.

8.29 Both the common carrier and the hotelkeeper must accept all persons who request transport or services, and both are excepted from this obligation when: (1) all facilities have been filled or reserved or (2) the person applying is in a condition deemed improper and dangerous to the other guests or passengers.

8.30 Gratuitous bailments lack the element of consideration in their creation, and consideration is necessary in the formation of enforceable agreements. Thus, either the bailor or bailee may terminate the bailment at any time, as long as termination does not endanger the parties or the bailed goods.

8.31 Not necessarily. If an attendant keeps the car and its keys and gives the owner a claim check that must be presented before the car is returned, a bailment agreement may be created in the eyes of some courts. Other courts, however, may deem this and all other parking-lot arrangements as lessor-lessee agreements, in which the car's owner, as lessee, simply pays for the right to use space in the lot.

8.32 A tortious bailee is anyone who has wrongful possession of another's goods.

8.33 A person becomes a passenger on entering the premises of a common carrier with the intention of purchasing a ticket for a trip at that time. The person ceases to be a passenger when the destination printed on the ticket is reached and the passenger has left the carrier's premises.

8.34 (1) Trover is the proper action in seeking the value of goods held by a tortious bailee. (2) Replevin is the proper action when the owner wishes to recover the goods themselves. (3) Trespass is used to recover goods or their value *and* any profits the tortious bailee has received through wrongful use of the goods.

8.35 Common carriers serve the public and must offer services to all who desire them, with certain exceptions. Private carriers are contract carriers, who may select their customers and set charges for each service rendered. Common carriers operate under franchises awarded by some governmental body.

8.36 A safe chattel is property of a type that will not cause injury to one who possesses it. Among a bailor's obligations is that he or she must deliver a safe chattel to the bailee.

8.37 (1) The carrier's right to retain possession of goods until all charges have been paid by the shipper or the consignee. (2) A contract between a shipper and a common carrier that is negotiable: it gives an endorser the right to transfer title and possession of goods described therein to a third party. (3) A carrier's absolute obligation for payment of damages resulting from loss or damage of goods in transit. (4) The amount of care that a carrier must provide for its passengers. (5) Someone other than a trespasser who enters the carrier's premises for reasons other than doing business.

8.38 (1) Slight care; (2) great care; (3) ordinary care.

Legal Terms

Bailment. The delivery of goods by one person to another for a specific purpose; the goods are to be returned when that purpose has been accomplished.

Bailor. A party who willingly gives up possession of personal property to another party, known as the *bailee*.

Bill of lading. A standard form of contract, approved by the Interstate Commerce Commission or a state commission, stating the obligations of a carrier and shipper in the transport of goods for a fee.

Gratuitous bailment. Bailments in which the bailee or the bailor gives no consideration in return for services rendered by the other.

Insurer. A bailee who agrees to accept complete responsibility for returning the bailor's property and to pay all damages resulting from the bailment relationship regardless of the cause of the damages.

Mutual-benefit bailment. A bailment in which both the bailor and the bailee are to receive benefits from the other.

Pledge. A bailment of goods as security for a debt or some other obligation.

Reasonable care. The degree of care required of a hotelkeeper or common carrier in the protection of guests and passengers and their property.

Right of lien. A hotelkeeper's or common carrier's right to retain possession of the personal property of a guest, passenger, or shipper as security of payment for services rendered.

Slight, great, and ordinary care. In each case, the amount of care that the ordinary person of ordinary prudence would have used in the same situation, as in a bailment that is the subject of complaint for damages by the bailor.

Tortious bailee. A bailee having wrongful possession of another's property.

PART V: *Insurance*

Chapter 9

Insurance Law

People have always gathered together in an effort to give strength and confidence to one another in protecting their lives and property. The idea of distributing risks among the members of a group is an old one. To this day, groups of people band together in social or religious organizations whose members lend support to each other in times of trouble. An Amish farmer who loses his barn in a fire will automatically have it rebuilt and restocked by the fellow members of his sect.

Insurance spreads financial risks among large numbers of people. Losses suffered through death, fire, accident, or illness are offset by the contributions made by others—people whom an insured person does not even know. The risks are spread among people in all social and economic groups. And they are spread among people in different geographic areas. A local mishap that might deplete the resources of a small insurer would not seriously strain a large company with widely spread-out risks.

Large insurers have agencies throughout the United States, and thus insurance laws are generally similar in all states. With few exceptions, insurance operations are regulated by state laws, the common law, and judicial tradition, and each state has its own insurance commissioner or commission to oversee insurers. This chapter reviews the general provisions of insurance law found in practically all states.

9.1 What Is Insurance?

Insurance protection is provided by an *insurer,* often an insurance company, to an *insured,* in consideration of payment of fees called *premiums*. Payments of claims are made to *beneficiaries,* who are individuals or persons named by the insured in the policy itself.

EXAMPLE 1. Herak, age twenty-five, insured his life for $25,000 with the Faithful Assurance Company. Herak named his wife, Helen, as the beneficiary of the policy. Herak agreed to pay premiums of $250 a year for the first five years of the policy. Thereafter, the premiums would increase.

LIFE INSURANCE

9.2 Insurable Interest in Life Insurance

A policy of life insurance will be issued only to one who has an *insurable interest* in the life of the person being insured in the policy. People have an insurable interest in another's life only if the death of that person would cause them a financial loss, such as the removal of income, nonpayment of a debt, or failure to complete a contract. Business partners, for example, have insurable interests in each other.

EXAMPLE 2. Greenfield paid premiums on a life insurance policy of $10,000 in which he named Faith Presbyterian Church as the beneficiary. On Greenfield's death, the insurance company claimed that the policy was invalid because the church did not have an insurable interest in Greenfield's life. It is not required that a beneficiary have an insurable interest. Greenfield, the insured, had an insurable interest in his own life and may name even the most distant stranger as beneficiary, should he like. Faith Presbyterian Church has every right to demand payment of the $10,000.

9.3 Insurable Interest in Business Associates

A corporation or a partnership has an insurable interest in the officers, key personnel, or partners in the business. Death of such persons may result in financial losses to the business. A partnership business may insure each partner to protect the firm from any claims against the partnership by a deceased partner's family, creditors, or the like.

EXAMPLE 3. American Chemical Industries employed Downie, a research chemist, to direct several long-term projects. These projects involved an investment of $500,000 by American Chemical. American insured Downie for $100,000, an amount considered reasonable because her death might delay further research and development. American Chemical had an insurable interest in Downie's life.

9.4 Creditor's Insurable Interest in Life of Debtor

Creditors have an insurable interest, up to the amount of money or obligation owed, in the life of each of their debtors.

EXAMPLE 4. Farmers Bank & Trust Company loaned $7,500 to Walther on Walther's unsecured ninety-day note for that amount. Added to the note was an interest charge plus an additional fee covering insurance of $7,500 for ninety days on Walther's life. The bank had an insurable interest in Walther's life because his death could have made collection of the note difficult or impossible.

9.5 Rights of Beneficiary

A person does not have the right to claim the cash value of a policy that names him or her as a beneficiary, nor may such a person use her or his beneficiary rights as security for a loan. Only the insured or one with insurable interest may exercise such rights.

EXAMPLE 5. LaMond insured his daughter, nine years old, for $5,000. The policy premiums were paid each year. When the daughter was twenty-five years of age, she wrote to the insurance company seeking payment of the cash value of the policy at that time. Only LaMond, the father, could submit a claim to the insurer for the cash value of the policy. The father had an insurable interest in his daughter's life, had the right to insure her life, and is the only one with an *equity investment* in the life policy.

9.6 Policy Validity after Passing of Insurable Interest

An insurable interest need not continue for the duration of a life insurance policy. It is only necessary that the one buying the policy have an insurable interest in the insured's life at the time the policy is issued.

EXAMPLE 6. Mrs. Smolke applied for a $5,000 ordinary life insurance policy on the life of her husband, who had never purchased life insurance. Mrs. Smolke named herself as sole beneficiary of the policy. Three years later, the two were divorced. Mrs. Smolke continued to pay the premiums on the policy, even though she received no further support from her husband. Smolke died, and the insurance company claimed that Mrs. Smolke lacked an insurable interest and that the policy was therefore void. Mrs. Smolke will be paid the full face value of the policy, $5,000. She had an insurable interest when the policy was issued, and her later change of status did not invalidate the policy.

9.7 The Incontestability Clause

Most states require that ordinary life insurance policies contain the two-year *incontestability clause*. This clause states that an insurer may not invalidate a policy for reasons of fraud in the application unless the fraud is discovered within a two-year period after the policy is issued. (There are some exceptions; see Solved Problem 9.8.)

EXAMPLE 7. Union Insurance Company issued an ordinary life policy to Darlington for $25,000. Darlington's wife was named as the sole beneficiary. Darlington died three years later. Union discovered that the cause of death was a blood condition that Darlington did not disclose when he applied for the policy. Had disclosure been made, the policy would not have been issued. Although Darlington had defrauded the insurer when applying for the policy, Darlington's widow will be paid the $25,000 face amount of the policy.

9.8 Grace Period in Life Insurance

Failure to remit life insurance premiums on the due date will not automatically invalidate a policy. In most states and in all but a few policies, a *grace period* of thirty or thirty-one days is allowed. For this period, the policy continues in force.

EXAMPLE 8. Bayard's life was insured under a $10,000 policy issued by Harcum Insurance Company. Premiums were payable annually on February 21. Bayard neglected to pay a premium when it was due. He died on the following March 15. Harcum incorrectly refused to pay the claim, stating that the policy had expired. Harcum will be required to honor the beneficiary's claim because the insured's death came within the grace period allowed by state law and the terms of the policy itself.

9.9 Misrepresentation of Insured's Age

Fraud in the disclosure of an insured's correct age in an application for insurance will not void a policy already issued. The insurer's obligation is reduced to payment of only that amount that the premiums paid would have bought at the actual age of the insured.

EXAMPLE 9. Freedman applied for an ordinary life policy for $10,000. At that time, he stated in writing that he was thirty-one years old. Premiums were paid each year for twelve years, and then Freedman died. It was learned that at the time of his death he was fifty-two years old. Thus, Freedman had actually been forty years of age when the policy was issued. Freedman's beneficiary will be paid only that amount of coverage that Freedman could have bought at age forty with the premiums he had been paying.

9.10 Invalidating the Insurer's Obligation

Life insurance policies contain provisions exempting payment of claims when death results from certain specified reasons. Death resulting from one's commission of a felony, from accidents in other than regularly scheduled commercial flights, from action in military service, and from execution for conviction of a crime are the exceptions contained in most policies. Low-premium policies usually contain even more restrictions.

EXAMPLE 10. Corrozi had been insured for twenty-two years under a $20,000 life policy in which his wife was named as beneficiary. He turned to a life of crime and was shot and killed during a bank robbery in which he participated. Corrozi's beneficiary will be denied the claim for the $20,000 face value of the policy. However, she will have returned to her the premiums already paid plus interest.

9.11 Death through Negligence of Insured

Death resulting from the negligence of the insured does not give the insurer a defense against payment of the face value of a valid policy. (A policy, through mutual agreement, might include this exemption, but it would be rare.) Accidental death under circumstances that indicate intentional death (suicide) would give sufficient grounds for investigation and rescission within the provisions of suicide contained in the policy.

EXAMPLE 11. Integrity Insurance Company issued a policy to Dunlap, insuring Dunlap's life for $50,000. The policy named Coburn University as beneficiary. Several years after the policy had been issued, Dunlap was killed when his car went through the iron railings of a high-level bridge over the Mississippi River. Witnesses testified that Dunlap had been drinking heavily and was intoxicated and belligerent just before he drove from his home. Integrity delayed payment of the $50,000 claim until it determined that the accident was not intentional and suicidal, but due instead to Dunlap's gross negligence under conditions of anger and intoxication.

9.12 Right to Change Beneficiary

An insured may not change the beneficiary in a life policy unless such a right is granted in one of the provisions of the policy. Most policies issued today give the insured this right.

EXAMPLE 12. Reitz was married for ten years. During this time, he paid premiums on a life policy in which his wife, Kathleen S. Reitz, was named as beneficiary. The two were subsequently divorced, and Reitz sought to make his second wife the beneficiary. The policy did not contain a provision which gave Reitz the right to change the beneficiary. Only with the consent of his former wife would Reitz be permitted to make the change.

9.13 Effect of Extraneous Changes of Beneficiary

Extraneous letters, promises, and contracts assuring a change of beneficiary have no valid claim against a life policy; any change of beneficiary must be made in the policy itself.

EXAMPLE 13. Rutledge borrowed $5,000 from Mitchell and signed a promissory note for that amount. In the note, Rutledge stated that Mitchell would be the beneficiary of the $5,000 life policy he (Rutledge) held with Engineers Mutual Insurance. The policy was still payable only to the beneficiary named in the policy, and not to Mitchell.

9.14 Changing Beneficiaries during the Life of the Insured

Beneficiaries of life insurance policies may be changed only during the life of the insured. An insurer may not pay someone other than the named beneficiary, even when instructed to do so by the insured's will.

EXAMPLE 14. Morton had a $25,000 life policy in which he named his son as beneficiary. The son later had outstanding financial success, and Morton wrote a will in which he stated that he was willing the proceeds of the policy to his brother, who was in dire financial straits. He did not change the policy to show his brother as beneficiary. Morton's intention, as contained in the will, did not change the insurer's obligation to follow the instructions in the policy.

9.15 When Death of Insured Is Caused by Beneficiary

A beneficiary who has intentionally caused the death of the insured loses all rights to a claim on a policy.

EXAMPLE 15. Mrs. Nichols was the named beneficiary in a $100,000 life policy taken out by her husband. Many years after the policy was issued, Mrs. Nichols, in a fit of rage, shot and killed her husband. She was indicted on a charge of first-degree murder. The trial was delayed for many months. The insurer would be granted the right to refuse payment of the $100,000 to Mrs. Nichols until after the outcome of the trial. If she was found guilty, the insurer would not have to pay to her the face value of the policy.

9.16 Beneficiary with Insurable Interest in Person Insured

Only the owner of a life policy has the right to seek a change of beneficiary. The beneficiary has no vested interest in the policy unless he or she is also the owner of the policy and has an insurable interest in the insured.

EXAMPLE 16. Roche paid premiums on a life policy in which he named his son Raymond as beneficiary. The son fell into financial difficulties. Raymond's chief creditor agreed to forestall further collection demands on Raymond's promise to change the name of the beneficiary to that of the creditor. Raymond's intentions were relayed to his father by the insurer. Roche changed the beneficiary from Raymond to another son, Henry. Raymond had no authority or right to change the beneficiary. He had no vested (current) rights in the policy. His "rights" were only futuristic and hopeful—not actual.

EXAMPLE 17. State Bank paid premiums on a $5,000 life policy insuring Murray, a man who had borrowed $5,000 from the bank. The bank was named as beneficiary. State Bank requested a change in beneficiary when Murray's $5,000 note was sold to Southern Trust Company. State Bank was the owner of the policy and had a vested interest even though the policy insured another's life. The bank had an insurable interest, and its right to change the beneficiary would not be disputed unless denied by a provision in the policy.

9.17 Claims of Creditors of Deceased against Beneficiaries

An insured's creditors have no rights to the cash payments made to the beneficiary of a life insurance policy. The funds belong to the beneficiary and are *not* considered to be part of the deceased's estate.

EXAMPLE 18. Marsland died, leaving claims of more than $35,000 by his creditors. All of his known assets totaled no more than $30,000, leaving less than $20,000 after medical bills, hospital bills, and funeral expenses were paid. Marsland's widow was named as beneficiary in the deceased's life policy of $100,000. (The policy had been issued many years before his financial troubles became evident.) Creditors would have no success in attempting to make collections from the $100,000 paid to Marsland's widow.

9.18 Presumption of Death

An insured who disappears mysteriously and who cannot be located through reasonable search for a continuous period of seven years is presumed to be dead. Life insurance policies on which premiums have been paid and which have been kept in force are valid and collectible at the end of such a seven-year period.

EXAMPLE 19. Holland, an insured, did not return to his home from work on January 16, 1969. Continued investigation by the police and his employer, relatives, and friends turned up no trace of the man. His wife continued to pay premiums on a $25,000 life policy. (Holland had purchased the policy years before, making Mrs. Holland the sole beneficiary.) On February 1, 1976, Mrs. Holland applied to the insurance company for payment of the $25,000. A court order declaring Holland to be dead was issued on the beneficiary's petition, and the $25,000 payment was approved and paid.

FIRE INSURANCE

9.19 Insurable Interest in Fire Insurance

The owner of a fire insurance policy must have an insurable interest in the property that is insured. The validity of a fire insurance policy ceases as soon as the owner of the policy no longer has an insurable interest in the insured property; in this respect, fire insurance is different from life insurance.

EXAMPLE 20. McGee applied for a fire insurance policy on a three-story house located at 2937 North Lincoln Street. The house was owned by Reynolds Realty. McGee had installed a new heating system in the Lincoln Street property and had registered an artisan's lien of $4,795 against the property. On March 18, Reynolds Realty paid McGee the $4,795 and received a receipt marked "Paid in Full." On March 19, the Lincoln Street house burned to the ground. McGee petitioned the insurance company for payment according to the terms of his policy. Receipt of the $4,795 by McGee on March 18 removed any insurable interest that he might have had up to that time. The claim will not be paid.

9.20 Insurer's Obligation on Binders

An insurer's *agent* may obligate the insurer before a policy is actually issued by giving a *binder* to a customer. Binders are usually written on binder slips, but they may be oral. A binder provides full coverage of insured property during the time it takes to apply for and pay for a policy and the actual delivery of the policy.

EXAMPLE 21. O'Donnel, an agent for Mutual Fire & Casualty Company, gave Turner a receipt for a premium when Turner applied for fire insurance on his house and garage. The receipt contained O'Donnel's notation that the insurance was in force from that moment. Early the next evening, Turner's house was damaged by fire. The binder in the receipt issued by O'Donnel obligated the insurer to reimburse Turner for his fire loss.

9.21 Oral Promise to Issue a New Policy

By orally agreeing to issue a new policy to replace one that has expired, insurance agents create binding obligations upon their companies.

EXAMPLE 22. Because Miles failed to pay premiums due on April 3, a fire insurance policy on his home expired. Miles called his insurance agent on June 1, asking that a new policy, similar to the expired one, be issued. The agent agreed. The agent's oral agreement with Miles would create coverage immediately. To confirm such an agreement, the agent would have to verify in writing that Miles requested the new policy.

9.22 Agents *versus* Brokers

Agents are representatives of insurers and have the right to obligate the insurers for whom they work or sell. Insurance *brokers* are *agents for the insured*. Statements by a broker who is not also an agent do *not* obligate the insurer.

EXAMPLE 23. Carter called his insurance broker and requested that the broker secure for him a fire policy to cover his furniture store. The broker agreed to secure the policy for Carter. Until the broker actually obtains the policy, however, Carter's store will *not* be covered. The broker has an obligation to use diligence and care in securing the policy. If he is negligent in doing this, Carter, in the event of a loss, may have a claim against the broker.

9.23 Friendly Fires

Fire insurance does not protect the insured from losses resulting from *friendly fires*. A friendly fire is one that is intended to be burning and that is confined to the place provided by one controlling the fire.

EXAMPLE 24. By mistake, William tossed a valuable wood carving into a burning fireplace. (The carving had been carelessly left atop William's woodbox.) William may not claim coverage because the loss resulted from a friendly fire.

9.24 Hostile Fires

Losses from other than friendly fires are the result of *hostile fires*. Hostile fires are any that are not intended and are not under the control of a responsible party.

EXAMPLE 25. Harris started a fire in a fireplace that had been out of use for several months. He neglected to clean out the chimney, and due to an obstruction heat built up and caused considerable fire damage in the walls of Harris's home. The damage resulted from a hostile fire, not a fire confined in the fireplace. The insurer would therefore be obligated, even though Harris had been negligent.

9.25 Damage Caused in Extinguishing Fires

The damage caused by water or some other substance used by fire fighters to extinguish a fire is covered by a fire policy. Damage caused by an explosion that is the result of a fire is also covered by a fire policy.

EXAMPLE 26. Parkaid Drug Store caught fire. The fire company poured thousands of gallons of water under high pressure into the blaze to extinguish the fire. Loss from water was far greater than that attributed directly to burning. Parkaid's fire policy will provide coverage for both the fire damage and the water damage.

9.26 Fire Losses Resulting from Order of Civil Authorities

Firebreaks ordered by a fire marshall, the burning of personal property contaminated with communicable disease germs, and other reasonable emergency measures may be taken by civil authorities.

Fire insurance policies, unless they include special provisions, do not cover losses that result from the orders of a civil authority.

EXAMPLE 27. A house in the town of Centreville had been occupied by several persons who died from yellow fever. The house was declared off-limits to all persons. By order of the state health authorities, all furnishings, clothing, and personal property in the house were removed and burned under supervision of the Centreville Fire Company. Owners of the property will not be reimbursed for losses through fire insurance covering the contents of the dwelling.

9.27 Effect of Insured's Negligence on Fire Damage Claim

An owner's negligence in the care and use of insured property will not give the insurer a defense against paying a claim for fire damages. (Exceptions would be the failure to abide by a policy's restrictions against storing gasoline, dynamite, or other inherently dangerous materials as outlined in the policy. The unsafe electrical wiring of an insured building, without the use of proper materials and without required inspection, may also exempt the insurer from payment for fire losses resulting from such wiring.)

EXAMPLE 28. Livelli lived in a rural area. On a fall day, he raked his lawn and put the leaves into a huge pile, which he set afire. A wind was blowing, and burning leaves were carried to the roof of his house. The house burned to the ground. Livelli's actions were grossly negligent, but the fire loss was not intentional. Livelli's negligence does not preclude him from securing reimbursement for the loss of the house and its contents.

9.28 Obligations for Fire Damage to Vacated Premises

Vacating premises for a period longer than that allowed in a fire policy exempts the insurer from obligation for losses during the period or voids the policy in its entirety. Permission given by the insurer in an endorsement on the policy will avoid this risk of loss. The time limits for insurance coverage of vacant premises are rarely longer than ten weeks.

EXAMPLE 29. Jackson and his family left their home in the city to spend three months at a vacation resort on the Atlantic Ocean. The family packed necessary furnishings and clothing, locked up the city house, and left it unattended for the entire summer. Fire destroyed the upper floor of the house and much of the contents after the family had been away for more than ten weeks. Without any kind of endorsement written into the policy by Jackson's agent, there would have been no reimbursement for the fire loss reported.

9.29 Appraisal of Fire Loss

The *cash value at the time of loss* is used as the guide in making an appraisal of loss. Sentimental value, the cost at the time of purchase, or the replacement value is not used unless specified in a policy.

EXAMPLE 30. Fire and smoke ruined the contents of Mahler's apartment. The contents of the apartment were fully covered by insurance. Mahler submitted a claim totaling $12,575 for damage to furniture, rugs, expensive clothing, books, and other furnishings. An insurance adjuster revised the claim, using the present cash value of the articles destroyed. The appraisal reduced the claim to less than $6,000, which was paid to Mahler.

9.30 80 Percent Coinsurance Clause

Most fire insurance policies contain an *80 percent coinsurance clause*. Such a clause states that the policy gives coverage to 80 percent of the insured's property and that the insured is responsible for the other 20 percent. Thus, a boat valued at $10,000 should be insured with such a policy for only $8,000, since that is the maximum amount the company will pay. (Certain fire insurance policies with very high premiums do not contain such a clause.)

EXAMPLE 31. Bailey insured a house and its contents with Fire Casualty Mutual for $60,000, the maximum amount payable under the policy. Fire destroyed the entire house and its contents. An appraisal of the damage showed that the entire loss totaled $70,000. The insurance claim will be approved at 80 percent of the loss, or $56,000. Had Bailey's policy been for only $56,000 (the maximum amount payable for total loss) he would have received that amount. Bailey was thus overinsured.

9.31 Fraudulent Claims in Settlement of Fire Losses

Making false claims in the settlement of an insured loss constitutes fraud on the part of the insured. Fraud relieves the insurer of any obligations under the policy.

EXAMPLE 32. Romano entered a claim against his insurance company for fire loss of personal property alleged to have been destroyed in his home. Romano intentionally "padded" (inflated) the claim and included expensive items that had not existed. Discovery of the fraud released the insurer from *all* claims by Romano.

9.32 Right of Subrogation in Fire Insurance

An insurer is *subrogated* to the rights of the insured. In other words, the insurer may pursue a suit against those who cause the losses for which the insurer reimbursed the insured.

EXAMPLE 33. Devine's house was damaged by fire caused by hoodlums who threw a firebomb through one of the basement windows. Devine was paid $5,700 under an 80 percent coinsurance policy. Insurance investigators located those responsible for the loss. They were sued by the insurance carrier for the $5,700 and for other expenses the insurance company had incurred. A judgment would be given the insurer against those responsible for the fire.

9.33 Assignability of Fire Insurance Policies

Fire insurance policies, with rare exceptions, are *not* assignable. A policy's life lasts only for that period of time during which the original owner of the policy continues to have an insurable interest in the insured property.

EXAMPLE 34. A building owned by Ballenberg was insured with the Eagle Fire Insurance Company for $85,000. Ballenberg sold the building to Geran. Ballenberg signed a document that purported to assign all insurance on the property to Geran. Fire destroyed the roof of the building, and Geran filed a claim of loss with the insurance company. It was correctly held that the assignment was ineffective and that Geran's property was not insured.

9.34 Insurer's Settlement Options

Fire insurance policies often give the insurer the option of either making a cash settlement for fire loss or rebuilding the property. The insurer has the right to choose which option will be taken and does not need the approval of the insured.

EXAMPLE 35. Ahearn's house suffered fire loss due to a faulty heating system. Appraisal of the loss showed that the house could be returned to its prefire state through the expenditure of $11,000. Ahearn claimed a loss of $16,000, citing estimates made by contractors he had consulted. Ahearn demanded payment of the $16,000. The insurer would be foolish to accept Ahearn's claim. Its responsibility to Ahearn could be met by hiring a contractor to do the repair work. The insurer may not, however, do a less-than-satisfactory job in choosing to rebuild the house rather than to reimburse the owner.

AUTOMOBILE INSURANCE

9.35 Automobile Collision Insurance

Collision insurance on a motor vehicle covers losses arising from collision with other vehicles or losses incurred from any accident that occurs while the vehicle is being driven.

EXAMPLE 36. A pick-up truck owned and driven by Campbell was demolished when it hit a culvert, turned over, and rolled into a ditch. The insurer incorrectly resisted paying the claim by arguing that the loss resulted not from a collision but rather from a faulty steering mechanism. Campbell is fully covered by the collision policy.

9.36 Effect of Insured's Negligence in Automobile Insurance

As with life and fire coverage, the insured's negligence does *not* give the insurer a defense against payment of claims resulting from damage. Disputes may legitimately arise, however, in determining whether damages resulted from an *intentional* act or merely through negligence and carelessness.

EXAMPLE 37. Grossman drove her sports car along a treacherous stretch of road at speeds of more than seventy-five miles per hour. She was not able to manage a sharp curve in the road, and the car vaulted over a guard rail and was demolished. Grossman had failed to obey ordinary rules of safety and was inexcusably negligent. The insurance carrier may not use this as a defense against Grossman's claims for loss as covered by her collision policy. Grossman will be disciplined, however, in seeking future insurance coverage. Her premium rate will be increased to a level that would make insuring another car extremely expensive.

9.37 Cash Value in Collision Settlements

Insurance claims under a collision policy will be paid according to present cash value, less any deductible clause provided by the policy. Cash value is in most cases determined by reference to the *Blue Book*, which is available to all dealers and insurers. The insurer has, in most cases, the option of either making payment or repairing reported damages.

EXAMPLE 38. Jonas, who drove only a few miles each week, owned a car that was ten years old. It was in excellent condition, and the total mileage shown on the odometer was less than 35,000 miles. The car skidded on a wet patch of roadway, swung around, and hit a tree. One whole side of the car was torn up. The estimated cost of repair was $1,200. The *Blue Book* value of the ten-year-old car was only $175. Obviously, the insurer would pay Jonas the value of the car, $175, rather than have it repaired.

9.38 Right of Subrogation in Automobile Insurance

An insurer has the right of subrogation against the person who causes damage to an insured's motor vehicle. The action is taken in the name of the insured, but it is not necessary to obtain the insured's consent to sue.

EXAMPLE 39. Stevens, who had collision insurance on his car, left it on the street in front of his home. Anderson, who was intoxicated, drove his car into Stevens's parked car and demolished it. Stevens was reimbursed for his loss, and the insurer brought an action against Anderson for the amount that had been paid to Stevens. Thus the insurer is subrogated to all of the rights of the insured against the person who caused the damage.

9.39 Damage Caused by Riot and Public Disturbance

Collision insurance does not cover damages caused by riots and public disturbances. Civil authorities, in some cases, agree to *idemnify* (act as insurers for) citizens who experience such losses.

EXAMPLE 40. Aiken's car was turned over and burned by a rioting group of students following a victorious football game. The car was a total loss, and Aiken entered a claim with his insurance company. The collision provisions in his policy did not protect him in this case, and he was not paid.

9.40 Comprehensive Auto Coverage

Comprehensive motor-vehicle coverage reimburses the owner for losses resulting from riot, fire, storm, flying objects, vandalism, and other causes except collision. Most important is the coverage given in event of theft. Theft coverage relates to the car and its integral parts—parts that are built in. It does not cover personal property left in the car.

EXAMPLE 41. Pritchard's car was left in a parking lot in the middle of Philadelphia. When he returned to get the car, he found that it was missing. The manager of the lot suggested that Pritchard make an immediate claim to his insurance company, which was responsible for coverage under a comprehensive policy. The insurer may later decide to seek recovery from the parking lot, under the right of subrogation, if the parking lot failed to meet its obligation in protecting Pritchard's car.

9.41 Medical Payment Coverage in Auto Insurance

Medical payment coverage included in the motor-vehicle insurance covers only those expenses directly related to injuries received in an accident. Coverage does not include payment for incidental losses.

EXAMPLE 42. Greenfield was seriously injured when her car was struck by another on a highway. She had medical coverage included in her car insurance policy. The insurer accepted her claims for ambulance costs, hospital bills, medical and surgical bills, therapy, and medicines. The insurance company denied claims related to her loss of salary while she was incapacitated.

9.42 Public Liability Insurance

Liability insurance makes the insurer liable for sums, not exceeding a fixed limit, for which the insured might be sued. Terms of liability are expressed in the maximum amount that will be paid to one person and the maximum amount that will be paid to all persons claiming damages from any one accident.

EXAMPLE 43. Hollis struck another car when he failed to apply his brakes in a line of traffic. The driver and three occupants of the other car were injured and required hospitalization. Hollis was insured under a $10,000/$20,000 liability policy. Hollis's insurer would pay no more than $10,000 to any one occupant of the other car. Neither would the insurer pay more than $20,000 in total claims made by all the occupants of the other car. Any claims exceeding the liability covered by the policy would become Hollis's personal liability.

9.43 Family Auto Use Coverage

Liability insurance protects the owner of an insured vehicle from claims resulting from damages caused by the insured, members of the insured's family, and others living under the insured's roof. Such policies also provide coverage when the vehicle is driven by others who have the permission of the insured owner.

EXAMPLE 44. Shilling's car was being driven by his wife when she negligently ran into a small boy riding a tricycle in the street. The car was in Shilling's name alone, and all insurance was issued to him. Shilling's insurance coverage will give protection in any damage claims made on him on behalf of the injured boy.

9.44 Liability Coverage while Operating Another's Vehicle

Most (but not all) liability insurance policies cover an insured who is operating someone else's vehicle, as long as the insured is operating the vehicle with the owner's consent.

EXAMPLE 45. While driving a car owned by Peltz, McCann struck another car. McCann alone was responsible for the accident. Peltz had no liability insurance, and McCann was enjoined in a suit for damages brought by the owner of the other car. McCann's own liability policy will protect him in a claim for damages.

9.45 Insured's Admission of Liability

An insurer has the right to deny liability on behalf of an insured who (1) admits his or her liability or (2) fails to report an accident as required in the policy. An insured must protect an insurer by giving the insurer the opportunity to use every possible avenue of defense against liability.

EXAMPLE 46. Durkin, an elderly widower, was involved in an accident with Wells, an attractive young woman. Wells persuaded Durkin to absolve her of any blame and accept all responsibility for the accident himself. Durkin later received notice of a claim against him for damages to Wells's car as well as a claim for injury to her back. Durkin's admissions to Wells gave Durkin's insurer the right to deny liability on the policy.

9.46 Uninsured Motorist Coverage

Uninsured motorist coverage, provided in some policies for an additional premium, is written in conjunction with ordinary auto liability insurance. It provides reimbursement for personal injuries resulting from an accident with an uninsured driver. Coverage is for personal injury only, not for damage to the vehicle.

EXAMPLE 47. Lerch's insurance included the uninsured motorist provision. Lerch was involved in a highway accident. The other car was not insured, and the owner-driver had no assets from which Lerch might have recovered damages if he sued. Lerch entered a claim for damages to his car and for medical expenses related to his personal injury. The uninsured motorist's coverage will reimburse Lerch for expenses related to personal injuries only. Collision insurance, if he had such, would cover damages to his car, less any deductibles written into the policy.

9.47 No-Fault Insurance

No-fault insurance laws require all registered motor vehicles to be covered with minimum liability insurance. In no-fault states, it is illegal to register a motor vehicle without proof of a minimum amount of liability coverage. No-fault usually (but not always) pays claims for personal injuries, not for property damage to the insured's vehicle. Regardless of fault, the insured's own carrier pays bills resulting from personal injury.

EXAMPLE 48. Strawbridge lived in a state that required all motor vehicles to have auto liability insurance with no-fault coverage. Strawbridge was involved in an auto accident in which he was entirely at fault. He claimed $700 medical expenses and $1,200 hospitalization costs. Strawbridge's insurer will honor the claim and reimburse Strawbridge for his expenses related to personal injury. Collision insurance, if Strawbridge owns it, will reimburse him for the costs of repairs to the vehicle itself.

Solved Problems

9.1 Casper paid premiums on a fire policy covering his cattle barn. The face of the policy was for $89,000. Provisions of the policy stated that it was an *open policy*. The barn was struck by lightning and burned to the ground; nothing was salvaged. Casper claimed full benefits of $89,000. Will he be paid this amount, the face value of the policy?

In an *open policy*, the insurer is obligated to pay the insured for losses suffered, but never more than stated on the face of the policy. If the claim adjuster proves that the loss was less than $89,000, Casper will be paid only for the actual loss, whatever it may be. A *valued policy*, on the other hand, is one wherein the insurer is obligated to pay the full face value of the policy in the event of total loss. The premium charged for a valued policy is higher than the premium for an open policy.

9.2 Herrington signed an application for a liability policy. He was given a low premium rate, as a "preferred risk," because he signed a statement declaring that he did not drink any kind of alcoholic beverage. Herrington ran head-on into another car, and the police proved that he was intoxicated at the time. Herrington sought the protection of his insurance company against claims made by others for their injuries and property damage. Will Herrington be successful in his claim?

An insured's definite guarantee of an existing fact or specific promise regarding the future may be included in a policy; such a guarantee or promise is called a *warranty*. If an insured breaches a warranty, and if the insurer can prove so, the policy may be voided. Herrington obviously breached his warranty, and the insurer may void the policy. Herrington will not be successful in his claim.

9.3 Stapleton purchased fire insurance on his house and attached garage. Such a policy usually restricts any insured from storing gasoline or naphtha within insured buildings. The insurer agreed in writing to *waive* this restrictive clause in Stapleton's policy. A fire in the garage caused extensive damage, and the insurer denied liability due to the presence of naphtha in the garage at the time of the fire. Will Stapleton recover his fire loss?

The insurer may waive a right or a defense to liability contained in a policy. Waiving a right estops insurers from claiming a defense they would otherwise have. Stapleton will be awarded full recovery on proof of the waiver.

9.4 Hargrove received and paid the premiun on a $25,000 life insurance policy on the life of his neighbor, Kelvington. The agent who sold the policy to Hargrove assured him that the usual requirement of insurable interest was waived. Kelvington died several years later, and Hargrove claimed payment of $25,000 as the named beneficiary of the policy. Will Hargrove be successful in his claim?

Requirements of the law may not be waived, even if both the owner of the policy and the insurer agree to such a waiver. Insurance law requires that the owner of a life policy have an insurable interest in the insured at the time the policy is issued. Hargrove would fail in any demand for payment of the $25,000. At most, the insurer would be required to repay Hargrove the total of all premiums paid, with interest for the period in which the money was held by the insurer.

9.5 Waller insured his wife, Helen, for $50,000 on an ordinary life policy. Helen was aware of the existence of the policy and had agreed to it. Four years later, she died of natural causes, and Waller claimed the $50,000. The insurance company rejected his claim, saying that Waller had no insurable interest in his wife's life because he suffered no financial loss as a result of her death. Was the insurer correct?

No. A husband has an insurable interest in the life of his wife, just as a wife has an insurable interest in the life of her husband. Waller's claim will be paid.

9.6 On April 5, 1976, a life policy was issued to Jablonsky on his own life. The face value of the policy was $75,000, and Jablonsky's wife was named as beneficiary. In completing the application of the policy, Jablonsky had described his physical condition as good. Specifically, he declared that he had never had any heart or pulmonary diseases that required the care of a physician. On August 10, 1977, Jablonsky suffered a heart attack and died. It was discovered that he had had a history of three previous heart attacks and had been under a specialist's care for many months prior to April 1976. Must the insurance company pay Jablonsky's widow the $75,000?

Jablonsky died within two years of issuance of the policy. His widow is therefore not protected by the two-year incontestability clause included in most policies. The insured was guilty of misrepresentation in applying for the policy. The estate will no doubt be reimbursed for the amount of the premiums already paid, with interest, but the face value will not be paid.

9.7 Charlton paid premiums on an ordinary life policy over a period of twenty-five years. Premiums for the twenty-sixth year were due on May 2, but Charlton neglected to pay them. On June 25, he was killed in an explosion. The insurer refused to pay a claim presented by his widow, the named beneficiary. The insurer contended that the policy had lapsed after nonpayment of the premium through the grace period. May Charlton's widow contest the company's decision?

Yes. The insurance company may not summarily cancel the policy in this manner. The beneficiary is a proper claimant in the cash value of the policy, which must have reached a considerable sum over the twenty-five-year period. This would be the minimum paid to her. A second solution, required by the laws of most states, would be the continuance of the policy in full force as long as the cash value would be sufficient to satisfy the unpaid premiums. A third solution would be the issuance of a fully paid-up policy for an amount that the cash value of the policy would pay at the time of default.

9.8 Thomlinson applied for a $50,000 ordinary life policy, making his wife the beneficiary. Thomlinson was then thirty-three years of age. Because he suffered from a form of cancer, he paid Jarvin $25 to take his place in getting the required medical examination. The policy was issued and remained in force for eighteen years, at which time Thomlinson died of the cancerous condition. When the insurers learned of Thomlinson's fraud, they would not pay his widow. She in turn claimed that she was protected by the two-year incontestability clause in the policy. Who was right?

Thomlinson's *misrepresentation* was not ordinary in any sense of the definition. He exercised a degree of fraud that will not be excused even under the incontestibility clause. The insurer will refund all premiums and interest to Thomlinson's estate, but will not pay the face value of the policy.

9.9 Only July 15, 1970, Draughton purchased a $100,000 policy on his own life. Six years later, in a despondent state of mind over serious financial setbacks, Draughton committed suicide. The insurer denied liability on the policy. May Draughton's beneficiary demand payment of the $100,000?

Most life policies include a clause that relieves an insurer of liability if the insured commits suicide. Such clauses, however, usually cover only a two-year period from the issuance of the policy because it is not generally believed that an insured would plan a suicide more than two years in advance. Draughton's beneficiary may rightfully claim the $100,000 face value of the policy.

9.10 Minnich contracted for a $25,000 ordinary life policy, paying additional premiums for *double indemnity*. Minnich made fraudulent statements in the application for the policy. Five years later, Minnich was killed in an airplane accident, which was included in the double-indemnity provision of the policy. The insurer agreed to pay Minnich's beneficiary only $25,000, not the $50,000 included in double indemnity. May the beneficiary contest this reduction in light of the two-year incontestability provisions of the policy?

The two-year incontestability provision does not have any effect on the double-indemnity portion of a life policy. The insurer will be obliged to pay the face of the policy ($25,000) but not the $50,000 that would have been paid in the absence of Minnich's fraudulent statements.

9.11 Erickson owned a $25,000 life policy that named his son as sole beneficiary. The son, who was building a new home, borrowed $25,000 from Erickson. As part of the loan agreement, Erickson's daughter was to replace the son as the sole beneficiary of the life policy. Before this change could be made in the policy, however, Erickson died. May the daughter petition the insurance company for payment?

No. Only the owner of a policy has the right to change the beneficiary. Erickson failed to change the name from that of his son to his daughter. The son remains beneficiary of the policy.

9.12 Saunders was insured under a life policy that named his wife as sole beneficiary. Saunders's wife died before he did, but Saunders never bothered to name another beneficiary in the policy. When Saunders died, the insurance company sought the advice of a court in determining payment. To whom would the company make payment?

The proceeds of the policy will be paid in full to Saunders's estate. The money will be distributed according to the terms of his will, or by law if Saunders had not left a will.

9.13 Donovan took money belonging to the Straughn Company, her employer, and purchased an annuity from which she would receive, at age sixty-five, a monthly income for the rest of her life. Investigators for the company discovered the theft after Donovan retired. They also traced the use of the funds. Could the Straughn Company have itself named recipient of any income from the annuity provided in the policy issued to Donovan?

The money used for the purchase of the annuity was money owned by the Straughn Company. The complainant, then, is the rightful recipient of the proceeds of the policy. In theory,

Donovan would be considered a trustee of the Straughn Company's funds in the creation of income actually due to her employer.

9.14 In a state that required real estate contracts to be both signed and under seal, Tribbett signed an agreement to purchase a house offered by Stoops Realty. Tribbett signed the agreement but neglected to place his seal on the document. Tribbett also insured the property against fire loss. Before the date of settlement, the house was destroyed by fire. Did Tribbett have an insurable interest that would support his right to collect for the loss?

The sales agreement was not enforceable by either Tribbett or the Stoops Realty Company because of the lack of the required seal. Tribbett did not hold an enforceable agreement. He therefore had no real legal rights in the property and no insurable interest. The policy would not be enforced. Tribbett would receive back only the premium he had paid to the insurer.

9.15 Balston Grocery Store was covered by fire insurance. A serious fire engulfed the store, and shortly afterwards someone entered the basement of the building and removed valuable goods stored there. Balston claimed payment for the loss of these goods from the fire insurance carried. Would Balston succeed?

No. Theft of goods from a burning building is not usually covered in a fire policy. The fire did not cause the loss, it merely made the theft easier to accomplish.

9.16 Patterson's home was covered by an ordinary fire insurance policy. A flash fire started in the recreation room. Patterson, assisted by fire fighters, removed furnishings from the burning room and placed them on the lawn. Some of the belongings were taken by thieves, who took advantage of the excitement caused by the fire. Does Patterson have a valid claim, under his fire policy, for the loss of this stolen property?

The furnishings were removed as part of an effort to keep fire losses to a minimum. Removal of the goods was directly related to an effort to fight the fire. Patterson would have a rightful claim for goods taken under these circumstances.

9.17 A fire broke out in the kitchen of Thurber's home. Thurber and a guest undertook to fight the fire themselves. They did not call the fire department for assistance until the fire spread and caused serious damage to the structure. Was the insurer fully liable for damages that Thurber claimed under his fire policy?

Thurber's failure to call the fire department amounted to gross negligence. Thurber should not be criticized for trying to fight or contain the fire, but he should have used common sense and sought help. The insured has an obligation to prevent loss. The insurer may deny at least part of Thurber's claim for damages.

9.18 Howell operated an employment agency from the front room of his residence. He insured the building against fire loss, paying commercial rates that were applicable to his case. Later, without notifying his insurance carrier, Howell changed the nature of his business by installing printing equipment. This greatly increased the risk of fire. In the event of a fire loss, could the insurer deny liability on its policy with Howell?

Yes. Howell voided his original policy by changing the nature of his business operation. Had Howell informed the insurer, there would have been an adjustment of rates to reflect the increased risk. Only this new policy would have been valid.

9.19 English insured personal property in his home against losses by fire, theft, and vandalism under a homeowner's policy. A basement fire destroyed a workbench, lathe, and power saw that three years before had cost him $785. He claimed $785, less depreciation of $150, for his loss. The adjuster found that the same equipment could be purchased in second-hand shops, in good condition, for as little as $250. What kind of settlement will English receive for his loss?

The insurance company pays the insured an amount equal to the actual cash value of that which has been destroyed. The actual cash value, according to a legitimate survey, was in the neighborhood of $250. Payment will be made in line with this figure, not with that provided by English.

9.20 A fire in the kitchen of Lenhart's home required that all the walls and woodwork be refinished. The house was fully covered by fire insurance. The fire loss occurred on January 10. Lenhart did not realize that his fire policy would cover the loss until talking with an associate two months later. Lenhart entered a proof-of-loss statement and a claim on March 25. Is the insurer obligated to pay Lenhart's claim?

Insurance policies usually contain provisions requiring that proof-of-loss statements be entered with the insurer within sixty days of the date of the loss. Under this provision, Lenhart's insurer would be justified in not accepting the claim for payment.

9.21 Sterling applied for fire policies with two different companies. Both policies were issued, and Sterling paid premiums to both companies. Each policy had a face value of $35,000. Sterling's property was completely destroyed by fire, so he entered a proof-of-loss statement and a claim for $35,000 to each company. Will Sterling be fully reimbursed for his loss by both companies?

No. Neither company will be required to pay Sterling for the full loss. Each insurer will accept a proportional amount of the loss. If the proven loss was $35,000, each insurance carrier would pay Sterling $17,500.

9.22 Overhill Insurance Company received a proof-of-loss statement and a claim from Huber ten days after a fire had damaged his house and its contents. Listed in the inventory was $379 in cash, a novel he had written but had not yet submitted for publication, one-hundred shares of stock, and $2,000 in U.S. Savings Bonds. Should these items be included in the insured's claim for payment?

Contract claims, manuscripts, cash, legal documents, commercial paper, stocks, bonds, and other securities are not covered in ordinary fire policies. Overhill will deny payment for the loss of these items.

9.23 Grimshaw carried collision insurance on his car. He loaned the car to Salinger, who drove it off a bridge and into a river. The car was demolished. Will Grimshaw be paid for this loss, in view of the fact that the car was being driven by someone other than Grimshaw himself or a member of his family or household?

Collision insurance is not voided merely because the vehicle in question is not being driven by the insured or by a member of the insured's family or household. Grimshaw will therefore receive payment for repairs or the current *Blue Book* value of the car.

9.24 Illers carried collision insurance on his station wagon, which he parked outside of his bookstore every day. A truck swerved into the station wagon and demolished it. Can the insurer, because the insured vehicle was parked and not being driving, disclaim responsibility by saying that no collision occurred?

No. There was a collision even though the vehicle was parked. Illers may rightfully claim coverage under his collision policy.

9.25 Flynn was involved in an accident in which Webb's car suffered $500 worth of damages. Because he felt that he was not at fault and would not be called on to pay for repairs to Webb's car, Flynn did not bother to report the accident to his insurance company. Later, he was sued for $500 in damages and was ordered to pay Webb, the plaintiff. Can Flynn, after he has paid Webb the $500, seek reimbursement from his insurance carrier?

No. Flynn failed to report the accident. He also failed to report the suit against him. By failing to report either of these events, he prevented the insurance company from offering a defense. Flynn has thus waived his right to a claim for the $500.

Review Problems

9.26 What is a *binder*, as related to fire insurance?

9.27 Is insurable interest in a life policy the same as insurable interest in a fire policy?

9.28 What effect does the two-year incontestability clause have on a life insurance policy?

9.29 Does no-fault insurance cover both physical injury and property damage?

9.30 What options does the insurer have in the settlement of a claim of damage in a fire loss?

9.31 (1) May the insured collect the face value of an open fire policy when total destruction is proven? (2) In a similar situation, may the insured collect the face value of a valued policy?

9.32 What recovery is allowed when the same building is covered by two policies issued by two different fire insurance companies?

9.33 Do a broker and a company agent have the same responsibilities to an applicant for insurance?

9.34 In auto insurance, is the insurer permitted to refuse payment of a claim because of an insured's gross negligence and carelessness?

9.35 What are the rights of a beneficiary to a policy that has been kept fully paid when the insured has not been seen or heard from for a period of years?

9.36 What is meant by a *waiver* in a fire policy?

9.37 Will misrepresentation of age in a life insurance application void the policy once it has been issued?

9.38 May the owner of a building collect a loss resulting from a fire marshall's attempt to create a firebreak as a means of saving other properties?

9.39 Under what conditions is the insurer responsible for an insured's personal property that is stolen during a fire?

9.40 Is an injured pedestrian limited to the amount of a driver's liability insurance in pressing a claim for damages?

9.41 What are the rights of a beneficiary who is found responsible for the death of one whose life insurance names her or him as beneficiary?

9.42 What disposition is made of proceeds of a life insurance policy when the named beneficiary predeceases the insured and a new beneficiary was not named by the insured?

9.43 What is a *friendly* fire? Are losses resulting from friendly fires covered under an ordinary fire insurance policy?

9.44 Does collision coverage cover a parked motor vehicle that is damaged by a vehicle in motion?

9.45 What are the insurer's rights when the insured knowingly "pads" the proof-of-loss claim with items not actually destroyed?

9.46 Should the owner of property purchase fire insurance in an amount equal to the real value of the property?

Answers to Review Problems

9.26 A binder is a promise of an insurance company, through its agent, to be responsible for losses between the date of application and payment of the initial premium and the date on which the policy is issued and delivered to the insured.

9.27 No. The owner of a life policy must have an insurable interest only when application is made and when the policy is issued. The owner of a fire insurance policy must have a *continuing* insurable interest.

9.28 Fraudulent statements made in the application (with some exceptions) will not void the insured's rights if the policy has been in force for a number of years (usually two years).

9.29 No-fault usually covers only physical injuries and related expenses, not property losses.

9.30 The insurer may (1) pay cash for the adjusted loss; (2) repair the property and return it to its former state; or (3) replace the property destroyed with property of the same kind and in the same condition.

9.31 (1) No. (2) Yes.

9.32 Each insurer will pay the insured a share of the actual loss proportional to the face value of each policy held by the insured.

9.33 No. A broker is considered the agent of the one applying for insurance. A company agent is the agent of the insurer. The insurer is held responsible for agreements made between the agent and the insured. The broker, not the insurance company, is solely responsible for agreements made between the applicant and the broker.

9.34 No.

9.35 After an earnest but unsuccessful search for the insured has been made, the insured may be declared *legally dead* by a court of proper jurisdiction. The court may direct the insurer to pay the beneficiary.

9.36 A waiver is an expressed exclusion of some standard provision written into a policy; it relieves the insured of certain responsibilities that might otherwise give the insurer a right to cancel the policy.

9.37 No. Payment of any claim on proof of death will be calculated on the amount of insurance the premium would have purchased at the insured's actual age.

9.38 No. Destruction of property by order of civil authorities is not covered by an ordinary fire policy.

9.39 The insurer is liable only when the theft has been achieved through conditions that are directly related to the fire itself or through the insured's efforts to protect property endangered by the fire.

9.40 No. The injured person may sue for *all* actual and incidental damages related to the other's negligence or willfully wrongful acts. Any judgment awarded in excess of the amount of the liability policy becomes the defendant's personal responsibility.

9.41 All rights and claims by the beneficiary are denied.

9.42 The insurance company pays the proceeds of the policy to the estate of the deceased.

9.43 A *friendly* fire is one that has been purposely created by the insured and is under the insured's control. Losses from friendly fires are not protected by an ordinary fire policy.

9.44 Yes.

9.45 The insurer may cancel the policy and dishonor the entire claim.

9.46 No. Doing so is usually buying too much insurance. The buyer of the policy should take into account the standard coinsurance provision of ordinary fire policies.

Legal Terms

Beneficiary. The party named in an insurance policy as the one who is to receive the benefits and payments guaranteed by the policy.

Binder. An insurance agent's written or oral promise that a policy applied for is enforceable from the time and date of application, rather than from the time and date on which the policy is actually issued.

Comprehensive insurance. Automobile insurance that covers all damages resulting from riot, fire, flying objects, vandalism, and other causes besides collision.

Friendly fire. A fire intentionally created to serve a legal purpose of a person whose property is insured against loss by fire; losses resulting from a friendly fire are not covered in fire policies; fires of any other kind are *hostile fires*, and are covered by fire policies.

Grace period. A period of thirty or thirty-one days subsequent to the date an insurance premium is due; during this time, the policy will remain in force even in the absence of payments.

Indemnity. An agreement by which one person engages to secure another against anticipated loss or damage.

Insurable interest. Proof of personal financial loss that could result from the death of an insured person or from damage to real or personal property; anyone who is to benefit from an insurance policy must have an insurable interest in whatever is being covered.

Insurer. The party, usually a company, that issues a policy of insurance to the *insured*.

No-fault insurance. The statutes of some states require all owners of motor vehicles to be insured with liability coverage protecting persons injured (or sometimes property damaged) by motor vehicles; no-fault reimbursement is made without the necessity of a court decision, which would otherwise be required to determine the party at fault.

Premium. The consideration paid for insurance.

Presumption of death. The mysterious disappearance of an insured person for a continuous period of seven years results in the "legal death" of the insured; a beneficiary may then make a claim of payment under the provisions of the insured's life policy.

Subrogation. The right of the insurer to proceed against a party who has caused damage to the insured property of one of its clients; the insurer thereby may prosecute the party who caused such damage and use all rights and evidence that would have been available to the insured.

Two-year incontestability clause. A provision contained in most ordinary life policies, this clause states that an insurer may not refuse a claim on grounds of fraud in the application for a policy if the policy has been in effect for a period of two years or more.

Examination II

Commercial Paper, Bailments, Insurance

1. Henderson, a minor, borrowed $100 from Kirby. Henderson gave Kirby his negotiable promissory note for $100, payable in thirty days. Kirby transferred the note for value to a holder in due course, who presented the note to Henderson on the due date. The holder claimed, as a holder in due course, that the right of collection could not be disputed. Was the holder correct?

   No. Incapacity is a real defense, which a maker may use against both immediate parties and those who qualify as holders in due course. The minor, Henderson, may legally disclaim any obligation to anyone presenting the note for payment.

2. Central Bank honored a check presented for payment by one who identified herself as the rightful holder. The maker had been negligent in writing the check, permitting a subsequent holder the opportunity of raising the amount of the check from $50 to $500. Is the bank liable to the maker of the check for having honored the holder's demand for payment of $500?

   No. The material alteration of the check was made possible by the negligence of the maker. Thus the bank is relieved of its usual obligation to a depositor. Had the check been written in a way that would have made any alteration obvious, the decision would be different.

3. Peltz borrowed a portable color television set from Watkins because his own set was being repaired. Watkins loaned the set as a favor to Peltz, due to their friendship. While Peltz was away from his apartment, someone broke in and stole the television set and other valuables. Watkins demanded that his friend replace the stolen television. Peltz denied any legal responsibility in the matter. Was Peltz correct?

   Yes. There was no indication of negligence or lack of care on the part of the bailee, Peltz. This was a bailment for the sole benefit of the bailee, requiring great care and obligating the bailee if there is proof of even slight negligence. Unless Watkins could prove that Peltz had left doors or windows unlocked or had not followed the usual precautions expected of others in the same neighborhood, Peltz would be free of any legal obligation to his friend.

4. During an intercity flight on a commercial airline, Padgett was injured and all of his luggage was lost when the aircraft crashed on landing. The crash resulted from causes beyond the control of airline personnel. Padgett filed a complaint against the airline, seeking recovery of financial loss resulting from his injuries and the destruction of his luggage. Will Padgett be reimbursed on both claims?

   No. Common carriers are insurers of their passengers' luggage. But responsibility for injuries to the passengers is limited to situations in which the carrier has failed to exercise reasonable care in transporting the passengers. Padgett will be reimbursed for the proven value of his luggage, within limitations set by law or by the airline. There is no proof, however, that the crash in any way resulted from the carrier's lack of care in the operation or maintenance of the aircraft. It is doubtful, then, that recovery will be permitted for injuries. (It is the usual practice of common carriers to accept claims for minor injuries of this type as a public-relations effort.)

5. Foley Builders sold a new house to O'Henry for $42,000. When settlement was made and O'Henry had received a deed to the property, he paid Foley $38 for fire insurance that Foley had purchased to protect the property. A fire loss of $1,800 was thereafter reported to the insurance company by O'Henry. The insurer refused to honor the claim. Was the insurance company justified in this decision?

Yes. Fire insurance law requires that the insured have a continuing insurable interest in property covered. Foley Builders lost their insurable interest when the property was deeded over to O'Henry. Had Foley's insurance policy been canceled and a new one issued to O'Henry, the claim would have been honored.

6. Wirt's new car, which was parked, was destroyed when it was struck by a speeding car. There was no question of the cause of the loss, and Wirt's insurance company paid in full under a nondeductible auto policy. The insurance company then proceeded to sue the driver who caused the accident. He claimed this could not be done because all damages had already been settled and paid to Wirt. Was the driver correct?

No. An insurance company is always *subrogated* to the rights of the insured. Thus, because Wirt had a right of action against the owner-driver of the other car, his insurer had the same right. Wirt, under the doctrine of subrogation, would be required to cooperate with his insurance company in its action against the driver who had caused the damage. In the present case, it is obvious that the insurance company will recover, through subrogation, all money paid to Wirt through his claim.

7. Daniels rented a power boat from the Chesapeake Marina. In the rental agreement he stated that he and his friends would take the boat to a nearby beach for a day's outing. Daniels was persuaded by the others to extend the trip several miles further downriver, beyond the point originally intended. During this extended trip, the boat hit a submerged rock that caused it to sink. Daniels proved he was absolutely free of any negligence or lack of care in the handling of the boat. With that proof, will he be free of liability to the Chesapeake Marina?

No. Daniels was, at the time of the accident, a tortious bailee. His agreement with the bailor limited the use of the boat to a trip to the nearby beach. In going beyond that point, Daniels had exceeded his rights as bailee. This made him an insurer, completely responsible for any loss or damage to the bailor's property. Daniels has no defense against the rightful claim of Chesapeake Marina for the entire loss.

8. Abruzzi, an agent for the Kinkaid Mutual Fire Insurance Company, accepted Henry Brothers' application and premium for fire insurance on their store building in Milford. Abruzzi noted on the receipt given to Henry Brothers that the property was fully insured at the precise time and date on which the receipt was issued. (1) In the event of a fire loss prior to delivery of the actual policy, is the Henry Brothers' store covered? (2) If Abruzzi had been a broker, would the answer be the same?

(1) Yes. An agent of the insurer has the power of issuing a binder, placing the insurance in force prior to the actual issuance of the policy. Henry Brothers' store would be covered and a claim would be paid. (2) No. A broker is the agent of the insured. Thus, the broker has no power to issue a binder.

9. Hollowell and Sterling were previous holders of a promissory note that was held by Coover when it became due. Coover presented the note for payment on the due date, but it was dishonored by the maker. A week later, Coover gave notice of dishonor to both Hollowell and Stevens, who had endorsed the note. May Coover recover his loss from these previous endorsers?

No. The holder of commercial paper that has been dishonored is obligated to give notice of dishonor to prior holders-endorsers before the end of the third business day after the day of dishonor. Coover was at fault in not meeting this obligation. Both Hollowell and Sterling are therefore released from liability on the note.

10. Dukes left an Orlon sweater with Century Cleaners for cleaning. She received a receipt for her property. When she returned to get the sweater, she found that it was ruined. The cleaner denied any responsibility, claiming that the problem resulted from materials used in manufacturing the sweater. A label attached to the sweater by the manufacturer gave specific instructions for cleaning that the cleaner had not followed. As the bailee of the sweater, would Century Cleaners be liable to Dukes for this loss?

Yes. Dukes and Century Cleaners had entered into a mutual-benefit bailment. Ordinary care was required on Century's part, and Century would be liable for any losses resulting from negligence. The custom of the market place would require a cleaner to read and be directed by labels attached to garments accepted for cleaning. Not having read the label constituted negligence on Century's part, making the cleaner liable to Dukes for the value of the sweater.

PART VI: **Agency**

Chapter 10

Types of Agency and Their Creation

We live in an age of specialization. Today it would be impossible to meet someone who could truly be called "jack of all trades." In our complex society, we must often count on the skills and talents of other people to help us meet our obligations and needs. People constantly depend on one another to carry out their responsibilities and to achieve their goals. Organizations are interdependent in the same way—they are always relying on one another.

An *agency* is created whenever people or organizations appoint some other to do a job on their behalf. Agency law cannot be separated from the other branches of law that we have already reviewed. Contracts are required in the creation of agency relationships. A bailee is often a bailor's agent. Salespeople are agents who sell goods or services that belong to someone else. An insurance broker is the agent of an insured.

This chapter is a review of the basic types of agencies and their creation. The three subsequent chapters also review principles of agency law.

TYPES OF AGENTS

10.1 General Agents

A *general agent* is one who has been given general powers of overseeing and executing assignments for another, called a *principal*. A general agent, in most cases, has the right of making decisions in carrying out those assigned duties. Store managers, department managers, administrative personnel, and salespeople are included in this category.

EXAMPLE 1. Hanlon was hired as manager of the Syracuse branch of the Home Products Company. He did all hiring, advertising, financial planning, and general managing for the store under his supervision. During the holiday season, Hanlon hired four extra clerks and an additional cashier for a one-month period. The regional manager complained of Hanlon's hiring additional help without first obtaining the approval of the home office. Hanlon was a general agent with *powers of discretion*. Discretion in decision-making is not unlimited, but would include the right to increase the number of employees required to operate the branch store properly.

10.2 Special Agents

Agents appointed to carry out specific duties according to prescribed instructions are *special agents*. Special agents, with few exceptions, have no discretion in determining the means of execution of the duties assigned. Within the restricted scope of the duties to be performed, a special agent may be granted a limited right of decision-making.

EXAMPLE 2. Clay worked as an attendant in the City Parking Garage. His duties were to accept cars for parking, drive them to open spots on one of the five floors of the garage, and return the car keys to the office on the ground floor. Clay is a special agent, with specific instructions for carrying out the duties of the job. His judgment and discretion would be limited to selecting a spot in which to park a car.

10.3 Independent Contractors

Independent contractors are agents over whom a principal reserves no right of supervision during the execution of the agency agreement. However, a principal does have the right to inspect and accept or reject work performed by an independent contractor. Any damages to third parties caused by the independent contractor's methods are the contractor's, not the principal's, liability unless the principal has been negligent in choosing a competent and reliable contractor.

EXAMPLE 3. After submitting a bid, the Dunmon Roofing Company was chosen to repair the roof of the Continental Warehouse Company. Dunmon was given specifications, a date for starting the job, and a completion date. All other matters were left with the contractor. Payment by Continental was to be made upon notification of completion of the job and after Continental's independent inspection and final approval of the new roof. Dunmon Roofing Company was an independent contractor, with full and complete supervision in execution of the contract.

10.4 Gratuitous Agents

A person volunteering to perform duties without compensation is a *gratuitous agent*. Gratuitous agents are not bound by their promises of future performance because such promises do not contain the element of consideration, which is essential in all enforceable agreements. Obligations resulting from a gratuitous agent's acts, however, are enforceable by the principal or a third party.

EXAMPLE 4. Kirby's Stables accepted Shirley's offer to help train riding horses for the owner. Nothing was said about pay. Shirley offered her services only because of her love for horses and riding. After working for three weeks, Shirley informed Kirby's Stables that she was leaving and would not return. Kirby's Stables would have no rightful claim for damages against Shirley because there was no consideration supporting their agreement.

10.5 Brokers

A *broker* is an agent appointed for the purpose of bringing together two contracting parties. A broker must show good faith in dealing with both parties. A broker may accept payment from both the principal and the third party only with the full knowledge of both.

EXAMPLE 5. Selby listed his house and farm with Truitt Realty. Truitt Realty had no title or other interest in the property. Larimore had previously commissioned Truitt to locate a farm for purchase in the same county. Both Selby and Larimore had contracted to pay Truitt commissions. It was Truitt's obligation, as a broker acting in good faith, to inform each party of the commission arrangements made with the other.

10.6 *Del Credere* Agents

An agent who guarantees to the principal that the third party will pay money owed under the agent's contract is a *del credere agent*. In return for the agent's guarantee of payment, the principal is charged an additional sum by the agent.

EXAMPLE 6. Rowe & Rowe, a food broker, accepted fresh produce from Hubbard Farms. Rowe & Rowe sold the food to retail stores in the area. Hubbard Farms, seeking a guarantee against losses that might result from bad accounts, paid Rowe & Rowe 1½ percent additional commission on all sales for Rowe & Rowe's guarantee that all accounts receivable resulting from the sales would be paid. Rowe & Rowe would thus be classified as a *del credere* agent.

10.7 Attorney in Fact and Power of Attorney

A principal may give an agent the power to negotiate the principal's contracts, to buy and sell the principal's real property or securities, and to carry out the principal's business with authority to use independent judgment. Such an agent is called an *attorney in fact*. The appointment of an attorney in fact is usually made with an agreement written and signed by the principal and under seal. The agreement itself is known as a *power of attorney*.

EXAMPLE 7. Stanbaugh planned an extensive trip abroad. She owned, in her own name, stocks, bonds, and other holdings whose values fluctuated from day to day. She appointed the vice-president of the Guaranty

Bank as her attorney in fact, with the right to sell, buy, and transfer her holdings within the bounds of good judgment and reasonableness. The agent, armed with a power of attorney, would be responsible for the safe and sound investment of Stanbaugh's funds until such time as she returned or canceled the power of attorney.

CREATION OF AGENCY

10.8 Oral Contracts in Agency

An agency contract, like other ordinary agreements, may be created by the principal's oral appointment of the agent. The principal or agent may later be called upon to prove the appointment, in which case evidence of the agreement may become important.

EXAMPLE 8. Reynolds hired Lusby to work in Reynold's Service Station during weekend rush-hours. Lusby was assigned to work on the service islands and to assist in lubricating and washing customers' cars. The agreement, with all details of pay and hours to be worked, was made orally. There is no question of the validity of the agreement if both parties were competent to contract and the contract was not in violation of any federal, state, or local laws or ordinances.

10.9 Written Agency Agreements

A contract of agency that is to continue for more than one year from the date of the contract must be in writing, under the provisions of the statute of frauds and the Uniform Commercial Code. Failure to have the agreement in writing does not make it illegal but does make it unenforceable. (State laws concerning written agency agreements vary.)

EXAMPLE 9. Stravinsky accepted a position as a research chemist with the Research Scientific Corporation. He was hired to lead a five-year basic research project. After two years, Stravinsky announced that he was leaving for another job. Only if the agreement were in writing would it be enforceable against Stravinsky.

10.10 Equal-Dignities Rule

By the *equal-dignities rule*, an agent's appointment and authority must be created by a contract equal in kind and formality to that which the agent is to negotiate with a third party. In cases where the contract made for the principal and a third party must be in writing and under seal, the agent's contract with the principal must also be in writing and under seal. If the contract with a third party must be in writing, the agent's agency contract must also be in writing.

EXAMPLE 10. Standish worked as a salesman for the Central Realty Company. He negotiated with prospective buyers of commercial and industrial properties. Standish represented Central in the sale of a $175,000 warehouse. All sales agreements were properly written, signed, and sealed by all parties. Standish signed for the seller in each case. Either Central or the buyer could void this agreement by showing that Standish had never received his authority by any means other than an oral agency agreement. Once the contracted obligations were executed, however, this complaint would have been waived by both parties.

10.11 Competency of Principal

Agents may do for principals those things that the principals are competent to do for themselves. Incompetent principals do not strengthen or weaken their positions by having competent agents act for them.

EXAMPLE 11. Roswald had been declared mentally incompetent by a state court. Although incompetent, he was not irrational and was permitted to live at home. Roswald hired Sturgeon to sell certain valuable books to a rare-book dealer. Roswald gave Sturgeon authority to sell the books at any price the dealer offered. Sturgeon did as requested, returning and giving the money received to Roswald. Roswald's guardian disapproved of the sale and sought to have the books returned. One declared insane is incompetent to make *any type of contract*. Although Sturgeon was fully competent, he had acted for Roswald, not for himself. The contract is invalid, and the guardian may demand the return of the books upon tender of the money received in the sale. (Had the book dealer taken advantage of Roswald's mental condition, a court might render a judgment allowing Roswald to retain the money received.)

10.12 A Minor's Contract Made by an Adult Agent

A minor's contract made by an adult agent is voidable just as if the minor had made the agreement without the agent. It is the minor's contract, not the agent's.

EXAMPLE 12. In a state where minors were prohibited from buying alcoholic beverages, Chapman, a legal adult, agreed to buy a six-pack of beer for Young, who was sixteen years old. Chapman made the purchase but decided not to deliver the beer to Young. Instead, he returned the money to Young. This agreement was void from its inception. Chapman's maturity may not be the means of extending the minor's rights under the law. Young would have no legal right to complain of a breach by Chapman.

10.13 Competency of Minor

It is not necessary that an agent have the capacity to contract. The agent need only have the physical and mental awareness to understand and carry out the principal's instructions. Contractual capacity must be with the principal, not with the agent.

EXAMPLE 13. DeGrange requested one of her high school students to go to a nearby store and buy a CB radio for her. She gave the student $127.50 in cash to make the purchase. DeGrange was not satisfied with the radio and sought to return it on grounds that it was purchased by a minor, who had no capacity to contract. DeGrange would fail. DeGrange was the principal and she alone was bound by the terms of the sales agreement.

10.14 Husband-Wife Agency Relationship

Marriage, of itself, does not create an agency relationship between the wife and husband. An exception to this rule would be those cases in which the husband fails to provide his wife and children with the necessities of life. In such cases the law will imply an agency relationship, permitting the wife to make purchases for necessaries and obligating the husband to pay for them.

EXAMPLE 14. Olander owed Sheer $500. Olander visited Sheer's home, intending to repay the $500, with interest. Sheer was not at home, and Olander gave the money to Mrs. Sheer. She never gave her husband the cash, so Sheer sued Olander, claiming that the debt had not been paid. Sheer's wife is not his agent for making collections. Olander actually appointed Mrs. Sheer *as his agent*. Olander was responsible for the acts of his own agent and thus could not claim that the debt was repaid.

EXAMPLE 15. Dougherty failed to give his wife the regular grocery allowance which she used to buy food for their family. Repeated demands did not produce any funds. Mrs. Dougherty purchased needed food and provisions for the family, charging them to her husband's account. Dougherty will be held responsible for these debts. A wife may act as her husband's agent in those cases where necessity requires that another act for the husband in carrying out his legal responsibilities to his family.

10.15 Implied Agency

An agency relationship may be created by the representations or even by the simple acts of two people, one of whom becomes the principal while the other becomes an *implied agent*. The principal in such a case may not disclaim or disavow the acts of the implied agent.

EXAMPLE 16. After a snowstorm, Guernsey started cleaning snow from the sidewalks surrounding Heubner's Market. Heubner had not requested Guernsey's help, but he did watch Guernsey through the windows of his store and made no effort to stop him. Guernsey injured a passerby with his careless shoveling, and Heubner's Market was correctly asked to pay the injured's medical bills. Guernsey was the implied agent of Heubner's Market. By permitting Guernsey to continue his work, Heubner implied that it was a satisfactory agency arrangement for which he would be responsible.

10.16 Apparent Agency

Under some circumstances a third party might reasonably suppose that a person is an agent of one believed to be a principal. Such an agent, who is not appointed by the apparent principal and who acts without the principal's knowledge or authority, is known as an *apparent agent*. A principal is bound by any of the apparent agent's actions that affect a third party.

EXAMPLE 17. On several occasions the manager of a gasoline station had ordered McKinney to keep off the premises and stop offering his assistance to customers. McKinney persisted and in one instance exploded a customer's tire by overinflating it. McKinney was neither an express nor an implied agent of the station's management. However, the customer *had a right to believe* that McKinney was an employee. The service station could be held responsible for the negligence of its *apparent agent*.

10.17 Agent's Scope of Authority

An agent's *scope of authority* may be reasonably inferred from the circumstances by a third party. However, the third party must use ordinary prudence in judging whether or not an agent is acting within the scope of his or her authority.

EXAMPLE 18. Humboldt was working as a clerk in a women's apparel shop. Signs in the store window announced "drastic reductions." Humboldt sold a jacket with a price tag of $95 for $45. The store manager had instructed Humboldt not to discount any merchandise unless there was a small red "D" on the price tag. This secret code marking was missing from the jacket's price tag. Humboldt had exceeded her scope of authority in discounting the jacket, but the customer could not have known that Humboldt had no authority to give the discount. Humboldt, although working outside the scope of her authority, had the apparent authority to discount the price during the "drastic reduction" sale. The owner of the apparel shop had no enforceable complaint against the customer.

EXAMPLE 19. A salesman for Jordan Sales showed a customer a new Lincoln Continental priced at $15,600. Anxious to make the sale, the salesman offered to give the customer a $5,600 allowance on her ten-year-old Mercury, which had been driven 189,000 miles. Contracts were signed and the customer gave the salesman a deposit of $500. The owner of the sales company correctly claimed that the customer should have surmised that the salesman went way beyond the scope of his authority in making such a generous offer. The agreement signed by the customer and salesman was therefore voidable.

10.18 Acts Outside Scope of Authority

Principals may defend themselves against unauthorized agreements made by agents when the agreements clearly contradict the ordinary *custom of the market place*. A third party who is suspicious of an agent's authority has the obligation to confirm the agent's representations by contacting the principal.

EXAMPLE 20. Waldron acted as a handyman for the Rubin Realty Corporation. He made small repairs and did painting on rental units. While working in Bronson's apartment, Waldron offered to accept Bronson's rent, which he promised to remit to Rubin Realty. Waldron spent the rent money, and Bronson refused to pay rent a second time. Bronson had no right to assume that the handyman had authority to make rent collections. If anything, Waldron was Bronson's agent, appointed by Bronson to deliver the money to Rubin. Bronson is still obligated to pay Rubin.

10.19 Agent's Scope of Employment

An agent may be outside the *scope of authority* but well within the *scope of employment*. Although given implicit instructions and restrictions by the principal, the agent may perform unauthorized acts which solely benefit the principal and for which the principal will be responsible.

EXAMPLE 21. Reed worked as a private detective for Healey's Department Store. He was given strict orders not to lay a hand on any suspected shoplifters but to bring them to the manager's immediate attention. Reed spotted a woman picking up merchandise and putting it in her handbag. He accosted her by pinning her to the counter and caused her physical injury. Reed had exceeded his authority, but he was still working within the *scope of his employment*. A complaint of the use of unnecessary force in making an arrest could result in a suit for damages against the store.

10.20 Acts Outside Scope of Employment

An agent will not obligate the principal for damages resulting from acts or representations made by the agent outside the scope of the agent's employment.

EXAMPLE 22. Giles worked as a cleaning woman in the Armstrong Building, where offices were rented to a variety of businesses. While sweeping a corridor, Giles spotted a man who had damaged her car several months before. The man had never offered to pay the cost of repairs. Giles chased the man down the corridor and hit him with a heavy broom, injuring him. Armstrong would not be liable for Giles's acts because she had left the scope of her employment. The agent in this case was not engaged in the scuffle through loyalty or service benefitting the principal.

EXAMPLE 23. Suppose, in Example 22, that Giles had been hired without any research into her past experience or any references from her former employers. Suppose also that Giles had a serious record of violent antisocial behavior set off by seemingly unimportant contacts with other people. Armstrong could be made responsible for having employed such an individual to work in areas used by persons entering the building. Failing to check a potential employee's background may be considered negligence on the part of the principal..

10.21 Apparent Authority to Negotiate Commercial Paper

Possession of another's unendorsed negotiable note does not in itself establish the holder's right to demand payment of the note. A third party may not claim that the holder's mere possession of a note gave the holder apparent authority.

EXAMPLE 24. Young shared an apartment with Chapman. Young saw a $250 negotiable demand note on a dresser in the apartment. The note was made out to Chapman and signed by Freemont. Young, representing himself as Chapman's agent, took the note to Freemont and demanded payment. Freemont is not obligated to pay Young. If Freemont did pay Young, he would still not be released from his obligation to pay Chapman $250.

10.22 Agent's Right to Issue Check in Principal's Name

An agent may not issue a check in the name of a principal unless the agent has specific authority to do so. Checks issued by agents without authority create neither implied nor apparent authority.

EXAMPLE 25. During the owner's absence from Smith's Variety Store, a c.o.d. shipment of toys arrived. The amount due on the delivery was $235. Harper, the assistant manager, went to the safe, took out the checkbook, and made out a check for that amount. Without authorization, he signed and issued the check. Both the bank and the owner of the store refused to honor the check when it was presented. The assistant manager had neither express, implied, nor apparent authority to issue the check. Under these circumstances, the assistant manager would be personally liable on the check.

10.23 Effect of Secret Partnership Agreements

Third parties are not bound by *secret agreements* contained in articles of copartnership that designate each partner's rights and restrictions under the partnership agreement. Each partner is considered to be the agent for the other partners in contracting on business matters with outside parties.

EXAMPLE 26. Hambleton, Joslin, and Grabowski were partners in a commercial printing business. By agreement, Hambleton alone was responsible for all financial matters. Joslin was responsible for sales, advertising, and public relations. Grabowski was responsible for all production and plant operation. Hambleton signed a contract with a magazine for a series of advertisements that would cost the partnership $5,320 over a two-month period. Joslin sought to rescind the agreement, claiming that Hambleton acted without authorization. The partnrship would be held liable under the agreement. The magazine had no way of knowing about the restrictions on any of the partners in the printing business. The magazine had acted in good faith in treating Hambleton as the agent of the printing company.

EXAMPLE 27. Suppose that the magazine in Example 26 had done business with the printing company many times before and had always been referred to Joslin in matters concerning advertising. In this case, the magazine's advertising director should have questioned Joslin about Hambleton's offer to sign a contract for advertising. The magazine would be required to be *on guard* and to inquire into this new and unexpected division of responsibilities. If the magazine failed to do this, the Hambleton agreement would not necessarily bind the partnership to the contract.

10.24 Agency by Estoppel, or Implication

An *agency by estoppel*, or *implication*, is created when a "principal" acquiesces in or fails to deny an "agent's" false representations of an agency relationship. People who act in a way that leads innocent third parties to reasonably believe that someone is an authorized agent are prevented, or estopped, from claiming later that such a person is not, in fact, an authorized agent.

EXAMPLE 28. In the presence of Abbott, the owner of an antique desk, Jackson tried to convince Carson that he ought to buy the desk. Jackson pointed out the craftsmanship in the desk and its great value. He offered to sell it to Carson for $3,900. Abbott remained silent throughout Jackson's presentation. When Carson finally agreed to buy the desk, Abbott informed him that there had been no serious intention to sell it and that he was merely interested in knowing if Jackson would be successful in his sales efforts. Ruling out arguments that might be based on the statute of frauds, Carson could claim a valid, enforceable agreement because Abbot permitted him to believe that Jackson made a genuine offer.

AGENCY THROUGH RATIFICATION

10.25 Ratification of Unauthorized Acts

One who is not a principal may *ratify* (but does not have to ratify) the acts and promises of another who claims to be her or his agent. Notification of approval to a third party is not required because the third party innocently believed all along that an agency relationship existed.

EXAMPLE 29. Miles worked for the Price Heating Company as an oil-burner mechanic. While cleaning and adjusting Paxton's burner, he suggested that Paxton purchase a new burner being sold by Price. Paxton agreed and placed his order with Miles. Miles was not authorized to sell burners, but Price was pleased with the sale and called Paxton to confirm the agreement. Although Miles acted outside of his authority, Price's confirmation ratified and made valid and enforceable the agreement with Paxton. Had Price felt differently, he could have denied any obligation on the agreement under the defense that it is not the *custom of the market place* that a burner mechanic is authorized to make sales contracts with customers.

10.26 Revocation Prior to Ratification

A third party has the right to revoke any agreement prior to its ratification upon discovering lack of authority.

EXAMPLE 30. Suppose Paxton, in Example 29, had learned that Miles was *not* authorized to contract with Price's customers. Had Paxton desired, he could have revoked any agreements he had made with Miles as long as Price had not yet notified him.

10.27 Ratification by Principal of Unauthorized Acts

Ratification of an unauthorized act or agreement implies a principal's knowledge of all that transpired between the third party and the agent. The principal becomes responsible for all acts, representations, and promises made in his or her behalf.

EXAMPLE 31. Lerner, a wheel-alignment expert, worked for Midtown Motors. During the absence of the shop foreman, Lerner inspected Calvin's truck, wrote up a service order, and made an appointment for Calvin to return to have the work done. Lerner had been told *not* to contract with customers, but the foreman approved the service order anyway. It later developed that Lerner had promised that there would be no charge for any parts needed in aligning the truck's wheels. Midtown Motors, in ratifying Lerner's agreement, *ratified all of it*. It is no defense that the shop foreman was not aware of Lerner's promises. Unless the copy of the estimate given to Calvin contained specific terms that contradicted Lerner's offer, Midtown would be obligated on the agreement Lerner made with Calvin.

10.28 Responsibility of Agent for Unratified Acts

A principal's refusal to ratify the unauthorized acts or promises of an agent will make the agent liable to the third party for any damages thereby caused. Agents are liable in such cases as though they had been working for themselves.

EXAMPLE 32. Stauffer, a real estate salesman, represented himself as having authority to sell a property at 2935 Lincoln Drive. He drove a potential buyer to the address, and they viewed the property from the car. Stauffer anticipated the possibility of convincing the owner of a profitable sale. The interested buyer signed a purchase agreement. Stauffer was not able to consummate the sale. Stauffer made himself liable to the buyer for any damages resulting from the false representation.

AGENCY BY OPERATION OF LAW

10.29 Agency by Necessity

The law will create an agency in bankruptcy proceedings, in connection with contracts made by a deceased, in matters necessary to a family in the absence of a provider, and in other emergencies in which an agency is necessary to protect life or property.

EXAMPLE 33. Slaughter refused to give his wife funds for buying meats, groceries, and provisions for herself and their three children. The family had previously purchased goods on credit at Handler's Supermarket. Mrs. Slaughter made purchases which were both reasonable and necessary for the family's welfare. All purchases were charged to Slaughter's account. Slaughter will not be permitted to deny his responsibility for the purchases charged to him. By law, a wife is an agent for her husband in making agreements for necessaries not supplied by him.

Solved Problems

10.1 Thurston, an attorney, agreed to represent Smith in an action against Smith for damages resulting from the libel of a business associate. Thurston was called away from the area at the time Smith's case was coming to trial. Thurston appointed another attorney to represent Smith. Smith complained of Thurston's action. Was Smith's complaint justified?

One obligated to performance in a contract for personal services of a professional nature may not appoint another to carry out those obligations. Without Smith's approval, Thurston may not appoint another to carry out the professional services she had agreed to perform herself..

10.2 Lawlor, a middle-aged woman with a mental age of 11 years, accepted employment with Hurlock's Restaurant. Hurlock sent the woman to a nearby market to make purchases for the restaurant. He later denied responsibility for her acts, claiming that she was incapable of making valid agreements because of her mental condition. Was Hurlock obligated to the market?

Yes. Anyone may be appointed as an agent, with certain exceptions where licensing and other requirements are set forth by statute. Incapacity to contract is related to a principal, not to an agent.

10.3 The daughter of the Home Finance Company's manager often visited her father's office and spent time using one of the office typewriters. Although never given authority to do so, she often accepted premium and installment payments brought in by customers. After making two payments to her at different times, Galloway made his third and final payment, which the girl kept and did not turn over to the office manager. Home Finance demanded that Galloway pay the last installment again, stating that the girl had no authority to accept money from the firm's clients. Must Galloway pay again?

No. The daughter would be considered an apparent agent of the Home Finance Company. Because of Home Finance's ratification of the girl's acts in other collections, Home Finance would now be estopped from denying her authority to accept for the company the payment made by Galloway.

10.4 Apple Construction Company contracted to build a market for Ace Stores. In this case Apple was an independent contractor, responsible only for the delivery of a complete building conforming to specifications supplied. During construction, a pedestrian was injured by a falling timber dropped from the roof of the building. Ace Stores denied liability, claiming that the job was under Apple's supervision. Investigation showed that Ace Stores had accepted the lowest bid and had not sought information on the reliability of Apple Construction Company. May Ace Stores be held liable for the injury to the pedestrian?

Yes. Hiring *anyone* as an independent contractor does not relieve a principal of an obligation for damages resulting to third parties. Care and discrimination must be exercised in selecting a contractor known to be responsible and skillful. Ace was interested only in the lowest price and had made no inquiries. If further investigation indicated that Apple Construction had fumbled on other jobs and was not reliable in safety practices, Ace Stores could be held accountable.

10.5 Wilson promised that he would help Cain plant a field of tomato plants during the weekend. Wilson and Cain often helped one another when they had jobs. Cain, as was usual, was not to pay Wilson for his time. Wilson failed to show up at the time promised, causing Cain the loss of two-hundred expensive plants. Cain demanded damages. Was he successful?

No. Wilson was a *gratuitous agent*. No consideration was promised by Cain, so Wilson was not bound to an enforceable contract. Cain had no more than a moral obligation to assist his friend.

10.6 Economy Clothes hired Cleaver as general manager of its retail outlet. Cleaver contracted with City Electric for the installation of new lighting in its sidewalk display windows. The cost of materials and labor amounted to $9,763. Economy's owners were not aware of Cleaver's improvement plans until the work was finished and a bill was submitted. May Economy refuse to honor the bill?

Yes. City Electric, aware that Cleaver was a general agent in charge of store operations, should also have been aware that he did not necessarily have authority for major changes of an expensive and lasting nature. Such decisions are not ordinarily within the scope of a store manager's authority. City Electric had the responsibility of confirming Cleaver's decision with the owners or executive management before starting work. Cleaver, who represented himself as one with authority, may be called upon as a defendant in City Electric's action for the $9,763.

10.7 Wessels was appointed purchasing agent and contract representative for the City of Rehoboth. His authority, without further confirmation by the City Council, was limited to purchases and contracts in amounts no more than $500. Wessels contracted to buy for the city a combination road grader and snow plow costing $39,000. Delivery of the machine was refused by city authorities. Is the city of Rehoboth responsible for the contract of its agent?

The authority granted a public official is recorded in public documents available for inspection by those dealing with such persons. Persons dealing with public authorities are, therefore, *on notice* of the public agent's rights and authority in any matter. Officials are free from personal actions against them. This freedom from liability is not the case in situations where a business agent misrepresents his authority to another person's injury or damage.

10.8 City Bank & Trust Company cashed a paycheck supposedly issued by Peninsula Van Lines to Albert Harris. Harris, dressed in the uniform of Peninsula's drivers, had cashed the check without being asked for other identification. Peninsula demanded that the bank reimburse them for the amount of the check when they found that blank checks and a uniform had been stolen by Harris. City Bank claimed that the check was cashed by one who was Peninsula's *apparent agent.* Was the bank correct in this claim?

No. Peninsula Van Lines had done nothing to encourage the bank's decision in cashing the check. They were at no time aware of the hoax and had in no way acted to weaken the bank's position in the matter. Harris was not an appointed, implied, or apparent agent of Peninsula. The bank alone must bear responsibility for the loss.

10.9 Carver worked as a collection agent for the Howard Furniture Company. He was fired for embezzling funds, but this fact was never made public. Two days after his dismissal, Carver visited some of Howard's regular accounts and made collections, which he pocketed. Howard Furniture sought to collect payments from these same customers, claiming that Carver was not working for them at the time of these last collections. Did Howard succeed?

No. Carver was an apparent agent. Howard had the responsibility to inform all third parties with whom Carver had had previous contact that he no longer worked for the store. Howard Furniture would have the right to bring a civil suit for damages against Carver. Howard could also sign a warrant for Carver's arrest on the grounds that he obtained money under false pretenses.

10.10 Ames asked Ellington, with whom he shared an apartment, to purchase a washer and refrigerator for him. Ellington did as he was asked and signed an agreement for the purchase of the two units with Hilton Household Supplies. He signed his name, Harry S. Ellington, followed by the word "agent." Will Ames be liable if Hilton attempts to enforce the agreement?

No. The seller knows only Ellington, who signed the agreement. Merely using the title "agent" does not obligate an unnamed principal. Ellington should have signed the contract: "Ames, by Harry S. Ellington, agent."

10.11 Central Taxi Company hired Svenson as one of its drivers. He was given careful instructions in the operation of the taxi assigned to him. At no time was he to exceed the company's speed limit of 35 m.p.h. He was also to observe all local and state traffic regulations. He signed an employment agreement in which he accepted these obligations. In an effort to deliver a fare to the airport in time to meet a plane, Svenson drove at 50 m.p.h. An accident resulted. Central Taxi denied responsibility on the grounds that Svenson had exceeded his authority in breaking the speed limit. Was Central liable?

Yes. An agent may exceed the scope of authority but still remain within the scope of employment. Svenson was exceeding the speed limit in an attempt to please a fare. Persons injured as a result of the accident could seek damages from the cab company.

10.12 Brandeis drove a delivery truck for Clover Dairies, serving 250 homes each day. He made regular collections every Monday, when there were no deliveries. One Monday, when he collected $628, he left town with the money and could not be located. Clover Dairies then sought to collect the same bills from Brandeis's customers. Was Clover successful?

No. Brandeis was a special agent for the delivery of his principal's goods and a general agent in making collections. His customers had a right to believe that the driver-salesman, as is the custom of the market place, had the right to collect. Clover would be permitted recovery only from their former agent—if they can find him.

10.13 Harrington, Swartz, and King were partners in the ownership and management of a beauty salon. King, during the absence of the other partners, agreed to sell all of the shop's hair dryers to a used-equipment dealer. Harrington and Swartz refused to honor the contract made with the purchaser. Was the used-equipment dealer correct in making this agreement with King?

No. Knowing that he was dealing with a partnership business, the dealer should have realized that one partner alone did not have the authority to liquidate the equipment necessary for the shop's operation. King could bind the other partners to contracts reasonable in the operation of the shop. Selling the shop's assets, however, should arouse suspicion in the mind of a purchaser and suggest the need of confirmation by the other partners.

10.14 Flood, a used-car salesman, was warned by Union Park Sales not to make promises to customers that went beyond conditions stated in the regular sales contracts. Flood induced Chambers to buy a used Mustang that had been driven 75,000 miles by writing into the printed contract an additional warranty covering the car against any mechanical defects for the next 50,000 miles. Was Chambers successful in attempting to enforce the warranty?

No. Chambers, as a person of ordinary intelligence, should recognize that Flood had made a guarantee that went far beyond the scope of employment granted to anyone selling used cars. Flood's unauthorized warranty, written into the sales agreement, went far beyond the custom of the market place, and Chambers should have checked it with the management of Union Park.

10.15 Mrs. Talbot made purchases of expensive shoes and clothing from several stores. She charged the purchases on accounts that had been approved by her husband. Although arguments over the purchases developed between Mr. Talbot and his wife, he paid the bills after warning her to stop making *any* purchases unless the items bought were necessary. Several days later, Mrs. Talbot bought a new coat and a spring suit, with accessories, billed at $469. Talbot refused to pay the bill for this purchase, claiming that as a husband he was responsible only for necessaries sold to his wife. Was Talbot's defense against payment adequate?

Talbot's acquiesence in paying other uncalled-for purchases set a pattern of apparent willingness to accept his wife's purchases as though he had approved the purchases himself. Therefore Talbot may not disclaim responsibility. He should have informed all creditors that he would no longer be responsible for purchases made by Mrs. Talbot unless he was contacted and confirmed such purchases.

Review Problems

10.16 How does *apparent authority* differ from *implied authority*?

10.17 In what ways are agencies created?

10.18 Who may be a principal?

10.19 What is meant by the agent's *scope of employment?*

10.20 Explain the *equal-dignities rule* in agency agreements.

10.21 Who may be an agent?

10.22 How does *scope of authority* differ from *scope of employment?*

10.23 Is a gratuitous agent obligated to render promised performance?

10.24 In what cases is a wife the agent of her husband?

10.25 Name three situations in which agency is created through *operation of law*.

10.26 Is a principal responsible for damages to third parties resulting from the negligence of an independent contractor?

10.27 In what way is a special agent different from a general agent?

10.28 May an agent performing professional services delegate the responsibility of performance to another?

10.29 When must an agent's contract be in writing and under seal?

10.30 Is a partner *always* deemed to be the agent of the partnership in *all* contracts made in connection with the partnership business? Explain your answer.

Answers to Review Problems

10.16 *Apparent authority* is actually no authority. It is derived through impressions permitted by the principal and allowing a third party to believe that the agent's acts and promises are made with the principal's approval, whereas they are not. *Implied* authority is actual authority. It is derived from the principal's unspoken approval of the agent's acts or promises. Authority is intended here, whereas in apparent authority the principal's intent is lacking.

10.17 They are: (1) expressed, (2) implied, (3) apparent (or by estoppel), or (4) created by operation of law.

10.18 Anyone with the capacity to contract and act for himself or herself may be a principal.

10.19 Scope of employment includes all activities and promises for the benefit of an employer within the boundaries of an agent's appointment. Scope of employment can usually be defined by the custom of the market place.

10.20 The contract between a principal and agent must be evidenced by agreements equal in formality to those agreements made with any third parties.

10.21 Anyone possessing the physical and mental abilities to carry out duties may be an agent. (An agent need not have the capacity to contract.)

10.22 Scope of authority consists of the principal's instructions to be followed by an agent in pursuance of employment. The authority may be express, implied, or apparent.

10.23 No. Absence of consideration renders gratuitous acts and promises unenforceable.

10.24 A wife is implied to be the agent of her husband in acts and promises necessary to the operation of their home and the care of their family. The wife is given powers, by operation of law, to contract in the husband's name for those things not supplied by the husband but necessary to the health, welfare, and safety of their home and family.

10.25 Agency is created through the operation of law in connnection with contracts made by a deceased, in bankruptcies, in cases where a husband fails to provide necessaries for his family, and in other emergencies.

10.26 No. Only when the principal has delegated duties to an independent contractor who is known to be irresponsible is the principal liable.

10.27 A special agent is appointed for the performance of a specific task. A general agent, in contrast, is given overall supervisory powers. He or she may make independent judgments in carrying out the principal's instructions, and has wide authority in decision-making within reasonable bounds.

10.28 No. Without the principal's permission, performance may not be delegated.

10.29 A seal is required when the agent executes contracts for the sale of real property for a principal in states that continue to require the use of the seal in formal contracts.

10.30 No. Partners are usually restricted by articles of copartnership. A partner's apparent authority binds the partnership only to those agreements considered reasonable within the custom of the market place. Third parties must be reasonable and must follow the custom of the market place in dealing with any individual partner in the absence of the others.

Legal Terms

Agent. Anyone possessing the physical and mental ability to carry out duties assigned by a principal. Legal capacity is not required of an agent, nor will an agent's legal capacity to contract be in any way effective in conferring legal capacity on an otherwise incompetent principal.

Apparent agency. An agency relationship reasonably supposed to exist by outside parties who observe the actions of one believed to be a principal and another believed to be an agent.

Attorney in fact. An agent with the authority to make contracts for a principal.

Del credere agent. An agent who guarantees to a principal that a third party will pay money owed under the agent's contract; if the third party defaults, the agent becomes liable to the principal.

General agent. An agent with powers of discretion and decision-making in carrying out the wishes of the principal.

Gratuitous agent. An agent who works without any promise of consideration.

Independent contractors. Agents working under the authority of a principal who has waived all rights of supervision and control during the performance of the agency agreement.

Power of attorney. A written instrument by which a principal appoints an agent and empowers the agent to contract for the principal.

Principal. One possessed of the legal capacity to do those things that have been assigned by her or him to an agent for actual performance.

Ratification. Approval of another's acts which were performed outside of an agency relationship. Ratification obligates a principal to all acts, representations, and promises made on the principal's behalf.

Scope of authority. The accepted area of authority of an agent, derived from both the express and the implied instructions and prohibitions of the principal.

Scope of employment. The acts of an agent performed for the principal's benefit, including those outside of the agent's scope of authority but within the custom of the market place.

Secret agreements. Instructions and powers made between a principal and an agent but not known by third parties.

Special agent. An agent appointed to carry out a special assignment, with specific instructions but with no powers of discretion or decision-making.

Chapter 11

Rights and Obligations of Parties in Agency

Each party in agency—the principal, the agent, and the third party—has obligations to the other two. These obligations are established by agreement, custom, or law.

An agent's powers are included in the scope of the agent's employment and in the more detailed scope of the agent's authority. These matters of authority are generally understood and agreed to by the principal and agent, but a third party's knowledge stems only from what she or he hears, reads, and is led to understand by the others' actions. Thus, a third party's understanding of an agent's authority may be very different from the authority actually delegated to the agent by the principal. Lack of communication and understanding that concern all three parties results in disputes that can be solved only by established laws and customs regulating various agency relationships.

The failure of a principal or agent to respect the rights of the other may result in the termination of an agency agreement. Termination of agency will be reviewed in Chapter 12.

PRINCIPAL AND THIRD PARTY

11.1 Knowledge Imputed to Principal

Information known to an agent is accepted as information also known by the principal. The agent's failure to use good judgment, inspect merchandise purchased, or to do those other things expected of a responsible agent impute poor judgment, failure to inspect, and other careless practices to the principal as well.

EXAMPLE 1. Rogers, an agent for Sullivan Hardware, allowed $50 to a customer who traded in an old power saw and purchased a new one. The customer had stated that the old saw was in excellent condition, and Rogers had accepted this statement without question or inspection. Rogers could have easily tested the saw before striking a bargain. Sullivan Hardware discovered that the old saw's motor had burned out and was not even worth repairing. Sullivan brought an action of fraud against the customer but was unsuccessful. Rogers had had an opportunity to examine the saw but had made no effort to do so. Rogers's failure to inspect became the principal's failure to inspect. *Caveat emptor* would rule out Sullivan's chances of recovery against the customer.

11.2 Collusion between Agent and Third Party

Information received by an agent is not imputed to be information known by the principal when there is collusion between the agent and the third party for the purpose of defrauding the principal. The agent's conflict of interest and collusion with the third party defeats any effort to impute knowledge to the principal.

EXAMPLE 2. Dr. Marcels entrusted his nurse with $500 to be used to buy a new air conditioner for his office. The nurse found an air conditioner on special sale. Its price was only $300. The owner of the appliance store agreed to give the nurse a receipt for $500 on the condition that she would split with the store the $200 saved. The air conditioner did not operate properly, and Marcels discovered that the machine delivered was a manufacturer's reject. He also discovered the cheating that had gone on between the seller and the nurse. The seller denied any responsibility or liability, claiming that information given to the nurse, who was acting as an agent for the buyer, was considered as having been given to her employer. The nurse had a conflict of interest when she joined the third party in perpetrating the fraud. This defeated the seller's argument. Dr. Marcels may demand the return of all the money received by the seller ($400) and by the nurse ($100).

11.3 Principal's Responsibility for Acts of Subagent

A principal may not deny responsibility for damage caused to a third party through the acts or promises of the principal's *subagent*—one hired by the principal's general agent.

EXAMPLE 3. Owens, the owner of an electronics supply store, hired Josephs as general manager of the store. Josephs hired Walton as a counter salesman. Walton, a subagent, injured a customer when he negligently dropped a case of batteries on the customer's foot. Owens denied liability, stating that he had not personally hired Walton and was therefore not obligated as Walton's principal. Owens is responsible in that, as principal, he had delegated hiring and firing duties to his agent, Josephs.

11.4 Delegation of Nonprofessional Duties

Duties of a nonprofessional nature may be delegated by a professional without endangering the contract between the principal and such a professional agent. Duties directly involving professional or artistic competence and skill may not be delegated to another.

EXAMPLE 4. Lucas retained Pell as his attorney in the prosecution of a suit for damages arising out of a breach of contract. Pell assigned the work of researching legal problems in the case to a paralegal assistant. Pell supervised and directed his assistant in the research project. This did not establish grounds for a complaint by Lucas because the paralegal did not make any decisions requiring a lawyer's skill and judgment.

11.5 Principal's Responsibility for Agent's Performance

A third party may sue only the principal, not the agent, when the agent has been careful and prudent in carrying out the principal's instructions in matters that might affect third parties.

EXAMPLE 5. Olson, the manager of the City Cab Company, hired Solomon as a cab driver. Careful checking of references and Solomon's driving record disclosed no information that might have made him a poor risk. Solomon negligently hit another car, causing considerable damage. Action was brought by the owner of the other vehicle against Olson. Olson is not liable to the third party. Only City Cab Company, the principal, may be sued for Solomon's negligence.

11.6 Principal's Responsibility for Acts of Agents

The principal is responsible for damages to third parties caused by agents who are working *within the scope of their employment* but *outside the scope of their authority.*

EXAMPLE 6. Costello worked in the shipping department of the Donovan Plumbing Supply Company. After receiving a shipment of pipes, Costello forgot to close the metal trap doors in the sidewalk that led to the store's basement. Anthony, a pedestrian, fell into the opening and was injured. Costello had been given specific instructions to close the sidewalk doors after each use. Donovan Plumbing denied responsibility for Costello's negligence, claiming that he had not followed instructions. Donovan Plumbing is responsible. Costello was performing duties within the scope of his employment when he opened the doors. Costello's negligence is Donovan Plumbing's negligence.

11.7 Principal's Responsibility in Selecting Agent

In selecting agents, the principal is obligated to use care and discretion in an effort to hire persons whose references and records of previous employment assure the principal that they will be good risks in dealing with third parties.

EXAMPLE 7. Goddard Shoe Store hired a shoe salesman who applied because he saw a "Help Wanted" sign in the store's window. Goddard Shoe had not investigated the applicant's employment history, which was filled with violent incidents. One day, one of Goddard's customers offended the new clerk, and he slapped her in the face. Goddard denied any responsibility for the clerk's actions, claiming that the private argument between the two had no relation to the store's business or to the clerk's job. Goddard was liable, however, because he had endangered customers (third parties) by hiring an imbalanced individual who had a history of distressing and even injuring others. Goddard should have investigated the man's employment record and either not hired him or employed him in an area where he would not come into frequent contact with other people.

11.8 Responsibility for Negligence of Independent Contractor

In most cases, the principal is not responsible to third parties for injuries resulting from the negligence of an independent contractor. The principal must, however, use care in selecting a reputable contractor.

EXAMPLE 8. Jolly hired Acme Plumbing Contractors to connect his home's plumbing to the county sewer line. Acme left an open and unguarded trench adjacent to the roadway when they finished their first day of work on the job. Adams, walking along the road at night, fell into the ditch. Adams sued Jolly for damages. Adams will not recover against Jolly. Acme Plumbing worked as an independent contractor and thereby accepted full responsibility for any injuries caused by their work.

11.9 Principal's Obligations for Torts of Independent Agents

A principal is not responsible for damages resulting from the ordinary torts of salespeople who: (1) work on a commission basis *and* (2) are not under the direct supervision of the principal *and* (3) provide their own transportation without reimbursement *and* (4) work according to their own time schedules.

EXAMPLE 9. Harvey sold vacuum cleaners for the SewVac Company. He was paid a commission, worked a protected territory, chose his own work schedule, and made calls in his own car at his own expense. Harvey struck and injured a pedestrian as he was hurrying to keep a sales appointment. The injured woman sued Sew Vac. Harvey was an independent contractor in his type of employment. The third party had no right of action against the principal. Action must be brought against Harvey.

11.10 Passenger-Guest Statutes

A *passenger-guest,* under the guest statutes now in force in many states, may not recover damages for injuries resulting from the driver's negligence unless such negligence was gross and amounted to wanton and intentional misconduct.

EXAMPLE 10. Hilyard took Sanford, his date, to a drive-in movie. During the evening, Hilyard drank heavily and became intoxicated. Against Sanford's wishes, Hilyard insisted on driving her home. In an accident, the car was thrown into a bridge abutment, and Sanford was seriously injured. Because of his gross negligence, Hilyard will be held responsible for damages; he will not have the usual protection given by the guest statutes.

11.11 Liability of Agent of Undisclosed Principal

An agent acting for an undisclosed principal may be held personally liable for all acts and promises made to a third party who is unaware of the existing principal-agent relationship.

EXAMPLE 11. Freund was anxious to purchase a property adjacent to his estate. Fearing that the owner would inflate the price if approached by him, Freund appointed Rawley as his agent to make the purchase. Rawley's authority was spelled out in an agreement both signed and sealed by Freund. Rawley was sworn to secrecy and he agreed to make the purchase in his own name. After the contract with the neighbor was made, Freund backed out. Rawley was sued by the seller. Rawley is vulnerable in a suit for damages because it was Rawley's contract, reputation, and assurances that encouraged the neighbor to sell. Rawley, of course, armed with the contract with Freund, may in turn sue Freund.

11.12 Right of Third Party to Sue Agent of Undisclosed Principal

A third party who discovers that an agent had worked for an undisclosed principal may opt to sue either the agent or the principal, depending on which gives greater promise of a successful judgment and satisfaction after a judgment.

EXAMPLE 12. Churchman operated a farm for its owner, Stanbridge. Churchman was known by all local business people as the owner as well as operator of the farm. Stanbridge never visited the area and his name was never used in connection with agreements related to the farm's operation. Churchman ordered ten tons of fertilizer from Ridgley Farm Supply. When Churchman did not pay, Ridgley Farm Supply sued him. Search of the records of the county recorder by Ridgley's attorney disclosed that Stanbridge was the owner of the operation. Ridgley Farm Supply might have better success in collecting a judgment from the previously undisclosed principal than from Churchman. A suit against Stanbridge would probably be the better decision, but a suit against Churchman would also be allowed.

EXAMPLE 13. Suppose, in Example 12, that when Churchman was requested to pay the fertilizer bill he issued a note, signing his own name as maker. Churchman did not honor the note on the due date, and Ridgley Farm Supply sued Stanbridge after learning his identity. Stanbridge will not be liable on the note. This is Churchman's personal note, and he alone will be held accountable.

11.13 Husband's Liability for Wife's Torts

A husband is not liable for damages resulting from his wife's torts unless he aided his wife in the commission of the tort or openly condoned her acts. A tort action against a husband and wife for damages resulting from the use of a motor vehicle may involve both parties when both are joined as owners of the damaging vehicle.

EXAMPLE 14. While Sewell was at work, his wife became engaged in a heated argument with the wife of a neighbor. Both women, in a fit of rage, struck one another. Each caused injuries to the other. Mr. Sewell was sued by the neighbor, and a countersuit was entered against the neighbor's husband for injuries to Mrs. Sewell. In this case, neither husband can be a party to the actions as a defendant for the injuries inflicted by his wife. While a wife is the agent of her husband in many respects, she is not within the scope of authority *or* employment when battling with other persons.

11.14 Liability for Children's Torts

Parents, in the absence of corrective statutes, are not responsible for the torts of their children except when the children are in their *tender years*—are less than seven years of age. Only if the parents instruct or guide the child in the commission of a tort are they liable.

EXAMPLE 15. Robert, age 13, batted a ball that went through a neighbor's $300 picture window. The accident was neither willful nor intentional. Robert's parents were sued for the expense of replacing the window. The parents are not responsible. The boy was not acting as their agent in playing ball. Suit could be made only against the boy.

EXAMPLE 16. Suppose Robert, in Example 15, admitted that he did not like the neighbor and in hitting the ball he hoped that it would break her window. Today, many states have legislation making parents liable for such a *malicious tort* of one of their minor children. These laws set limits of responsibility, usually not more than $300 for any one tort. Under this law, parents are held accountable to the injured third party to the amount permitted by statute.

AGENT AND THIRD PARTY

11.15 Agent's Responsibility for Principal's Breach of Contract

An agent working within the scope of his or her authority will not be liable if a principal breaches a contract made for and in the name of the principal.

EXAMPLE 17. Wayne represented Eastern Shore Canneries in contracting with farmers for the purchase of green beans, peas, tomatoes, and other field crops. Wayne, as an agent, signed all contracts in the firm's name. Because of an extra-large crop, Eastern Shore Canneries refused delivery of 2,500 baskets of ripe tomatoes. A farmer sued Wayne for the breach. Only Eastern, the principal, may be sued by third parties in this situation. The agent's relationship with the third party had been honest, truthful, and in good faith at all times.

11.16 Liability of Agents Who Hold Themselves Out as Principals

Third parties may seek damages from agents who falsely represent themselves as principals. Third parties may also seek damages against agents who admit that they represent others but refuse to disclose the names of their principals.

EXAMPLE 18. Morris negotiated with Hawthorne Jewelry Stores for the purchase of precious gems the store was selling for the Hubert Estate. The amount of money involved made it obvious that Morris was not buying for himself, but for some unnamed other person. Morris signed contracts that were later breached, when Morris's principal failed to give him funds at the time of settlement. Morris was personally liable to Hawthorne, the third party, for any damages resulting in the breach. Morris, of course, could seek a recovery from the principal if proof of their relationship existed.

11.17 Agent's Liability for Unauthorized Statements

Agents may be held liable for any statements they mistakenly or willfully make outside the authority granted by the principal.

EXAMPLE 19. Miller requested Allied Sales to sell his television at a price of no less than $200. One of Allied's salesmen secured a buyer by mistakenly offering the set for $100. Miller refused to let the set be sold at that price, and the interested buyer sued Allied Sales for damages caused by the salesman's mistake. Allied Sales was held liable.

11.18 Agent's Contracts in Name of Incompetent Principal

An agent may be held personally liable for agreements made on behalf of a principal who is declared insane by civil authorities. Lack of knowledge of the insanity decree does not give the agent a defense against damages claimed by an injured third party. Representing one declared insane is little different from representing one who is deceased. Neither is competent to make contracts of any kind. It is an agent's responsibility to discover a potential principal's competence to contract.

EXAMPLE 20. Curtis, declared insane by a state court but rational in all outward respects, illegally drove a car titled in his name to a used-car lot. He asked the car-lot dealer to sell it for $1,800. The dealer agreed and secured a buyer. Curtis's legal guardian learned of the transaction, canceled the agreement, and demanded the return of the car. The dealer may be held responsible to the purchaser of the car.

11.19 Collusion of Principal and Agent

An agent who willingly joins a principal in a fraud as a means of securing a third party's agreement may be held personally liable to the third party for damages resulting from the fraud.

EXAMPLE 21. Parkinson appointed Thrush, a licensed real estate salesman, to sell his house. Parkinson disclosed to Thrush that the house was infested with termites but that their presence could be concealed from any potential buyer. With this knowledge, Thrush negotiated a contract of sale with Higgins. After moving into the house, Higgins discovered the fraud and sued Thrush. Because he *knowingly* and *willfully* participated in the concealment, Thrush made himself personally liable for the buyer's proven damages.

11.20 Responsibility of Agent for Willful or Negligent Acts

Third parties have a right of action against either a principal or an agent for the agent's willful or negligent acts performed while working within the scope of employment. An agent who leaves the scope of employment and authority is solely responsible for his or her acts.

EXAMPLE 22. Hubbard Grocery employed Richards as a delivery truck driver. While intoxicated, Richards exceeded a local speed limit by 20 m.p.h. and ran the truck off the road. It hit a frame house and caused $8,000 in property damage. The owner of the property sued Richards, who was known to have assets out of which a judgment might be collected. Richards is guilty of the commission of a tort for which he may be held liable. (The third party could have elected to sue Hubbard, the principal.)

EXAMPLE 23. Suppose Richards drove the truck to a part of the town in which there were no deliveries to be made. He picked up friends and took off on a joy ride. Richards thus left the scope of authority and employment. A damage suit resulting from an accident under these circumstances would fall solely on the agent, with no responsibility to the principal. (State laws differ as to the liability of those involved in motor vehicle accidents and must be consulted in cases of this kind.)

11.21 Liability for Damages if Agent Was Not Negligent

An agent is not liable to third parties for damages in which the agent is not found to be negligent or intentionally harmful. Damages imputed to the principal's negligence may not be transferred to an agent who has no knowledge or intent of wrongdoing.

EXAMPLE 24. Industrial Painting Contractors hired Thornton to burn off blistered paint on the Haley Building. Thornton was given equipment, including a twenty-pound tank of LP gas, a hose, and torches. While Thornton was working, the tank exploded and caused a fire that burned down the Haley Building. Thornton was not aware of a defect in the tank. (Industrial, however, had been warned of the defect by a former employee.) Thornton is free of liability. Only Industrial is responsible for the third party's loss.

11.22 Agent's Right of Suit for Third Party's Breach of Contract

An agent has no right of suit against a third party who has breached an agreement made on behalf of a known principal. An agent is not in *privity* and has no actual *property right* in the principal's contract.

EXAMPLE 25. Andover acted for Whann in the sale of Whann's used living-room suite. The agreement was signed by the buyer and by Andover, as agent for Whann. The buyer breached the agreement, and Andover tried to sue him. Andover's suit would not be allowed because he had no real interest in the agreement. Only Whann may enter the case as a plaintiff.

11.23 Right of Suit by Agent of Undisclosed Principal

An agent acting for an undisclosed principal has the right to sue a third party who has breached a contract made with the agent. This is true even if the third party has been made aware that the agent represents someone else.

EXAMPLE 26. Coleman acted for Kauffman in securing the purchase of Cedar Grove Estates. Owners of Cedar Grove had an intense dislike for Kauffman and would not have sold to Coleman had he disclosed that he worked for Kauffman. After all contracts were signed, Cedar Grove's owners discovered that the property would go to Kauffman. They refused to deliver a deed. Coleman may sue Cedar Grove in his own name.

11.24 Agent's Right to Protect Bailed Property

Agents may not seek damages from third parties on contracts made in the name of a principal. Agents may, however, demand protection of their rights as bailees when the principal's goods are removed from the agent's possession by illegal and unwarranted acts of third parties.

EXAMPLE 27. Poland worked as a salesman for the Strassburg Jewelry Company. He carried expensive samples on his rounds. The samples were stolen from his car. They were later found to have been bought by Taylor, an innocent purchaser. Taylor refused to give up the jewelry to Poland, claiming that Poland was only an agent and not the owner of the jewelry. Poland's responsibilities as a bailee give him the right to demand from Taylor the return of the jewelry.

11.25 Injuries Caused Agent by Third Party

An agent has the right of recovery against third parties who have caused the agent injury. Another source of recovery may be workmen's compensation, through the employers' obligations to employees. (See Chapter 13.)

EXAMPLE 28. Whittington worked in a printing shop. One of his jobs was to trim and square printed booklets on a paper cutter. The new paper cutter, because of a defect, closed on Whittington's hand and removed the ends of two of his fingers. Whittington chose to sue the machine's manufacturer (a third party), under the law of product liability, rather than accept settlement under workmen's compensation laws. (This is a right provided to persons other than the buyer when manufactured products fail to perform properly and cause injury to a person other than the buyer.)

PRINCIPAL AND AGENT

11.26 Agent's Obligations to Principal

An agent is obligated to follow the instructions given to him or her by the principal. Failure to follow instructions makes the agent liable to the principal for damages that might result. General agents have more latitude in decision-making than do other agents, but they must still keep their decisions within the reasonable bounds of the principal's instructions. Similarly, gratuitous agents are not excused from this duty to follow the principal's instructions, but they do not have to *continue* to perform promised services because there is no consideration that binds them to service.

EXAMPLE 29. Woodring worked as an outside salesman for the Home Products Company. He was given specific instructions that prices could be discounted no more than 10 percent in any attempt to close a sale under difficult competitive conditions. In one sale, Woodring gave a customer a 20-percent discount to meet the offer of a competing salesman. The cash loss to Home Products amounted to $38.50. Woodring had not followed instructions and thus made himself responsible to Home Products for the $38.50 loss.

EXAMPLE 30. Elliott, general manager of Koleman Kitchen Kontractors, had instructions to clear all prospective employees through the firm's regional office in Detroit before hiring them. As the result of an intensive advertising campaign of the firm's products and services, Elliott was faced with the immediate need for an assistant in the shipping department. He hired Godfrey on a day-to-day basis, at $30 a day. Elliott had not followed his principal's instructions. However, his responsibilities as general manager, the need for immediate additional help, and the benefit resulting to the principal would excuse him for his acts.

11.27 Agent's Delegation of Duties to Subagent

An agent may delegate duties to a subagent except in contracts for personal services of a professional nature or those involving personal choice.

EXAMPLE 31. Arnold agreed to paint the exterior of Abram's house. Arnold hired Seybrand, another painter, to do part of the work. Delegation of part of the work to the subagent was within Arnold's agency powers.

EXAMPLE 32. Consuelo, a portrait painter, was commissioned to do a portrait of the president of the First National Bank. Consuelo did the basic painting and hired Grohs, an apprentice painter, to do the background and fill-in work. Consuelo exceeded his authority in delegating part of such professional work to another.

11.28 Using Agency for Personal Gain

An agent must exercise loyalty and good faith in all services for the principal. The agent may not use the agency relationship for personal profit or self-interest.

EXAMPLE 33. Stahl worked as a salesman for Avenue Used Cars. A customer told Stahl that she wanted to buy a good used Volkswagen. Stahl took advantage of the buyer's interest and sold her his own Volkswagen. Stahl violated his responsibilities to Avenue Used Cars. He could be held liable for losses that developed because he had served his self-interest when he should have been representing the principal.

11.29 Agent's Duty to Keep Principal Informed

An agent is obligated to the principal for any damages resulting from giving the principal false information or failing to give the principal information important to the principal's business.

EXAMPLE 34. Hershey was employed as a bookkeeper by Henry Brothers. Hershey's friend Arnold owed Henry Brothers $350. Arnold's account was listed in the company's ledgers, but Hershey never included it in the monthly report of bills past due. Arnold's unpaid account finally passed the statute of limitations period, which rendered any claims for payment voidable by Arnold. Hershey had concealed information valuable to her employer. Hershey could thus be held liable for the company's loss of $350.

11.30 Agent's Right to Remuneration from Both Principal and Third Party

Agents may not accept remuneration or commission from both the principal and a third party. The agent cannot be loyal to two parties in the same transaction. The only exception to this rule is when both the principal and the third party are aware that the other is giving compensation to the agent.

EXAMPLE 35. Brooks Realty Company received a request from Hinkson to seek out a particular kind of house for her. Hinkson agreed to pay Brooks $200 for this service. Brooks already listed a property, owned by Minotti, of the type Hinkson desired. Brooks sold Hinkson the house, receiving a sales commission from Minotti and the $200 from Hinkson. Both Hinkson and Minotti have a rightful claim against Brooks because Brooks failed to advise each party that he was working for the other.

11.31 Agent's Obligation of Good Faith and Loyalty to Principal

An agent may not buy property of the principal for the agent's own profit and benefit. Competing with the principal in any way violates the agent's obligation of good faith and loyalty.

EXAMPLE 36. Toulson worked as a saleswoman for Colonial Antiques. Colonial held several valuable pieces of furniture in its shop. The pieces were priced very attractively in a competitive market. Toulson made a pretense of buying the pieces for her own home. Actually, she was buying them for resale to a collector, who paid her a price that gave her a 50-percent profit. Colonial Antiques may seek damages from Toulson. She had used her position of trust for her self-interest and personal advantage.

11.32 Agent's Obligation to Exercise Care, Skill, and Diligence

An agent must render services with the care, skill, and diligence reasonably expected of other persons rendering service in the same type of work. The agent is personally liable to the principal for damages resulting from a lack of the skill indicated by the agent in applying for employment.

EXAMPLE 37. Central T.V. & Appliance hired Mears, who had answered the store's advertisement for an experienced television mechanic. Mears indicated knowledge and skill in the repair of both black-and-white and color television sets. If Mears damaged sets owned by Central's customers because he lacked reasonable and ordinary skills, he could be held liable by Central for losses that developed through third-party complaints.

11.33 Agent's Obligation to Keep Accurate Records for Principal

An agent is responsible to the principal for keeping accurate records and accounts of all monies handled in connection with the principal's business. Failure on the part of the agent to keep such records makes the agent liable in damages for the amount of any resulting losses.

EXAMPLE 38. Coppock made c.o.d. deliveries for Halda's Market. The amounts he collected daily were often more than $1,200. In a hurry to finish up his work one day, Coppock failed to record the amounts paid by various customers. Halda's Market was not able to accurately record payments in its books. Coppock is fully responsible to Halda's Market for losses resulting from his failure to perform his duties and follow instructions with care and diligence.

11.34 Principal's Obligation to Compensate Agent

A principal, except in gratuitous agency agreements, has an obligation to compensate the agent for services rendered. If the amount of compensation has not been predetermined by contract, it should be in an amount deemed reasonable and proper in the market place.

EXAMPLE 39. Parklyn Theatre hired Maloney, a projectionist, for three evenings because the regular projectionist was ill. No agreement was made determining Maloney's pay. At the end of the three days, Parklyn's manager handed Maloney a check for $20. Maloney may ask for more reasonable compensation, basing his request on the sum usually paid projectionists in the area in which he worked.

11.35 Agent's Right to Reimbursement for Reasonable Expenses

The principal is obligated to reimburse the agent for reasonable expenses incurred by the agent in carrying out the principal's instructions.

EXAMPLE 40. Pollard was asked to represent the Holland Florist Shop at the regional meeting of the National Florists Association. Travel expenses in Pollard's own car and his hotel and meal expenses totaled $225. Pollard also submitted a bill for $55 for a new tire to replace one that blew out during the trip to the meeting. The $225 expense is justified. The $55 for the tire may be questioned by Holland on the grounds that it was not justified as part of Pollard's immediate and necessary expense in attending the meeting.

11.36 Principal's Responsibility for Agent's Injuries and Losses

The principal must indemnify the agent for losses resulting from and directly related to the agent's activity in carrying out the principal's instructions.

EXAMPLE 41. Suppose, in Example 40, that Pollard was made ill from food eaten at the Association's banquet. A doctor's visit and medicines cost Pollard $35. Pollard, as agent, would be justified in asking Holland for indemnification for these expenses. If damages were proven, the principal (Holland) would be justified in seeking payment from the hotel on grounds of negligence in food preparation.

11.37 Agent's Right of Lien

An agent has the right of lien against the principal's property for money owed the agent by the principal. This is also known as a *bailee's right of lien.*

EXAMPLE 42. Cleveland Auto Sales hired Reardon to drive to Detroit in his own car to pick up certain documents. Reardon was to turn over the documents to Cleveland on his return. Cleveland refused to compensate Reardon for his time and expenses when he came back from Detroit. Reardon had a right to retain the principal's property until payment was made. (Had Reardon originally agreed to be paid at some later date, he would have waived this right of lien.)

11.38 Agency Coupled with an Interest

Agency agreements may be terminated at any time. The principal may terminate the agent's employment with or without reason. An agency terminated without cause may give the agent the right to seek damages for breach of an executory contract.

The principal may not terminate an agent's contract, however, where there is an *agency coupled with an interest.* The interest may be either in the authority or in the subject matter. An *interest in authority* exists when an agent has been given authority by the principal to collect funds owed to the principal and to retain the funds in payment of a debt owed to the agent by the principal. An *interest in the subject matter* exists when the agent has a lien on the principal's property as security for a debt and is then appointed to sell the property and retain the money received to extinguish the principal's debt.

EXAMPLE 43. Hempstead Apartments, Inc., owed Blackburn $5,000 for tax and accounting services Blackburn had performed. Blackburn was given authority to collect rents to liquidate the $5,000 debt. Blackburn's agency was *coupled with an interest* (an interest in *authority*). Hempstead may not terminate the agency until Blackburn has collected sufficient rentals to cover the $5,000 owed plus the expense of collecting the money.

EXAMPLE 44. Hargrove was employed as an agent by Dorado Properties, Inc., after he loaned Dorado $10,000. He received as security a mortgage containing a clause authorizing him, in case of default on the debt, to sell the mortgaged property. Dorado has in this case given Hargrove an immediate legal interest in the *subject matter* of the agency, which cannot be taken away. Dorado may not terminate the agency. In a situation such as this, Hargrove may proceed with a sale of the property *in his own name*. (If only the agency had been given Hargrove as security for the loan, he would, in case of default, have to exercise his authority in the name of the principal.)

Solved Problems

11.1 Saylor, an attorney, acted as an escrow agent by holding the new deed to Fisher's house, which was being sold to Landers, until Landers tendered his certified check for the purchase price of the house. Is Saylor the agent of Landers or Fisher?

An *escrow holder* (or *escrow agent*) is not really the agent of either the seller or the buyer in the ordinary definition of agency. Saylor, as escrow holder, is not under the control of either Landers or Fisher. Saylor must abide only by the agreement made between Landers and Fisher. However, if Landers tenders his check, Saylor will become his agent and will either deliver or hold the deed for Landers. If Landers fails to tender his check, Saylor becomes the agent of Fisher and holds or returns the deed according to Fisher's wishes.

11.2 Sanders Construction Corporation loaned a front-end loader and an operator to the Haber Company for one day. The agreed-on price was $230. Haber was to direct all work performed by the operator. The operator's lack of attention to Haber's instructions resulted in serious damage to the foundation of a building adjoining Haber's work area. The owners of the damaged building sued Sanders for the negligence of his agent, the operator of the machine. Is the Sanders Construction Corporation liable?

No. The problem comes within the area of the so-called *loaned servant* doctrines. The party obligated to the owner of the damaged building is the one under whose control and supervision the agent was working when the damage was done. Haber had full control and gave the operator all instructions. This made Haber responsible for the damage.

11.3 Suppose, in Problem 11.2, that Sanders provided the machine and the operator to do work for Haber, but that Haber did nothing more than point out to the operator where there was work to be done. Haber did not give specific instructions and did not keep close to the job and direct the operator in his task. Would the decision be the same as in Problem 11.2?

In this case, the operator continues to be the agent of Sanders. Haber has not intervened as a principal. Sanders's relationship to Haber is analogous to that of an independent contractor, not an agent. Sanders, in this case, would be liable for damages caused by his own employee.

11.4 Mrs. Lawlor had been separated from her husband for a period of three months because of domestic problems. Lawlor failed to provide his wife with the necessities of life during this period. Mrs. Lawlor purchased food and necessary winter clothing and billed these items to her husband. He informed creditors that he no longer lived with his wife and that he was not responsible for the contracts made by her. Was Mrs. Lawlor an agent of her husband in making these purchases?

Yes. A husband continues to be responsible for his wife's necessaries if they are separated. Failure to provide necessaries permits a wife to make purchases for her personal welfare as an agent of her husband.

11.5 Foster was authorized by Pennington to purchase a five-acre tract from Berl. Pennington warned Foster that he did not want his name used in connection with the purchase. Foster made the purchase, informing the seller that he was representing a principal without disclosing the principal's name. When Berl later learned from Foster that Pennington was the principal, he brought action against Pennington for Foster's breach of contract. Pennington's defense was based on the claim that he could not be made a party to a suit on a contract he did not sign. Was Pennington correct?

No. When the principal's identity is learned, the third party may opt to sue either the agent or the principal. Although Pennington's *name* did not enter negotiations, Berl did know that Foster was representing a principal. Even though the agent later exceeded his authority by disclosing the name of the principal to the third party, the principal will nevertheless be liable.

11.6 Argo was sued by a third party on a contract she had made in her own name. The contract was actually made for Roberts, Argo's undisclosed principal. Does the plaintiff (the third party) have rights against both the agent and the undisclosed principal? What are the three options open to the third party as plaintiff?

Yes. (1) If during the trial the identity of the principal is disclosed and made known to the third party (the plaintiff) for the first time, the third party has the option of continuing the suit against the agent or dropping that suit and commencing an action against the principal. (2) If the third party discovers the identity of the undisclosed principal after the final judgment has been made but before the judgment has been paid, then the plaintiff may, in most states, discharge the action against the agent at this point and commence suit against the now-disclosed principal. (3) If the third party discovers the identity of the undisclosed principal after judgment has been made and satisfied by the agent, the third party may not seek a judgment against the previously undisclosed principal.

11.7 Geiss was an agent for Carlisle, an undisclosed principal. Geiss agreed to make a cash payment for merchandise he bought for Carlisle. Payment was promised for April 15. Geiss failed to tender the money owed, and the seller canceled the contract on the grounds of Geiss's breach. Now Carlisle, the undisclosed principal, offers payment to the third party and demands delivery. Is the third party now responsible to Carlisle?

No. The seller negotiated with Geiss, knowing nothing of Carlisle. The third party has no obligation to a principal who had never been even partially disclosed. The breach by Geiss was sufficient reason for the seller to cancel.

11.8 Crossan was an agent of Market Motors. He accompanied Howard on a test drive of a used car offered for sale to Howard. Howard's negligence resulted in an accident that injured Crossan. From whom may Crossan seek damages for injuries and expenses related to the accident?

The agent has the option of suing the third party (Howard) in a tort action for negligence. Crossan may also demand indemnification of damages from the principal, Market Motors.

11.9 Anderson Contractors asked its office manager, Reilly, to purchase a typewriter and an adding machine for use in the office. Reilly had both items at her home. She took them to the office, pretended that they were purchased from an office supply house, and submitted a bill of $237.50. Anderson discovered that Reilly was acting for herself in this transaction. What are the rights of the principal in this situation?

An agent must at all times be loyal to the principal and act in good faith in all matters connected to the principal-agent relationship. The agent may not use her position for her own benefit and profit. Reilly did not inform the principal of the fact that the machines being purchased were her own property. Anderson would be under no obligation to keep or pay for the machines.

11.10 City Credit Associates hired Groom as a collection agent. Groom made regular collections each week on a list provided by City Credit. In turning in receipts on one day's collections, Groom was unable to account for collections and for his own funds, which had been intermingled with City Credit's money. What are the principal's rights in this matter?

An agent must make an accounting to the principal for all funds handled for the principal. When the agent's personal funds are intermingled with those of the principal and separation cannot be made, all of the funds become the property of the principal. Groom therefore has no right to any of the funds in his immediate possession.

11.11 Callahan worked as a helper for Minotti Plumbing Services. Callahan spoke with Minotti's customers, warning them that they might be overcharged when they received their bills for work done. Callahan had no grounds on which to base such statements. What are the rights of the principal?

Callahan has displayed an attitude of disloyalty to his principal. He had no grounds for the statements he made. Neither was it his duty to speak to customers about the practices followed by his employer. Callahan has breached his duty of loyalty and good faith to Minotti Plumbing Services and would be subject to dismissal.

11.12 Ludwig left his car with Midtown Motors. The company had agreed to do needed body and fender work for which they had given Ludwig an estimate. Midtown sent the car out to a body and fender shop that did the actual work. The work was poorly done, and the car was further damaged through efforts to improve its appearance. Midtown denied any responsibility, claiming that Ludwig should seek damages from the body and fender shop, not from Midtown. What are Ludwig's rights?

An agent may delegate work to a subagent except in those cases where performance is of a professional or artistic nature. Midtown had the right to delegate performance of the body and fender work to another. However, as agent, Midway is directly responsible to Ludwig for the work done by the subagent. Ludwig's damages are the responsibility of Midway. Midway, in turn, may seek damages from the body and fender shop that actually did the work.

11.13 Katz was employed as a general purchasing agent for Kauffman & Company. Kelley, a salesman for the Manufacturer Supply Corporation, gave Katz and his family free use of an ocean-front vacation cottage for the month of August. Katz responded to this favor by giving preference to Manufacturer Supply's bids over those submitted by competitors. What were Katz's obligation in this situation?

Agents are not permitted to use their positions for their own profit and benefit. The position of the principal must be considered first. Katz's acceptance of the cottage placed him in a position that may have deprived him of the freedom of choice required in his purchasing job. Katz has exceeded his authority in his acts and may be liable to discipline or discharge by the principal.

11.14 Bleyer worked as an auditor for Slay & Company. He visited the firm's branch offices in many parts of the country. On one trip, Bleyer purchased first-class airline reservations and hired a chauffered Lincoln Continental from a car agency located at the airport. Bleyer's employer refused to approve payment for these items on the expense account. Must Slay & Company reimburse Bleyer for his expenses?

The principal must reimburse its agents for reasonable and necessary expenses related to the performance of the agent's instructions. Ordinary practice would have required Bleyer to reserve tourist-class, not first-class, airline accommodations and to rent a car that would have provided him with safe and comfortable transportation, not with luxury travel. Slay & Company would reimburse Bleyer only for an amount that would have provided what was necessary and reasonable.

11.15 Schenck Milling Company authorized Juhrgen to purchase, on the open market, 10,000 bushels of wheat at not more than $3.15 per bushel. Juhrgen was able to purchase the wheat for $3.32 a bushel, a price he was advised would be the bottom price available during the year. Schenck Milling was held to the agreement signed by Juhrgen. What are Juhrgen's obligations to the principal?

An agent is obligated to the principal for all damages that result when the agent exceeds the authority given by the principal. Juhrgen, although acting in good faith and with the intention of benefiting the principal, had exceeded his authority in obligating the principal to a price over $3.15 per bushel. Juhrgen had *apparent authority* to make such an agreement, and thus the seller had a right to hold Schenck Milling Company to the $3.32 price. Juhrgen himself is liable to Schenck.

11.16 Barlow was a wholesale shoe salesman for the Brockton Shoe Company. He carried sample shoes on visits to retailers in the area assigned to him. In an effort to please a new customer, Barlow sold him twelve pairs of expensive sample shoes for $25. Barlow had no authority to do this. Brockton Shoe Company brought an action of replevin against the buyer for the return of the shoes. May the third party refuse to give up possession of the shoes purchased?

No. Shoe buyers in the retail trade should be aware that wholesale representatives do not have the authority to sell and transfer title to the samples they carry. Thus, the third party (the buyer) was not actually an innocent purchaser, with no knowledge of a defect in the sale. The buyer would be obligated to give up possession of the shoes. (The buyer would be reimbursed for the $25 paid the agent.)

11.17 Ream was under contract as an engineering representative for the Petroleum Products Company. Two years before the expiration of his contract, Ream was induced to break the contract and become a salesman for a competing firm. Petroleum Products sought damages from the third party who caused the breach of the employment contract. Will Ream's former principal recover on this claim?

Third parties are responsible for damages when they induce an agent to break a valid executory employment or agency contract. Ream, as agent, is directly responsible for breaching his agreement, but the third party is also responsible for having alienated the agent from his previous employer.

11.18 Keith acted as agent for Blythe. He was under written authority to purchase a new car for Blythe. Keith bought the car, signing Blythe's name and his own as agent. Blythe rescinded the agreement under her right as a minor. (She was only 17 years old.) Is Keith, as agent, in any way liable to the car agency?

Yes. An agent contracting for another makes an implied warranty that the principal represented is capable and competent to contract. Keith would be responsible to the seller for damages resulting from failure to disclose that he was working for a minor.

11.19 Wayne worked as a foreman for the Square D Ranch. In many ways, he was in charge of ranch operations. Eastern Provision Company, through its representative, contracted with Wayne for the purchase of 300 head of Black Angus cattle. The cattle were to be shipped to Eastern's receiving yard in Lancaster, Pennsylvania. Square D Ranch refused to approve the contract, and Eastern thus sued the ranch on a breach of contract. What are Eastern's rights?

Third parties dealing with an agent often have an obligation to confirm the agent's authority. Reasonable conditions, the custom of the market place, previous negotiations, and other circumstances determine the obligation to check with a principal. Eastern Provision should have concluded that a ranch foreman did not have even apparent authority to contract to sell livestock from the ranch. Square D Ranch would, in all probability, be relieved of any obligations under this agreement.

Review Problems

11.20 How does collusion between an agent and a third party affect the obligations of a principal?

11.21 What obligation does a principal have to a third party for the wrongful acts of someone hired by the principal's general agent?

11.22 May duties of a nonprofessional nature be delegated by an agent to a subagent?

11.23 Is a principal responsible for third-party damages caused by an agent working outside the scope of authority but within the scope of employment?

11.24 How are independent contractors different from ordinary agents in obligating a principal for damages caused to a third party?

11.25 What are the three courses of action open to an injured third party who is seeking recovery from the agent of an undisclosed principal?

11.26 Is a wife the agent of her husband in *all* contracts made by the wife with third parties?

11.27 Are parents responsible for the torts of their children after the children have reached the age of seven?

11.28 Is an agent responsible for damages to third parties when the damages are the result of the principal's lack of competence to contract?

11.29 May an agent be held liable for damages to third parties when the agent has willingly entered into fraudulent schemes with the principal against such third parties?

11.30 Who is responsible for an agent's torts committed outside the agent's scope of employment?

11.31 May an agent working for an undisclosed principal sue a third party on an agreement made for the undisclosed principal?

11.32 Are gratuitous agents excused from damages resulting from failure to follow the principal's instructions?

11.33 Under what circumstances may an agent accept remuneration from both the principal and the third party?

11.34 To what degree of skill is an agent held in the performance of duties for a principal?

11.35 What is the difference between *reimbursement* and *indemnification* as related to a principal's obligations to an agent?

11.36 Does an agent ever have the right of lien over goods owned by the principal but in the agent's rightful possession?

11.37 What is an *agency coupled with an interest?*

Answers to Review Problems

11.20 A principal is not bound by any agreements made in his or her name by an agent and a third party who are working in collusion.

11.21 The principal is obligated as if he or she had hired the subagent directly.

11.22 Yes.

11.23 Yes.

11.24 The principal is *not* liable for the torts of an independent contractor who is acting within the scope of employment. The principal *is* liable for torts of ordinary agents acting within the scope of employment.

11.25 (1) A third party suing an agent may drop that suit and instead sue the previously undisclosed principal, whose identity is disclosed in the course of the trial. (2) After judgment has been rendered but before collection has been made, the third party may waive rights under the judgment and proceed against the now-disclosed principal. (3) If a judgment has been rendered and collection has been made, the third party must accept the judgment and may not then proceed against the now-disclosed principal.

11.26 No.

11.27 No, but special legislation in most states does place limited responsibility on parents for the *malicious torts* of their children.

11.28 Yes.

11.29 Yes.

11.30 Only the agent is responsible.

11.31 Yes, because it is the agent's contract.

11.32 No. Their responsibilities and liabilities are no different from those of other agents in this respect.

11.33 The agent must inform both the principal and third party of the payments from the other.

11.34 The agent must show skill equal to that of persons of reasonable ability in the same trade, business, or profession.

11.35 An agent is *reimbursed* for those expenses necessary and reasonable in carrying out the principal's instructions. An agent is *indemnified*, or paid for, any injuries or damages suffered by the agent in carrying out the principal's instructions.

11.36 Yes. When the principal has not reimbursed and/or indemnified the agent for money owed the agent in connection with assigned duties, the agent may retain possession of the principal's property already in the agent's rightful possession until payment is made.

11.37 It is an agent's interest either in the *authority* or in the *subject matter* of an agency agreement. The agent's interest may involve a right of lien, a security interest in the subject matter of the agency, or authority to collect funds to be applied to a debt owed to the agent by the principal.

Legal Terms

Agency coupled with an interest. An agent's interest in either the authority or the subject matter of an agency agreement; such an agency may not be terminated at will by the principal.

Agent's right of lien. The agent's right to withhold the principal's personal property as security for the payment of compensation owed the agent as a result of the agency agreement.

Delegation. An agent's right to assign to a subagent the performance of work that is not of a professional or artistic nature.

Guest statute. Laws, now in force in many states, prohibiting an injured party's recovery of damages from the driver of a motor vehicle in which the injured party was a guest-passenger.

Undisclosed principal. A principal for whom an agent acts without disclosing to third parties the name or even the existence of the principal; the agent may give the impression that he or she is the principal, and not an agent acting on someone else's behalf.

Chapter 12

Termination of Agency

Agency agreements, like contracts and bailments, are subject to termination. An agency may be terminated by the mutual assent of the principal and the agent or by the decision of one party alone, as long as the other party has no justifiable complaint against termination. Thus, gratuitous agents may choose to terminate their agency obligations at any time except when such termination would do direct damage to a principal.

Agencies may also be terminated by operation of law or by certain changes of circumstance, both of which are reviewed in this chapter.

TERMINATION BY ACTS OF THE PARTIES

12.1 Termination by Original Agreement

A principal and agent may include in their agency agreement conditions of termination related either to time or to performance. In a general agency agreement, there is usually a condition that specifies a date on which the agreement will be either terminated or renewed. Termination of a special agency is usually dependent on the completion of certain tasks to be performed by the special agent.

EXAMPLE 1. Parsons contracted to work as a quality-control inspector for Western Electronics. His job was to approve or reject television components produced for Western by the Hill Products Company. Parsons' contract was for one year. Both parties agreed to negotiate an extension of the agreement at the end of the year if Parsons' skills were still needed. Thus, this agency contract would terminate at the end of one year by terms mutually agreed to in the hiring contract.

EXAMPLE 2. Handy Shoe Stores commissioned Joslin to do a series of twelve advertising layouts to be used in national publications. Joslin was to be paid $1,000 for each layout. All twelve layouts were to be finished and submitted within three months of the date of the agreement. Joslin was a special agent, and termination would coincide with his completion of performance. Although a time limit was included, the agreement could be terminated in a shorter period if the work were submitted and approved before the three months had elapsed.

12.2 Termination by Subsequent Agreement

The principal and the agent may terminate the agency agreement *at any time* without damage to either party when termination is approved by both. By mutual agreement, either the principal or the agent may secure the other's consent without additional consideration. Consent may also be secured by payment of an amount acceptable to the party whose agency is being terminated.

EXAMPLE 3. Darlington agreed to work for three months as a lifeguard at Ocean City. Two weeks after he began his duties at the beach, Darlington was offered another job that gave him a full-time career opportunity. Another guard was secured to take Darlington's place, and he was released from any further obligations on the three-month contract.

EXAMPLE 4. Dukes was under contract to the TriState Broadcasting Company to head up a news team. She was responsible for preparing and presenting two news reports each day. An agency contract for eighteen months was signed. Ten months later, Dukes agreed to accept a $15,000 cash settlement for her release of TriState from the remaining eight months of their existing agency agreement.

12.3 Termination by Breach

Termination without mutual consent is a breach of an agency agreement. The breaching party is subject to a claim for money damages resulting from the termination.

EXAMPLE 5. Padgett was employed under a three-year contract as general manager of the Tower Brand Cannery. Without cause, Padgett was relieved of his job. The daughter of a principal stockholder was appointed to his position. Padgett may claim damages equivalent to the amount of money he would have been paid if the contract continued for the three-year period.

12.4 Damage Limitations to Discharged Agent

A discharged agent may seek damages from a breaching principal. However, the agent must deduct from the total damages sought any income derived from employment secured elsewhere for the duration of the breached agreement. A discharged agent need not accept employment in fields not directly related to his or her skills and training. However, discharged agents who do not accept reasonably similar employment may have waived their rights to recovery of damages from the breaching principal.

EXAMPLE 6. Suppose, in Example 5, that Padgett was offered a position as the manager of another cannery within a reasonable distance of his present job. He was to do the same type of work, but at an annual salary $1,500 less than he was paid by Tower. Padgett's damages would be reduced to the difference between the income on this new job and the job he had with Tower.

12.5 Equity Action in Agency

Agents who leave their employment before the expiration of a contract may not be forced back to work by a decree of specific performance issued by a court of equity. (Similarly, a principal may not be forced to continue the employment of an agent.) However, a court of equity may, for the duration of a breached agreement, enjoin a breaching agent from performing for a new principal the same kind of work the agent performed for the original principal. Such an order from a court of equity is called a *restraining injunction*.

EXAMPLE 7. The Selectrons, a nationally known rock band, hired Foley as their lead vocalist under a two-year contract. Foley gained popularity through recordings and television appearances. He left the Selectrons to take a similar spot with another group, which offered him a large increase in salary. The Selectrons could not force Foley to return to his old job, but they could seek an injunction against Foley that would prohibit him from performing with another band for the duration of the contract with the Selectrons. They could also seek money damages from Foley in a court of law.

12.6 Notification of Termination to Third Parties

Revocation of an agent's authority by the principal must be communicated to third parties who might otherwise innocently continue negotiations with the agent. Renunciation by the agent must also be communicated to third parties to protect the principal from the agent's unauthorized and unwarranted acts.

EXAMPLE 8. Appleton Realty employed Peterson as agent for the collection of rents. After six months, Peterson was fired for dishonesty. However, after being discharged, Peterson collected $3,700 in rents, which he did not turn over to Appleton. Neither Peterson nor Appleton told the tenants that Peterson was no longer employed by Appleton. The tenants were therefore innocent of any wrongdoing when they paid Peterson. To protect the realty company's rights, Appleton should have informed the tenants that Peterson was no longer the company's agent. Appleton has no right to collect the $3,700 again from the tenants; the company's only recourse is to seek payment from Peterson.

12.7 Termination by Party's Manifest Acts

Direct communication of renunciation or revocation to a principal or agent is not necessary when the acts of either party manifest an intention to terminate the agency.

EXAMPLE 9. Tobin worked as warehouse manager for the Security Storage Company. Returning from a two-week vacation, Tobin discovered that all locks to the offices had been changed, that he could no longer enter his own office, and that his name had been removed from the door. As a reasonably intelligent person, Tobin would know that his agency had been revoked by Security Storage.

12.8 Agency Coupled with an Interest

A principal may not revoke an agency coupled with an interest. (See Chapter 11, Section 11.38.)

EXAMPLE 10. Consolidated Finance loaned Telford $2,300. As security for the loan, Telford appointed Consolidated as his agent for the collection of debts owed Telford until the $2,300, plus interest, had been liquidated. Telford has no power to revoke Consolidated's authority. Consolidated has an agency coupled with an interest. (In this case, the interest related to authority.)

EXAMPLE 11. Rappaport was in debt to Henry, who had done extensive motor and body work on Rappaport's car. Unable to pay the bill, Rappaport gave Henry authority to sell the car, deduct what was owed, and remit any balance to Rappaport. This, too, is an agency coupled with an interest, but with interest in the subject matter (the car). Rappaport has no power to revoke Henry's authority except by mutual agreement.

12.9 Abandonment of Agency

An agent may terminate or renounce an agency agreement in those cases where the principal makes unfair and unreasonable demands on the agent, beyond the bounds of the agent's obligations.

EXAMPLE 12. O'Donnell worked as a service representative for the New York Electric Company. When hired, he was expected to make ten service calls each day. Other service representatives were dropped from the company's payroll over a period of weeks, increasing O'Donnell's calls to more than twenty per eight-hour day. O'Donnell refused to carry such a work load and resigned without notice. O'Donnell was justified in renouncing his agreement and would not be subjected to the company's claims of resulting damage.

EXAMPLE 13. Suppose, in Example 12, that O'Donnell lost interest in his work and instead of making the ten calls daily, which was reasonable, he deliberately made no more than six each day. O'Donnell, in this situation, would have exposed himself to discharge for unreasonably abandoning his obligations to New York Electric.

TERMINATION BY IMPOSSIBILITY

12.10 Termination by Change in Circumstances

An agent's authority may be terminated temporarily or finally when circumstances that are known or that should have been known to the agent change the intent or the outcome of the agency relationship. The agent is bound to be aware of those facts that anyone in the same trade or profession would be expected to know.

EXAMPLE 14. Mensch authorized Dougherty & Sons, financial investors, to use $100,000 he had deposited with them to make first-mortgage loans. When he deposited the money with the firm, interest rates on mortgage loans were generally running around 6 percent. Soon afterwards, the interest rates increased dramatically to about 9½ percent. Dougherty & Sons, who had not yet invested Mensch's money, would be responsible for knowing about these new, higher rates and for investing Mensch's money accordingly. Care, skill, and diligence, as well as good faith and loyalty, are required of agents.

12.11 Performance of Dependent Acts

An agent is deemed to have notice of termination of authority to carry out instructions that are rendered useless because of surrounding circumstances.

EXAMPLE 15. Connell hired Smith & Smith Plumbing Company to drill an artesian well near his hunting lodge. The well was to supply water to the lodge, which was several miles from existing water mains. Smith & Smith were also instructed to install pipes and fixtures for a new bathroom and a kitchen. They were unsuccessful in drilling for water and, after several attempts, they abandoned that part of the job. They then proceeded to install pipes and fixtures in the house. Authority to do this work would have been terminated. Installing plumbing was an obvious waste because they had had no success in finding water.

12.12 Destruction of Subject Matter

The agent's authority is immediately terminated *without notice* when the subject matter of the agency has been destroyed and is no longer in existence.

EXAMPLE 16. Sun Associates were appointed agents to sell a two-engine aircraft owned by Midwest Sales Corporation. Sun procured a buyer and negotiated a contract according to the agency agreement. Two hours before the sales agreement was signed, and without Sun's knowledge, the aircraft was destroyed by a hurricane at an airport 1,500 miles from its home field. The contract negotiated by Sun was null and void because the subject matter of the agreement was not in existence at the time of the sale. Also, the agency contract of Sun and Midwest Sales was terminated for the same reason.

12.13 Change in the Law

Sometimes performance is made impossible by a change in the law. Such changes immediately terminate the agent's authority without the necessity of notice from the principal.

EXAMPLE 17. Sanitary Services, Inc., contracted to install a septic tank and a drainage system for disposal of sewage emanating from Bixler's house. The County Commission passed an ordinance forbidding the installation of private sewage-disposal systems in the area in which Bixler lived. By law, all houses had to be connected to the county's sewage system. As a result, Bixler's contract with Sanitary Services was automatically terminated.

12.14 Termination by Death

An agent's authority arises from the capacity of the principal and thus depends on the principal's continued existence. The death of a principal extinguishes his or her agency agreements. The death of an agent likewise extinguishes his or her agreements. Notice to third parties of a principal's death is not required for the protection of the principal's estate. (One exception is an agency coupled with an interest, which is not extinguished by the death of the principal.)

EXAMPLE 18. Quinlan authorized Hinkson to purchase a five-acre tract for him. Hinkson entered into negotiations with the owner at 4:00 P.M. on June 12, and within thirty minutes the two had signed a sales agreement. Unknown to either Hinkson or the owner, Quinlan had died at 3:00 P.M. the same day. The signed agreement had no validity because Quinlan's death had automatically terminated Hinkson's authority.

12.15 Bank's Payment of Deceased's Outstanding Checks

A bank has the right to honor the outstanding checks of a deceased depositor until ten days after the depositor's death. (An exception to this would be a case in which the executor of the deceased's estate or some other authorized party ordered payments to be stopped.)

EXAMPLE 19. Hurka had issued checks to Stevens, Conklin, and Bradbury. The checks were still outstanding at the time of Hurka's death. The bank honored the checks written out to Stevens and Conklin because the checks arrived at the bank three and eight days, respectively, after Hurka's death. The bank did not honor the check written to Bradbury because it arrived at the bank for payment fifteen days after Hurka's death.

12.16 Insanity

Insanity of either the principal or the agent after the creation of an agency agreement terminates the agency. Temporary insanity only interrupts the agency for that period of time during which one of the parties is insane.

EXAMPLE 20. Bernstein appointed Kovac his agent to sell his farm produce to local food stores. Bernstein was declared insane by the court on petition of members of his family. Bernstein's capacity to contract was thus terminated, as was the authority held by Kovac. Unlike in termination by death, the third party may rely on the agent's authority prior to learning of the principal's mental condition.

12.17 Bankruptcy

Bankruptcy of a principal or agent in most cases terminates their agency. Bankruptcy of the agent does not usually terminate the agent's power to deal with the property of the principal already in the agent's possession. In addition, those things *exempt* from bankruptcy may remain in the agent's authority. Articles and property not exempt and not in the agent's possession are passed over to the trustee in bankruptcy. The agent loses authority in such property *without notice.*

EXAMPLE 21. Ketter was requested by Burns to sell the equipment in Burns's office and the furniture in Burns's house. After Burns was put into involuntary bankruptcy by his creditors, Ketter's authority as the agent of the office equipment was terminated. At the time, Ketter did not have possession of any of the equipment. However, the household furniture, which was exempt from creditors' claims, continued to be the object of Ketter's agency.

12.18 Termination by War

An agency agreement between a principal and an agent whose countries are at war with each other is usually terminated. Termination often results because of impossibility of performance caused by the acts of war between the two countries.

A divergent view is expressed by the American Law Institute, *Restatement: Contracts 1932, Secs. 593–596:* ". . . there is no rule that war between countries in which the agent and principal dwell terminates authority." Thus, except where illegality creates an impossibility of performance and authority, the agent's authority will continue.

EXAMPLE 22. Hambright acted as purchasing and export agent for Oriental Steel Works, a foreign company that bought and shipped scrap metal purchased in the United States. An outbreak of hostilities and a declaration of war made operation and continuance of the agency agreement impossible. Hambright's rights and obligations to the principal would necessarily be terminated.

12.19 Termination of Authority of Subagents

Termination of an agency agreement also terminates the right of subagents working in the name of the principal. The same rules that apply to termination of the agent's agreement apply to termination of authority of the subagent. Although authority may be terminated between principal and agent, the third party may have rights against either the principal or the agent based on the rules of *apparent authority*.

EXAMPLE 23. Hampstead was regional manager for the Cycle Sales Corporation. By authority of Cycle Sales, Hampstead hired and instructed sales representatives, who were paid a salary and expenses for calling on dealers throughout their assigned territories. On May 1, Cycle Sales introduced new sales techniques, and all salespeople (subagents) were discharged. Any contracts made by subagents with third parties subsequent to May 1 were to be rejected. However, third parties dealing with subagents could rely upon the *apparent* authority of the subagents. Contracts with them would be valid in the absence of notice by the principal of the decision to terminate the subagents' authority.

Solved Problems

12.1 Despite repeated warnings from her husband, Mrs. Horgan continued to make extravagant purchases and charge them to him. Horgan continued to pay the bills as he received them. Finally, when he received a bill for an expensive fur coat, he refused to pay it. He claimed that a wife is not the agent of her husband except in purchases necessary to the family's health, safety, and welfare. Was Mr. Horgan correct?

Basically the husband is not responsible for contracts made by his wife except as the contracts may be necessary for herself and the family. Horgan, however, was liable for the coat on the grounds that his wife was his *apparent agent* in making purchases beyond those required. He had denied her permission to make expensive purchases, but third parties were not aware of this fact.

12.2 Bayard published an advertisement in the local newspaper that read: "From this date, I will not be responsible for any debts created by anyone other than myself." Bayard's wife made purchases on Bayard's credit. He refused to pay for the purchases, basing his defense on the published advertisement. Does the advertisement protect the husband from creditor's claims?

Communication of termination of an agency must be complete to be effective. There is no proof that Bayard's creditors read his advertisement or were aware in any other way of his intentions. Publishing a notice denying liability for debts created in a person's name by another is not conclusive in terminating an agency. Direct communication to all creditors by certified mail would have accomplished Bayard's purposes.

12.3 Trimble owed Hanson $300 for work done by Hanson. As a means of clearing up the account, Trimble authorized Hanson to sell his car, valued at $2,500, with the right to retain for himself the $300 owed. Before the car was sold, Trimble died and the executor terminated Hanson's agency. May Hanson demand continuance of his agency agreement?

Yes. Death or insanity of the principal terminates most agency agreements, but not an agency coupled with an interest. Hanson had an interest in the subject matter of his agency agreement. He may demand reinstatement, with the same rights authorized when Trimble was alive.

12.4 Henry Used Car Sales authorized George to paint a late model Ford that it had for sale. Before George had time to pick up the car, one of Henry's salesmen sold it to Rayburn. Did an agency agreement still exist between Henry and George?

Loss of any interest in the subject matter by the principal terminates an agency agreement *without notice*. Transfer of title to Rayburn deprived Henry of any interest in the car. The agency was thus terminated. George may, however, still exercise his rights against Henry Used Car Sales on the breached agreement by suing for damages (anticipated profit on paint job).

12.5 Landing requested Stewart to buy groceries and provisions for him at the local food market and to charge them to Landing's account. Stewart did as ordered. Landing later denied any obligation to pay for the food on grounds of insanity. Landing had never been declared insane but was known by all of his friends to be "odd and somewhat different." Had insanity made impossible and invalid the agency agreement with Stewart?

One not declared insane by the court may make agency agreements that would be reasonable and necessary for that person's health, safety, and welfare. Stewart, acting as an agent for Landing in the purchase of necessary foods, was acting with authority. Landing must pay for the groceries.

12.6 Involuntary bankruptcy proceedings were brought against the Summit Coal Company, Inc., by their creditors. Armstrong, a geologist employed by the company, continued to report for work after the corporation was declared bankrupt. May Armstrong hold the coal company liable for hours worked during this period?

Armstrong's working contract was terminated automatically upon the bankruptcy of Summit Coal. He worked, therefore, without a contract and may not obligate the defunct corporation for wages or salary.

12.7 Romberg, an alien, was employed by General Aviation Design, Inc., as a test pilot on new military aircraft. Hostilities broke out between the United States and the nation in which Romberg still held citizenship. Is Romberg's position protected from termination?

No. Agency agreements are terminated by operation of law in those cases where the agent's position may threaten the security of the government and the nation. Romberg's exposure to vital secrets in the development of aircraft would dictate the termination of his working agreement with General Aviation.

12.8 Newmark worked as general manager in one of ten beauty salons owned by Beauty Care, Inc. Beauty Care's new president indicated that all present management personnel were being replaced. Newmark continued to receive her weekly paycheck from the main office and continued to work. Was she within her rights?

Yes. A principal's intentions must be manifested by facts known or understood by the agent. In the absence of a clear expression of termination, Newmark may continue to work.

12.9 Stanley, an attorney, represented the Galsworthy Corporation in all of its court cases. Stanley had failed to renew his license for the practice of law, and he received notice that his license had been withdrawn subject to further investigation and examination of his case. What effect did this have on Stanley's association with the Galsworthy Corporation?

Expiration of a license terminates an agency in cases where a license is required by law. Stanley's agency agreement with Galsworthy is thus terminated, even if only temporarily. Until the license fee has been paid and Stanley has been reinstated as a legally licensed attorney, he may not act as Galsworthy's attorney in court.

12.10 Stein engaged Larkin as agent to supervise all of Stein's business activity in the Atlanta area. Stein fell seriously ill and was forced to remain in a medical facility for several months. Does Stein's illness affect the agency agreement?

Not necessarily. A principal's illness, when it does not deprive the principal of the capacity to contract, does not cause the termination of an agency agreement. Physical illness that affects mental capacity may terminate an agency agreement.

12.11 Ross agreed to sing in a series of concerts being promoted in colleges throughout the South. The booking company had arranged concerts at ten different schools over a period of three weeks. A serious throat ailment threatened Ross with irreparable damage to her voice if she carried out her agreement. What are the rights of the parties?

Impossibility of performance may terminate an agreement involving personal services. Absence of intent or negligence on Ross's part negates any possible action against her for breach of contract.

Review Problems

12.12 How does apparent authority affect the termination of agency?

12.13 Does termination of an agent's authority also terminate authority vested in a subagent?

12.14 What agency agreements may not be revoked by the principal?

12.15 Does death always revoke an agency?

12.16 How may subsequently legislated laws terminate an otherwise valid and legal agency agreement?

12.17 May a bank honor outstanding checks issued by a depositor now dead?

12.18 Under what conditions may an agent *abandon* agency obligations without fear of suit for damages by the principal?

12.19 Does the law automatically terminate contracts between principals and agents living in countries at war with each other?

12.20 When will insanity terminate an agency agreement?

12.21 What is meant by termination through *change in circumstances?*

12.22 May a principal require an agent to continue performance by securing a decree of specific performance in a court of equity?

12.23 When may a principal revoke or an agent renounce an agency agreement?

12.24 By what two types of agreements may agency be terminated without subjecting either the agent or principal to damages?

12.25 What restrictions may a court of equity impose on an agent who has breached a personal-service agreement?

12.26 To what extent may an agent seek damages on grounds of the principal's breach of contract?

Answers to Review Problems

12.12 Third parties who have not been advised of the termination of an agency may still rely on the apparent agent's right to bind the principal.

12.13 Yes.

12.14 Agency coupled with an interest either in authority or subject matter.

12.15 No, not when there is an agency coupled with an interest.

12.16 Authority vested in an agent is terminated when the purpose of the agency has been made illegal, even by laws passed after the agency was created.

12.17 Yes, until ten days after the death of a depositor unless a stop-payment notice is served on the bank by the executor or some other authorized party.

12.18 When the principal makes unreasonable demands on the agent, beyond the agent's agreed scope of employment, the agency may be abandoned.

12.19 Not entirely; only when performance of the agency is impossible or is deemed illegal or when its operation would constitute a threat against the safety of the countries involved in the hostilities.

12.20 When the principal or the agent has been declared insane by proper state authorities, the agreement may be terminated.

12.21 When circumstances of law or facts make performance of the agency illegal, impossible, or highly unreasonable, the agent's authority, as initially given, is terminated.

12.22 No.

12.23 At any time, but with the possibility of a suit for damages resulting from the termination.

12.24 This may be achieved (1) by mutual assent contained in the original agreement or (2) by a subsequent agreement of both agent and principal.

12.25 The agent may be enjoined from performing for another principal what he or she contracted to perform for the original principal.

12.26 The agent may seek only money damages experienced from the principal's termination of the agent's authority. The court will deduct from damages sought all income received by the discharged agent during the unexpired period of the breached agency agreement.

Legal Terms

Abandonment. In agency, the agent's renunciation, with or without cause, of an agency agreement.

Impossibility of performance. Termination of an agency agreement when circumstances make performance impossible; automatically releases both parties from their agency obligations.

Restraining injunction. An order from a court of equity that restricts a breaching agent from performing for some other principal the same work the agent was to perform for the original principal.

Revocation. The recall of some power, right, or privilege previously conferred.

Termination of subagent's authority. Termination of an agency agreement also terminates the authority of a subagent working in the name of the principal.

Chapter 13

Employer-Employee Relationships

This chapter is a review of the basic principles of employer-employee relationships. Strictly speaking, employer-employee relationships are not the same as agency relationships. However, there are enough similarities between the two types of relationships to make this a logical place to discuss the duties and obligations of an employer and an employee to each other.

Employees are hired for the purpose of working under the strict control of their employers. Agents, on the other hand, are authorized to represent their principals in negotiations with third parties. Some employees, like the driver-salesman of a laundry truck, are also agents. The driver-salesman is an employee in the pickup and delivery of customers' goods, but becomes an agent in making collections of money for the principal.

Agency depends to a great extent on the common law and the law of contracts. Employment also depends on contract law, but today it is also regulated to a great extent by federal law and state statutes. Agency often relies heavily on the personal relationship between a principal and an agent. In contrast, thousands of employees may be represented in collective bargaining with their employers by elected or appointed union representatives.

As you review this chapter, keep in mind how agents and employees are similar to and different from each other in their rights and responsibilities.

THE EMPLOYMENT CONTRACT

13.1 Contract Elements in Employment Agreements

To be enforceable, employment agreements must contain: (1) mutual assent, (2) capable parties, (3) consideration, and (4) valid subject matter. The agreements may be either express or implied.

EXAMPLE 1. Brittingham Drugs employed Steelman as a chemist. Steelman agreed to all the terms of the employment contract. She was to be paid $1,100 per month, for which she would work eight hours a day, five days a week. She held a pharmacist's license and agreed to dispense drugs only on prescriptions signed by physicians. This agreement satisfied all of the requirements of contract law.

13.2 Volunteer Services

Sometimes people volunteer their services to businesses in the hope of receiving tips from customers. Such persons are employees of neither the customers nor the businesses. They create no obligation on the part of either a customer or a business in the event of injury to a third party.

EXAMPLE 2. Fargo Markets permitted porters to serve customers who purchased orders of groceries from the market. The porters assisted customers in transferring purchases from shopping carts to waiting automobiles. Customers showed appreciation by voluntarily tipping the porters for their services. Should one of the porters injure someone while performing this service, only the porter would be responsible. There is no employment contract with either the store or with the customer who is being served.

13.3 Self-Service Customers Are Not Employees

Persons who wait on themselves in self-service stores, cafeterias, and other public consumer outlets are not to be deemed employees of such establishments for the purpose of holding the businesses responsible in the event of injury or accident. No contract of employment is intended by either party.

EXAMPLE 3. Griffith shopped at Central Food Market, where she waited on herself. She fell when she walked into a shopping cart that had been left in an aisle by another customer. Griffith could not claim damages on the theory that she was working for the market and that the market had not provided a safe place for her. She was not an employee by any description. She could, however, recover in an action based on her rights as a *business guest.*

13.4 Borrowed Employees

One who *borrows* employees from another employer, even for a short time, may be deemed an employer with full responsibility for that period of time. To be held responsible, the one who borrowed the employee must be the one who has the power of supervision and control over the employee during the temporary loan period.

EXAMPLE 4. Samson's Service Station permitted Stover, one of its employees, to go next door and help Andrews, a real estate broker, repair a sign hanging over the front entrance of his office. Stover dropped the sign and injured a passerby. A claim for damages was placed against Stover's employer. Stover had been *loaned* to Andrews for work done under Andrews's control and supervision. Andrews, not Samson's Service Station, is liable for Stover's negligence.

13.5 Union Contracts

Members of a union are represented by union representatives in *collective bargaining* with management in negotiations for employee contracts. Employees may approve or disapprove contract terms presented by the union. Individual employees are not directly involved with management in these contract negotiations.

EXAMPLE 5. Overland Trucking Company's employees were members of the Transport Workers Union. Contract negotiations were carried on by a union representative. Ambroy, who had years of seniority as a driver, voted against the contract offered by the union. He was outvoted and given the option of either working under the new contract or looking for work elsewhere. If representation had been unfair and biased, Ambroy could make a complaint to the National Labor Relations Board.

13.6 Statute of Fraud Requirements

A contract of employment must be in writing if it is to last more than one year from the date of the making of the contract. (The written agreement need not be formal to satisfy the requirements of the statute of frauds.)

EXAMPLE 6. On April 10, Hunter verbally agreed to accept a position as an administrative secretary with the Stevens Corporation. She was to report for work on Monday, April 15, and agreed to work for one year. Because the contract could not be completed within one year of the *date of making,* neither party could enforce the agreement. The agreement should have been written.

13.7 Restraint-of-Trade Clause

An employment contract may contain a restraint-of-trade clause. With such a clause, an employer can restrain a former employee from accepting work with a new employer who is engaged in the same type of business as the original employer. The restraints may pertain to both a certain time period and a specified geographic area. To be valid, a restraint-of-trade clause must be reasonable. One employer may not permanently restrain an employee from working for and earning a living from another employer.

EXAMPLE 7. The Whatnot Furniture Company employed Steubens as sales manager in one of its local retail outlets. Steubens's employment agreement stated that he would not be permitted to work in sales for any competing firm within a one-hundred-mile radius for a period of five years after leaving Whatnot's employ. The agreement may be voided because it is too broad in its restraint over a former employee.

13.8 Rights and Restraints in Contract Writing

Parties are permitted to include any legal provisions desired in an employment contract. (They are restricted, for example, in that the purpose of the agreement must be legal and that neither the employer nor the employee may be deprived of rights under federal, state, local, or common law.)

EXAMPLE 8. Krandall took a job as a truck driver. He agreed to make two round-trip hauls from Atlanta, Georgia, to New York City each week. The schedule required him to drive continuously for periods of ten or more hours. Although acceptable to both Krandall and his employer, the agreement was in conflict with Interstate Commerce Commission rules and regulations and was therefore unenforceable.

DUTIES AND OBLIGATIONS

13.9 Rendering Services

An employee is obligated, by the terms of an employment contract, to render or stand ready to render those services agreed to. Readiness and willingness on the employee's part are required even if the employer is unprepared to accept the employee's service at the time and place agreed upon.

EXAMPLE 9. Bayless signed on as a plumber's helper with the Deep-Well Plumbing Company. He was to start work on Monday morning, and was to work eight hours a day for $4.80 per hour. When Bayless reported for work Monday morning, Deep-Well informed him that he would not be needed that day because scheduled jobs had been canceled. Bayless had fulfilled his obligation. The employer's disaffirmance resulted in a breach.

13.10 Using Work Hours for Other Activities

An employee may not divert his or her employer's time to other matters. Using *company time* for personal gain or in the interest of another is an indication of a lack of good faith and honesty on the part of the employee.

EXAMPLE 10. Steam Turbines, Inc., employed Raskin as a welder of high-pressure steam lines. Raskin spent more than an hour of his time welding a broken cast-iron part that had been brought into the shop by a friend. Raskin had exceeded his rights as an employee and would be subject to discipline by Steam Turbines, Inc.

13.11 Employee's Liability for Damage to Employer

An employee is personally liable to the employer for damages resulting from the employee's misconduct, negligence, or disobedience.

EXAMPLE 11. Schofield drove a delivery truck for the Roman Bakery. One day, while out making scheduled deliveries, he drove to his own house on a personal errand. Schofield left the ignition keys in the truck and went into his house. The truck was highjacked and was never recovered. Schofield may be held liable by Roman Bakery or by Roman's insurance company for money damages resulting from this negligence and disobedience.

13.12 Obligation of Care, Skill, and Diligence

An employee is obligated to perform promised services with the degree of care, skill, and diligence ordinarily attributed to a person engaged in the same type of work or trade.

EXAMPLE 12. Mullins applied for a job as an electrician with Bates Electrical Contractors. He was hired as an experienced journeyman and was assigned to install a three-phase motor and a relay switch in a 440-volt line. Faulty installation caused an electrical fire. Inspectors discovered that Mullins's work showed that he was unskilled and without experience and knowledge in the trade. In applying for the job, Mullins had warranted that he had ordinary skills in the electrical trade. He may be held responsible by Bates Electrical Contractors for the resulting damage.

13.13 Obligation to Protect Employer's Trade Secrets

An employee is forbidden to reveal to third parties *trade secrets* valuable in the employer's business. This does not include general knowledge or skills, but only information that would be damaging if shared with other companies in the same business.

EXAMPLE 13. Lord worked as a clerk in the advertising department of the Cortese Shoe Company. She listed in proper files all inquiries coming to the firm as the result of newspaper, radio, and magazine advertising. Lord sold duplicate lists to a competing shoe company that served the same wholesale market. She thus violated her duties of loyalty and would be subject to discharge and a claim for damages. Cortese Shoe Company had additional rights against the third party who encouraged Lord and paid her for the unethical and illegal theft of her employer's confidential and valuable information.

13.14 Employer's Right to Inventions

The employee's obligation to the employer for inventions resulting from work done within the scope of employment depends on the conditions contained in the employment agreement. The employer has a right to such inventions when such a right is reserved and agreed to by both parties. When such is not stipulated in the contract, the employer has a nonexclusive right to the use of the invention without payment of royalty or license rights to the employee. Employers anticipating the occurrence of such an event often include in the employment contract the right to inventions patented by an employee within a specified time after terminating employment.

EXAMPLE 14. Jefferson Chemical Company employed Steininger as a chemist. He was assigned to test samples of products produced by the company. While using the firm's materials in carrying out his duties, Steininger discovered a time- and money-saving process of testing the strength of certain acids. Steininger's invention is his own in the absence of conditions in his employment agreement. Jefferson Chemical, however, may use the process without the obligation to pay Steininger any license or royalty fees.

13.15 Employee Lien and Credit Preference

State laws usually give employees rights superior to those of other creditors in claims and liens against the employer's property. Laws that give employees this preference usually limit the extent of the employees' claims.

EXAMPLE 15. The McCann Foundry ceased operations because of financial difficulties. The firm's assets did not equal its liabilities, and claims were filed by creditors, including workers who had not been paid for their final month's work. Liens against the firm's property and other assets were filed by employees. These liens were given prior rights over the liens of other creditors.

13.16 Pension Reform Act of 1974

The Federal Pension Reform Act of 1974 provides protection to employees in pension plans administered by employers. Included in the Act are: (1) the employee's right to a limited *portability* of pension rights when the employee switches from one employer to another; (2) employer contributions determined by actuarial computations assuring the employee of pension promises; and (3) a plan of insurance that protects the employee in those cases where the employer terminates the business. These rights have been provided in order to prevent a continuance of the employee-pension losses experienced prior to the passage of this legislation. The operation and enforcement of the Act comes within the authority of the Secretary of Labor.

EXAMPLE 16. Catalina works as an itinerant steel rigger. He goes to any part of the country where employment in bridge construction is offered. Over a period of twenty-five years, he has worked in thirty-five states and for twenty-one different construction companies. The Pension Reform Act of 1974 now permits Catalina to have a pension fund that all the different companies he works for will contribute to.

13.17 Occupational Safety and Health Act of 1970 (OSHA)

OSHA gives the Secretary of Labor powers in setting safety and health standards for employees. State laws provide similar employee protection in cases where the federal law does not apply. Regardless of OSHA, an employer has an obligation to provide safe working conditions and to point out to employees those hazards of employment that would not otherwise be obvious.

EXAMPLE 17. The Klaus Motor Company operated a machine shop for grinding and polishing steel shafts used in motors. Brenner lost the sight in his right eye when working on a grinding wheel. No safety glasses had been issued to employees. Inspectors also discovered that safety switches, gear guards, and dim lighting had contributed to other accidents in the plant. Under OSHA regulations and local safety rules, Klaus would be required to redesign its plant with all of these safety features. In addition, Brenner could recover damages from the Klaus Motor Company.

13.18 Common Law Defense against Employee's Claims

Prior to state workmen's compensation laws and the Federal Employers' Liability Act, employees injured in the course of employment were in most cases denied damages claimed for injuries related to employment. Common law defenses included: (1) contributory negligence of employee; (2) assumption of risk; and (3) acts of a coworker.

EXAMPLE 18. Larkin worked as a lineman for a power company. While working he made contact with a high-tension power line and was thrown forty feet to the ground. Although Larkin was seriously injured, the employer was not obligated to indemnify him for any expenses or for permanent physical injuries suffered as a result of the fall. Larkin's assumption of risk as an employee and possible contributory negligence on his own part deprived him of a claim against his employer.

13.19 Workmen's Compensation

Employees, with certain exceptions, are protected financially from injuries they receive while they are engaged in their employment. Benefits are guaranteed to the injured worker or to the worker's survivors in the event of death. (Common law defenses are now outlawed.) Provision is made for specified payments for losses of body members. Occupational diseases of specific kinds are also included. Deliberate, self-inflicted injuries and injuries resulting from intoxication are not covered, however.

EXAMPLE 19. Had Larkin, in Example 18, worked today, under workmen's compensation, he would have received benefits covering medical expenses, including hospital care. He would also have been compensated for losses resulting from his inability to work. Had he been killed, his survivors would have received compensation.

13.20 Justifiable Discharge by Employer

An employee may be discharged without a right to suit against the employer under the following conditions: (1) for failure to carry out assigned duties; (2) for misrepresentation or fraud exercised in getting the job; (3) for disobedience to instructions; (4) for lack of loyalty and good faith toward the employer; (5) for misconduct on the job; (6) for incompetence; and (7) for disability.

EXAMPLE 20. Fitzhugh was appointed as a draftsman by Central Design Associates. In applying for the position, he claimed that he was a graduate of two engineering schools and had advanced degrees. He also claimed ten years of experience in the type of work for which he was hired. All of this information was fraudulent. Discovery of the misstatements would subject Fitzhugh to dismissal from his job, and he would have no grounds for a suit against Central.

13.21 Justifiable Abandonment of Job by Employee

An employee may abandon employment without giving the employer grounds for legal action under the following conditons: (1) employer's breach of contract; (2) mistreatment of employee by employer; (3) employer's demand for services not included in the employment agreement; (4)

employer's acts barring employee from work; and (5) unsanitary and unsafe employment conditions.

EXAMPLE 21. Bush worked as a radio operator for a commercial radio station. During a heavy storm, the station manager ordered Bush to climb to the top of an antenna tower and restring a lead wire that had broken loose. Bush had never agreed to do such work under his employment contract. Continued demands that he perform this duty gave Bush the right to abandon his job. (He would not, in compliance with federal regulations, be permitted to leave his post. The station manager, however, could not order Bush to climb the antenna tower.)

13.22 Discriminatory Hiring Practices

Federal and state laws prohibit employers from practicing discrimination based on the race, creed, color, national origin, sex, or age of an applicant for employment. Other legislation requires equal wages for equal employment, regardless of an employee's sex, and prohibits employment advertising in which any of the above are made requisites of selection.

EXAMPLE 22. Allen Manufacturing Company advertised for production workers in its Michigan plant. The advertisement specified that applicants must be white, male, and not over thirty-five years old. The advertisement would be prohibited under present nondiscrimination laws.

EXAMPLE 23. Harvey was hired by the Allen Manufacturing Company at an hourly rate of $4. She learned that her hourly rate was lower than that paid men in the company who did the same work. Allen Manufacturing Company would not be permitted to discriminate against female employees by paying them less for equal work and equal performance. Harvey could bring suit against the company for its illegal practices.

Solved Problems

13.1 Hinton watched a window cleaner wash the display windows of his store. It took the man almost an hour to complete the job. Hinton thanked the man but did not offer to pay him anything. Was there any employer-employee relationship between the two parties?

Yes. An implied contract of employment may develop from the actions or absence of action manifested between two parties. Hinton was aware that the services being rendered were not of a gratuitous type. There was an implied acceptance of the worker's services because the store manager permitted the man to continue his work.

13.2 Royal Beauty Salon sought the assistance of the owner of a nearby moving company. Royal asked the owner to send one of his men over to help move some heavy appliances in the beauty shop. The mover accompanied one of his employees to the shop and instructed him in all he did. The loaned employee caused injury to a client of the beauty shop. Royal Beauty Salon was asked to pay damages to this customer. Was Royal liable for this claim?

No. An employer is responsible for the acts and injuries caused by an employee who remains under the employer's control and supervision. The man who caused the injury was a borrowed employee, but Royal did not supervise and control his acts and work. The client's only recourse would be an action for damages against the employer of the loaned employee and, of course, against the employee himself if his actions were outside the scope of his employment.

13.3 Carver was employed as a floor foreman in the Security Warehouse. Although he noticed that the lock on an outside door was not functioning properly, he failed to report the matter to his employer. Burglars entered the building through the unprotected door and carried off goods. What responsibility did Carver have to Security?

An employee must be honest, loyal, and act in good faith to the employer at all times. Information of importance to the employer possessed by the employee must be communicated to the employer. Carver did not meet his responsibilities to his employer. He is subject to discharge and may be held accountable for Security's loss from the burglary.

13.4 First National Bank hired Selby as a teller for its Brookside branch. Selby agreed to follow the rules of conservative appearance and conduct that were explained to her by the personnel director. One week after starting the job, she appeared for work in blue jeans and a sleeveless shirt. She refused to return home and change, stating that it was her constitutional right to choose her own dress. What are Selby's rights?

Constitutional rights as a member of a free society are not the same in employment as in one's personal life. Selby had agreed to the rules to be followed when she was interviewed for the job. The rules were reasonable for persons working in a professional environment. Selby's disobedience gave the bank grounds for her discharge.

13.5 Bailey worked as a motorcycle mechanic for three years at Freeman's Cycle Shop. Freeman was conscientious and capable and taught Bailey all of the "tricks of the trade." At the end of the three-year period, Bailey was a skilled motorcycle mechanic. Bailey then left Freeman and took a job with a competing shop. Freeman attempted to enjoin Bailey from disclosing the skills he had learned. Was Freeman successful?

No. An employee may not be prevented from using general knowledge and skills learned and perfected through contact with and training from a previous employer. (The employee may *not* divulge trade secrets, confidential records, and other information at the expense of the previous employer and may be enjoined from so doing.)

13.6 The Hagen Chemical Company had a written agreement with Jergen, a chemist working for them. Jergen agreed, for fair consideration, to assign to Hagen Chemical any inventions or discoveries he might make within a period of six months of the termination of his contract with Hagen. One month after leaving Hagen, Jergen invented a new process for producing one of Hagen's products. He refused to assign the patent, claiming that the assignment agreement was unreasonable, invalid, and illegal. Was Jergen correct?

No. Contracts that assign the rights to inventions and discoveries to a former employer are valid if they are reasonable. Jergen's agreement was for only a six-month period and would not be deemed unfair or unreasonable in his profession. Hagen may enforce the agreement with Jergen.

13.7 Moreau, who worked for the Harlan Department store, owed $924 to the Ender Furniture Mart. The bill was three months in arrears, and Ender commenced *garnishment proceedings* against Moreau and the Harlan Department Store. Harlan threatened to discharge Moreau because of the garnishment threat. May Harlan do so because of the inconvenience caused them by being involved in Moreau's financial difficulties?

Title III of the Consumer Credit Protection Act (CCPA) prohibits an employer from discharging an employee whose wages are being garnished *for the first time*. Continued garnishments, which may subject an employer to extra bookkeeping expenses and inconvenience, may result in the employee's justifiable discharge. If Moreau was having his salary garnished for the first time, he could not be fired by Harlan.

13.8 Suppose, in Problem 13.7, that Harlan Department Store was ordered to pay Ender Furniture Mart the $924 by deducting 75 percent of Moreau's pay each week until the bill was satisfied. May such an amount be taken from an employee's earnings?

Under the Truth in Lending Act (CCPA), an employee is protected from garnishment that deducts an unreasonable amount of earnings from his or her pay. The usual formula permits a garnishment of no more than 25 percent of the employee's take-home pay. Title III of the CCPA exempts from weekly garnishment an amount equal to thirty times the minimum hourly rate as set by federal law. The order to deduct 75 percent of Moreau's weekly take-home pay was illegal under the standard set by the Truth in Lending Act.

13.9 Simpson worked as a cook and maid in DeHaven's home. Without switching on a light, she went into the basement of the house and fell over an empty basket. Simpson was injured. DeHaven denied liability, using as a defense the claim that Simpson's injuries resulted from her own contributory negligence. Could Simpson claim damages under workmen's compensation laws that outlawed this common law defense?

As a general rule, agricultural and domestic workers do not come under workmen's compensation laws. Without this employee protection, the employer is not barred from using an employee's contributory negligence as a defense against liability for the employee's injuries received on the job. It is doubtful that Simpson would recover damages for her accident and the resulting injuries.

13.10 Forest Products employed Manwiller as an operator in one of its plants. Manwiller was assigned to control the flow of hydrochloric acid into vats used in the plant operation. He was not given protective gear and was not warned of the hazards connected with the job. What action might be taken by the Department of Labor in this matter?

The Federal Occupational Safety and Health Act of 1970 gives the Secretary of Labor jurisdiction in setting standards of safety in matters such as the one presented here. Forest Products would be liable for any injuries befalling Manwiller, who had not been informed about or protected from the hazards of his job. The Department of Labor would be within its rights in making a complete inspection of the plant, ordering the correction of Manwiller's situation, and ordering that all other safety and health infractions in the plant be corrected.

13.11 Santow drank two six-packs of beer while working the late-night shift at the Rogers Fabrication Corporation. The punch press that Santow worked on conformed to OSHA standards. Santow, in an intoxicated condition, seriously injured his right hand while operating the punch press. Is Santow protected under workmen's compensation?

No. Not allowed by workmen's compensation coverage are claims for injuries to an intoxicated worker and claims for willfully self-inflicted injuries connected with employment. Santow will receive no compensation for the injuries reported here.

13.12 Hill worked as a sales clerk in the Haines Merchandise Mart. Without provocation and without warning, a customer struck Hill with her fist and knocked him to the floor. Was Hill successful in seeking recovery for damages from the Haines Mart?

An employer is not responsible to an employee for injuries caused by the unprovoked attack of a customer. Haines was in no way responsible for the third party's assault. Hill's course of action would be against the woman who struck him.

13.13 Suppose that, in Problem 13.12, the owner of Haines Merchandise Mart knew of the troublesome customer's presence in the mart and had reason to believe that her presence might lead to injuries to employees. Would these facts affect Haines's responsibility to the employees and Haines's liability for any damages or injuries caused by the pugnacious customer?

An employer has the responsibility to protect employees from known hazards. The negligence of the management in permitting the third party to wander through the mart without surveillance of some kind would make Haines liable to Hill for injuries received.

13.14 Peltz served as a chauffeur for members of the State Department. He provided transportation for representatives of foreign nations visiting the United States. While on an official trip, Peltz carelessly ran into a pedestrian who was crossing the street at a busy intersection. To whom will the injured third party address a claim for damages?

Under the Federal Torts Claims Act, the United States is responsible to third parties for injuries caused by federal employees driving motor vehicles of the U.S. Government. The act also prohibits claims against the federal employee personally. Peltz will not be sued; the claim will be against the United States.

13.15 Richmond Industries employed Gumpert as an engineering consultant under a five-year contract. Representatives of the Conway Corporation induced Gumpert to leave her job after only two years. What options does Richmond Industries have in seeking damages for Gumpert's unjustified termination of the five-year agreement?

An employer may claim damages from a third party who induces an employee to terminate, through breach, an executory employment agreement. (The employer may also seek damages from the employee herself for the breach of contract.)

13.16 Nabor was discharged from her job at the Woodring Knitting Mills. The reasons given for her dismissal were lack of good faith and loyalty to her employer. Nabor had worked with other employees in an effort to organize a union. Was the employer justified in this action?

The Labor-Management Relations Act (the Taft-Hartley Act) protects employees from an employer's disciplinary action resulting from an employee's efforts to organize a union. Nabor may appeal to the Labor-Management Relations Board for an order to reinstate her in her position.

13.17 The Northeast Packaging Company employed fifteen women to assemble boxes that would be used in interstate shipments. The employees were paid $1.85 an hour for a work week of forty-four hours. Does this arrangement conform to the regulations of the Federal Fair Labor Standards Act?

The Federal Fair Labor Standards Act regulates labor practices in the employment of persons in interstate commerce. The Northeast Packaging Company has erred in two matters under the act. First, the minimum wage standards were not met by payment of only $1.85 per hour; the rate should have been at least $2.30 per hour. Second, persons working more than forty hours per week must be paid time and one-half for time worked over forty hours per week.

13.18 Foster worked in a neighborhood lunchroom as a waitress. She was paid a wage of $1.50 an hour. She was required to divide all tips with the owner-manager. She went to representatives at the Federal Fair Labor Standards office and sought an increase of wages under the minimum-wage provisions of the Federal Fair Labor Standards Act. Was she correct in doing so?

Foster was not working in interstate commerce, and her employment is not included in the minimum-wage regulations. Only if a state law provides for minimum wages, as many states do, would Foster be entitled to file a complaint.

13.19 A television producer hired Angela, six years old, to appear in a series of advertisements. She was paid $250 for her part in each segment of the series. A complaint was made by

an interested party. The complaint stated that one of such a tender age should be prohibited from accepting employment. Was the complaint justified?

The Fair Labor Standards Act provides specific regulations covering child labor. It prohibits employment of any persons under the age of 16. Exceptions are permitted in agricultural labor, in employment by parents or guardians, for child actors, and in the delivery of newspapers. Angela's employment may not be interrupted as long as the employer works within the framework permitted in the hiring of a six-year-old actor.

Review Problems

13.20 What is the major difference between principal-agent and employer-employee relationships?

13.21 When is a party who borrows an employee liable for the wrongful acts of that employee?

13.22 How does the statute of frauds relate to an employment contract?

13.23 Are employment contracts that are in restraint of trade enforceable?

13.24 How much of an employee's working time must be devoted to the employer's benefit?

13.25 How much care and skill must an employee have in any particular type of job?

13.26 Does the employer have a property right in all inventions perfected by an employee during the employee's working hours?

13.27 Does an employee have preferential rights in claims and liens filed along with those of other general creditors against the employer?

13.28 How has the Pension Reform Act of 1974 benefitted today's employees?

13.29 List the common law defenses that protected employers prior to the introduction of the state workmen's compensation laws.

13.30 When is an employee justified in abandoning a job?

13.31 In what ways may an employer discriminate in the selection of employees?

13.32 May an employer discharge an employee because the employee is engaged in organizing a union within a non-union shop?

13.33 What federal law provides for the regulation of child labor?

13.34 Does the Taft-Hartley Act afford any advantages to labor?

Answers to Review Problems

13.20 Principal-agent agreements usually relate to the employment of those who will deal in some way with third parties. Employer-employee contracts are those in which the employee remains under the strict control and supervision of the employer and has little or no contact with third parties.

13.21 He or she is liable when the borrowed employee is acting under the supervision and control of the borrower rather than the regular employer.

13.22 All employment agreements that cannot be completed within one year of the date of making must be evidenced by a written agreement.

13.23 They are enforceable and valid only when reasonable in duration and in the geographic area over which the contract restricts the employee's rights.

13.24 100 percent

13.25 An employee must show the care and skill of an ordinary employee engaged in the same type of work.

13.26 No. Employers have such rights only when the employment contract specifically gives them the rights. Without such an agreement, the employer has the nonexclusive right to use of the invention without payment of royalties or fees to the inventor-employee.

13.27 Yes. With a few exceptions, the unpaid employee has preference over other general creditors.

13.28 The Act gives some portability to the pension rights of an employee who changes employment. It also assures safety in the employee's future pension rights and in contributions to the pension.

13.29 The defenses were: (1) contributory negligence; (2) assumption of risk of employment accepted; and (3) injuries resulting from acts of coworker.

13.30 The employee is justified when there is: (1) employer's breach of contract; (2) mistreatment by employer; (3) demand for services not included in the employment agreement; (4) employer's acts that bar employee from work; or (5) unsanitary or unsafe employment conditions.

13.31 An employer has the right to select employees only on the basis of skills, experience, education, and other factors that qualify one for a job. The employer may not discriminate in *any* other way.

13.32 No. The employee is protected under the provisions of the Taft-Hartley Act.

13.33 The Fair Labor Standards Act

13.34 Yes. The Taft-Hartley Act gives fair and equal rights to both labor *and* management.

Legal Terms

Borrowed employees. Employees whom one employer lends to another on a temporary basis.

Care, skill, and diligence. The qualities required of an employee in carrying out instructions of employment; the degree of care, skill, and diligence expected of an employee is determined by the custom of the market place.

Collective bargaining. The process of securing a workers' labor agreement with management through representation of the workers by a union or other appointed bargaining agent.

Company time. The working hours agreed to by an employer and employee. Loyalty and good faith require the employee to use these hours for the employer's sole benefit.

Employee's lien. An employee's superior right over most other general creditors in claims against the employer's property.

OSHA. The federal Occupational Safety and Health Act of 1970, which assures employees of minimum safety and health standards determined by inspectors under the Secretary of the U.S. Department of Labor.

Restraint-of-trade clause. Provisions in an employment contract that restrict a former employee from accepting employment with a competing employer for a specified period of time and over a predetermined geographic area.

Self-service customers. Persons doing business with a store who are permitted to wait on themselves; such persons are not deemed to be employees of the store.

Workmen's compensation. Financial protection provided by law for employees injured in the course of their employment. Compensation is provided to the injured employee or to survivors in the event of death through accident or illness attributed to the job.

PART VII: *Business Organizations*

Chapter 14

Sole Proprietorship and Partnership

Almost all businesses in the United States are operated as sole proprietorships, partnerships, or corporations. In this chapter, we will review the laws relating to sole proprietorships and partnerships.

Laws governing the operation of sole proprietorships are very much like the laws relating to contracts, sales, and agency. The sole owner of a business is recognized as a principal, and the people who work for him or her are recognized as agents or employees. Sole proprietorship requires little review in this chapter because the laws relating to it are so similar to the laws relating to agency and employer-employee relationships.

A partnership is a more complex business organization—it represents the combination of the capital and/or skills invested in a business by two or more people. Contract and agency law are important to the operation of a partnership. Each partner is an agent for the other partners, and may bind them to contracts and torts related to the partnership business. The express, implied, and apparent powers of many different kinds of partners determine the personal liability that each partner might face should the partnership be unable to meet the demands of outside parties.

As you read this and the next chapter, keep in mind the advantages and disadvantages of each type of business organization.

14.1 Sole Proprietorship

One person, acting alone as the owner of a business enterprise, is a *sole proprietor*. A sole proprietor's activity is restricted only by the law, his or her abilities, and his or her financial strength. A sole proprietor answers to no one other than himself or herself and makes all decisions, receives all profits, and is liable for all claims against the business. A sole proprietor may name or change the name of the business at will and may personally decide what goods or services the business will offer at any time.

EXAMPLE 1. Rolph operated a catering business that employed twenty persons and served a varied clientele. On January 3, for reasons known only to himself, he discontinued the catering service, laid off all of his staff, and sold all the business equipment. A short time later, he opened a men's clothing store called the Buckeye State Clothing Center. All of these decisions and acts required no more than Rolph's own approval. Both businesses were legal in nature. Rolph, as a sole proprietor, was not restricted by the obligations of a partnership business or a corporation.

PARTNERSHIP

14.2 Nature of Partnership

A *partnership* organization is created when two or more competent parties combine their assets, labor, and/or skills for the purpose of carrying out a lawful business. Partners agree to share their profits and losses.

EXAMPLE 2. Roland, Jefferson, and Cartney contributed $100 each toward the purchase of Christmas candies they planned to sell during the holiday season. Each one agreed to solicit orders from friends and relatives. When all the candy was sold, the money collected was divided equally among them. Although no formal or written agreement had been drawn, the three had created an operating business partnership.

14.3 Partnership Law

To establish uniformity, many states have, through their legislatures, adopted the Uniform Partnership Act (U.P.A.). States that have not adopted the U.P.A. continue to regulate partnerships under the common law and existing statutes. The Uniform Partnership Act and other partnership laws are very similar to agency law.

EXAMPLE 3. Dugan and Crouch entered into a partnership agreement for the purpose of conducting a landscaping business. A short time later, Dugan began ordering Crouch around and assigned a disproportionate amount of work to him. Partners, under both the Uniform Partnership Act and the common law, are agents for one another but are not considered to be each other's employees. Dugan exceeded his authority in assuming complete leadership.

14.4 Proprietary Interest

One is not a partner unless he or she has a *proprietary interest* in the business—interest resulting from the contribution of capital, service, or both. The proprietary interest creates a right to profits and a liability for losses.

EXAMPLE 4. Larson provided $25,000 capital and Romberg agreed to use all of his engineering and scientific skills to create a new builders' consulting business. Larson and Romberg had each made substantial contributions to the new venture, and they would be considered partners.

14.5 Partnership Agreement

Partnership agreements may be oral, written, or implied. Only in special cases, where the statute of frauds or other legislation makes it mandatory, must the partnership agreement be in writing. A partnership may result from the actions and agreements of parties, without the actual expression of an intention to create a partnership.

EXAMPLE 5. Lodge operated a furniture-repair business. He was assisted by Quarles, a skilled cabinet maker who worked on a weekly salary. Lodge suggested that Quarles invest money in the business, with the right to share in the management of the business and in any profits at the end of the year. Quarles accepted. They may not have intended to create a partnership by their agreement, but they did. Both Quarles and Lodge now are agents for the partnership business.

14.6 Articles of Copartnership

A written agreement between parties which outlines the rights and obligations of each partner is termed the *articles of copartnership*. The articles should contain: (1) the names and addresses of the partners; (2) the nature of their business; (3) the capital investment by each; (4) the duties and salaries of each; (5) the division of profits and losses; and (6) provisions for the dissolution of the partnership and the withdrawal of a partner.

EXAMPLE 6. Jackson and Archino each invested $15,000 in a new beauty shop. Jackson's duties were to manage the financing and other business. Archino was in charge of the day-to-day schedules and operations. No provision was made in the articles of copartnership for the division of profits and sharing of losses. Although Archino did 80 percent of the work and brought in most of the business, partnership law would provide an equal distribution of profits because no other distribution was provided for in the articles of copartnership. Anticipating inequalities of time and effort expended, the parties should have provided for a more equitable distribution of profits and losses in the articles.

14.7 Minors as Partners

Minors may be partners in all but a few types of businesses. However, minors have the right to avoid contracts, so a minor may withdraw from a partnership before becoming of age. The minor may not, however, withdraw her or his investment if such an action would weaken the business.

EXAMPLE 7. Carson, a minor, was an active partner with Sharp in a dog-care and grooming business. Both had invested $800 in the venture. Carson announced that she was "getting out" and demanded the return of her $800 and any profits due her. Sharp could deny Carson the return of her investment until such time as the business would not be threatened by Carson's withdrawal. Sharp would not, however, have a right of suit against Carson for terminating the partnership agreement.

TYPES OF PARTNERS

14.8 General, or Real, Partners

Persons who are active in the management of a business and who share in its gains and losses are *general*, or *real, partners*.

14.9 Silent, or Secret, Partners

Persons who are active in the management of a business but who are not known to be partners by outside parties are *secret partners*.

EXAMPLE 8. Smith and Dale were general partners in an auction business. Jay, another auctioneer, was always present at all auctions and participated in running the sales. Jay was actually a partner with a one-third interest, but he preferred that his interest not be known. (His regular employment was that of a high school teacher and coach.) Thus, Jay was a silent partner in this auction business.

14.10 Dormant Partners

Persons who are partners in a business but who take no active part in the business and who are not known as partners to outside parties are *dormant partners*. Such a person is usually an investing partner or one who is included in the partnership because of skills in directing and counseling the other partners.

EXAMPLE 9. Seisman, a mathematician and physicist, invested $50,000 in a partnership venture organized for the purpose of producing instruments used in measuring light waves. Because of his professional status, Seisman preferred to remain "behind the scenes." He was most instrumental in offering advice and guidance, but was never mentioned to outside parties as a member of the firm. Seisman was a *dormant partner*.

14.11 Nominal Partners

Persons sometimes permit a partnership business to use their names as a way of lending public appeal and attractiveness to the business. Such persons, if they are in no other way a part of the venture, are *nominal partners*. Outside parties may conclude that such persons are general partners, thus making them liable to the partnership's creditors.

EXAMPLE 10. Harvey, a popular professional basketball player, permitted his name to be used, with two general partners' names, as a nominal partner in Harvey, Richards, & King Sports Outfitters. On the strength of Harvey's name, credit was extended to the partnership in the purchase of merchandise for the store. In case of financial reverses, creditors could call on Harvey, the nominal partner, for payment of the partnership accounts.

14.12 Limited, or Special, Partners

Persons who have no share in the management of the business and whose liability is limited to the amount of their investment in the business are *limited*, or *special, partners*. State laws provide requirements for qualifying as a limited partner. The requirements usually include the filing of a *certificate of limited partnership* in a public office, announcement of the partnership formation in a newspaper of general circulation in the county, and membership of at least one general partner in the partnership. (Limited, or special, partners are those who usually have only an investment interest in the business.)

14.13 Partnership Name

Partnerships organized for purposes other than trading with the public may operate without a name. For identification, convenience, public relations, and buying and selling goods and services, partnerships usually have names. There are no restrictions on names chosen, as long as they do not infringe on already-copyrighted names and as long as they conform with local statutes. Some states declare it illegal to include in the partnership name the names of persons who are not real partners. Other states restrict the use of the words "and company." When a partnership is sued, the suit is brought in the name of the individual partners, not the partnership name. By common law, real property is held in the name of partners. The Uniform Partnership Act does permit real property to be held in the name of the partnership, however.

EXAMPLE 11. Lambert and George invested $30,000 each in a music store that sold instruments and music. Stationery, signs, and window displays carried the name "Amateur Artist Music Center." Neither partner's name was included in the name of the business, but the name was satisfactory.

RIGHTS AND DUTIES OF PARTNERS

14.14 When Partners Have No Written Agreement

In those partnerships where there is no agreement as to the partners' rights and duties, the law will apply obligations similar to those existing between a principal and an agent. Partnership law is based on the principle that each partner is an agent acting for the other partners. The rights and duties concerning outside parties are similar to a principal's and agent's relationship to third parties.

EXAMPLE 12. Smultz and Kurfirst were general partners in an auto-repair shop. They had no formal agreement but worked successfully as partners. Against the wishes of Kurfirst, Smultz ordered a machine for grinding brake drums. Although Kurfirst did not agree to Smultz's act, the seller of the machine had the right to believe that Smultz acted with authority, as provided for under the apparent-authority principle in agency law. The partners, thus, are equally liable for payment to the seller of the machine.

14.15 Rights and Duties in Articles of Copartnership

Partners' rights and duties, as provided for in the articles of copartnership, usually include the right of each partner to: (1) participate in management; (2) share in profits; (3) indemnity or contribution for injuries or expenses; (4) the return of cash advances and capital investment; and (5) inspect the partnership accounts and records.

Also specified in most articles are these duties: (1) honesty and good faith in the partnership relationship; (2) exercise of care, skill, and diligence; and (3) a promise to observe and follow the terms of the partnership agreement.

14.16 Powers of the Partners

Partners may have: (1) powers that are expressed or implied in the partnership agreement or (2) apparent powers that outside parties have a right to believe the partners have. Partners may also have powers granted them by secret agreements contained in the articles of copartnership; these agreements are not necessarily binding on outside parties.

EXAMPLE 13. Sentry and Palmer signed articles of copartnership. Only Sentry was authorized to make contracts and extend credit to the partnership's customers. During Sentry's absence from the store, Palmer agreed to sell a CB radio and car antenna to Humber for $195. The terms he gave were $50 cash with the balance due in thirty days. Sentry demanded the return of the radio on the grounds that Palmer had no authority to extend credit to a customer. It would be *apparent* to a customer, however, that a partner would have the right to extend credit. The secret agreement was not known to Humber and he would have no obligation to agree to any changes in the deal he made with Palmer.

14.17 Implied Powers of Partners

Although certain powers may be restricted by terms of the articles of copartnership, it is ordinarily implied that each partner has the right to: (1) hire agents and employees; (2) receive money due the firm; (3) incur debts within the scope of the partnership business; (4) bind the firm to contracts within the scope of the business; (5) purchase goods normally used by the business; (6) make, accept, and endorse negotiable instruments issued in the firm's name; (7) sell or mortgage the firm's personal property; and (8) reduce a debt owed to the partnership.

14.18 Limitations of Partners' Authority

Unless given specific authority by the articles of copartnership, a partner acting alone may not: (1) dispose of the business's goodwill; (2) set off a personal debt against a debt of the firm; (3) sell real estate held in the name of the partners; (4) make a confession of judgment on behalf of the partnership prior to a trial verdict; (5) give the firm's guaranty of a personal debt or the debt of a third party; (6) assign the firm's entire property to pay the partnership debts.

14.19 Partner's Personal Liability

A partner is *jointly liable* with the other partners for contracts entered into by any partner within the scope of the partnership business. Partners are *jointly and severally* liable for the partnership's torts against outside parties.

EXAMPLE 14. Benson, a partner in Benson and Hawley, injured a customer in the partnership store during a demonstration of a compressed-air drill. The injured party has the option of suing Benson and Hawley jointly (together) or severally (either one alone).

14.20 Execution of Judgment against Partnership

The personal assets of the partners may be taken to satisfy a judgment when the assets of the partnership are not sufficient. The satisfaction of a judgment may first be sought by confiscating the personal property of one partner. If that step is insufficient, the same partner's real property may be attached. When a judgment is satisfied out of the property of only one partner, that partner may institute an action for *contribution* against the other partners, demanding that each partner share proportionally in the satisfaction of the judgment.

EXAMPLE 15. Financial failure resulted in a judgment against Thomas and Riley, who were equal partners. A deficiency of $13,000 remained after all of the partnership assets were disposed of. The creditor proceeded to collect the deficiency by securing a judgment against Riley personally, attaching Riley's personal property. Riley may now seek a $6,500 contribution from Thomas.

14.21 Liability of a Retiring Partner

A retiring partner is personally liable for a proportionate share of the debts of the partnership incurred during the time in which she or he was a partner. (This is true because credit had been extended to the partnership partly on the strength of the retiring partner's personal assets.)

EXAMPLE 16. Durham retired from the partnership of Durham & Gregg, Florists. At the time of his withdrawal, there were debts of $7,500 outstanding against the partnership. Durham may be held jointly liable with Gregg for the $7,500 accounts payable in the event that the business fails to meet this obligation.

14.22 Informing Outside Parties of a Partner's Withdrawal

It is the duty of a partnership or a retiring partner to inform outside parties with whom the partnership has been doing business of a partner's retirement. Failure to communicate such notice permits outside parties to consider the retiring partner as an apparent partner, with continuing liability for partnership debts.

EXAMPLE 17. Suppose, in Example 16, that Durham had not notified outside business associates of his withdrawal from the partnership. Any contracts entered into under the name of Durham & Gregg would be made on the assumption that Durham was still a member of the firm. Durham would be jointly liable with Gregg on these new contracts.

EXAMPLE 18. Suppose that an announcement made in the public press indicated that Durham had retired from Durham & Gregg, of Example 16. Thereafter, Durham & Gregg contracted with a new firm to buy floral vases. Even though the new firm had not read the announcement in the paper, Durham would *not* be held liable. In the case of *new* outside parties, the law holds that such a *constructive notice* is sufficient. (This is an exception to the rule illustrated in Example 17.)

DISSOLUTION OF PARTNERSHIP

14.23 Dissolution by Partnership Agreement

Similar to an agency contract a partnership may be dissolved: (1) by mutual agreement; (2) by terms of the articles of copartnership; (3) by the assignment of one of the partner's interest in the partnership; (4) by completing performance of the purpose for which the partnership was formed; (5) by passing the originally agreed-to dissolution date; and (6) by withdrawal of a partner.

EXAMPLE 19. Allenby, a partner in the Rhodes Drug Stores, sold his partnership interest to Brimshaw. The original partnership was thus terminated. Partners have the right to select their fellow-partners. In this case, the remaining partners may elect to accept Brimshaw as a partner, thereby forming a *new partnership.*

14.24 Dissolution by Operation of Law

Without regard to the wishes of partners, a partnership is sometimes dissolved by the operation of law. Dissolution may, in some cases, result in the formation of a new partnership, as when a partnership is formed by the surviving partners upon the death of a partner.

Partnerships are dissolved by operation of law when: (1) a partner dies; (2) a partner is declared insane; (3) a partner is declared bankrupt; (4) new legislation makes the partnership operation illegal; or (5) the partnership itself is bankrupt.

EXAMPLE 20. Stapley and Kile were licensed to operate a hearing-aid center. They were general partners. Neither partner was a trained audiologist. A state law requiring that hearing aids be sold and serviced only by licensed audiologists was passed. The partnership of Stapley and Kile would be dissolved automatically by this new legislation.

14.25 Dissolution by Court Decision

A partnership may be dissolved by court decision as well as by the enactment of new legislation. Cases in which a court may declare a partnership dissolved include those in which: (1) a partner is declared insane and is thus not capable of contracting; (2) there is a serious disagreement between partners, and they petition the court to dissolve the partnership; and (3) a partner is guilty of dishonesty, fraud, and the like.

EXAMPLE 21. A successful furniture business was operated as a partnership by Henry, Dukes, and Lyons for fifteen years. Dukes, who was in charge of public relations, decided to contract for television commercials. Henry and Lyons would not agree. The argument became serious among them and resulted in a loss of customers and a decline in business. Henry and Lyons petitioned the court for an order dissolving the partnership. If it was granted, there would be a division of assets, capital, and profits. Henry and Lyons, thereafter, would be free to form a new partnership without Dukes.

14.26 Liquidating Partners

The partners remaining after other partners have left the business, have been expelled, have died, or have been removed by court decision are called *liquidating partners.* It is the responsibility of these partners to liquidate the assets of the former partnership, pay all bills and accounts, and divide what remains among the surviving partners. Surviving partners may, if they desire, purchase a deceased partner's share and thus continue the business under a new partnership arrangement.

14.27 Distribution of Partnership Assets

Liquidating partners, when a partnership is discontinued, have the responsibility of distributing the remaining assets of the business to all partners and to the executor of any deceased partner's estate. These partners, after paying all claims, distribute the remaining assets as follows: (1) to creditors other than the partners themselves; (2) to any partner who made a personal loan to the firm; and (3) to the partners, in proportion to their individual investments.

EXAMPLE 22. Longview Farms was owned and operated as a partnership by Larrimore, Truman, and Harper. The value of their land and the taxes on it increased to a point that made farming unprofitable. The sale of the land and an auction sale of machinery, growing crops, and personal property netted the partnership a total of $987,653. Assets exceeded the firm's liabilities. All taxes, liens, notes, and outstanding accounts were paid. The remainder was divided among the partners.

Solved Problems

14.1 Harvey worked as the store manager for Roberts Supply, which was owned and operated by Sam Roberts. Harvey's salary was 30 percent of the store's profits each month. Roberts controlled all management matters, giving Harvey specific instructions to be followed. Is Harvey a partner in the business?

By the definition of a partnership adopted by the Uniform Partnership Act, Harvey is *not* a partner. He does not participate in management, and his salary is merely calculated as a percent of each month's current profits.

14.2 Livelli and Freedman, in the presence of Miller, ordered merchandise from Mitchell, permitting Mitchell to believe that Miller was a member of their partnership. Miller made no effort to deny that he was a partner, which he was not. When the merchandise was not paid for, Mitchell sued all three as partners. Could Miller deny responsibility?

Miller was fully aware that he had been presented to Mitchell as a partner and did nothing to correct Mitchell's mistaken impression. Miller is thus a *partner by estoppel* and would be liable, with the others, to Mitchell.

14.3 Parsons and Price operated a partnership under the name of Central Hardware Store. Outside parties claimed that Parsons and Price were operating the business fraudulently by not disclosing the names of the owners of the partnership. Have the partners been in violation of their obligations?

As a general rule, partners operating a business under a name other than their own names must file in a public office a declaration that shows the names of the owners. State laws vary in this regulation, however. Parsons and Price might, in some states, be guilty of a misdemeanor and be fined.

14.4 Thornton and Walton verbally agreed to start a magazine-distribution agency as partners. The partnership was to continue for a period of four years, at which time they would

renegotiate their arrangement. After one year, Walton announced that he was withdrawing from the business. Could Thornton successfully sue Walton for breach of their partnership agreement?

No. The Uniform Partnership Act states that "rules of law and equity" will be followed in all matters not specifically contained in the Act. Thus, the statute of frauds applies to the partners' agreement. Because they had no written contract, the agreement did not bind them after one year from the date of the agreement.

14.5 **Bowman and Mahler worked as partners in selling untaxed cigarettes purchased in an illegal operation. Mahler stole money from the partnership. (Bowman discovered this when he examined their books and found that $8,500 could not be accounted for.) May Bowman sue Mahler in an attempt to recover this money?**

No. Persons engaged in illegal activities may not seek the protection of the law in any matters related to their operations. The expression that a plaintiff "may not go into court with dirty hands" is a respected legal maxim. In this case, Bowman has no legal rights enforceable against Mahler.

14.6 **Hearn and Greenfield were partners in a dry-cleaning business. At the end of the first year's operation, the business showed a profit of $12,000 after deduction of the partner's salaries and all other expenses. Must the partnership pay federal or state income tax on this profit?**

No. The profits from a partnership are divided among the partners as personal income. The partners themselves pay income tax to federal and state governments. A partnership makes only an *information return,* not a tax payment, to the Internal Revenue Service.

14.7 **Darlington borrowed $6,300 from the First State Bank. He planned to use the money to purchase merchandise for Darlington & Rosfield, Clothiers. Darlington signed the note in his own name, not using the name of the partnership. Is the partnership business liable on the note?**

No. The note was Darlington's, and was not collectible against the partnership firm. Actually, Darlington himself had procured $6,300, which had been turned over to the firm and might be treated as a personal loan to the firm by Darlington. The note to the bank, however, was Darlington's personal note.

14.8 **Chase and Collins were partners in a hardware business. During Chase's absence, Collins signed a lease with a realtor. He planned to move the business from Centreville to Denton, four miles away. Did Collins have the authority to make this decision alone?**

No. Basic changes in partnership operation require the consent and approval of all partners or a majority of partners. Collins, acting alone, exceeded his rights in the decision to move the business to another town.

14.9 **Marsland, McGee, and Lofink were partners in a law firm. McGee and Lofink agreed that a new set of the *Corpus Juris Secundum* was needed in the firm's law library. Marsland disagreed. Must all partners agree in making such decisions in the day-to-day operation of the partnership?**

By majority rule, partners may make and execute decisions in matters relating to the operation of the business. The purchase of books needed in the library did not constitute a major or basic change in the business. The decision of McGee and Lofink was sufficient to override Marsland's objection.

14.10 By agreement of all four partners in a business, it was decided that only Dunlap, one of the partners, would have the authority to grant credit to customers. One of the other partners granted credit to Elliott. Dunlap later disapproved this act. What are Elliott's rights?

Outside parties who are not informed of each partner's rights and powers will not be bound by secret agreements made among the partners. Elliott, as a reasonably prudent person, would have the right to believe that all partners had the right to make credit decisions. The partnership is bound by the decision of the partner who acted outside his authority.

14.11 Conte, Newton, and Offutt were partners in a crop-dusting venture. The partnership owned two airplanes. Newton, acting in the names of the other partners, sold one of the specially equipped airplanes to Massey Air-Dusters, Inc. The sale had not been authorized by the other partners. Conte and Offutt demanded the return of the aircraft from Massey. Were they justified in this demand?

Outside parties must be prudent in deciding what powers any single partner has in making contracts for the partnership. Massey Air-Dusters, Inc., should be aware that one partner alone would not ordinarily have the power to sell one of the airplanes being used in the ongoing business. Massey, then, was *not* an innocent purchaser and would be required to return the aircraft after receiving back all monies it had paid.

14.12 Curtis and Crossan, painting contractors, applied two coats of outside white paint to DeFelice's house. DeFelice was billed $2,100 for the job. DeFelice complained to Crossan that the charge was excessive. Crossan disagreed and refused to reduce the bill. Later, DeFelice convinced Curtis to lower the charge to $1,900, which DeFelice paid. If Crossan found out about this could he still collect the $200 difference from DeFelice?

No. As far as outside parties are concerned, a partner has the apparent authority to *adjust* a customer's complaint without advice and approval from any other partner. Curtis's agreement to accept the $1,900 as full payment of the *disputed* account bound the partnership.

14.13 Cortese and Riggin were partners in a repair business. They worked on foreign cars and motorcycles. They were general partners, each working five days a week and receiving a salary and a one-half share in the business's year-end profits. Riggin opened the shop on three consecutive Saturdays and did work for persons who paid him directly. Cortese heard of Riggin's activity and demanded that the money received be placed in the partnership account. Was Cortese correct in his demand?

Partners, like agents, must act in good faith and do nothing that might advance their own profits at the expense of the partnership. Riggin's activity, without Cortese's knowledge, was dishonest and in direct competition with the firm's business. Riggin is obligated to deposit the added income to the account of the partnership.

14.14 Seeley, Bedwell, and Shidler opened an office as equal partners. They served as public stenographers to businesses located in the Fountain Building. Shidler became ill a few months after the business operation started and was not able to return to the office for six months. Seeley and Bedwell increased their own efforts, and the firm realized an excellent net profit at the end of the first year. Was Shidler correct in demanding an equal share of the profits with the other two?

Yes. Unless the articles of copartnership have different conditions, each partner is entitled to an equal share in the partnership profits. In anticipation of the possibility of the excessive absence of a partner, partners should include provisions for a different distribution of earnings.

14.15 A supermarket operated as a partnership by Hearn, Lovell, and James employed ten persons as clerks and assistants. As required by law, the business was covered by workmen's compensation. Lovell was injured while working and applied for workmen's compensation benefits. Will he receive the benefits?

Workmen's compensation laws vary from state to state, but in most cases partners are *not* covered as employees. Lovell would probably not receive benefits under workmen's compensation laws.

14.16 Eastburn withdrew from the partnership of Eastburn, Hawley, and Grimes. Two weeks later, Grimes negligently ran into James with the firm's delivery truck. (Grimes had been delivering merchandise for the partnership.) James held that Eastburn was jointly liable for damages because he had not informed outside parties that he had severed his connections with the partnership. Was James correct in this claim?

No. Eastburn is not liable in any way for the torts of former partners after his withdrawal from the partnership. This is in contrast with his liability for *contracts* based on a former partner's apparent continuing association with the partnership, in which case notice of withdrawal must be given to certain outside parties.

14.17 Grover secured the approval of two of his three associate partners to admit Harold to their partnership. One of Grover's associates would not agree to the proposal, however. May the new partner be admitted on the basis of majority rule?

No. Admitting a new partner actually created a *new* partnership. Grover could not gain the admission of the new partner without the approval of every member of the partnership.

14.18 Suppose that Grover, after his disappointment in Problem 14.17, decided to sell his *interest* in the partnership to Harold. May the other partners prevent this sale of the interest?

No. The Uniform Partnership Act does not restrict a partner from selling an *interest* in a partnership—a property interest that one has the right to sell to others. However, Grover may not *assign* his partnership rights and powers to another. Thus, the sale of Grover's interest does not make the buyer of the interest a partner.

14.19 Willoughby and Simpson were partners in an apparel shop. Simpson died, and her husband, as sole legatee to the estate, claimed the right to take her place in the business. Was Mr. Simpson correct in his assumption?

No. The death of a partner automatically dissolves a partnership. Simpson was, of course, the heir to his wife's interest in the firm, but he could not unilaterally declare himself to be Willoughby's new partner.

14.20 Geiss was a general partner with Holly and Moss in a printing business. Geiss fell far behind in his personal debts and filed for voluntary bankruptcy. His petition was granted. Did this affect the partnership business?

Yes. Bankruptcy of a partner, whether voluntary or involuntary, dissolves a partnership.

14.21 Wyncoat and Spruce operated a private airport in Newcastle County. Due to extensive apartment construction in the area, the county zoning board had the airport's land zoned residential, making it no longer available for flights. How did this ruling affect the partnership?

A partnership is dissolved by operation of law when a new law makes the purpose of the partnership illegal. Unless overturned by a court, the zoning authority's ruling would render the partnership dissolved.

14.22 Wyncoat and Spruce, in Problem 14.21, were required to liquidate their firm. Financial reports showed that the partnership had assets of $400,000 and liabilities of $275,000, not including the partners' investments. Outside creditors were paid, and Wyncoat and Spruce received all back salaries and expenses and repayment of personal loans to the firm. Each had invested $100,000 in the business. How was the $125,000 remaining balance distributed?

There was $125,000 remaining after distribution of the $275,000 to various creditors. Based on the equal contribution of $100,000 each from Wyncoat and Spruce, each will receive a settlement of one-half the remaining amount, or $62,500.

Review Problems

14.23 What are the advantages of a sole proprietorship over other types of business organizations?

14.24 What are *secret partners?*

14.25 Do partnership businesses pay federal income taxes?

14.26 (1) May a partner sell his or her interest in a partnership? (2) May a partner assign her or his partnership rights and powers?

14.27 What is a partnership?

14.28 What is the Uniform Partnership Act? How does the Act become operative in any state?

14.29 What special provisions may state laws make for limited partnerships?

14.30 Does a nominal partner share in the profits of a partnership?

14.31 What obligation does a minor have in withdrawing from a partnership business?

14.32 Is a retiring partner liable for the torts of former partners after he or she withdraws from the partnership?

14.33 Why is a knowledge of agency law necessary to one who becomes a business partner?

14.34 What is the obligation of a retiring partner to outside parties with whom the partnership has been doing business?

14.35 What are *dormant partners?*

14.36 Are there any restrictions in selecting a partnership name?

14.37 Under what laws are partnership operations regulated if they are not covered by the Uniform Partnership Act?

14.38 Why is it advisable to write articles of copartnership?

14.39 May a partner's personal assets be attached to pay the debts of an insolvent partnership?

14.40 What is the term used to describe the surviving partners who close out a partnership business?

Answers to Review Problems

14.23 The owner follows his or her own judgment and makes his or her own decisions in all matters related to the management and operation of the business.

14.24 Secret partners are those who are active in the management of a partnership business but who are not identified as partners to outside parties.

14.25 No. They merely file partnership information reports with the Internal Revenue Service.

14.26 (1) Yes. (2) No.

14.27 A partnership is the combining of two or more persons' finances, skills, and/or knowledge for the purpose of carrying out a lawful business with the intention of making a profit.

14.28 The Uniform Partnership Act consists of uniform rules for the regulation of partnership businesses. The Act becomes operative when it is adopted by the legislature of an individual state.

14.29 State laws may require the filing of a certificate of limited partnership in a public office for review and for the protection of outside parties.

14.30 No. Nominal partners are not really partners at all.

14.31 A minor must allow his or her investment to remain in the business until such time that it may be removed without threatening the business or its creditors.

14.32 No.

14.33 Agency law forms an important part of partnership law. Each partner is an agent of the others in making contracts and in managing the affairs of the business.

14.34 A retiring partner must give notice to creditors and other concerned parties that she or he is withdrawing from the business. Otherwise the withdrawing party becomes an *apparent* partner.

14.35 Dormant partners are partners who do not take an active part in the business and who are not know as partners to outside parties.

14.36 Yes. Copyright laws protect names already filed with the United States Patent Office. Also, partnerships may not use names that would be misleading to outside parties. Also, some states prohibit the use of such expressions as "and company" in association with the names of partners.

14.37 the common law and statute law

14.38 It helps to remove uncertainties about the rights and powers of partners and to establish procedures in anticipation of later dissolution.

14.39 Yes.

14.40 liquidating partners

Legal Terms

Articles of copartnership. A written agreement, subscribed to by business partners, outlining the rights and obligations of the partners.

Capital. Money and property invested in a business.

Liquidating partners. The partners remaining after other partners have left, been expelled, died, or been removed by court order. It is their responsibility to liquidate the remaining assets of the now-terminated partnership.

Partnership. A business created by two or more competent parties through the joining of assets, labor, and skills for the purpose of carrying on a lawful activity and of sharing both profits and losses.

Proprietary interest. A partnership requisite; achieved through the contribution of capital, services, or both to a partnership.

Sole proprietorship. A business venture owned by one individual, who operates it either alone or with the assistance of agents and employees.

Chapter 15

Corporations

Corporations and corporation law are an outgrowth of a New York State law which, in 1811, provided legislation making the corporation a valid type of business organization. (England adopted the corporate type of organization by an Act of Parliament in 1855.) Businesses operating under state laws are usually identified as corporations by the abbreviation "Inc.," which follows the name of the business. (English firms use the expression "Limited," or "Ltd.")

Corporations are legal entities with rights and duties almost the same as the rights and duties of persons. They differ from persons in that they are, of course, incapable of acting for themselves. They always perform their chartered activities through agents.

Corporations may be large or small. Large firms are usually organized as corporations because such an organization gives them greater powers to assemble the capital investment necessary in carrying on huge undertakings. A corporate type of organization is also attractive to the small business because its stockholders are protected by the "corporate veil," which prohibits creditors and other claimants from confiscating the shareholder's personal estates should the corporation become insolvent.

Corporations are not all operated for the purpose of making a profit. Welfare organizations, schools, colleges, hospitals, and numerous other institutions are chartered as nonprofit corporations. (Nonprofit corporations are not financed through the sale of stocks, bonds, or other securities.) Lodges, clubs, and other nonprofit social groups may also be formed through the issuance of a corporate charter.

Corporation law is essentially state law, although there are federal rules and agencies that regulate corporations engaged in interstate commerce. It is essential, therefore, to refer to the corporation laws of a particular state in determining the outcome of specific legal problems concerning corporate law in any one state. This chapter reviews the basic laws and principles common to most states.

TYPES OF CORPORATIONS

15.1 Public Corporations

Corporations created for governmental purposes are *public corporations*. Cities, as well as special departments of local and state governments, are usually governed under a corporate charter issued by the state. Public corporations issue no stock, receive no private investment, and declare no dividends.

EXAMPLE 1. In an effort to provide more efficient operation of the postal service, the United States Congress enacted the Federal Postal Reorganization Act of 1970. By this act, postal service in the United States was organized under a new public corporation, which has the right of almost independent action in all postal matters.

15.2 Quasi-Public Corporations

Quasi-public corporations are privately financed corporations that are created to provide public services, usually under a special franchise awarded by the incorporating state. Public utilities and public transportation systems such as toll roads, highway bridges, and ferry boats often come within this classification. Quasi-public corporations are carefully supervised by public authorities in matters of the rates they charge and their efficiency.

EXAMPLE 2. Queen Anne County had no telephone service. Private investors formed the Queen Anne Telephone Company, a quasi-public corporation. It was awarded an exclusive franchise by the state to provide telephone service within the county. The corporation was required by the state to serve *all* individuals and businesses that applied for service. In addition, the rates it charged had to be approved by the state.

15.3 Private Corporations

Private corporations are those formed by private interest either to carry on a business or to provide some charitable service. Unlike a partnership, a private corporation is a legal entity entirely separate from and independent of its owners.

EXAMPLE 3. Stetson, Riley, and Arthur were partners in a lumber business. The firm's expansion was limited by the amount of capital the partners were able to invest. The partners therefore incorporated the business, sold stock, and thus increased the financial strength of their company. The new corporation was a legal entity, separate from and independent of the former partners.

15.4 Domestic Corporations and Foreign Corporations

A corporation is a *domestic corporation* in respect to the state or country from which its charter is issued. When transacting business in another state or country, that same corporation is called a *foreign corporation*.

EXAMPLE 4. E. I. du Pont de Nemours, Inc., is incorporated under the laws of the State of Delaware, where it is a *domestic corporation.* When it does business in other states, it is deemed to be a *foreign corporation.* Constitutional protections give a domestic corporation the right to operate in all foreign states as long as the corporation's purpose is legal and the corporation conforms to the laws and requirements of the state in which it is doing business.

15.5 Alien Corporations

Corporations operating outside the confines of the country in which they are incorporated are know as *alien corporations.* Like alien persons, alien corporations must respect the laws of their host countries.

15.6 Close Corporations

Small firms, with stock that is not traded publicly but is closely held by a few stockholder-owners, are known as *close corporations*. Many states, such as Delaware, have special provisions regulating close corporations. Close corporations have very much the same corporate advantages that large, publicly traded corporations have.

EXAMPLE 5. Reneau operated an exclusive dress shop in New York. Her store served a discriminating and wealthy clientele. To protect her personal estate from confiscation in the event of the company's financial reverses, she secured a corporate charter for the business. Reneau held 90 percent of the common stock and issued the remaining 10 percent to members of her family, who were named officers of the corporation. Protection is thus given the owner of this business in the same way protection is given stockholders in multi-million-dollar companies.

15.7 Professional Corporations

Corporations may be formed by people who wish to combine their skills in the practice of law, medicine, architecture, and other professions. Those who are active in providing the professional services are deemed to be *employees* of the corporation. When a special license is required for the practice of a profession, the employee must apply for it; a professional license cannot be issued to the corporation itself.

EXAMPLE 6. Drs. Hill, Campbell, and Barton were specialists in the practice of ophthalmology. They worked as a team, occupied adjoining offices, and employed one medical secretary and one nurse among them. To allow a more efficient operation and to create certain tax advantages, the three doctors formed a close corporation, each taking one-third of the common stock. Each doctor was paid a monthly salary commensurate with services rendered to patients during that month.

15.8 Nonprofit Corporations

Nonprofit corporations, also known as *eleemosynary corporations,* are those created to provide educational, charitable, or health services. In contrast to other types of private corporations, no stock is issued, dividends are not declared, and special methods of accounting and reporting are followed. Nonprofit corporations, when they meet federal and state requirements, are granted exemption from payment of income taxes and other forms of operating and property taxes.

EXAMPLE 7. The Johnson School of Drafting was organized as a proprietary institution in 1918. It was operated for a profit and paid its owners regular dividends. The school's unexpected popularity and a growing respect for its accomplishments prompted alumni and other public-spirited individuals to buy out the founders and create a new, nonprofit corporation that took over the operation of the institution. All tuition fees and other income then went to the betterment of the school; no further profits went to outside owners.

15.9 *De Jure* and *de Facto* Corporations

A *de jure corporation* is one that receives its state charter after satisfying *all* requisites for the formation of a corporation under the laws of the state. A *de facto corporation* is an organization that operates as a corporation but that in some minor way has not satisfied all the requisites of state law. Only the incorporating state has the right to question the operation of a *de facto* corporation.

EXAMPLE 8. State law required newly chartered corporations to provide the state with a copy of the seal that would be used in signing all corporate contracts. Waste Paper Products, Inc., failed to do so. Although in noncompliance with this requirement, Waste Paper would be permitted to operate as a corporation after issuance of a charter. Only the state would have the right to question the corporation's legal existence.

FORMATION OF A CORPORATION

15.10 Corporation Promoters

Those persons who carry out all necessary preliminary steps in the formation of a corporation are its *promoters*. After a charter is issued, the new corporation will take over all contracts and agreements made on behalf of the corporation by the promoters. The promoters may be held personally liable to outside parties if their acts and representations are not afterward underwritten by the corporation.

EXAMPLE 9. Promoters of the proposed TransArctic Corporation made fraudulent statements to subscribers to the new corporate stock. After the charter was issued, certain subscribers realized the deception used against them; they therefore started suit. The action would be against the promoters. Only if the corporation knowingly accepted the wrong done by the promoters would the corporation itself be liable.

15.11 Incorporation Papers and Prospectus

All *incorporation papers* and a *prospectus,* which outline all phases of a new venture, should be prepared by a new corporation's promoters. Unless the corporation is to be an intrastate corporation, the prospectus must be approved by the Securities and Exchange Commission (S.E.C.), a federal agency. Any intrastate corporation's prospectus is usually reviewed by a state agency, which guards the welfare of those who might be interested in purchasing securities in new ventures.

15.12 Certificate of Incorporation

A *certificate of incorporation* is a formal document drawn up by a proposed corporation's promoters. The certificate contains detailed information, including the corporation's duration, the location of principal offices, and the names of directors and incorporators. The certificate also gives an account of the number of shares of stock subscribed to by each holder. The certificate is filed in the office of the secretary of state, from whom the charter is sought.

15.13 Corporate Charter

Approval of the certificate of incorporation, after study and investigation by the state, results in the formation of the new corporation. The certificate of incorporation becomes the *corporate charter,* or, as it is sometimes called, the *corporate franchise.*

15.14 Capital Stock of Corporation

The total *par value* of the shares of stock (each share in one issue must have the same value) specified in the corporate charter is called the *authorized capital stock.* A corporation is restricted from selling more shares than the number allowed by the charter. The sale of additional stock may be authorized later by a petition to the secretary of state by the existing stockholders.

EXAMPLE 10. The Harbor View Apartment Corporation sold ten-thousand shares of $100 par-value stock. The money from the sale was to be used for the construction of apartment buildings. Inflationary trends increased building costs, and another $50,000 was needed to complete the job. A petition to the secretary of state resulted in permission being granted the corporation to sell five-hundred new shares of capital stock.

15.15 Stockholders' Rights

Stockholders are entitled to participate in the corporation's profits in accordance with dividend provisions contained in the stock certificates and according to whether their stock is *common* or *preferred.* Stockholders have a right to vote at stockholders' meetings and to share in the distribution of corporate assets should there be a dissolution of the corporation. The corporate charter designates the voting rights that each type of stock will carry. Stockholders may not, however, enter into direct management of the corporation. (They are represented in management by the board of directors.) Owning stock does not authorize the stockholder to be an agent of the corporation.

EXAMPLE 11. Wexler owned one-thousand shares of common stock in Steam Turbine, Inc. He traveled five-hundred miles to visit the company's main plant. During a tour of the plant, he demanded, as a stockholder, that convenient rest areas be provided for all employees over fifty years of age. Wexler may make such a suggestion, but he has no power to manage and direct the corporation. All that management would owe him would be the same courtesy shown to anyone else who might tour the plant.

15.16 Board of Directors

Directors are nominated and voted upon by stockholders at their annual meeting. A stockholder's vote may be in person or by proxy. The corporation's directors, sitting as a board, determine the policies of the business and make all major management decisions. Officers of the corporation are directly responsible to the board. One director, acting as an individual, has no power to direct the firm's activities or to be an agent of the corporation.

EXAMPLE 12. Shawn was elected to membership on the board of directors of the Chicago Coke Company, Inc. One of her first acts, as director, was to write to the president of the company to demand a change in the corporation's logo. Shawn had no authority to direct the president in any action unless appointed to do so as a representative of the board.

EXAMPLE 13. Rugby, a member of the board of directors of the Cardboard Box Corporation, asked the board to discuss the current problem of securing secretarial help in the firm's main office. The chairman refused to include this discussion in the board's agenda. The board of directors, except in rare cases, does not enter into the day-to-day operation and problems of management. The board's responsibility is in the area of overall policy-making and in deciding on major changes in the corporation's operation.

15.17 Qualification of Directors

Corporation laws in most states require that a board of directors be made up of at least three members. Membership qualifications are at times set forth in the corporate charter. Unless prohibited by the charter, membership may be extended to anyone: nonresidents, minors, and persons who own no stock in the corporation. The bylaws of the corporation may, however, specify certain qualifications of board membership.

EXAMPLE 14. The Eugenia Cosmetic Corporation selected for its board of directors a biological chemist of national reputation. She was not a stockholder, lived in a state distant from the corporation headquarters, and had no real financial interest in the corporation's growth. This new member on the board of directors would be valuable to the corporation in the professional guidance and direction she could give to the board as a whole.

15.18 Powers and Liability of Directors

As representatives of the corporate entity, the directors have the power to appoint agents to act for the corporation, to delegate authority to carry out the wishes of the board, and to elect the officers of the corporation. Directors are not personally liable for acts performed in the conduct of corporate business. Stockholders may, however, hold a director liable for losses attributed to the director's negligence, fraud, or neglect of duty, or if the director exceeds the authority of his or her office.

EXAMPLE 15. The directors of the Jennings Corporation appointed a new president of the corporation. The appointment was made solely on the basis of representations made by the applicant himself. The new president made several bad decisions and was directly responsible for the financial difficulties that depleted the firm's surplus account. The directors could be held personally responsible for the losses resulting from the inexcusable manner in which the new president was chosen. A stockholder's suit against the directors would probably follow.

15.19 Officers of the Corporation

The corporate officers, selected by the board of directors, are responsible for implementing the policies and plans handed down by the board. Their positions are those of general agents: they have the right to use discretion in making day-to-day judgments about the operation and management of the corporation. All other agents and all employees are subagents of the officers.

CORPORATION STOCK

15.20 Common Stock

Common stock gives its owners voting rights in the corporation. Income from the stock is not guaranteed. Dividends are paid out of surplus funds after preferred stockholders have been paid the dividends indicated in their preferred-stock certificates.

EXAMPLE 16. McFall owned five-hundred shares of common stock in the Mobility Corporation. The firm showed profits of \$765,000 in one year. After paying interest on outstanding bonds, dividends to preferred stockholders, and reinvesting \$210,000 in the company, there was nothing left for dividends to McFall and the other owners of common stock. McFall has no right to complain of this distribution, unless he can prove that the \$210,000 reinvested was unreasonable and unnecessary for the corporation's growth and financial security.

15.21 Preferred Stock

The term *preferred stock* designates stock that is given preference, in one way or another, over other kinds of stock. The preference given may concern dividend payments, the division of assets on dissolution, or any other express matter. The preferred stock of most corporations does not give its owners the right to a stockholder's vote.

15.22 Treasury Stock

Stock that has already been issued and is returned to the corporation as a gift or through purchase is called *treasury stock.* Dividends are not paid on treasury stock.

EXAMPLE 17. The Copper Products Corporation was involved in financial difficulties caused by very competitive pricing in a period of inflation. To guarantee the firm's survival and to reduce its credit obligations, a majority of the stockholders turned in 15 percent of their stock holdings, which became treasury stock. This stock was then sold on the market by Copper Products in an attempt to regain the financial strength it needed to carry on the business.

15.23 Lost Stock Certificates

A stockholder whose stock certificates have been lost or stolen has the obligation to notify the corporation and to seek the issuance, at his or her own expense, of new certificates. An owner may not hold the corporation responsible for registering lost or stolen certificates in the name of a new "owner" if notification of loss has not been given. Owners petitioning the corporation for the issuance of new certificates must post an indemnity bond with the corporation to protect the corporation from losses that might arise through the loss of the original certificates.

15.24 Dividends

The board of directors declares dividends as a way of distributing profits to stockholders. Directors are expected to use discretion in declaring dividends, withholding sufficient profits to provide for payment of anticipated expenses. Capital assets may *not* be sold as a means of collecting funds to be distributed as dividends. Dividends may be in the form of cash payments or in the form of additional stock.

EXAMPLE 18. The board of directors of the Sanford Corporation sold some of the corporation's real estate and machinery as a means of securing funds that might be distributed to both common and preferred stockholders, who were dissatisfied with the profits being realized by management. The sale of such assets for dividend purposes would be illegal and would subject the directors to a stockholders' suit.

15.25 State and Federal Regulations

The interstate sale of securities is regulated by the Federal Securities Act of 1933. All new stock issues must be accompanied by a prospectus filed with the Securities and Exchange Commission. Approval for sale by the S.E.C. does *not* carry any investment recommendation. Approval signifies only that the S.E.C. has found the information in the prospectus to be truthful. Securities sold within the incorporating state are protected in most states by so-called "Blue-Sky Laws," which operate in much the same fashion as the S.E.C. regulations.

15.26 Federal Securities Exchange Act

The Federal Securities Exchange Act (1934) requires all stock exchanges engaged in the sale and transfer of securities to register with the Securities and Exchange Commission. Registered exchanges are forbidden to sell any securities disapproved by the S.E.C.

15.27 Margin Sales under Federal Reserve

The Federal Reserve Board has discretionary powers in setting the *margin* (minimum cash payment) required in the sales of securities through an exchange. Economic conditions and the condition of the market determine decisions of the Federal Reserve in adjusting margin rates.

EXAMPLE 19. During a recessionary period, the Federal Reserve Board granted a more liberal margin in the sales of securities. The more attractive margin brought buyers into the market, to some degree reversing the downward trend of the market.

OPERATION OF CORPORATIONS

15.28 Express and Implied Corporate Powers

Corporations derive powers from their charter. Express powers, specifically stated, are included in the charter. Implied powers consist of those that would be reasonably interpreted as necessary and consistent in carrying out the express powers.

EXAMPLE 20. Youth Styles, Inc., was chartered to operate a business for the design and manufacture of women's casual clothes. Youth Styles announced plans for adding a fabric-testing laboratory to its already complex operation. A stockholder's suit sought to enjoin the firm from this action on grounds that it was not permitted under the corporate charter. The importance of testing fabrics before purchase and use would be reasonably implied as a necessary addition to the firm's successful operation. The power to do so would be *implied* by the corporate charter.

15.29 *Ultra Vires* Acts

Ultra vires acts are those that are outside either the express or implied powers of a corporation. *Ultra vires* acts are in some ways analogous to a minor's agreement for necessaries. Thus, an *ultra vires* contract will not bind a corporation on grounds of legal incompetency. Once an *ultra vires* contract has been executed, however, neither the corporation nor the other party may rescind it.

EXAMPLE 21. Suppose, in Example 20, that Youth Styles contracted to manufacture a full line of men's wear. After the contract had been performed and all new merchandise was delivered by Youth Styles to the buyer and was paid for, the buyer attempted to rescind the agreement, demanding the return of money paid. Although Youth Styles had exceeded its express and implied powers, any action to have the executed contract rescinded would be discharged.

15.30 Stockholders' Rights

Stockholders have certain rights assured to them during the operational phase of the corporation's existence. These include: the right to receive notice of stockholders' meetings; the right to inspect the corporation's books when such an inspection is made in good faith and for a legitimate purpose; the right to vote at stockholders' meetings; the right to transfer stock; the right to receive dividends; the right to subscribe to new shares issued by the corporation; and the right to a fair share of assets distributed upon dissolution.

EXAMPLE 22. The annual stockholders' meeting of the Grimshaw Corporation was scheduled for April 15 by the board of directors. Notices of the meeting were not mailed until April 10. Stockholders protested the disregard of their right to receive notice a reasonable time prior to the meeting. The meeting was rescheduled, and new notices were sent out a month in advance of it.

15.31 Stockholders' Liabilities

By virtue of being a stockholder, a party is liable to the corporation for: any unpaid portion of a stock subscription; unpaid wages to employees (in some states only); and damage to corporate creditors resulting from unlawful distribution of the corporation's assets as dividends.

EXAMPLE 23. During a period of financial reversals, the Steel Products Corporation sold certain of its patent rights and large amounts of raw materials from its inventory as a means of collecting funds to be distributed as dividends. A dividend of 75¢ per share was declared on all common stock. As a result of this dividend, creditors could not be paid what was owed them by the corporation. A suit by the creditors could result in a judgment ordering the return of all dividends thus paid. The funds from these returned dividends would be used to pay the creditors.

15.32 Claims against Stockholders' Personal Estates

A distinct advantage of investment in a corporation over investment in a sole proprietorship or partnership is the protection of the stockholder from confiscation of his or her personal estate to satisfy the corporation's creditors. Only in rare instances, usually caused by a stockholder's fraud and deception, is a creditor's claim against a stockholder's personal property upheld. This is known as "piercing the veil."

EXAMPLE 24. Suppose, in Example 23, that the Steel Products Corporation fell far short of being able to meet its obligations to creditors even after the dividends were returned. Creditors would be barred from seeking judgment against the stockholders for money still owed. Stockholders may lose no more than the investment they have made in the business.

DISSOLUTION OF CORPORATIONS

15.33 Surrender of Charter

By a unanimous vote of stockholders or by a vote of the directors and two-thirds of the stockholders, it may be agreed to dissolve a corporation. Application is then made to the secretary of state for permission to carry out the dissolution.

15.34 Expiration of the Charter

Corporations may be chartered to continue in existence for a limited time or for a period required for the performance of powers granted in the charter. Unless the state is petitioned for a renewal, the charter expires automatically, and the corporation loses any power or authority to continue operating.

EXAMPLE 25. A historic-preservation group incorporated itself as a fund-raising entity to collect contributions for the restoration of historic buildings built before 1776. The group's goal was $2,500,000. When the goal was reached and the funds were put to their intended use, the corporate charter expired without the necessity of surrendering the charter.

15.35 Forfeiture of Charter

Quo warranto proceedings, carried out by the courts, may demand forfeiture of a charter for reasons of a corporation's insolvency, failure to use the franchise granted, charter abuse, wrongful or fraudulent acts, or other infractions of powers, rights, and the law. Through *quo warranto* proceedings, a court will declare the charter forfeited and will terminate the life of the corporation.

EXAMPLE 26. Charleston Electric and Power Company was chartered by the state and given an exclusive franchise to generate and distribute electric power to customers in the city of Charleston and those living less than three miles beyond the city limits. Delay caused by indecision among directors and stockholders deprived the area's people of electric service for three years. Action was brought in the courts against Charleston Electric, resulting in forfeiture of the charter and the issuance of a charter to another group certified to be ready to carry out the powers granted.

Solved Problems

15.1 Jefferson, King, and Lodge petitioned the secretary of state for a charter for a new corporation, which they planned to call the Financial Association. The charter was not issued because of the name chosen. Did the state have the power to deny the association a charter on these grounds?

Yes. Laws of most states make it mandatory that a corporation's name include such words as "company," "corporation," or "incorporated." Outside parties have a right to know that the "Financial Association" is a corporation and that they are not dealing with what might be construed as a partnership. "Financial Association" would be acceptable only if the certificate of incorporation included one of the descriptive titles required by state law.

15.2 Although Jefferson, King, and Lodge, in Problem 15.1, failed to receive a charter, they nevertheless represented their company as a corporation to outside parties. A contract with the Service Mailing Company was breached, and the firm sued Jefferson, King, and Lodge as individuals. May the three be sued as individuals?

Yes. Service Mailing Company had been deceived by the three owners, who were well aware that their company was not a corporation. They had acted as the *apparent agents* of a nonexistent corporation, making themselves personally liable to innocent outside parties.

15.3 Suppose that in Problem 15.2 Jefferson, King, and Lodge actually believed that their company was a corporation. In such an event, would Service Mailing Company have a right of action against the three individuals?

No. The company, in this case, was not a *de jure* corporation but was a *de facto* corporation to all concerned.

15.4 The certificate of incorporation for the Harley Henderson Company stated that the new firm would have *perpetual existence*. On an interpretation that "nothing can last forever," the charter was denied by the secretary of state. Had the incorporators' rights been denied in this situation?

"Perpetual existence" is allowed as a corporate-charter provision under the laws of *most* states. In only a few states is the life of a corporation restricted in time. In most states, then, the secretary would have erred in not issuing the charter containing this provision.

15.5 Chambers Boat Company, Inc., was chartered to build and sell luxury cruisers. A surplus of undistributed profits was invested in real estate located in a growing residential community. Stockholders complained that the corporation was engaged in an *ultra vires* act by going outside its chartered rights. Were the stockholders correct?

No. Corporations are permitted to invest surplus funds by the powers granted under the law. Chambers Boat Company was not entering the real estate business; it was merely investing funds in expectation of a reasonable return on the investment. This, then, was not an *ultra vires* act and was not illegal.

15.6 Suppose, in Problem 15.5, that the Chambers Boat Company entered into subsequent contracts whereby they were going to build one-hundred middle-income homes on the property purchased. Would this be within the corporation's powers?

No. This is different from the previous case. The corporation is here entering an entirely separate and distinct type of business. This would be objectionable as an *ultra vires* act and may be halted by the stockholders.

15.7 Sortman was one of the incorporators of the Brandywine Medical Center. Before Brandywine received a charter, Sortman contracted with Interior Decorators, Inc., to supply furnishings for the new medical building that was being built. When Brandywine Medical Center received its charter, its directors refused to ratify the contracts may by Sortman. Would Brandywine Medical Center, Inc., or Sortman be liable to Interior Decorators, Inc.?

Sortman. A nonexistent corporation has no capacity to contract. Contracts made for such a business are not enforceable against the corporation when and if the charter is issued. The promoter (Sortman) may be held personally liable for contracts with Interior Decorators, Inc. Had the directors acted to approve the contract with Interior Decorators, Inc., the decision would have been different.

15.8 Harrison was the sole owner of all shares of stock in the Avenue Service Center, Inc., a neighborhood business that serviced vehicles brought in for repairs. A pneumatic lift malfunctioned and dropped Bristow's car to the ground. Bristow sued Harrison for damages to her car, preferring to avoid a suit with the corporation itself. Is Harrison, as sole owner of the corporation, personally liable to Bristow?

Bristow may not "pierce the corporate veil" and bring this tort action against the owner rather than the corporation. A corporation is not one and the same with the owner of its stock. Harrison is not liable in this action; the complaint must be made against Avenue Service Center, Inc.

15.9 Albright secured a corporate charter under the name of Household Sales, Inc. Albright owned all of the company's stock. Albright did not, however, appoint any directors, and there were no other officers. Income to the corporation went directly into Albright's personal checking and savings accounts. No records were kept that might distinguish the corporate assets from Albright's assets. May an outside party "pierce the corporate veil" and sue Albright for damages resulting from the corporation's acts and contracts?

Yes. Albright and Household Sales, Inc., are one and the same. There was no way to distinguish one from the other. The assets, liabilities, and the contracts of the company could have been for either Albright or the company. The "corporate veil" would be nonexistent and give no protection to Albright.

15.10 The incorporators of the Arrow Company offered subscriptions to interested buyers of the new firm's one-thousand shares of common stock at $100 par value. One of the promoters received a subscription from Lukins, who offered to take two-hundred shares of the stock at $85 per share. May the incorporators agree to accept this offer?

Stock offered at a par value may not be sold for less than that value. To have sold Arrow Company's $100-par-value shares at $85 would have been illegal.

15.11 Giles orally agreed to subscribe to two-hundred shares of the Arrow Company's $100-par-value shares. Directors of the Arrow Company voted to accept Giles's subscription. Giles later refused to accept the stock, claiming that the order had not been made in writing. Is Giles released on these grounds?

The only restriction on oral agreements in the sale of stock arises from the statute of frauds requirement that agreements must be in writing if they are to last more than one year from the date of making. Giles's agreement was not of such duration. His subscription, although oral, is enforceable. (A few states take exception to this rule, requiring that subscriptions be in writing.)

15.12 Randall agreed orally to sell seventy-five shares of stock he owned in the Centrex Corporation to Zurko for $238 a share. Randall refused to deliver the stock on the agreed date, and Zurko sued Randall. Is Randall liable on the oral agreement with Zurko?

No. Transferring already-issued stock is not the same as subscribing for the unissued stock of a new corporation. Oral agreements for the sale of stock are *not* enforceable. Only if Randall had signed an agreement to sell the shares to Zurko would the agreement have been enforceable.

15.13 Stevenson purchased two-hundred shares of the Bold Company's $100-par-value stock. Stevenson paid for the shares with his check for $5,000 and a six-month interest-bearing promissory note for the balance of $15,000. Other shareholders entered a complaint of illegality on this stock transaction Was the sale valid?

Such a transaction was not valid because there was a delayed payment, represented by the promissory note. Only that part of the sale covered by the $5,000 payment is legal and enforceable.

15.14 The Trembly Machine Company bought back as treasury stock five-hundred previously issued shares of their own stock. The par value of a share was $100. At a later time, two-hundred-fifty of these common-stock shares were sold to Shivers for $85 a share. Shareholders complained that the sale was illegal because the shares were sold for a price below par. Were the stockholders correct in their complaint?

No. Treasury stock may be sold at prices below par. Such a sale is legal and is not to be confused with the sale of stock to initial subscribers of par value stock, as illustrated in Problem 15.10.

15.15 The Standard Wares Company submitted a certificate of incorporation to the secretary of state. The company also submitted a prospectus to the Securities and Exchange Commission because it planned to sell corporate securities in other states. The directors of the new corporation authorized the mailing of the prospectus to potential investors before getting final approval from the S.E.C. Was this a proper action by the directors?

No. A prospectus of a new security issue must be approved by the Securities and Exchange Commission *before* being issued. It is not sufficient that it has only been *filed* with the Commission.

15.16 Clifton printed counterfeit stock certificates on the Carlton Corporation. He sold two-hundred shares of the fake Carlton common stock to Heubert. Heubert mailed the counterfeit certificates to the Carlton Corporation, requesting that he be registered as the new owner and that a new certificate be issued in his name. Is Carlton liable to Heubert?

No. Counterfeit stock certificates are without value to anyone. The corporation is not liable to anyone on counterfeit certificates. Clifton is liable to Heubert on grounds of fraud. As one transferring a stock certificate, Clifton has given an implied warranty that the certificate is genuine. Clifton is also subject to a criminal complaint.

15.17 Southern Bank & Trust Company stock was signed by the responsible bank officers and held in the bank's vault. The certificates were ready to be filled in with the names of subscribers who would buy the stock. Ormesby, an attendant, stole a certificate and filled it in to represent two-hundred shares. He then sold the stock to Billings at its current value. The bank later denied Billings's right to the stock, claiming that there had never been a legal transfer of the certificate to Billings. Was the bank correct?

The bank corporation, through its officers, had made possible the fraud against Billings. Billings did not possess a counterfeit certificate. He had received a valid certificate showing ownership of two-hundred shares. Southern Bank & Trust Company must respect Billings's right to the shares.

15.18 Rubin endorsed his certificate to one-hundred shares of the Reading Company stock. The endorsement was in blank because Rubin anticipated sale of the stock to Thurston. On the way to Thurston's office, Rubin lost the certificate, which was later found by Higgins. Higgins sold the shares to Rawlins for cash. Rubin attempted to regain the shares from Rawlins, the innocent purchaser. Would Rubin succeed?

No. A blank endorsement on a share of stock is no different from a blank endorsement on a check or any other kind of negotiable instrument. One who purchases the certificate for value, with no notice of any defect, becomes the rightful owner. Rubin would not be permitted to reclaim the shares from Rawlins, the innocent purchaser.

15.19 Light & Power, Inc., through its board of directors, declared and paid an illegal dividend out of capital assets of the corporation. The company shortly thereafter became insolvent, and creditors sought to hold the directors liable. How will the court determine the liability of individual directors?

(1) Directors who knowingly voted an illegal dividend may be held liable. (2) Directors innocent of the illegality for good reason would not be liable. (3) Directors without specific knowledge of the illegality but professionally capable of recognizing illegality would be liable. (4) Directors whose "no" vote on an illegal dividend is recorded are not liable. (5) Directors not attending and not voting, with an acceptable excuse for absence, are not liable. (6) Directors not attending and with no excuse for absence may be held liable.

15.20 The president of the East Manufacturing Company surreptitiously borrowed the firm's money and used it for private investment. Directors friendly to the president were aware of his acts but did not report him or stop him. Shareholders learned of the illegal borrowing and brought action against both the president and the directors for losses to the firm. Are the directors liable?

Yes. The directors had a duty to the firm and to its stockholders to correct an illegal matter of which they were aware. While not a party to the president's illegal acts, they had a duty of loyalty and good faith to the shareholders.

15.21 The Dye Products Corporation spent $500,000 on the development of new dyes that showed great commercial promise. The president, with the consent of the directors, promoted the dyes, but without success. The market was not ready for acceptance of the new product. Are the president and directors liable to stockholders for this loss?

No. Officers and directors are *not* personally liable for losses not related to carelessness and grossly poor judgment. Careful research indicated possible profits for the Dye Products Corporation. Officers and directors are not endowed with abilities to determine the outcome of *all* ventures undertaken in the operation of a business.

15.22 The Cosmetic Supply Corporation, by vote of the stockholders, began dissolution proceedings. After the assets had been liquidated, all demands from creditors, workers, and others were studied for payment. In what order of preference are the obligations of the corporation paid off?

After payment of salaries due employees, the distribution of the corporation's cash will be made in the following order: (1) payment of all taxes to federal, state, and local governments; (2) full settlement of all secured liabilities, such as mortgages, liens, and bonds issued by the corporation; (3) payment of unsecured debts; (4) payment to stockholders who are preferred as to assets; (5) payment to common stockholders of cash remaining.

15.23 Buy-by-Mail, Inc., did business in all fifty states through the direct-mail distribution of catalogues and promotional material. Several hundred families in one state enjoyed doing business with the mail-order firm. The attorney general of that state demanded that Buy-by-Mail establish a residence office in the state to comply with laws regulating corporations operating within the state. Must this order be followed?

A corporation that is not engaged in carrying on a business within a state but is engaged in interstate commerce need not register as a foreign corporation. Buy-by-Mail's business was not carried on *within* the particular state. All of its transactions were between its headquarters address and customers located in almost every area of the country.

15.24 Suppose, in Problem 15.23, that Buy-by-Mail, Inc., decided to establish retail outlet stores in several different states. Leases were acquired, and a staff was hired to manage and operate the stores. Would Buy-by-Mail, Inc., now be required to register as a foreign corporation in each of these states?

Yes. Establishing resident business locations in foreign states would constitute a foreign corporation's operation in each of those states. Buy-by-Mail, Inc., would be required to register in each of these states and appoint a resident agent, on whom legal process could be served if necessary.

15.25 Vacation Lodges, Inc., operated motels throughout the Midwest. The firm was incorporated under the laws of one state that had issued its charter. The incorporating state claimed corporate income tax from Vacation Lodges, Inc., for all profits made by the corporation in all states where motels were established. Vacation Lodges, Inc., defended itself by claiming that the state law was unconstitutional. Was the state authorized to collect these taxes?

Yes. The state does have the right to demand a tax on all of the profits of Vacation Lodge, Inc., regardless of where the money was earned.

15.26 Suppose Vacation Lodge, Inc., of Problem 15.25, invested heavily in real property in the many states in which it was doing business. Local taxes and assessments against real property were billed to the foreign corporation for these holdings. Vacation Lodge, Inc., complained of the illegality of imposing these taxes on a foreign corporation. Were the taxes and assessments legally charged?

Yes. The assets of a foreign corporation may be taxed according to tax levies within the state where the property is located. However, a foreign corporation's assets that are located outside the state are free of such taxation.

15.27 Vacation Lodge, Inc., realized excellent profits from its operation in a particular state. The state collected income taxes from corporations and all businesses operating within the state. Vacation Lodge, Inc., sought protection from this income tax levy on the grounds that it was a foreign corporation. Would Vacation Lodge succeed in this claim?

A state may levy income taxes on those profits of a foreign corporation realized from operations within the state. The corporation must actually be engaged in operating a business to be subject to the tax. Establishing a sales office as a contact point for business between that state and the corporate headquarters would not bring such a foreign corporation under the income-tax provisions of the foreign state.

Review Problems

15.28 In what ways is a corporate type of organization better than a partnership?

15.29 What state official is usually petitioned for a corporate charter?

15.30 What is meant by the expression "piercing the corporate veil"?

15.31 May par-value stock be sold below par when it is first issued to a subscriber?

15.32 How are officers elected in a corporate business?

15.33 Are directors, by virtue of their positions, considered agents of a corporation?

15.34 What is an *ultra vires act?*

15.35 Distinguish between a *domestic* and a *foreign* corporation.

15.36 When must a foreign corporation register with a state with whose citizens the corporation may be doing business?

15.37 What is a *certificate of incorporation?* What is a *corporate charter?*

15.38 What is meant by a *quo warranto* proceeding in connection with corporations?

15.39 How does a *de facto corporation* differ from a *de jure corporation?*

15.40 Explain how dividends are distributed to preferred stockholders.

15.41 What liability does a shareholder have for claims related to a lost stock certificate?

15.42 When are corporation directors personally liable to stockholders for losses to the corporation?

15.43 May dividends be declared out of a firm's liquidated capital assets?

15.44 Do state laws usually prohibit the formation of corporations for a perpetual period of time?

Answers to Review Problems

15.28 A stockholder's personal assets may not be confiscated by a corporation's creditors. Also, by joining many persons together in a corporation, much more capital may be made available for investment and business growth.

15.29 The secretary of state of the incorporating state is usually petitioned.

15.30 It is the rare right of creditors and claimants to confiscate the property of the stockholders of a corporation in settlement of claims against the corporation.

15.31 No. This is an illegal sale.

15.32 Officers are elected by the board of directors at the annual meeting or when necessary.

15.33 No, they are not except when they are given special authorization to act on behalf of the corporation.

15.34 It is an act that is outside the powers granted the corporation in its duly issued charter.

15.35 Corporations are *domestic* as to the state in which they are incorporated. They are *foreign* when operating in states outside the incorporating state. A corporation receiving its charter from the State of Delaware is a domestic corporation in Delaware. In all other states, it is a foreign corporation.

15.36 A foreign corporation must register when it actually operates within the foreign state.

15.37 A certificate of incorporation is the document prepared by the promoters and incorporators and submitted to the secretary of state as a petition for a charter. The certificate of incorporation, when approved, becomes the corporate charter.

15.38 *Quo warranto proceedings* are court proceedings whereby a corporate charter is dissolved for reasons of illegality.

15.39 A *de jure corporation* is one that has been created in compliance with all of the requirements contained in the incorporating state's laws. A *de facto corporation* is one that for all intents and purposes is a corporation, but in reality has failed to comply with some minor legal requirement as prescribed by state law.

15.40 Preferred stockholders are paid dividends according to provisions contained in their stock certificates. They are paid before any dividends are paid to the owners of common stock.

15.41 The owner of a lost certificate is usually estopped from making any claim of ownership if the lost certificate has been sold and negotiated to an innocent purchaser by the one who found it.

15.42 They are liable when they are guilty of fraud or negligence in the observance of their obligations as representatives of the stockholders. Careless management, dishonesty, and the like will subject the directors to personal liability. Losses to the corporation resulting from errors of considered judgment do not subject them to personal liability.

15.43 No. This is illegal.

15.44 No. Only a few states restrict the life of a corporation to stated periods of time.

Legal Terms

Certificate of incorporation. A formal document, filed with the secretary of state, petitioning for the creation of a new corporation; the certificate contains all the information the state needs to decide whether or not it should grant a corporate charter.

Charter. A state's grant that permits a corporation to exist.

Close corporations. Small firms whose stock is not traded publicly, but is closely held by a few persons (often restricted to family ownership).

De jure corporations. Corporations receiving a state charter after having satisfied *all* legal requirements of the incorporating state.

Dividends. Payments, taken out of earnings, that are distributed to stockholders by vote of a corporation's board of directors.

Federal Securities Exchange Act. Federal legislation of 1934 that requires all stock exchanges engaged in the sale and transfer of securities to register with the Securities and Exchange Commission (S.E.C.).

Private corporations. Corporations formed by private interests to carry on a business for profit.

Public corporations. Corporations created for governmental, not private, purposes.

Quasi-public corporations. Privately-financed corporations providing public services, education, welfare, and the like; they are not organized for profit and do not issue stock.

Quo warranto proceedings. Court procedure seeking the forfeiture of a corporate charter because of charter abuse, wrongful or fraudulent acts, or other infractions of powers, rights, and the law.

Ultra vires acts. Activities of a corporation not granted either through the express or implied powers under the corporate charter.

Examination III

Agency, Business Organizations

1. The McCann Taxi Company hired Perrotti as a regular driver on the night shift. The night foreman gave Perrotti strict orders not to exceed a speed of thirty-five miles per hour while driving within the city limits. Perrotti picked up a fare and, while driving her to the railroad station, had a serious accident at a busy intersection. Evidence showed that at the time of the accident the cab was being driven at a speed between forty and forty-five miles per hour. McCann denied any liability for Perrotti's actions, claiming that he had not followed instructions and had been outside the scope of his authority in driving faster than thirty-five miles per hour. May the McCann Taxi Company be held liable?

   Yes. Perrotti had exceeded instructions and was not within the scope of his authority. He was, however, carrying out his duties in transporting a fare and was within the scope of his employment. McCann Taxi, as principal and employer, is liable as a defendant in any action brought by the injured passenger or others claiming damages caused by the accident.

2. Thornton and Madden were general partners in a roofing and siding business in Plainfield. Business reverses and a court judgment against the partnership reduced the assets of the partnership to less than $300. Bills of more than $1,000 were charged by other creditors to the business. Thornton and Madden disclaimed any personal liability for these debts, informing creditors there was only $300 remaining for settlement of the business debts. Were the partners correct in this assumption?

   No. General partners are personally liable for their partnership debts. Confiscation of their personal assets may occur when there are not sufficient business assets to pay the firm's debts. Thornton and Madden, either together or singly, may be personally sued for any balance unpaid after the depletion of the partnership assets.

3. Gunther Brothers Contractors were the successful bidders on a proposal to install a concrete roadway leading to the Maddox Merchandise Mart. In all contracts and agreements, Gunther Brothers were identified as independent contractors. Kadis, who was not associated with either party, was injured by the negligence of one of Gunther Brothers' employees during their work on the roadway. Kadis entered suit against the Maddox Merchandise Mart for money damages. Is Maddox Mart liable as a defendant in this suit?

   No. Gunther Brothers were employed as independent contractors. They had complete and full supervision of the contract and were responsible to Maddox Mart only for an acceptable job. Gunther Brothers Contractors, not Maddox, should have been named as defendant in this suit. Only in rare circumstances is the principal who hires an independent contractor liable in damages for the torts of the contractor.

4. The Credit Furniture Mart employed Haggerty as its collection agent. He was to make collections from more than one-hundred active charge customers. Difficulties arose, and Haggerty was dismissed from his job. He then called on several of his former accounts and collected more than $500 of Credit Furniture's money. Credit Furniture never received

these collections and demanded a second payment from the customers who had innocently paid Haggerty. Do Credit Furniture's customers have any defense against these claims?

Yes. The customers from whom Haggerty made wrongful collections had no knowledge that he had been fired from his job. Haggerty continued to be an *apparent agent* of the Credit Furniture Mart. Those who made payments did so with no knowledge of any wrongdoing. They have no obligation to make additional payments.

5. The Crawford Realty Company was indebted to Turner for $1,850. To liquidate the debt, Crawford Realty appointed Turner as its rental agent. She was to collect rents from tenants and had the power to retain one-half of all the rentals she collected until the $1,850 she was owed was collected. In addition, Turner was paid a salary of $150 per week. Before the debt had been cleared, and with no apparent reason, Crawford terminated Turner's agency agreement. May Turner demand reinstatement into her job?

Yes. Turner had an agency coupled with an interest—an interest in the subject matter. A principal is restricted from terminating such an agency until the *interest* element has been removed. Turner had a *vested right* to continue collecting rents and to apply one-half of the collections to the reduction of the $1,850 owed her. Crawford Realty Company would be required to continue the agency relationship.

6. Hanby was a majority stockholder and a member of the board of directors of the Northern Mining Company. On one of his frequent visits to the firm's main office, he demanded that changes be made in the accounting system being used. He also ordered the office manager to fire two bookkeepers employed in the office. Did Hanby's position on the board of directors and his ownership of stock give him the power to order these changes?

No. Owning stock and being a member of the board of directors does not give an individual the power to enter into the active management of a corporation. Hanby was not an officer or an agent of the corporation. His instructions to the office manager were without authority and need not be carried out. Hanby's desires could be expressed at a board meeting, in which he could *seek* changes through the regular channels of management.

7. The Sweet Sounds Record Company appointed Carpenter as a general agent in charge of its retail store in Baltimore. The regional manager instructed Carpenter not to hire any additional sales personnel without first getting approval from the main office. Carpenter hired two additional salespeople, without first getting approval, to handle a great increase in business created by the store's Christmas advertising campaign. The regional manager later disapproved this unauthorized hiring and refused any salary or commission payments to the new employees. May the new employees recover the compensation that was promised by Carpenter?

Yes. Secret agreements between a principal and agent do not bind third parties who have no knowledge of such agreements. General agents, such as store managers, have the apparent authority to make decisions necessary for the best operation of the store. Carpenter did nothing unusual. His hiring practice would not have created any suspicion of wrongdoing to those hired. Sweet Sounds was obligated by Carpenter's acts. Carpenter disobeyed the regional manager's instructions, subjecting only him personally to discipline by Sweet Sounds' manager.

8. Bradley, Miller, and Harris owned and managed, as general partners, a television sales and repair shop. Financial difficulties in Bradley's personal life resulted in his petition for voluntary bankruptcy to the United States District Court. Bradley was declared bankrupt. Did Bradley's situation have any effect upon the partnership?

Yes. Bankruptcy of a partnership or of one of the partners terminates a partnership. The partnership of Bradley, Miller, and Harris was automatically terminated by operation of law. If they desired it and if it was possible, Miller and Harris could subsequently write new articles of co-partnership and thus establish a new partnership business.

9. Reuther was employed by Harris Realty as a salesman for new homes in a housing development called Mockingbird Hills. His oral agreement gave him full rights to develop sales and execute contracts with prospective buyers visiting the model homes. Carter signed a contract for a home and agreed to pay $57,000 when the house was complete and ready for occupancy. Carter later changed his mind and demanded the return of his $1,500 cash deposit. Was Carter's contract enforceable?

No. The equal-dignities rule requires that the contract between a principal and agent be equal in formality to contracts that the agent will execute with others in the name of the principal. The statute of frauds requires that all contracts for the sale of real property be in writing—and, in many states, under seal. Reuther's agency agreement was oral. Thus, the contract executed by Reuther with Carter would have no validity, and the $1,500 would be returned to Carter.

10. The National Tire Company, following three years of financial difficulties, experienced a year of sales upturns and reasonable profits. The board of directors voted to retain all profits, which were to be used for research and the advertising of new products. Stockholders demanded that the profits be distributed as dividends. Did the board of directors act within its powers in the decision to reinvest the profits?

Yes. A board of directors has the authority to decide how a corporation's profits should be used, just as long as the board's decision is reasonable and is in the best interest of the corporation. The use of profits to assure the continued upturn in business in a highly competitive field was in the best interest of the corporation.

PART VIII: Property

Chapter 16

Types of Property

Life, liberty, property, and the pursuit of happiness are sacred to all free people. Under English and American law, these fundamental rights are assured to all persons. In this chapter and the three following chapters, we will review property law.

Included in this chapter are discussions of the differences between real and personal property and tangible and intangible property. Also included in this chapter is a review of the various kinds of *estates,* or property rights, that a person may have in real property.

Property rights are not unlimited. One person's property rights may come into conflict with another person's property rights or with the interests of the community at large. In addition, one party (called a *grantor*) who sells or gives property to another (called a *grantee*) may limit the grantee's rights to the property.

In this country, the basic principles and specific regulations of property law can be found in the United States Constitution, state constitutions, state statutes, and local ordinances. As you read this chapter, keep in mind the fact that specific property statutes differ from state to state and from locality to locality.

PERSONAL PROPERTY

16.1 Personal Property Defined

Personal property includes all things that are not real property or accepted as a part of real property. Personal property that is attached and made a part of real property becomes part of that real property. Personal property is in most cases moveable, not fixed.

EXAMPLE 1. Darwin rented an apartment for one year. During the year, he put a new air conditioner in the bedroom window, built bookcases into the living room wall, and installed a portable dishwasher in the kitchen. At the end of the year, he started moving all of these additions out of the apartment. The air conditioner and the portable dishwasher continued to be personal property, which Darwin would be permitted to remove. The bookcases, however, had been permanently built into the living room. They were thus real property, which the landlord could prohibit Darwin from moving.

16.2 Tangible Property

Tangible personal property consists of those things that are discernible to touch, sight, hearing, and taste. They have physical dimension and are valuable for their own characteristics and use. Tools, appliances, books, perfume, tape recordings, automobiles, and steamships are all examples of tangible personal property.

16.3 Intangible Property

Intangible property consists of *rights* rather than things. It includes stock certificates, contract rights, currency, leases and deeds, and such other documents which are not valuable in themselves, but which represent certain powers or rights.

EXAMPLE 2. Wentzle rented a safe-deposit box, in which he placed the following: the deed to his house; his life- and property-insurance policies; patent rights to inventions that paid him a regular income; promissory notes; contracts; and cash. Not one of the items deposited was valuable in itself. The value of each item was in the rights it represented. (The cash gave the owner the power to acquire property.)

16.4 Lost Property

Tangible or intangible personal property missing and not in its owner's possession is considered *lost property*. Owners who misplace or lose their personal property do not lose their title rights to the property.

EXAMPLE 3. Kovel lost his wristwatch while playing golf. The watch was found by another golfer. The finder claimed the watch and would not return it to Kovel. The watch still belongs to Kovel, and he may demand its return. Failure of the finder to return it could result in a criminal action against the finder.

16.5 Fruit of Industry

Growing things that are one-season crops and that the owner intends to harvest are called the *fruit of industry*. Examples of such fruits of industry are annual flowers and most garden vegetables, which must be planted and then harvested each year. Fruits of industry are considered *personal property*. (See Section 16.11.)

EXAMPLE 4. Farmer Jones sold his farm, together with all real property, to Baker. Before giving up possession, Jones harvested thirty acres of winter wheat and a heavy crop of early potatoes. Baker demanded reimbursement for these growing things removed from the farm he had already purchased. Jones had *not* removed any real property to which Baker was entitled. The crops removed were one-season crops, and were therefore personal property.

16.6 Choses in Being, or Chattels

Choses in being consist of personal property now in existence. *Chattel* is another term for choses in being.

16.7 Future Goods

Future goods include those goods which have been ordered but which have not yet been manufactured, as well as fish in the sea and wild animals that have not been taken into captivity. One may not claim title to fish, animals, and the birds of the air until they have been captured and brought under control. Future manufactured goods become *choses in being* only after they have been produced and are accepted as existing goods.

EXAMPLE 5. Reed, a hunter, grazed a deer with a shot from his rifle. The deer was not mortally injured and continued off through the woods. Boyd, seeing the fleeing deer, shot the animal and brought it down. Both Reed and Boyd claimed the deer. Boyd brought the deer down, and it is his. Although Reed might have weakened the animal and made it easier for Boyd to subdue, it was Boyd who brought the wild animal under control. This gave Boyd superior title rights.

16.8 Fixtures as Personal Property

Fixtures consist of those things attached to real property by either the owner or a tenant. A fixture that is not permanently attached and is not intended to be a permanent part of the real estate continues to be personal property. However, a fixture that is permanently attached becomes a part of the real estate and is considered real property.

EXAMPLE 6. Arnold Brothers rented a store, into which they carried shelving, counters, and other furnishings needed in carrying on a retail shoe business. Not one of the items was fastened to either the walls or the floor. The furnishings remained personal property, and Arnold Brothers would have continued title to them.

REAL PROPERTY

16.9 Real Property Defined

Real property consists of land and all things permanently affixed to the land. Buildings, houses, and structures that are intended to be permanent, as well as any contents that are also intended to be permanent, are real property.

EXAMPLE 7. Archino purchased a mobile home, which he kept in back of his permanent residence during the winter months. In the summer, he transported it to a beach area. Although used as a summer residence, the mobile home would not qualify as real property.

EXAMPLE 8. Suppose, in Example 7, that Archino decided to leave the mobile home on his beachfront lot all year. He built a concrete-block foundation, landscaped the installation, and installed permanent hookups to water, sewage, and electrical services. What had previously been considered personal property is now real property and would be subject to assessment for real-property taxes.

16.10 Chattels Real

Chattels real include those items of personal property that are so closely related to and dependent on the real property that they themselves are said to be real property. The keys to a house would come within this definition. Although moveable and not intended to be permanent, keys are so much related to the realty that they are termed to be real property. Blackstone, in his *Commentaries,* also included rights in another's lands or the right to live in another's house as chattels real.

EXAMPLE 9. Hanby Realty purchased a dozen blank keys from a hardware store. A maintenance employee ground the keys to fit apartment locks in the Harcum Arms development. The keys were delivered to tenants for their use. When purchased from the hardware store, the keys were personal property. After being fitted to the apartments and given to tenants for use, the keys became chattels real. If the apartment buildings were sold, the buyer would have the right to demand the keys as part of the real property purchased.

16.11 Fruit of Nature

Those things growing or planted with the intention that they remain growing from year to year are said to be the *fruit of nature* and are *real property.* Trees, perennial crops, and fields of alfalfa and grazing grass return each year and are thus included in this grouping.

EXAMPLE 10. Jackson sold his suburban home to the Trimble Realty Company. After he had signed all agreements but before he moved out, Jackson started digging out all daffodil bulbs, small flowering trees, and dwarf fruit trees that he had planted only a year before. All of these items had become the property of Trimble Realty through its purchase of the real property. Jackson would be obligated to return them to the soil or to pay the buyer money damages for their removal.

16.12 Fixtures as Real Property

Personal property attains the status of real property when it is attached to real property with the intent that it is to become a part of the realty. It is often difficult to determine what is personal and what is real in this situation. Courts use the following guidelines in establishing whether a chattel has changed to real property. A chattel is real property if: (1) the owner has installed the chattel in a way that indicated permanency; (2) the chattel has been adapted to the use of the real property; or (3) the express, implied, or apparent intent of one affixing the property has been that it is to be a permanent addition and therefore real property.

EXAMPLE 11. Katz rented a house and installed a television antenna on its roof. He did a very thorough job, using guy wires and roof braces to secure the antenna. At the end of his leasehold, Katz informed his landlord that he intended to remove the antenna. The landlord claimed that the antenna was a permanent part of the building because of the way in which it had been installed. The landlord was correct. The permanent, professional installation of the antenna had made it part of the building and hence real property that belonged to the building's owner. Katz should have made previous arrangements with the landlord by writing into the lease a clause that would give him the right to install and then remove the antenna.

ESTATES IN REAL PROPERTY

16.13 Freehold Estates

An estate that is held by its owner "forever" or for the owner's life is called a *freehold estate*. Persons having freehold estates may sell their interest or give it to another. They may do with the property as they wish, providing they observe restrictions and limitations imposed by law or by a previous owner.

EXAMPLE 12. City Realty sold a condominium to Fletcher. He was deeded a freehold estate. Although recognized as the uncontested owner of the condominium unit, he was bound by mortgage obligation to a bank, by rules imposed on all who lived in the condominium building, and by other restrictions created by local, state, and federal laws.

16.14 Freehold Estate of Inheritance

Also known as an *estate in fee simple,* a *freehold estate of inheritance* is one that is owned outright and forever. Ownership may be *devised* (transferred) to others by a will or through laws designating others' rights should the owner die without leaving a will. Within the restrictions imposed on the use of the property by law or by deed, the owner may use the property in any way he or she desires.

EXAMPLE 13. Waters, an architect, owned a house and land, holding a deed that showed her to be the owner of an *estate in fee simple.* After taking title to the property, she started immediate alterations on both the interior and exterior of the house. Neighbors objected to the new style of architecture and sought to stop her. Investigation showed that she had not disregarded any zoning laws, restrictions in the deed, or any other ordinance or law. Nor could it be proved that her project was offensive or a nuisance to the neighborhood. Waters would be permitted to proceed with her plans to redesign and reconstruct her house.

16.15 Freehold Estate of Less than Inheritance

Ownership under a *freehold estate of less than inheritance* is limited by the terms of deed or will under which the owner has taken title. One receiving this type of estate is aware of the next owner in line, who is known as the *remainderman.*

EXAMPLE 14. Elizabeth, the unmarried daughter of Lippincott, received her father's house on his death. Two of Elizabeth's younger sisters also survived their father. The will stated that Elizabeth would have a freehold estate of less than inheritance—during her lifetime. On her death, the property was to descend to her two sisters or to their natural heirs if the sisters predeceased Elizabeth. Elizabeth had full ownership of the property only during her own lifetime.

EXAMPLE 15. Elizabeth, in Example 14, decided to move to California, where she had many friends and a job opportunity. She put the house up for sale and sold it to Ross. Ross received no better rights to the property than had been held by Elizabeth. On *Elizabeth's* death, Ross would lose all rights to the property, and it would automatically go to the surviving sisters or their heirs. Ross would have the additional obligation to preserve the property in good condition for those who would take title to it after Elizabeth's demise.

16.16 Less than a Freehold Estate

One having less than ownership rights in a property has *less than a freehold estate.* Tenants holding the property under a *leasehold* come within this definition. Such persons have the legal right of enjoyment of the property over the period of time indicated in the tenant's agreement with the owner.

16.17 Reversion Estate

A freehold estate of inheritance that is to *revert*, or return, to the grantor under certain expressed conditions is called a *reversion estate.* It may be a *life estate* or an estate containing any other legally acceptable conditions imposed by the grantor.

EXAMPLE 16. Raymond, a young man, bought a house for his dependent mother. The deed received by the mother stipulated that the house would revert to the son at such time as the mother died, remarried, or moved from the house. This was a reversion estate, which protected Raymond's investment in the property.

16.18 Remainder Estate

Some deeds and wills contain stipulations that specify a party other than the grantor to whom the estate will descend. Such a stipulation, which may be based upon the termination of a life or on some other condition, creates what is called a *remainder estate.*

EXAMPLE 17. Cortland's will recited his intention to leave his mansion to the City of Newport. The mansion was to be used to house his collection of early American furniture and curios for public display. The will further stated that should the city ever abandon its responsibility in maintaining the house as a museum, the property and contents would be sold, and the proceeds would go to the Newport Historical Society. Cortland has, thus, specified a *remainder estate* in the name of the Newport Historical Society.

16.19 Estates in Severalty

An estate in land owned by one person alone is called an *estate in severalty.*

16.20 Estates in Common

Also known as a *tenancy in common,* an *estate in common* is one in which two or more persons have equal rights of ownership and possession of an undivided share of real property. It is permitted that one co-owner have more than *equal rights* when such is expressed in the deed. Co-owners under an estate in common have independent rights in selling or giving away their shares of the property without interference from the other co-owners. A co-owner may devise his or her share of the estate to another by will. In the event a co-owner dies without a will, his or her share descends to his or her heirs, *not* to the surviving owners of the estate.

EXAMPLE 18. Helen and Grace Johnson, who were sisters, operated a beauty shop. They owned the business building as co-owners in an estate in common. Helen withdrew from the business and informed Grace of her intention to sell her one-half share in the building. Helen gave Grace first rights in buying the property at a price set by Helen. Should Grace not take up the offer, Helen would have the right to put her half interest on the open market, for sale to anyone who might be interested.

16.21 Joint Estates

Joint estates differ from estates in common. In a joint estate, the right of survivorship to any co-owner's share goes to the *surviving co-owners* rather than to one named in a will (or, through descent without a will, to the deceased co-owner's heirs). Joint ownership also differs in other respects. It requires what are called *four unities*: (1) each co-owner has an *equal interest*; (2) names of all co-owners must appear together on the deed; (3) co-ownership must have commenced at the same time for all; and (4) equal rights of ownership and possession are guaranteed all co-owners. Some deeds do not specifically state whether they are joint estates or estates in common. Statutes in many states today declare such a deed to be an estate in common. Joint estates usually contain the abbreviation "W.R.O.S.," meaning "with right of survivorship." This expression follows the names of the co-owners on the deed.

EXAMPLE 19. Brown, Baldt, and Zebley, as joint tenants, purchased the Black Cat Casino, a popular night club and bar. The deed contained the words "with right of survivorship" immediately after their three names. Baldt and Zebley were killed in an automobile accident, and their wives each claimed a one-third right in the Casino. The wives have *no right* in the property, even though such a right was expressed in the wills of their deceased husbands. The entire property reverts to the one remaining owner, Brown.

16.22 Estate by the Entireties

An estate held jointly by a husband and wife is an *estate by the entireties.* An estate by the entireties requires a *unity of person* in addition to the four unities outlined for joint estates in

Section 16.21. In the sale of this type of estate, both husband and wife must sign the deed transferring the property to a grantee. Action by a creditor against *one* of the parties gives no right to confiscate the property to satisfy the judgment. On the death of either the husband or the wife, the property automatically becomes an estate in severalty, in the name of the survivor, without legal costs and the inconvenience of administration.

EXAMPLE 20. Ronald and Katherine Crouch, an elderly couple, owned their home as joint tenants with the right of survivorship. Shortly after his ninetieth birthday, the husband died. The property immediately reverted to this wife, Katherine, with no need for the administration of a will or any other legal transfer. Had Ronald at any time during his lifetime attempted to sell the property without his wife's permission and signature, he would have been stopped. He could not issue a proper deed to any grantee without first getting his wife's approval and signature.

LIMITATIONS IN OWNERSHIP

16.23 "A Man's House Is Not His Castle"

Ownership, even in fee simple, does not give the owner complete rights or complete freedom in the use of a property. Owners are limited in use by terms in the deed, by law, and through the rights that outsiders may have developed in the estate.

16.24 Restrictions Contained in Deed

A deed may restrict an owner in the use of his or her property. (Such a restriction may also regulate all future owners of the property.) Restrictions are valid and enforceable against an owner as long as they are reasonable and do not interfere with the owner's constitutional rights. In addition, restrictions are not enforceable if they are in conflict with local, state, or federal laws.

EXAMPLE 21. Sherwood Development Associates imposed restrictions and limitations on all persons who purchased lots or houses in their development. Included were the following: (1) no laundry may be hung outside the house for drying; (2) no animals may be kept on the premises, either inside or outside a house; (3) no more than four people can occupy any house at one time; (4) no apartments or two-family houses could be constructed on the unimproved lots that were to be sold; and (5) houses or lots could not be sold to anyone except members of the Caucasian race. The courts would in most cases uphold all restrictions with the exception of (3) and (5). Restriction (3) would probably be ruled unreasonable and unenforceable. Restriction (5) could not be enforced or respected due to the Civil Rights Act of 1964 and Supreme Court decisions related to civil rights.

16.25 Easements

An *easement* is a right in the lands of another. Such a right may be created by a mutual agreement between seller and buyer or between an owner and another party. (Easements may be included in a deed.) The property having rights over another property is known as the *dominant estate*. The other property is called the *serviant estate*. Easements may also be created by *adverse use*. Easements come within the jurisdiction of equity courts. A party with a so-called *equitable estate* may petition a court of equity to have easement rights written into the deed of a dominant estate. To acquire ownership through adverse use or possession, one must prove: (1) continuous use over a period of years set by statute; (2) without interruption by the owner; (3) with the owner's knowledge; but (4) without the owner's consent.

EXAMPLE 22. The Grable & Stark Company operated a foundry adjacent to lands owned by Hurley. For many years, condensed steam from the plant was exhausted into a sluice that emptied into Hurley's meadow and formed a stream that emptied into a nearby creek. This continued for a period of twenty years, and though known to Hurley, was neither interrupted by him nor done with his expressed permission. Grable & Stark had established an easement over the lands of Hurley. Hurley could terminate this easement only through mutual agreement with the dominant estate, perhaps by offering money to Grable & Stark as consideration for giving up its rights.

16.26 Air Rights

By common law, the owner of land owned *all* air rights above his or her property. There was no limitation as to how far into the heavens the landowner had title. With the advent of commercial aviation, the Supreme Court restricted the owner's air rights to a height over which it could be determined the owner had reasonable control. This is usually a reasonable number of feet above the highest structure erected on the land. The owners rights are also restricted, in certain heavily trafficked areas, to a height that will not interfere with the flight of aircraft. This latter rule is especially important when applied to property adjacent to an airport.

EXAMPLE 23. Compton owned a house and five acres of land in Willingboro. The local telephone company began installing poles nearby and stringing a cable that passed over Compton's property. The company did not secure Compton's permission. The wires were passed over his property at a height of only thirty feet from the ground, lower than the gables of his house. Compton, through a petition in equity, could enjoin the company from trespassing over his lands and could force the company to remove the wires. Compton, without question, owned air rights up to the height of the gables. (Through eminent-domain proceedings, a public utility may secure rights to enter another's property for uses claimed to be in the public good and not solely for private profit.)

EXAMPLE 24. Commercial aircraft owners were charged with the invasion of Compton's air rights when flying at 32,000 feet over his five-acre estate. Prior to the Supreme Court decision that restricted a landowner's air rights, Compton could have demanded nominal damages and enjoined the aircraft from any future invasion of his property. Today, however, Compton would not be successful in such a claim.

16.27 Subterranean Rights

One who has title to land has title to all beneath the land to a point determined to be the middle of the planet Earth. Landowners are at times restricted in the exercise of their subterranean rights, such as when former owners sold mineral and oil rights or easements to other parties. Such conditions are recorded in the deeds of properties and may severely restrict the present owners' use of areas below their properties.

EXAMPLE 25. Jordan purchased a farm in the vicinity of Scranton, Pennsylvania, a center of the anthracite coal industry. Only after making the purchase did Jordan carefully read his deed. The deed contained a description of the land and specified that all subterranean and mineral rights had been deeded over to the Lehigh Coal Company seventy-five years before. Jordan had taken the land with restrictions. He would not be prohibited from digging root cellars, house basements, and the like, but he would have no right to start a mining operation.

16.28 Percolating Waters

Landowners are prohibited from taking water from underground springs and rivers except when such water is needed for the operation of the household, barns, and other buildings on the land. A landowner may not draw such *percolating waters* for use at locations away from the land when such use seriously reduces the water supply of others depending on the same sources.

EXAMPLE 26. The Artesian Water Company, serving thousands of residences and businesses over a twenty-five-mile area, drilled three wells in the vicinity of Mount Cuba. When Artesian started their pumping operation, numerous property owners in the vicinity complained that their wells had dropped to a level that did not leave sufficient water for their own domestic uses. Artesian Water Company would be enjoined from excessive pumping that would endanger the water supply of all others who depended on the same water supply.

EXAMPLE 27. The Community Swim Club built a swimming pool that was to be used by its members. The pool was to be fed by an artesian well that operated eighteen hours each day. Neighbors claimed that their wells were going dry because of the club's use of so much subterranean water. The Club would be enjoined from its practice of excessive pumping, which resulted in damage to others who depended on the same water source for the operation of their homes and businesses.

16.29 Riparian Rights

Owners of property near a navigable stream may not dump refuse or waste into the stream to the damage of others whose property also abuts the stream. Neither may such owners divert water from the stream to an extent that deprives downstream owners of a water supply for either domestic purposes or recreation. These are the owners' *riparian rights*. On other than navigable and tide waters, the owner of adjacent lands has title to the bottom of the stream or lake to a point halfway across the body of water. Riparian rights do *not* give property owners title to the water itself. Their use of the water is restricted in a manner similar to that explained for percolating waters in Section 16.28. Ice formed in such waters, however, *does* become the property of owners of land adjoining the body of water. The owners have property rights to a point halfway across the frozen body of water.

EXAMPLE 28. Marcy lived in Maine in a house adjacent to Moose Lake. Each winter, property owners nearby cut ice from the lake and stored it for summer use. Harris, who owned land on the opposite shore from Marcy, cut ice to a point ten feet beyond the middle of the lake. Harris would be guilty of confiscating Marcy's property rights in the ice. He may be enjoined from further trespass and assessed damages for encroaching on Marcy's property rights.

16.30 Eminent Domain

Land and other real property may be taken from its owners for purposes that enhance the public good. Owners are compensated for land taken according to a valuation determined by a land commission. Offers from such political bodies may be contested and reviewed in the courts. Eminent domain is also granted, in carefully regulated situations, to public utilities when it is necessary for them to go through private property with electric and telephone transmission lines and pipelines carrying petroleum or natural gas.

EXAMPLE 29. Harvey's Service Station was located at the intersection of Milltown and Limestone Roads. The service station was a very profitable business. The State Highway Department planned to widen the intersection to relieve traffic and to make it safer. The state took Harvey's Service Station through eminent-domain proceedings. Harvey suffered the loss of a profitable business and received less for his land than he was forced to pay for a less attractive location elsewhere. He could appeal to the courts for the fair market value of his property.

16.31 Police Powers

Persons are not permitted to use their lands in ways that might endanger the health, safety, or welfare of the general public. Governments have *police powers* in the form of zoning laws, sanitary regulations requiring connection to public sewer lines, and even the power to destroy private property to prevent the spread of disease or fire.

EXAMPLE 30. A fire raged out of control in the city of Cornish. To stop the spread of flames, the fire marshall ordered the dynamiting of a row of homes in the path of the fire. By doing so, the fire was contained and hundreds of other homes and businesses were saved. Under police powers, fire marshalls have this authority, although they must be extremely cautious in making such decisions. Fire marshalls may be held personally liable if they use poor judgment in ordering the destruction of property.

16.32 Taxes and Assessments

Real property is subject to taxation. Many of the tax dollars collected are used to provide funds for public services such as police protection, schools, fire departments, and the like. Unpaid taxes create a lien on the property subject to the tax. Unpaid taxes may eventually lead to the selling of the property through a sheriff's sale to satisfy the unpaid tax. Assessments may also be placed upon properties in a separate area where new street lights, sidewalks, and other improvements are made. Such assessments are often levied on the basis of the total footage a property has facing the street.

EXAMPLE 31. Hampton County required the building of a new high school that would serve the entire county. To finance construction, bonds were sold and the county increased taxes in an amount sufficient to cover the interest and the reduction of principal on the bonds over a period of years. Property owners had no choice in determining their individual obligations in this tax increase.

16.33 Overhanging Trees and Other Encroachments

Adjacent property owners are responsible for tree branches that overhang into neighboring properties. Also, it is a trespass to have water drainage from one's roof falling onto a neighbor's property, even without apparent damage. The serviant property owner has the right to remove overhanging branches from another property. However, the owner of the serviant property is liable for money damages should such removal kill or harm an otherwise healthy tree.

EXAMPLE 32. Miller planted four Norway maple trees just inside his property line, only two feet from Wilson's residential lot. Ten years later, Miller's trees had grown large and full, and their long branches extended several feet over Wilson's lawn and flower beds. Wilson may demand the removal of the branches overhanging his property, to be accomplished at Miller's expense. Wilson himself may remove the branches, but he will endanger his own legal rights if he harms the trees.

Solved Problems

16.1 Donovan deeded a property to Dukes. The deed stated that the property was deeded to "Dukes, his heirs, and assigns forever." Shortly before his death, Dukes sold the property to the Downs Realty Corporation. Dukes's sons and daughters objected to the transfer and sought to have it set aside on grounds of the words used in the deed when Donovan transferred the property to their father. Were the objections of Dukes's children correct?

No. The words "to Dukes, his heirs, and assigns forever" created a freehold estate of inheritance in Dukes. He owned the estate in fee simple, with the right to sell it, give it away, or do anything else with it without limitations or restrictions, just as in a life estate.

16.2 Dykes owned a farm from which he selected five acres to be deeded to St. Paul's Church. The deed stated that the land would revert to Dykes if it was not used for religious purposes. St. Paul's Church prospered, and its directors decided to erect a new church building closer to the population center that it served. The church board contracted to sell the present church to another religious group. May Dykes demand the return of the land because of the church's decision to move?

Dykes's deed provided for a reversion to him should the property not be used for religious purposes. It did *not* confine this use to the St. Paul's congregation. St. Paul's may sell the land and building to another group under the same restrictions that had been imposed on the original grantee.

16.3 By deed, Woodward granted an easement to the Greenbank Company for a mill race, which was to be constructed through part of his property to provide power for operating a textile mill. The deed stated that the mill race would revert to Woodward or his heirs should the milling operation ever be terminated. The textile mill was later sold to a community group that proposed using water from the race to supply a swimming pool for its members. Do the new owners have a legally enforceable right to keep the mill race in operation?

No. By the terms of Woodward's will, provisions were made for either a reversion estate to the grantor or a remainder estate to Woodward's heirs. The condition that guaranteed continuance of the easement was terminated when the mill ceased operation. The new owners have no right to demand the continuance of a water supply from the mill race. Their recourse would be to open negotiations with Woodward, or his surviving heirs, to extend the easement under terms acceptable to both parties.

16.4 Weyman left a will devising a downtown office building to his wife. The will stated that should the wife remarry, the property would go to his son. The wife remarried one year later and made arrangements to sell the building. The son claimed that he now had a freehold estate of inheritance in the property. Was the son correct in his claim?

Yes. The wife had an estate in fee simple, conditioned on her continued unmarried state. Her second marriage terminated her interest in the property, which now rightly belonged to the son as a freehold estate of inheritance.

16.5 Franklin deeded a property to Peters. The property was to belong to Peters only during his lifetime. Peters died, leaving a will that left the Franklin property to Peters's son. Franklin and the son both claimed the property. Who will receive the property?

Franklin. Peters had *not* received a freehold estate of inheritance through Franklin's deed. His was a life estate only. Thus, Franklin continued to have a reversion right in the disputed property. Franklin's claim will supersede Peters's will.

16.6 For more than twenty years, the four successive owners of Nestlewood Acres had walked through Harris's property as a shortcut to the Brandywine School. Harris had never complained, although he did not approve of the practice. Harris now made plans to build a house on the lot at a point that would block the well-worn path. The present owners of Nestlewood Acres demanded that nothing be placed in the way of this long-used path. What are the rights of the parties?

An easement through adverse use developed through the continued use of the path over a twenty-year period, without Harris's permission but with his knowledge. Harris had never even tried to cut off the path during the twenty-year period. It makes no difference that the dominant estate (Nestlewood Acres) had been owned by several different parties over the twenty-year period. Harris would only have a right to negotiate with the owners of Nestlewood Acres in an effort to buy back their easement rights.

16.7 Talbot purchased one-half of a large parcel of land owned by Thomas. The portion deeded to Talbot had no access to a public road. She began driving her car over the Thomas property to reach her own land. Thomas later blocked her access to his private road. Does Talbot have any rights against Thomas?

With no other way out of the property, Talbot may claim an *easement by necessity* through Thomas's property. By mutual agreement, Thomas and Talbot would be allowed to select a road to be followed that would be suitable to both parties.

16.8 Through many years of continued use, Stansby established an easement right to drive her car over a right-of-way between the main road and Silver Lake. The surface of the right-of-way gradually deteriorated and became dangerous due to pot holes and wash-outs. Stansby demanded that the owner of the right-of-way grade and resurface the roadway. Was Stansby correct in these demands?

Dominant parties in an easement have no right to demand that a right-of-way be kept in repair for their safety. The only exception would be an easement granted by deed or license, in which the servient property owner, for a consideration, accepted such responsibility. Stansby's only recourse in this situation is to make the repairs herself or to cease using the easement right.

16.9 Galperin left a will by which his three children, Nancy, Arthur, and Robert, received his farm in equal shares. Nancy made arrangements to sell her share to Grover to secure funds for her college education. Arthur and Robert objected. They claimed, as co-owners, that she did not have the right to sell her share. Was Nancy correct?

Yes. The three surviving children were tenants in common. As a tenant in common, Nancy has the right to sell her one-third share of the farm. The only problem here would be the arrangement by which her share would be sold. The new owner would in most likelihood take a one-third interest in the entire property rather than a one-third share divided and separated from the other tenants in common.

16.10 Harold, Russell, and Steve, brothers, were tenants in common of a farm that they operated as partners. Last year, Steve did practically all the work, selling the crops and keeping the money. He argued that this was his right because he was the one who had made profits possible. Harold and Russell each demanded a one-third share of the profits. Were they correct in this demand?

Yes. Each of the tenants in common has a right to an equal one-third share of the net profits produced, even though only one of them made the profits possible. The division could have been more equitable had the brothers agreed to a different arrangement earlier, anticipating the labor to be contributed by each.

16.11 Suppose, in Problem 16.10, that Steve decided to sell his share and sought to have the court dissolve the tenancy in common. The other brothers objected, stating that this action required the decision of all three. Was Steve acting within his powers in seeking this dissolution?

Yes. A tenant in common need not be joined by the other tenants in petitioning a court to dissolve the common tenancy. This is the usual procedure when two or more persons get involved in a situation in which agreement is impossible.

16.12 Hubert and Joanna, husband and wife, owned their home as an estate by the entireties. Hubert, in his will, left all of his holdings to his son, Alexander. Does Alexander or Joanna have superior rights in the home?

Joanna, as wife and by the deed, suceeds automatically to complete ownership in the home. The will, in this case, has no reference to her right of ownership. Under an estate by the entireties, the wife and husband have joint ownership with right of survival.

16.13 Suppose, in Problem 16.12, that Joanna and Hubert had been divorced, and that Joanna elected to sell her share of the property to another party. May Hubert, her former husband and owner under a joint tenancy, object to the sale?

No. Upon the divorce of Joanna and Hubert, there is an automatic termination of the tenancy by entireties. It then becomes a tenancy in common. The former husband, in the absence of other provisions in the divorce decree, has no right to interfere with or delay Joanna's plans of selling her interest in the property.

16.14 Over a twenty-five-year period, seven different parties had owned the property at 506 Milltown Road. The property next door, 508 Milltown Road, had six owners during the same period of time. Those living at 506 had continuously used a path through the rear of

508 as a shortcut to a public swimming pool and recreation area. The owners of 508 now close off the path, much to the anger of their neighbors. Must this path be kept open?

Yes. Easements "run with the land." They are regarded as rights *in rem* ("against a thing") rather than rights *in personam* ("against a person"). It makes no difference that several parties have owned both the dominant and the serviant tenements. The important matter is that the dominant tenement has served the serviant tenement for a sufficient period of time to create an easement by adverse use. The present owner and all subsequent owners of 508 must observe the rights of 506 by keeping the path open.

16.15 Clause and Bracken owned adjoining lands. Surface waters from Clause's property ran over Bracken's property and caused erosion. Bracken brought in ten truckloads of topsoil to raise the surface of his yard. This backed up all the surface water on Clause's land. Does Clause have any rights in this matter?

Yes. A landowner is restricted from changing the natural course of surface waters to the damage of those on property above or below. Bracken damaged Clause's property by backing up a natural water course that had been formed by nature. Bracken's only solution would be to install drainage pipes that would carry the surface waters through his land to the lands of those below. This drainage must be achieved, however, without causing any damage to the property of those below.

16.16 Craven purchased a house in a residential area of Springfield. As a part-time venture, he built a shop in his basement for the repair of radios, televisions, and small electrical appliances. To advertise his business, Craven placed a small sign on his lawn. Neighbors objected and demanded that he curtail all operations due to existing zoning laws. Must Craven terminate his business?

If Craven's neighborhood was zoned "residential only," he would be enjoined from any further business activity in his home. In most cases, the only zoning-law exceptions are for professional persons operating physician's, dentist's, or similar offices in their homes.

16.17 Bolsky came home from work one day to discover that parking meters had been erected in front of his house and other houses on the same block. Bolsky disregarded the meter and did not insert the required coin. After he received a ticket, he defended himself by saying that by his deed he owned property to the middle of the street and could not be denied the right to park in the space in front of his house. Was Bolsky's contention correct?

No. Under its police powers, a local government has the right to regulate others in the use of property that exists for the general welfare and safety of the populace. Bolsky's rights are subjugated to the rights of the community.

16.18 Rachael and Paul Drummond owned their home as an estate by entireties. Paul was involved in a serious accident one evening when driving home after visiting a local bar. He had been intoxicated, and the accident was all his fault. His insurance did not cover the judgment against him. The sheriff started proceedings to take the Drummond house and sell it to secure money with which to satisfy the judgment. May this be done?

No. Paul Drummond was on an "excursion of his own" when he had the accident. His escapade had no connection with anything involving Rachael Drummond. The house may not, then, be confiscated and sold as a means of satisfying the judgment against Paul. Had the two been engaged in a "common venture," riding together in fulfillment of something beneficial to both, the result might have been different.

16.19 Conviction for the crime of larceny requires proof that the accused took *personal* property from another without permission and with the intent to keep it. Hayes, while walking through the country, went into an orchard, picked several apples from a tree, and then continued her walk. Was she subject to arrest for larceny? Suppose she had picked up apples that had fallen to the ground. Would the decision be the same?

Apples, while growing and still attached to the tree, are real property. Prosecution of Hayes on the charge of larceny could be defended on the grounds that she had taken *real*, not personal property. Had she picked up apples off the ground, she would have been taking *personal property*, which is the only grounds on which the crime of larceny could be charged.

16.20 Walters owned a home under a deed that stated that the property could never be sold to anyone other than a white person. He moved to another neighborhood and entered into a contract to sell the house to a black family. Other residents in the neighborhood sought to stop the sale, basing their claims on the restrictions contained in all deeds to houses in the community. May Walters go through with the sale?

Yes. Supreme Court decisions and the Civil Rights Act of 1964 have voided restrictions in deeds that prohibit the sale of property to people who are not members of one particular race. The restriction in Walters's deed was invalid and had no legal standing under today's laws.

16.21 Twenty families contributed money and time in constructing a swimming pool in a wide area of Sycamore Creek. They enjoyed the recreation until a paper mill located several miles upstream started to discharge waste products and chemicals into the stream. The group complained to the mill manager, who replied that as a property owner the mill had the implied right to use the stream for its purposes. Who was correct in this matter, putting aside for the moment modern environmental laws that prohibit the pollution of streams?

The downstream families were correct. Parties owning lands adjacent to a stream may *not* pollute the waters to the damage of those through whose lands the stream flows. The paper mill could be enjoined from dumping its wastes into the stream even without the complainants' recourse to modern environmental law.

16.22 Suppose that in creating a swimming area, the group in Problem 16.21 had cut off the flow of water in the stream to the damage of other parties living further down the same body of water. What are the rights of those living below the dammed-up stream?

Except by mutual agreement, one may not cut off the flow of a freshwater stream to the damage of those whose properties are located further downstream. If, after filling the dammed-up area, the stream's flow returned to normal, no damages could be sought.

16.23 Three individuals purchased a building in which they conducted a partnership business. Each invested $30,000 toward the purchase price. Would it be best for these individuals to create a joint estate or an estate in common when instructing their attorney to draw up the deed?

If each person were married and the $30,000 investment was important to the family survival should one of the partners die, it would be best to have an estate in common. On the other hand, an estate in common would introduce a wife or children into the partnership as a co-owner of the building. A better plan, for security and for the continuance of the business, would be to have a joint estate, with the partnership taking out three life insurance policies of $30,000 each in favor of each partner's wife and family in the event of the death of a partner.

16.24 The Allstate Chemical Corporation planned to build a new plant in an area selected by its engineers. Options for the purchase of the necessary land were secured except for one small lot, whose owner refused to negotiate with the firm's representatives. An action in eminent domain was started to force this one "holdout" to sell his land on the generous terms offered by Allstate. Will this owner be forced to give up his property?

No. Eminent-domain proceedings may be used only for the public good. They may not be used for purposes related to profit to be gained by individuals. Although the construction of the plant might give jobs to many and thus benefit the public, the project will not qualify for eminent-domain proceedings. The firm will have to make its own bargain with the "holdout."

Review Problems

16.25 How does the *fruit of nature* differ from the *fruit of industry?*

16.26 Under what conditions is a fixture said to be *real property?*

16.27 How does a *joint estate* differ from an *estate in common?*

16.28 Give an example of *chattel real*.

16.29 (1) What is *tangible personal property;* (2) *intangible property?*

16.30 For what purpose may eminent domain be used to take away one's property?

16.31 What powers are included under the so-called *police powers?*

16.32 To what point above the ground does a property owner exercise air rights?

16.33 What four points must be proven to establish an easement by adverse use?

16.34 Is an easement a personal right (*in personam*) or a right accompanying the land (*in rem*)?

16.35 In easements, what are the *dominant tenement* and the *serviant tenement?*

16.36 What particular name is given a joint estate owned by a husband and wife?

16.37 Is the water in a stream running through one's lands the property of the landowner? What about ice that forms in the stream or lake?

16.38 To what extent may the owner of an artesian well draw water from the well without encroaching on the rights of others?

Answers to Review Problems

16.25 Fruit of nature is real property; fruit of industry is personal property.

16.26 Personal property becomes real property when it is permanently attached to the real property, is adapted to the use of the real property, and has been affixed by the owner with the intent that it become a part of the realty.

16.27 Under a joint estate, the right of survivorship is to the surviving owners named in the deed. In an estate in common, the deceased's share survives to one named in the will of the deceased or to the deceased's heirs when there is no will.

16.28 The keys to a house or some other building are examples of chattel real.

16.29 (1) Tangible personal property includes those things that are discernible to the senses, have dimension, and are not a part of the realty. (2) Intangible property consists of rights rather than things; the value of intangible property is not in the property itself but in rights assured the owner of documents, negotiable paper, cash, and the like.

16.30 Eminent domain may be used only to acquire property required for the public good.

16.31 Police powers are those powers provided a government for protection of the health, safety, welfare, and good of the citizenry.

16.32 Air rights extend to a point above the highest structure over which the owner has reasonable control.

16.33 The four points are: (1) continuous use; (2) without interruption; (3) without the owner's consent; but (4) with the owner's knowledge.

16.34 It is a right accompanying the land (a right *in rem*).

16.35 The dominant tenement is the land served and benefitted by an easement. The serviant tenement is the land over which the other has developed or been granted rights.

16.36 It is called an *estate in the entirety*.

16.37 No. An owner merely has the right to the *use* of the water in the stream or lake. On the other hand, ice formed in the body of water belongs to the adjacent landowner to a point midway between her or his land and the lands of others.

16.38 The owner may draw what water is needed for maintaining his or her home, livestock, and other needs. The water that is drawn may not be used at locations other than the property on which the well is located.

Legal Terms

Air rights. An owner's rights in the space over his or her land and buildings; such rights extend to a point over which the owner has reasonable control.

Chattel. An article of personal property.

Chattels real. Those things usually designated as personal property but so closely related to the real property that they are considered real property; examples are the keys to a house, a deed to land, and the like.

Choses in being. Personal property now in existence, as opposed to *future goods*; also known as *personal property* or *chattels*.

Easements. Rights of persons other than the owner in the use of real property; may be created by deed or through *adverse use*.

Eminent domain. The right of the local, state, or federal government to divest an owner of lands that are required for public use and benefit; payment of a fair price for the land is required.

Fixtures. Personal property that has been affixed and attached to real property in a manner that implies that it may now be considered part of the real property.

Freehold estate of inheritance. Outright ownership of real property; also known as *estate in fee simple*.

Freehold estate of less than inheritance. Ownership under a deed or will that limits the grantee's rights to the conditions of ownership contained in the document; for example, a grantee's life estate that is to go to another at the grantee's death.

Fruit of nature. Things growing that remain in the ground over a period of years; classified as real property.

Life estate. The right to use property or to receive income from it for life.

Personal property. All things not included as real property. When attached to real property, personal property is considered to be part of the realty and is no longer personal property.

Police powers. The right of state or local government to restrict owners in their use of land; the owners may be prevented from using the land in a way that endangers the welfare and safety of others; police powers includes health regulations, zoning laws, mandatory connection to public sewer and water lines, and the like.

Real property. Land and those things permanently affixed to it.

Subterranean rights. A landowner's right to the exclusive use of the land beneath the surface of his or her property to a point determined to be the middle of planet Earth.

Chapter 17

Taking Title to Real Property

An individual or a nation can take title to real property in many ways—including the seizure of land through discovery or conquest. Christopher Columbus claimed title to all lands of the Western Hemisphere for the King and Queen of Spain, without regard for the rights of the natives who already lived there. During the last century, many bloody wars have been fought over lands that were overrun and claimed by invading armies.

In this chapter we will review some of the more peaceful and conventional ways in which people and institutions can aquire title to land and other forms of real property. Taking title to real property through purchases is the most common way in which property is transferred today, and this method of transfer is thus emphasized in this chapter. Steps in the purchase of real estate, pitfalls to avoid, and the various types of deeds are outlined in the following pages. Of special importance is the discussion of surveying a property and making a careful title search before signing a contract or deed.

The rights of married persons in property owned by a spouse and the rights of heirs to property descending through a will are discussed at length in this chapter. In addition, there is a discussion of the transfer of property rights through adverse use—a subject touched on in the previous chapter under the review of easements.

As you read and study this chapter, keep in mind the fact property law is an intricate and always-changing subject. In any transaction you might wish to make, consult local and state statutes, which may have superseded the common law in your area.

METHODS OF ACQUISITION

17.1 Title by Occupancy or Discovery

Nations have, since the beginning of history, claimed title to land through either *occupancy* or *discovery*. By force of arms one nation has overcome another, claiming all lands and property in the name of the conquering country. Title may also be claimed through discovery, as when Columbus declared the Americas to be the possession of Spain. Volcanic islands still may appear above the surface of the sea, and when this happens, they are declared to be the property of the country that first discovers and occupies them.

EXAMPLE 1. Prior to the outbreak of World War II, Mussolini directed his troops to invade lands in Northern Africa that for centuries had been under the government of the Emperors of Ethiopia. Ethiopia was defeated, and its lands were annexed to Italy. Following World War II, the lands were returned to the government of the Emperor of Ethiopia.

17.2 Title by Deed

The most common method of transfer of real property is by *deed*. The party transferring the property is called the *grantor*. The other party is called the *grantee*. To be effective, a prepared and signed deed must be delivered by the grantor to the grantee or to the grantee's agent. Deeds may be transferred either for consideration or as gifts.

EXAMPLE 2. Because he was of advanced age, Ralston decided to transfer his farm to his sons during his lifetime. A deed to the property was drawn and signed. It made the sons tenants in common to the farm and the buildings thereon. Delivery of the deed to the attorney representing the sons completed the transfer of the property.

17.3 Title by Judicial Sale

Land may be purchased through a judicial sale, which is authorized by a court as a means of satisfying any unpaid taxes, liens, mortgages, and the like. Such sales are advertised in local newspapers and are conducted by the county sheriff, usually at public auction. Statutes vary from state to state as to the title received under such a sale. In many cases, the title given is not accompanied by the usual warranties given in a private sale.

EXAMPLE 3. Hensley failed to make payments on a $15,000 loan secured by a first mortgage on his house. Foreclosure proceedings were started, and the result was the judicial sale of Hensley's property at auction to cover the indebtedness. Stoltz was the highest bidder, at $14,500. This left a deficiency of $500 that Hensley had to pay out of other assets. Stoltz received title to the property. (Hensley, however, through the process of equity of redemption, may be allowed to reacquire the property within a time fixed by law by reimbursing Stoltz for the amount paid at the auction, plus interest. See Section 17.33.)

17.4 Title by Adverse Possession

Title to land may be acquired through *adverse possession*, a legal doctrine respected by and enforced through the courts of equity. Title through adverse possession is acquired when one (not the owner) occupies another's land for a period of time (twenty years or as set by statute) without any interruption by the owner and without the owner's consent, but with the actual or constructive (inferred) knowledge of the owner. Such proof gives the user of the land an *equitable title* superior to the owner's *legal title*. The equitable title may later be included in a recorded legal title and deed. Title by adverse possession may not be enforced in many states against a municipal corporation or other governmental body.

EXAMPLE 4. Many people built vacation shacks along the Centreville beachfront, a state preserve facing the Atlantic Ocean. After more than twenty years had passed, year-round residents of the area complained of the presence of these people, who paid no taxes and yet enjoyed the privileges of local taxpayers. The *squatters* claimed title to the state lands on which they had settled with the knowledge of the state, but without the state's permission. State law did not recognize title by adverse possession on state property, and all persons were ordered to vacate the shacks immediately following a court order.

17.5 Title by Marriage

A husband and wife are vested with title rights in each other's real property if the property was owned at the time of marriage or acquired by either during the marriage. The rights of each spouse in the property of the other depends on whether they have residence in a *common-law* state or in one that provides for *community property* or some other statutes. (See Section 17.10.)

17.6 Dower Right

By *dower right*, the wife receives a one-third interest in real property possessed by her husband during her lifetime, unless other provisions are made for her by state law. Even though the property is recorded in the name of the husband alone, the wife's consent and signature are necessary for passing title to a grantee.

EXAMPLE 5. Yearsley, a real estate dealer, owned extensive holdings in real property in a state that provided for dower rights. He married Richmond on August 1. On August 15, he sold an apartment building that he owned for $300,000. Yearsley would be required to secure his wife's signature to the deed before transferring property to the buyer.

17.7 Contracts in Anticipation of Marriage

The law respects and will enforce contracts made between parties who anticipate marriage when such contracts (called *antenuptial agreements*) are in writing, as required by the statute of frauds. Such agreements are enforceable if they are consummated freely and without duress or undue influence. Persons with extensive real estate holdings should consider such agreements.

EXAMPLE 6. Suppose that Yearsley, the real estate dealer of Example 5, entered into an antenuptial agreement with Richmond. In the agreement, Richmond gave up her dower right in real properties traded by Yearsley in his business. Such an agreement is valid and enforceable. Richmond, later Mrs. Yearsley, could have reserved her dower right in their home and vacation residence, if such a reservation was acceptable to both her and her husband.

17.8 Curtesy Right

Curtesy right is a husband's right, under common law, to his wife's entire real-estate holdings. For curtesy right to be actionable, children must have been born of the marriage. The husband's right is limited to a life interest. Statutes in some states permit the wife to defeat the curtesy right by either selling her real property during her lifetime or by giving it to another through a will.

17.9 "In Lieu of Dower"

A will by a husband may include a bequest to the surviving wife with the phrase "in lieu of dower." Acceptance by the wife of such a bequest has the effect of eliminating her dower right in the real property titled to the husband alone. The surviving wife has the option of accepting or rejecting such a bequest.

EXAMPLE 7. Hornsby left a will in which he included a bequest of $75,000 to his surviving widow. The bequest was prefaced by the expression "in lieu of dower." Hornsby, in his own name, owned more than $500,000 in real estate, which was subject to the wife's dower right. The widow, using good judgment, refused the $75,000 and demanded her dower right.

17.10 Community Property

Some states have recently adopted *community-property* laws. Such laws state that property brought into a marriage continues to be owned by the one who had title to it prior to the marriage. Property acquired after the marriage by either spouse or by both is community property, and each spouse shares equally in its value. Arizona, California, Idaho, Louisiana, Nevada, New Mexico, Pennsylvania, Texas, and Washington are community-property states. Statutes in each state differ to some extent in the application of this concept.

EXAMPLE 8. Willin had assets, both real and personal, amounting to $18,000; Evans listed her assets at $25,000 prior to her marriage to Willin. After marriage, they both continued to work and they invested their savings in a new home and securities that eventually totalled $150,000. According to community-property statutes, only the $150,000 estate would be shared between them. Any other property, either real or personal, that each had brought into the marriage would not be shared.

17.11 Title by Descent

Property owned by persons who die without a will is distributed to heirs according to the provisions contained in the statutes of each state. As explained previously, provision is made first for a surviving spouse. The remainder goes directly to the closest *heirs* (blood relatives), usually children, grandchildren, or brothers and sisters. Spouses may not be included in this distribution because they are not *heirs* (they are not related by blood line).

EXAMPLE 9. Arthur and Lillian, husband and wife, were involved in a traffic accident in which Arthur (who had no will) was killed. The wife would receive her dower right or her right under community property. Their two children would share equally in the division of the remaining real property. Had Arthur died leaving a will, the division might have been much more equitable in terms of the wife's responsibilities for caring for the two children.

PURCHASE OF REAL PROPERTY

17.12 Sales Agreement

A sales agreement for the purchase of real property must be in writing, as required by the statute of frauds. In many states, the contract must be signed and must contain the seals of both the seller and buyer. The seal may be any mark or sign adopted by the signer as his or her seal. (Use of the word "seal" or the letters "L.S." following the signatures is sufficient as a seal.)

EXAMPLE 10. Avondale Estates sold a house and lot to Simpers. The agreement contained a description of the property, the method of financing, the purchase price, the date of settlement, and the amount of the down payment. Reference was also made to the disposal of the token down payment should either the seller or buyer breach the agreement. The agreement between Avondale Estates and Simpers now opens the way to further steps in fulfillment of the sale.

17.13 Engineering Survey

Buyers, to protect their interest, should contract for a civil engineer or surveyor to make an actual survey of the property to determine whether it conforms in dimensions to the description contained in the county recorder's office. Differences discovered between the description and the actual survey require further negotiation between the selling and buying parties. The survey should also bring to light any easements that may have developed through adverse possession or use. (Such easements may not be recorded or discoverable through mere inspection of the owner's deed.)

17.14 Title Search

Careful scrutiny of the legal history and condition of the property should be made by a buyer's attorney. A *title search* will uncover any unpaid taxes, liens, or other encumbrances against the property that will affect the buyer's interest in it. Discovering that the seller has only a freehold estate of less than inheritance or that there has been an unsatisfied claim of a dower right by the wife of a former owner may protect the buyer from later difficulty and suit. The title search should also include research into all former transfers of the property—by deed, will, or descent.

EXAMPLE 11. Williams retained an attorney to research the title to the Graymore Estates, which he had contracted to purchase. The attorney discovered that the present owner was involved in an action as a defendant in a serious auto accident in which the plaintiff was seeking damages of $250,000. It would be inadvisable for Williams to purchase the property with such a "cloud" over it. (The property could later be confiscated to satisfy a judgment against the present owner.)

17.15 Abstract of Title

The attorney making a title search provides the prospective buyer with an *abstract of title*. The abstract is a summary of information concerning the legal history and present legal status of the property's title. Based on the contents of an abstract, buyers can judge what rights and obligations they will assume should they go through with the purchase.

EXAMPLE 12. An abstract of title prepared for Seaman, the prospective purchaser of an unimproved city lot, disclosed that sewer, water, and gas pipes passed through the middle of the property, as permitted under an easement granted by a former owner. Seaman's proposed use of the lot required a very deep basement, which would not have been possible because of the pipes already installed. Seaman decided to call off further negotiations after reviewing the abstract.

17.16 Title Insurance

Title insurance is available to purchasers of real property. It insures their right to the property and guarantees that the insurer will defend the buyer against any claims made by other parties on matters not discovered in the title search. Title insurance gives the buyer greater security than does prosecution of an individual attorney who might have been negligent in the title search and the preparation of the abstract ot title.

EXAMPLE 13. Jamison purchased a house and lot. A title search showed that there was no flaw in the seller's title that might in any way damage Jamison's right to the property. As further assurance, Jamison purchased a title-insurance policy by payment of one premium. Four years after taking title to the property, Jamison was sued by the wife of a former owner. Her dower right had not been respected when the property was sold. Jamison's title policy will provide legal assistance in this suit and payment of any judgment that might be made against him as defendant.

DEEDS

17.17 Quitclaim, or Release, Deed

A deed that does nothing more than release one's rights in a property is a *quitclaim,* or *release, deed.* Such a deed gives no warranties or assurances of title to the grantee. It is unusual for this type of deed to be used in the sale of property today.

EXAMPLE 14. James received a one-third interest in a property through the will of his late father. His mother received a two-thirds interest. As a gesture of kindness to his mother, James signed a *quitclaim deed*, whereby he gave up all rights to his one-third interest. He did not warrant the property clear of encumbrances; he merely gave up what interest he had in the property.

17.18 Tax-Sale Deed

Tax-sale deeds are issued to the buyers of property that is sold to recover taxes, assessments, or other claims and judgments. The deeds are issued after a sheriff's sale. Such deeds are no different from quitclaim deeds. The buyer takes the deed, without warranties and subject to all and any claims that may exist against the property purchased.

17.19 Bargain and Sale Deed

A deed that transfers title to property but makes no warranties with respect to the title or to the use of the property is a *bargain and sale deed.* Such a deed names the amount of consideration given in exchange for the property.

EXAMPLE 15. Carlos sold an unimproved piece of land to Sanders. Neither party secured the services of an attorney to make a title search. Not wishing to be bound by any further claim against him by Sanders, Carlos transferred the property through a bargain and sale deed, in which the purchase price of $700 was named. In the event that flaws in the title developed, Carlos would be free of liability.

17.20 Simple Warranty Deed

By a *simple warranty deed*, the seller does nothing more than warrant to the buyer that he or she has good title to the property and that the buyer's legal rights to the property will not be threatened or disturbed. *Bargain and sale* and *simple warranty deeds* are not often used today in the transfer of real property.

17.21 Full Covenant and Warranty Deed

Sales of real estate in today's market are almost all accomplished through the issuance of a *full covenant and warranty deed.* This deed, unlike the types of deeds discussed above, gives the seller's assurances to the buyer of valid title and freedom from interruption of ownership rights. Covenants or warranties incorporated into this type of deed are assurances by the seller:

1. that he or she is the owner of the property in fee simple, with the right to convey title to another;
2. that the buyer will not be interrupted in the quiet enjoyment of the property;

3. that there are no undisclosed encumbrances on the property and that the seller will be liable on any claims made against the property by any creditor for debts existing prior to the transfer;
4. that the seller guarantees the title and will procure and give to the buyer any legal documents that might be necessary to perfect the title and that the seller will defend the grantee in these rights.

A seller may be held liable for breach of these warranties to the extent of any damage resulting to the buyer. Such a guarantee is backed only by the seller's financial ability to answer for damages; a policy of title insurance, on the other hand, gives the buyer more security and assurances against loss.

EXAMPLE 16. Glover Brothers purchased a warehouse, receiving a full covenant and warranty deed from Denver Realty Company, the former owners. Subsequent to the sale and transfer of the deed, Campbell Roofing Company placed a lien on the property to secure payment for work previously done on the building. Glover Brothers may enforce Denver Realty's warranty, contained in the deed, making them liable for payments due Campbell Roofing.

EXECUTION OF A DEED

17.22 Steps in Execution of Deed

The steps in the execution of deeds are regulated by the laws of each state. State procedures are not uniform in all details, but generally follow these steps:

1. Deeds must be in writing and signed and sealed by the seller(s). (In states where the use of the seal has been eliminated, only signatures are necessary.)
2. The instrument must contain words of intention of transferring title to the property being sold or given away.
3. The deed must contain an unmistakable and clear description of the property.
4. The deed must be witnessed.
5. The deed must be acknowledged by being signed in the presence of a notary public or authorized official, who will impress his or her official seal on the deed.
6. The deed must be delivered to and accepted by the buyer.

17.23 Final Settlement

The grantor must present a full and proper deed, and the buyer must tender payment on the date, at the time, and at the place agreed upon in a sales agreement. Either seller or buyer may be represented by an attorney or other authorized agent. Failure of the seller to present a deed or the buyer to tender the purchase price results in a breach for which the offender (seller or buyer) may be held responsible in damages.

EXAMPLE 17. Whitney and Grable were the seller and buyer, respectively, of the Whitney Estates. They agreed to make settlement at 10:30 A.M., April 23, at the office of Whitney's attorney, in the Land Title Building. It had been agreed that Grable would make payment with a certified check in the amount of $285,750. Whitney was prepared to deliver the deed. Grable, however, presented his personal check, without certification by his bank. Grable had breached the agreement. Whitney would have the option of declaring the contract breached or permitting Grable to have additional time to have the check certified before delivery of the deed.

17.24 Delivery of Deed

A deed to a grantee has no validity prior to delivery. Delivery may be made and accepted by authorized agents of the seller and buyer.

17.25 Delivery in Escrow

Delivery in escrow is a requirement under the laws of certain states. Such a deed is delivered to a disinterested third party, known as an *escrow agent*. The escrow agent is bound to deliver the deed to the grantee on performance of stated obligations or conditions, such as payment by certified check. The escrow agent is prohibited from returning the deed to the grantor until such time as it is proven that the grantee has refused it or has failed to perform a promised obligation.

EXAMPLE 18. Summit Realty sold a house to Hunter. Merchants Bank, selected as the escrow agent, was to hold the deed from Summit Realty from June 3 to June 5, during which time Hunter was to deliver his certified check for $59,000 in payment of the property. Summit Realty learned on June 4 that it could sell the property to the American Variety Stores Corporation for $100,000. Summit demanded the return of the deed on the morning of June 4, before Hunter had appeared. Merchants Bank would be liable to Hunter for damages had it returned the deed to the realty firm before the end of June 5.

17.26 Recording the Deed

To protect the new owner, the deed must be recorded in a public office immediately following settlement. Recording the deed gives notice to all interested parties of the transfer of title and the identity of the new owner. Failure to record the deed may estop the purchaser from making claim of ownership against a subsequent purchaser from the first owner (the *owner of record)*.

EXAMPLE 19. Suppose that Hunter, of Example 18, delayed having his new deed recorded in the county recorder's office for several days after receiving it. A sale by Summit Realty to a second innocent purchaser could occur. Examination of public records would show Summit Realty as the owner of record. Should the second purchaser have his deed recorded first, Hunter would be estopped in claiming superior title to the property. Summit Realty, obviously, would be guilty of a fraud by making the duplicate sale.

FINANCING THROUGH REAL ESTATE MORTGAGES

17.27 Real Estate Mortgages

Mortgages of one kind or another are the principal source of cash for financing the purchase of real estate. A mortgage consists of a document issued by a *mortgagor* (the debtor) to a *mortgagee* (the creditor), binding the real estate as security for a cash loan. Accompanying the mortgage is the mortgagor's note or bond, which makes the mortgagor personally liable on the debt.

EXAMPLE 20. Harmon purchased a $60,000 house, paying $20,000 in cash. The balance was borrowed from the Country Saving & Loan Association, evidenced by a mortgage for $40,000, at 8½ percent interest, amortized over a period of thirty years. Harmon also signed a note in the same amount. Should Harmon default on the mortgage payments, the property could be sold to liquidate the loan. If the property did not bring sufficient funds to pay off the mortgage, Harmon would be personally liable for any deficiency through the note that had accompanied the mortgage.

17.28 Title Search and Recording a Mortgage

Prior to approving a mortgage loan, creditors will demand a title search of the property as thorough as the one made by an attorney for the buyer of a property. The mortgagee must be satisfied that the property will represent sufficient security against the loan made and that no other preferred claims would weaken the security given.

A mortgage against a mortgaged property must be recorded in a public office. Such a record gives notice to any potential buyers or lenders of the claims already existing against the property. Second and third mortgages are often issued with the same property as security for a loan. Each mortgage has priority over the next in line in the event of foreclosure for nonpayment.

EXAMPLE 21. The Rolph Company purchased a building, financing it through a first mortgage loan of $150,000, which they secured from the First National Bank. Second and third mortgages secured two other loans of $50,000 and $35,000, respectively, which were granted by other lenders. The firm defaulted on its payments, and foreclosure proceedings were started. Sale of the firm's property brought $200,000. The first and second mortgages were satisfied through this amount, but the mortgagor remained indebted on the $35,000 third mortgage. A deficiency judgment would have to be paid from other assets, if any existed.

17.29 Obligations and Rights of the Mortgagor

A mortgagor—whether an individual, a partnership, or a corporation—is regulated by the following requirements, which may be recited in the mortgage or prescribed by law:

1. The mortgagor is respected as the owner of the mortgaged property and has the right of possession and use.
2. The mortgagor may sell, lease, or assign a property within the restrictions contained in the mortgage. The mortgagee usually reserves the rights to approve the sale of the property to a new owner.
3. The mortgagor is not restricted from borrowing additional funds by using the same property as security under second, third, or other subsequent mortgages.
4. The mortgagor is required to insure the building for an amount equal to the mortgagee's equity in the building as security of the loan. The mortgagor may also insure the building to an amount that equals his or her own insurable interest in the property.
5. The mortgagor must preserve the building in a manner that will not endanger the mortgagee's interest and security for the loan.
6. The mortgagor must make all pledged payments on the principal and interest.
7. The mortgagor is obliged to keep up all tax payments, meet special assessments, and in all respects use the premises in accordance with all laws regulating the use and protection of the property.

17.30 Mortgagee's Rights

A mortgagee has unqualified rights to sell, assign, or transfer a mortgage. As with other assignments and transfers, the transferee (assignee) "steps into the shoes" of the transferor (assignor), receiving the same benefits and rights previously held by the one making the transfer.

EXAMPLE 22. Monoghan held a first mortgage on a house and lot owned by Ferguson. Subtracting payments already made to Monoghan, the outstanding indebtedness was $14,643. Monoghan assigned the mortgage to the Security Trust Company, which bought the mortgage and note for that amount. In assigning a mortgage, the mortgagee need not consult the mortgagor or secure permission for the assignment from the mortgagor.

17.31 Foreclosure of a Mortgage

The mortgagee has the right to demand the sale of the mortgaged property if the mortgagor fails to fulfill her or his obligation on the loan. Sale through a foreclosure is processed through the courts of equity. Proceeds from the sale are applied to liquidation of the mortgage debt, interest, and other expenses. Any surplus remaining is used to satisfy secondary mortgages, if any, or is returned to the mortgagor. According to the terms of some mortgages, such a sale may be made without bringing a foreclosure action in the courts.

17.32 Deficiency Judgment

A *deficiency judgment* is a judgment by the court against the mortgagor when mortgaged property that was foreclosed does not bring sufficient funds to satisfy the mortgagor's debt. The deficiency judgment may be collected through the sale of the mortgagor's other assets or through garnishment of salary or wages due the mortgagor from an employer.

EXAMPLE 23. Hinds was in default in payments on a mortgage loan from the Bankers Trust Company. The mortgage debt, including interest, was $32,790. In a foreclosure action the property was sold at public auction, bringing only $26,850. A deficiency judgment of $5,940 was issued by the court against Hinds. Other assets belonging to Hinds were confiscated and sold, leaving a balance of $1,300. The balance owed was paid through garnishment of Hinds's salary.

17.33 Equity of Redemption

By statute in many states, the mortgagor is permitted to buy back his or her confiscated property from the purchaser in a foreclosure sale. Repurchase must occur within a time limit set by statute, and the repurchase price will include an interest charge. A deed is not issued to the foreclosure purchaser until after the expiration of the time period allowed for redemption. This process is known as *equity of redemption*.

EXAMPLE 24. Due to temporary unemployment, Krieg was not able to meet mortgage payments on his family homestead, which had been mortgaged with a loan several years before. A foreclosure action was commenced, and the property was sold to Langstrom for $28,000. The property had been in Krieg's family for many generations. Circumstances improved for Krieg, and within the time alloted by statute he was able to reimburse the buyer, with interest. Thus the debtor is permitted to regain a property that could not be duplicated elsewhere.

17.34 Purchaser Assumes the Mortgage

One purchasing a property on which there is an existing mortgage may *assume the mortgage*. By assuming the mortgage, the new owner accepts the assignment of all obligations related to the mortgage and liability on the seller's note. If, in a foreclosure, the property does not bring sufficient funds to cover the indebtedness, the *new owner* will be subject to any deficiency judgment that may be placed against him or her.

EXAMPLE 25. Spahr purchased a property, assuming a mortgage and note that then showed an indebtedness of $23,873 to the Avenue Trust Company. Spahr had financial reverses, his mortgage payments were in arrears, and the property was sold for $19,654 in a foreclosure action. By assuming the mortgage, Spahr also made himself liable for the deficiency of $4,219, to be paid out of any other assets that he still possessed or out of his future earnings.

17.35 Purchase Subject to the Mortgage

A new owner who takes a mortgaged property *subject to the mortgage* is not subject to a deficiency judgment in the event of a foreclosure.

EXAMPLE 26. Suppose that Spahr, of Example 25, had purchased the property *subject to the mortgage*. On foreclosure, Spahr's loss would be limited to the loss of the property. He would *not* have been required to answer for the deficiency judgment of $4,219.

17.36 Release of Mortgage

When a mortgage indebtedness has been satisfied by the mortgagor, a document known as a *satisfaction piece* is issued by the mortgagee as a receipt and release from further obligation. The satisfaction piece is then presented to the county recorder, who removes the lien from the property records. Failure to have the mortgage lien removed from the recorder's records leads third parties to believe that an indebtedness still exists against the property.

EXAMPLE 27. Zimmerman satisfied a mortgage of $58,000 recorded against his Lancaster County farm. A satisfaction piece was delivered to him by the Farmers Bank & Trust Company, the mortgagee. Zimmerman failed to exhibit the satisfaction piece to the county recorder, and the lien remained on the recorder's books as an indebtedness against the farm. Zimmerman later attempted to purchase a heavy-duty tractor on time payments. A credit check showed that the mortgage indebtedness still existed. Zimmerman's request for credit was therefore denied. Under the Consumer Credit Protection Act, Zimmerman would be permitted to demand reasons for the denial of credit, after which he could have the record corrected.

Solved Problems

17.1 Chapman deeded his farm to his son Daniel, who had assisted his father with the farm for more than twenty-five years. The completed deed, in proper legal form, was placed in a strongbox. Before giving Daniel possession of the deed, Chapman was killed in an accident. On examination of Chapman's papers, the deed was discovered. Other sons, who had never given support to their father, contested the deed. They claimed equal shares in the property. What would be the outcome of this case?

A deed has no validity unless it has been delivered to the grantee or to the grantee's agent. Despite the moral virtues of giving the property to Daniel, the other sons will share equally in the distribution of their father's estate unless a will that states otherwise is found.

17.2 Freid sold his property to Cressona and delivered a deed to him on June 12. Cressona, unaware of the necessity of having the deed recorded, locked it in his strongbox for safekeeping. Freid, aware of Cressona's ignorance of the law, sold the same property to Pomeroy. Freid issued a second deed to Pomeroy, who recorded it immediately. Pomeroy sought to have Cressona removed from the land, charging him as a trespasser. Was Pomeroy correct in this action?

Pomeroy was a purchaser in good faith. He had no knowledge that the land had already been sold to Cressona. Public records showed Freid, from whom Pomeroy received title, to be the owner of record. Cressona will be evicted from the land. His recovery, if any, will be in an action against Freid.

17.3 Worrel falsely represented himself as an agent authorized to sell Tallman's three-hundred-acre farm. Gantz, an interested buyer, bought the farm. Worrell signed the deed "Arthur Tallman, by Henry Worrell, agent." The deed was recorded. Tallman later sold the property to Kuhn, to whom he delivered a good and proper deed. Gantz maintained in a court action that he was the previous buyer and the owner of record as established in the county recorder's office. What are the rights of the parties?

The deed issued by Worrell had no validity because it was issued without proper authority. Recording a deed does not enhance its legality. A title search might have shown Gantz to be the owner, but he has no title rights whatsoever. Kuhn is the only person possessing a good and valid title from the owner, Tallman.

17.4. Butman had lived on a tract of land for thirty-five years but had never searched the title and was not fully aware of his right of ownership. He sold the land to Witman, giving only a quitclaim deed. Witman duly recorded this deed. Butman later affirmed his right to the land by a title search and sold it to Kline, giving a full covenant and warranty deed. Kline attempted to evict Witman, claiming that his deed was superior to the quitclaim deed held by Witman. Was Kline correct?

No. The quitclaim deed transferred to Witman Butman's complete and entire interest in the tract, for what it was worth. Although a full covenant and warranty deed is by far preferred, it gave Kline no superior rights in the land.

17.5 Robert and Mary married in Pennsylvania, a community-property state. Mary had undisputed and full title to five-hundred acres of woodland in Pike County. The land had been left to her two years prior to her marriage through her late father's will. A domestic dispute arose, and Robert claimed his one-half right of ownership in Mary's tract of land. Under community-property law, will he succeed in an equal division of the property?

No. Property owned by a spouse *prior* to marriage is not considered to be a part of the community property of a husband and wife. Robert has no right by marriage to make any claim to a one-half interest in his wife's five-hundred acres.

17.6 Myers mortgaged her lands as security for a debt of $53,750 that she had borrowed from the County Trust Company. The land contained approximately sixty acres of woodlands, principally hardwoods of high value. Myers made a contract with the Adirondack Lumber Company to come in and remove the seasoned trees at a mutually agreeable price. Will the County Trust Company have any interest in this transaction?

Yes. A mortgagor is not permitted to deplete the value of a mortgaged property at the expense of the mortgagee. Removing the trees depleted the value of the property and weakened the mortgagee's security in the event of a default by the mortgagor on her note and mortgage. The County Trust Company may enjoin Myers from fulfilling her agreement with the Adirondack Lumber Company.

17.7 Bunnell was mortgagor and Central Trust was mortgagee on a property owned by Bunnell. Bunnell had mortgaged the property as security on a loan of $17,500. During the term of the mortgage, Bunnell failed to pay tax bills levied against the property. Unpaid taxes plus interest amounted to $1,393. Bunnell failed to meet mortgage payments to the bank, and foreclosure proceedings resulted in the public sale of the property. The sale brought just enough to cover the bank's claim. The county made a concurrent claim for the $1,393 in unpaid taxes and interest. What priorities will be taken in the settlement of claims against Bunnell's mortgaged property?

In most instances, unpaid taxes take priority over a mortgage. Thus the county will receive $1,393 in unpaid taxes, leaving only $16,107 for the bank. A deficiency judgment of $1,393 will then be entered against Bunnell in favor of the bank, to be paid from his remaining assets or from his future earnings.

17.8 Suppose that, in Problem 17.7, Central Trust learned of Bunnell's tax problems, which had a detrimental effect on the bank's security. Central Trust, without consulting Bunnell, satisfied the tax bill. What are the bank's rights against Bunnell?

The mortgagor is under a duty to the mortgagee to keep the property free of tax liens resulting from unpaid taxes or property assessments. Failure to meet these obligations gives the mortgagee the right to pay them, holding the mortgagor responsible for the amount expended, plus interest.

17.9 Worrell borrowed $30,000 from the General Finance Company. Rather than take a mortgage secured by Worrell's apartment building, General Finance Company arranged for a *deed of trust* on the apartment building. How does a deed of trust differ from a regular mortgage?

By a *deed of trust*, the borrower conveys to a selected trustee the title to the property offered as security. The trustee holds the property for the benefit of the note holder, General Finance Company in this case. The trustee reconveys the property to the borrower when the debt is paid. If not paid, the trustee forecloses on the property and applies the proceeds of the sale to the payment of the secured debt. Under a deed of trust, it is important that the borrower reserve for herself or himself the right of possession and use of the property for the duration of the secured loan.

17.10 Denver decided to sell his home and buy either a cooperative apartment or a condominium. He inspected apartments under each type of ownership offered in an attractive community. What are his legal obligations and rights in making his selection of either the cooperative or the condominium?

If Denver decides to purchase a *condominium*, the agreement will give him a deed to his condominium unit and an undivided fractional interest in the common areas of the entire building. Denver's ownership rights and deed are very little different from those he would have if he purchased a dwelling standing independent of other structures. Each owner of a condominium unit is assessed a prorated fee for the upkeep and maintenance of the common areas. If Denver purchased an interest in a *cooperative*, he would buy stock in a cooperative corporation, receiving in return his living quarters. Denver would have no ownership in the cooperative's real estate, as he would have in a condominium. His ownership would be his intangible interest in the corporation, deemed a personal, rather than a real, property right. In a condominium, each owner may have his or her own mortgage, secured by a particular living unit. In a cooperative, there is only one mortgage; the cooperative corporation is the mortgagor, and the entire building is the security for the loan.

17.11 Grover, Kilgore, and Webb operated a private airfield on the outskirts of Oceanside. In the purchase of the land, they sought legal advice as to the best type of deed they should have to protect each one's family interest. What advice would an attorney probably give them in this matter?

To protect the interest of each partner's family, the attorney would probably advise that they seek a deed creating an estate in common. In that way, each partner's equal share would descend to his family, rather than succeed to the other partners.

17.12 Diffenbach died without a will. He possessed five large farms and two blocks of city real estate. His wife claimed ownership as his heir. By their marriage, there were also two surviving children. May Diffenbach's widow make a claim as an heir of her deceased husband?

A wife is not an heir of her husband. To qualify as an heir, there must be a *blood* relationship. The two children are Diffenbach's rightful heirs. The widow would have either a dower right (a one-third interest or as provided by statute) or a community-property interest in the property purchased or given to her husband after their marriage.

17.13 Byler and others built a hunting lodge on land owned by the Washington Lumber Company. They visited the lodge each year during the hunting and fishing seasons. No permission had been sought for building the lodge, but the lumber company's inspectors were aware of its presence and annual use. After twenty years, Washington Lumber Company officials ordered the men to dismantle the cabin and vacate the premises. What are the rights of both parties?

Byler and his friends had achieved property rights superior to those of the Washington Lumber Company through adverse possession and use. These rights protected their interest and prohibited the lumber company from having them evicted.

17.14 Mrs. Ulrich, the widow of John Ulrich, was threatened with eviction from her family home due to confusion on the right of ownership to the property. Mrs. Ulrich's three minor children were living with her at the time. Are there statutory provisions that will protect this woman and her children from eviction from their family home?

Some states, by statute, provide a life estate to a surviving spouse and to the children during their minority. Statutes vary, but in general the surviving spouse is permitted to enjoy, free of liability for debts and exempt from tax levy, a specified portion of real property being occupied as a residence. In such states, Mrs. Ulrich and her minor children would be assured a home during her lifetime. Some states determine the tax exemption by the property's area, others by its value. Others determine the exemption by both area and value.

17.15 Merryman married Swift in October. Swift, the wife, owned valuable property in her own name. The following August, a son was born to the couple. The son died only two weeks after birth. The mother died one month later, without leaving a will. Brothers and sisters of the deceased woman claimed title to her property. Merryman also claimed the right of ownership. To whom does the deceased woman's property descend?

Merryman. A husband has a curtesy right in the real property of his wife when it is proven that living children have been born of the marriage. It is *not* necessary that the child or children survive the mother. The curtesy right gives the surviving husband a life interest in the wife's real property. Had the child not been born to the Merrymans, the wife's property would have descended to her heirs. Likewise, Mrs. Merryman could have, in most states, deprived Merryman of these rights by leaving a will disposing of the property in any manner she chose.

17.16 The United States, through its space program, was the first nation to place a man on the Moon. In conformance with the law of acquiring real property by occupancy and discovery, could the Moon have been claimed as property of the United States?

Title by occupancy and discovery would at one time have given the United States the right to make claim to ownership of the Moon. However, by mutual agreement in the United Nations (as of December 1963), all member nations agreed to give up that right in the exploration of celestial bodies. By this agreement, such exploration is for the benefit of all the people of Earth.

17.17 Rosseau purchased a warehouse for $185,000. He took the property subject to a Bankers Trust mortgage of $130,000. Rosseau's business failed, and the warehouse was sold through foreclosure by the bank. At public auction, it brought only $110,000. Bankers Trust levied a deficiency judgment against Rosseau for the unpaid balance of $20,000. Must this be paid out of Rosseau's other assets and future earnings?

No. Rosseau purchased the warehouse *subject to the mortgage*. By these terms, his liability is limited to whatever is realized in the sale of the real estate securing the loan. He is not personally subject to the deficiency judgment. Had he *assumed the mortgage*, the deficiency judgment would have stood against him.

17.18 Sweitzer left two properties by his will. One, which went to his wife for her lifetime, was to be returned on her death to the estate and distributed among his surviving children. The other was left to the Harmony Grange, with the condition that if the Grange ever ceased using the property, for any reason, it was to go to the adjacent Limestone Presbyterian Church. How would one define these two estates?

The estate left to his wife was a *reversion estate* at her death. (The property would *revert* to his children.) In the second instance, a *remainder estate* would develop if the Harmony Grange gave up the use of the land.

17.19 Fantom sold a triangular piece of downtown real estate to the Spaulding Store for $29,000. Neither Fantom nor Spaulding cared to go to the expense of making a title search. Fantom merely gave Spaulding a quitclaim deed. Five years later, an heir to a former owner claimed title to the property through a will that had been left by his grandfather. His claim was supported by a court decision. Could Spaulding seek damages from Fantom?

No. Fantom's quitclaim deed transferred to Spaulding only what interest and ownership Fantom had in the property. A quitclaim deed contains no guarantees or warranties on which Spaulding might have made a claim.

17.20 Milligan agreed, by contract, to purchase for $10,000 two acres of unimproved land adjacent to his bakery. He planned to use the land as a parking lot. Milligan deposited $2,500 with the seller. The balance, $7,500, was to be paid on the date of settlement. The seller failed to present himself on the date of settlement, sending word that he had changed his mind and was returning Milligan's deposit of $2,500. What were Milligan's rights?

Milligan could bring an action in equity demanding specific performance of the contract. However, if he accepted and used the $2,500, he would waive his right to bring an action against the seller. By the court's writ of specific performance, the seller would be required, under threat of contempt charges, to deliver a full and proper deed to Milligan.

Review Problems

17.21 What is a *satisfaction piece?*

17.22 Explain what is meant by an *estate by the entireties*.

17.23 Explain the term *title by occupancy*. How does this affect exploration in outer space?

17.24 What is (1) a *dower right* and (2) a *curtesy right?*

17.25 Explain the expression "in lieu of dower."

17.26 What is an *abstract of title?*

17.27 What assurances relating to title does a seller give a buyer through a quitclaim deed?

17.28 Does a tax-sale deed warrant good title to the property sold?

17.29 What effect does nondelivery of a deed have upon the grantee's title rights?

17.30 Must real property deeds always be *signed and sealed* by the grantor?

17.31 In what court does a petitioner seek an order of specific performance?

17.32 What is a mortgagor? What is a mortgagee?

17.33 Explain equity of redemption.

17.34 How do *assuming a mortgage* and *taking subject to a mortgage* differ?

17.35 How does one achieve title through adverse possession?

Answers to Review Problems

17.21 It is a document, issued by a mortgagee to a mortgagor, signifying that the mortgage has been fully paid and satisfied.

17.22 It is a joint estate owned by a wife and husband, with the right of survivorship.

17.23 Title by occupancy is title achieved by discovery or conquest. Exploration of celestial bodies, by agreement of the United Nations, will be for the benefit of all mankind, not for the nation first occupying a planet or other celestial body.

17.24 (1) A dower right is the wife's statutory interest in the real property of her husband. (2) Curtesy right is the surviving husband's statutory right in all of the real property of the wife for his lifetime; it exists only if a child has been born of the marriage.

17.25 It is a provision in the will of a husband whereby he leaves money or other property to his widow in place of her dower right; the widow has the option of accepting what was left to her in the will or of claiming her dower right.

17.26 It is a document prepared by a lawyer who has searched the title to a real property; the document, if it is complete, contains a history of the property and lists all encumbrances and obligations existing against the property.

17.27 A quitclaim deed gives no assurances of title whatsoever.

17.28 No. The buyer is merely assigned such title as exists in the name of the present owner.

17.29 The deed is not valid if it is not delivered to the grantee or the grantee's agent.

17.30 They must be signed, but need not be sealed in those states whose laws no longer require the use of the seal.

17.31 An order of specific performance is sought in a court of equity.

17.32 A mortgagor is the party who pledges real property as security for a loan or some other executory promise. A mortgagee is the one making the loan or giving other consideration.

17.33 It is the right of a property owner, within a time set by statute, to recover his or her property after it has been sold through foreclosure of a defaulted mortgage.

17.34 *Assuming a mortgage* obligates the new mortgagor to a deficiency judgment if the property is ultimately foreclosed and does not bring sufficient funds, on foreclosure, to cover the note. Taking a property *subject to the mortgage* does not obligate the new owner to a possible deficiency judgment in the event of foreclosure and public sale.

17.35 Four qualifications are necessary: occupancy of the property or its use (1) for a period of twenty years or a time set by statute; (2) without interruption during those years; (3) without the consent of the owner; but (4) with the owner's knowledge.

Legal Terms

Abstract of title. A summary of all the conveyances, mortgages, liens, and other charges affecting a parcel of land; may be used as evidence on which the owner's title to the real property depends.

Community-property statute. Some states, by such a statute, automatically give each spouse a one-half right of ownership in both the real and personal property acquired after their marriage.

Conveyance. An instrument transferring title to real property; the transfer of title to real property from one person to another.

Curtesy right. By common law, the right of the husband to all of his deceased wife's real property for his life; this right exists only in those cases where a child living at birth has been born of the marriage.

Deed. A written instrument that conveys real property rights.

Dower right. The provision made by law for a widow out of her late husband's real property.

Encumbrance. A lien or liability attached to a property.

Equity of redemption. The statutory right of a mortgagor to buy back property sold at a foreclosure sale for the price paid by the buyer, plus interest.

Escrow agent. In the transfer of real property, one selected by the seller and buyer to take possession of the new deed with the obligation to refuse delivery of said deed until such time as the buyer has delivered the purchase price and other fees agreed upon in the sales agreement.

Foreclosure. The right of a mortgagee to sell property named in a mortgage to secure the unpaid pledge made by the mortgagor.

Mortgage. A lien on property by which the property is made security for a loan.

Quitclaim deed. A deed containing no warranties, granting to another whatever right the grantor may have in real property; also called a *release deed*.

Title. The right to property; evidence of ownership.

Title by occupancy and discovery. The right of a nation to claim title to lands it discovers or occupies; title by occupancy now comes under the close surveillance of the United Nations.

Title search. The tracing of the rights of all former owners of real property; done by an attorney to assure the rights of a new owner taking a deed to the property.

Trust deed. An instrument that transfers real property to a second party, who holds it in trust for the benefit of someone else.

Chapter 18

Leasing Real Property

As a rule, prospective tenants do not closely study the lease agreements they make in the rental of property. This is especially true of those who make residential lease agreements, which are short-term as compared to commercial leases.

Lease agreements are usually written by attorneys who specialize in the field of real property. Such agreements are usually attentive to the landlord's, not the tenant's, rights and obligations. It is rare that a tenant is aware of all the rights and obligations that he or she may have. The average tenant is most often aware of only two things—the obligation to pay a certain amount of rent at a certain time and the requirement to put down a security deposit at the beginning of a tenancy.

This chapter attempts to give a somewhat more balanced review of the rights and obligations of both tenants *and* landlords. As you review the principles and examples in this chapter, keep in mind the fact that state statutes and local ordinances should always be consulted in making any lease agreement.

THE LANDLORD-TENANT CONTRACT

18.1 The Lease

An agreement between a person (called a *lessor*) who owns lands and buildings and another person (called the *lessee*) who rents them is called a *lease*. Leases may be either oral or written. Leases for periods of more than one year must be in writing, however, as required by the statute of frauds.

EXAMPLE 1. Josephs rented an apartment from the Harris Realty Company for the nine months he would be attending Pacific University. There was no written agreement. After only four months, Josephs vacated the apartment, claiming that he had the right to do so in the absence of a written lease. Harris Realty could hold Josephs responsible for rent over the entire nine-month period agreed on. However, if Josephs were a minor, his contract might be voided through incapacity.

18.2 Lease Compared with License

A lease is less than a freehold estate, but it is a right in another's property. A *license* is a personal right, not a right in real property. A license provides the licensee with some special privilege in the use of another's land, such as the right to go hunting on the land or to use it for camping. A license, unlike a lease, is rarely in writing, is usually without consideration, and may be canceled at any time.

EXAMPLE 2. Hockessin Church Sunday School planned a summer outing along the banks of the Brandywine River. Wyeth, a landowner along that body of water, gave the group permission to use an open meadow facing the river. No real *property* rights had been given to the group by the owner. This was a license to use Wyeth's property, not a lease.

EXAMPLE 3. Suppose that the church group of Example 2 intended to use the meadow every week and planned to build bath houses, refreshment stands, and other buildings on the grounds. In such an event, the owner would enter into a lease agreement with the church. The agreement should be in writing and should outline the rights and responsibilities of the lessor and the lessee. Included in the lease should be any consideration to be paid and the duration of the agreement.

18.3 Tenancies

The executed lease creates what is called a *leasehold estate* between the owner and tenant. Leasehold estates may be of different kinds. The most common are: (1) tenancy for a definite period; (2) tenancy from year to year; (3) monthly tenancy; and (4) tenancy at will.

18.4 Tenancy for a Definite Period

Tenancies for a stated period may be for a month, six months, a year, or any duration agreed to by the parties. No intention of a date of termination of the lease is required. Some leases state that tenants have the obligation to inform the landlord of their intention to vacate. Tenants who sign such leases must inform their landlords on or before the date stated in the lease. Failure to inform the landlord makes the tenant a *tenant by sufferance*. A landlord may charge a tenant by sufferance as a trespasser. The landlord may also elect to extend the lease for a period equal to the time that has elapsed since the lease was first signed.

EXAMPLE 4. Rudnick rented a store to Patterson Clothes for one year. The lease required Patterson Clothes to give notice of their intention to vacate the premises in writing at least sixty days prior to the end of the leasehold. Patterson had not read this condition in the lease and did not write the required letter. Rudnick elected to hold Patterson Clothes to an automatic renewal of the lease for another year. The landlord, under such a renewal, is not permitted to increase the rent except by agreement of the tenant.

18.5 Renewal by Landlord's Acceptance of Rent

Acceptance of rent from a tenant who has overstayed his or her lease, when tenancy is for a definite period, gives the tenant the right to assert her or his claim to remain for an additional period equal to that agreed to in the original lease. The landlord is, in such cases, prevented from evicting the tenant until the expiration of the automatically renewed leasehold.

EXAMPLE 5. Suppose that Rudnick, of Example 4, intended to terminate the lease with Patterson Clothes. Patterson had not mailed in notice of intention to vacate. A rental agent accepted Patterson's check for another month, not being aware of Rudnick's intention to terminate. By accepting Patterson's check, the landlord's rental agent would restrict Rudnick from evicting Patterson for a time period equal to that stated in the original lease—in this case, one additional year.

18.6 Tenancy from Year to Year or from Month to Month

Tenancies from year to year or from month to month are terminated when notice by either party is given within limits set by local statute. On a month-to-month lease, notice from either the tenant or the landlord is usually required on the day the rent is due, with the understanding that the premises would be vacated one month hence. When the tenancy is from year to year, the statutory period of notice is usually three months.

EXAMPLE 6. Truman, an itinerant farm worker, rented an apartment on a month-to-month basis. The demands of his employment determined the time he could remain in any particular location. When he received orders to move to another location, he gave notice to the landlord of his intention to terminate the month-to-month tenancy. The termination was to coincide with the expiration of the next month's rent payments.

18.7 Tenancies at Will

A *tenancy at will* is one that does not cover any agreed-upon period and may be terminated at any time by either party, usually after giving required notice. Some states require a thirty-day notice to terminate a tenancy at will. Other states permit termination by either party without the necessity of giving any advance notice.

18.8 Assignment of Lease

A tenant may assign a lease to a third party without the consent of the landlord unless a statement prohibiting such an assignment is included in the lease. When assignment is made, the assignee "steps into the shoes" of the assignor. The assignor is responsible to the landlord as a guarantor of obligations required of the tenant under the terms of the lease.

EXAMPLE 7. Toulson occupied an apartment at the Arundel Apartments. Her written lease terminated on June 25 of the following year. Toulson, without the consent of the resident agent, assigned her lease to Alexander on November 25. Alexander was ordered to vacate the apartment by the renting agent because Toulson's lease prohibited assignment or termination except by mutual assent of landlord and tenant. Alexander was forced to move, and Toulson continued to be responsible for all rents over the ensuing seven months of her lease.

18.9 Rights and Duties of the Landlord

The landlord's rights include: (1) the right to collect rent; (2) the right to recover the property at the end of the leasehold; (3) the right to evict a tenant for nonpayment of rent, misuse of the property, disorderly conduct, destruction of property, or illegal use of premises; and (4) the right to take title to all fixtures added by the tenant that may be considered permanent additions and real property.

EXAMPLE 8. Young and Chapman rented a house in the Pike Creek Estates for one year. Two months after taking possession, they started a gambling operation on the premises. Gambling was illegal by state law, and use of the property as a commercial establishment was prohibited by local ordinances. The landlord would have legal grounds for evicting these tenants even though they had respected all other requirements of the lease.

18.10 Landlord's Right of Lien for Unpaid Rent

By the terms of most leases and by statute in many states, a landlord has the right of lien for unpaid rent on the tenant's personal property if it is housed in the rented premises. The technical term for this right is *distress for rent.* Personal property may be sequestered through proper legal procedure and retained until the rent is paid. If the rent is not paid within a reasonable or statutory period of time, the personal property may be sold through a court order.

18.11 Landlord's Duties to Third Parties

The landlord has the duty to give notice to a tenant or to any other persons entering the rented premises of hazards and defects that might endanger a person. No warranty, however, is usually given by the landlord that the premises are safe or suitable for the tenant's intended use. All states require warning of known hazards. Other states, by statute or judicial decision, make a landlord responsible for injuries resulting from hazards that he or she *should have been aware of* by virtue of her or his ownership of the premises.

EXAMPLE 9. Lehman, a mailman, delivered a package to Slicer, a third-floor tenant in the Hampton Hall Apartments. A worn stair-tread gave way, and Lehman fell to the floor below. It was determined that the owner of the building had not inspected the stairs for many years, during which time they became hazardous for those using them. Denial of knowledge of the hazard would be of little use as a defense if Lehman sued the landlord for injuries. A different decision would result if the mailman knew of the existing hazards in the stairs and failed to use care in climbing them.

18.12 Rights and Duties of the Tenant

A tenant has rights and obligations related to the tenancy. In addition to the fundamental rights and duties listed here, numerous other conditions are usually written into the leases for commercial housing and apartment rentals: (1) The tenant has the right to "quiet enjoyment" of the premises. This refers to the tenant's right to uninterrupted privacy. His or her legal rights include the sole right to entrance and occupancy of the rented property, excluding even the owner's right of entry without the tenant's express permission. (2) The tenant, unless prohibited to do so by the terms of the lease, has the right to sublet the premises. (3) The tenant must pay rents agreed upon, must respect the owner's right of title, and must make such repairs as are outlined in the lease agreement. (4) The tenant must respect restrictions of use as contained in the lease. When the premises are rented for a special use, no other uses may be made of the premises. Alterations of a permanent nature may not be carried out without the consent and approval of the landlord.

EXAMPLE 10. Valet, Incorporated, rented stores at two locations from City Realty. The lease stipulated that the two stores were to be used exclusively for the receipt and distribution of clothing left for cleaning, pressing, and repair. (Cleaning and pressing were not to be done at these locations, but at Valet's main plant.) Valet installed a pressing machine in one of the stores and hired an employee to do pressing of suits and dresses. Valet, Inc., thus breached its lease agreement and may be evicted by City Realty.

DUTY OF REPAIRS

18.13 Lessor's Obligation to Repair

By the terms of a written lease, the landlord's duties to repair are usually outlined and limited to the roof, walls, and general structure of the premises. A landlord may be held liable for injuries to a tenant or to third parties resulting from failure to repair conditions of which the landlord was aware. State and local laws enacted over the past decade place more responsibility upon the landlord than had been required under common law. (Under the common law, almost all kinds of repairs were the responsibility of the tenant.) In an apartment building, the landlord has the responsibility to repair all common areas, including hallways, stairs, entrances, fire escapes, elevators, and the like. Some local laws permit tenants to withhold rent when repairs are not made to heating systems, plumbing, and other services necessary for peaceful living in the building.

EXAMPLE 11. Chambers occupied a house rented by Oliver Realty. During an unusually cold spell, the automatic furnace cut off. No heat was supplied to the house, and Chambers and his family were threatened with serious illness if repairs were not made. Chambers, through appeal to the local housing authority, could force Oliver Realty to make the repairs without delay.

18.14 Tenant's Obligation to Repair

A tenant, by common law, is required to return the rented premises to the lessor in the same condition as they were received, with allowances for "ordinary wear and tear." Destruction of rented premises has, in some judicial decisions and by common law, required the tenant to rebuild the premises at her or his own expense. State laws and provisions included in some leases relieve the tenant of responsibility in the event of total destruction through such catastrophies as fire, hurricane, flood, and the like.

Destruction of premises due to misuse or negligence places *full responsibility* on a tenant to rebuild the rented premises. Such responsibility gives the tenant an insurable interest in the rented property. Rental of an apartment or a *part* of a building does not place this same responsibility on the lessee.

"Ordinary wear and tear" is interpreted as the depreciation that would ordinarily occur through occupancy by persons of prudence. Repairs required by other than ordinary wear and tear become the tenant's responsibility.

EXAMPLE 12. Thorogood rented a barn, in which he kept two riding horses. Lightning hit the barn, and it burned to the ground. The horses were killed, and everything stored in the barn was destroyed. If no relief was offered Thorogood by law or by a provision in the lease, he would be required to rebuild the barn at his own expense.

EXAMPLE 13. Three students rented an apartment close to their college. They used nails to hang pennants, pictures, and other materials on the walls. They used no care in cooking, and heavy grease saturated the walls of the entire apartment. They also spilled liquids on the carpeting, which was discolored beyond the point of cleaning or repair. These damages were beyond ordinary wear and tear, and the students could be held responsible.

18.15 Termination of the Lease Agreement

A lease is a contract and may be terminated in many of the same ways that other contracts are terminated. Leases can be terminated by: (1) expiration of the term agreed to in the lease; (2) mutual agreement of landlord and tenant prior to termination by terms of the lease; (3) the landlord's title through eminent-domain proceedings; (4) the tenant's or landlord's breach of conditions contained in the lease (a partial breach may lead to interruption of rent payment rather than termination, depending on local law); or (5) destruction of premises where the tenant is not at fault. This last condition of termination will be decided by reference to local laws or the common law.

EXAMPLE 14. Gallagher and Stultz, who were attorneys, rented a suite of offices in the Jefferson Building. A fire of undetermined origin gutted the entire building, burning out the lawyers' offices and destroying all of their records and their law library. Gallagher and Stultz would not be held to the duration of the lease. (Under some laws, the tenant remains liable for all rents if the tenant has leased the entire building, not just a part of it.)

Solved Problems

18.1 Eshelman rented a store to Hosler for three years on an oral lease. Rent was to be $250 a month. Hosler made improvements to the store through painting and other decoration, making the premises much more valuable. Eshelman gave Hosler notice to vacate after only fourteen months. Eshelman then entered into a written lease with Leffler, charging him $350 a month for the much-improved premises. May Hosler remain in the store?

Leases for periods of more than one year must be in writing to be enforceable. Hosler had no grounds for suit against his landlord, Eshelman. Moral rights do not give Hosler the right to stay in the store.

18.2 Suppose that Hosler, of Problem 18.1, had spent several hundred dollars in making extensive repairs to the run-down store, all with Eshelman's knowledge. Eshelman approved of the repairs and accepted rents over a period of eighteen months. He now ordered Hosler out on grounds of an unenforceable oral lease. Are the conditions the same?

Eshelman's agreement to his tenant's spending large amounts of money on the property, with full approval and knowledge of the work being done, could estop him in his denial of a valid lease. The tenant had relied entirely on Eshelman's approval of the expenditures of time and money in improving Eshelman's property. The prevention of the unjust enrichment of one person at the expense of another is the principle which lies at the foundation of this interpretation, which strictly speaking is contrary to the provision of the statute of frauds that specifies that leases of more than one year must be in writing.

18.3 Schrey rented a house to Diller for $235 a month on a one-year written lease. Rents were paid for several months, when Diller fell two months behind in rents. Schrey threatened to evict Diller unless all rents were brought up to date. Does Schrey have the right to evict Diller under these circumstances?

By common law, a landlord, acting on his or her own authority, may *not* evict the tenant for nonpayment of rent unless the lease gives the landlord that right. Statutes in some states have changed the common law, giving the landlord this right. The final decision as to Diller's rights would depend on where he lives. In any state, however, Schrey has the right to bring suit against the tenant for unpaid rents.

18.4 Schaut and Crouch rented a furnished apartment, where they often gave wild and crowded parties. The furniture in the apartment was given rough treatment; its springs were broken and holes were burned in the upholstery of the living room suite. The lease contained no conditions covering the care of or liability for the furniture. Could Schaut and Crouch be held liable to the landlord for these losses?

The tenants' possession of the lessor's furniture created a mutual bailment of personal property. In addition to their responsibility for repairs to the apartment, the bailees (Schaut and Crouch) have a responsibility for damages resulting from negligence and their failure to give ordinary care to the furniture. They would be liable to the landlord.

18.5 Kilmer rented a house from Scheimer for one year under a written lease that contained no provisions concerning the parties' rights and obligations in the event of the destruction of the house. The house burned to the ground seven months prior to the expiration of the lease, and Kilmer ceased making rent payments. Scheimer sued for rents for the remaining period of the lease. Will he succeed?

By common law, the tenant is responsible for all rent payments during the term of the lease. This is based on the theory that Kilmer is renting the ground in addition to the house. Kilmer would be excused of this obligation in states that have changed the common law to protect the tenant. Also, if Kilmer had insisted on a clause in the lease that would have relieved him of this obligation, Scheimer would have had no grounds for a suit.

18.6 Diltz rented an apartment in Elsmere Arms, a building containing ten efficiency apartments. Flood waters destroyed the building and all tenants were forced to vacate the premises. When Diltz discontinued rent payments, he was sued by the landlord. Must Diltz honor his one-year lease?

No. This case differs from the previous one in that Diltz rented and occupied only one small part of the building. He did not rent the land together with his apartment. The premises he formerly occupied were not any longer habitable, or even in existence. This fact terminated any obligation he might have had to Elsmere Arms.

18.7 Whaley rented rooms in a house owned by Sterling. Whaley renovated the rooms so that they would be suitable for the display of home-decorating materials and antique furniture that he proposed to advertise through the public press. Local inspectors learned of Whaley's intentions and informed him that he could not operate a business at that location, which had been zoned as "residential only." Whaley sought to break his lease on the grounds that he had rented the rooms specifically to run a business. Will he be released of his obligations under the lease?

No. Zoning laws are public information and are available to all who wish to consult them. Sterling was aware of the existing restrictions and had a moral obligation to inform his tenant of them, but he is not required by law to do so. There was no fraud or misconduct on the part of the landlord. Whaley may be held to the lease.

18.8 The Longacre Plumbing Company rented a warehouse and display room from Waples Realty for $500 a month. A ten-year lease was drawn up and signed. The location proved to be a bad choice for Longacre, and they vacated the premises and assigned the lease to another firm. The owner of Waples Realty intensely disliked the owner of the firm to which the lease had been assigned. The realtor therefore would not agree to the transfer. Nothing was included in the Longacre-Waples lease concerning assignment. Was the assignment valid and enforceable?

Yes. Unless restricted by a provision contained in a written lease agreement, an original lessee may assign rented premises. Waples had no legal argument that may defeat the assignment.

18.9 Suppose that in the previous case the lease written by Waples Realty contained an option for an additional ten-year period and that the option was the tenant's choice. The assignee of Longacre Plumbing's lease elected to pick up the option and renew the lease for another ten years. Waples strongly objected to this renewal by the assignee, whom he had wished to evict from the premises ten years before. May the assignee of the Longacre lease opt to renew for another ten years?

An assignee "steps into the shoes of the assignor." There was no restriction against assigning the Longacre-Waples lease; neither is there a restriction against the assignee taking up the option for renewal. Waples will have to accept the unwanted tenant's presence for an additional ten years.

18.10 Hillman assigned his five-year lease on a service station to Custer. At the time of the assignment, the lease had three more years to run. For eleven months, Custer paid rents and observed all other obligations of the lease. Then he moved out without notice. Hillman is now sued by the landlord for Custer's unpaid rent for the remaining two years and one month of this lease. Is Hillman obligated to pay the rent?

Yes. The assignor of an unexpired lease remains a guarantor of rents and other conditions imposed on the lessee by the terms of the lease. Hillman is responsible for the lease for the unexpired two years and one month.

18.11 Hurka and Young rented a run-down house for $75 a month for a period of four years. They were both professional carpenters and plumbers and immediately went to work improving the house. At the end of the leasehold, the house had appreciated at least $5,000 in value through their volunteer efforts. Before moving, they demanded remuneration from the owner for all improvements they had made over the four-year period. Will they succeed in their demands?

No. Hurka and Young acted voluntarily in making improvements which enhanced the value of the house. They had no contract with the landlord, who did not authorize or oversee the work and was under no legal obligation to reimburse the men for their time and the materials they used.

18.12 Zechman orally leased a cottage, starting September 1, for one year. The rent was $125 a month. The following September, Zechman tendered his check to the landlord for $125, representing the rent for that month. On Octobor 1, Zechman was given notice to vacate. He contended that he had the right to remain for another year by virtue of the fact that the lessor had accepted the September rent check. Was Zechman correct?

Yes. Zechman had a lease for one year on a *year-to-year periodic tenancy*. The lessor's acceptance of Zechman's check for September of the second year renewed Zechman's right to remain for another twelve months.

18.13 Stump rented an apartment from Thompson on a month-to-month basis. The rental was $110 per month. When Stump tendered her rent for the fourth month, Thompson informed her that the rent had been increased to $125, which he demanded immediately. Must Stump pay Thompson the $125?

No. The landlord, when renting on a month-to-month arrangement, usually must give one month's notice of any change or increase in rent. Stump may refuse to pay the $125 demanded. The following month, she would have the choice of either paying the $125 or moving out.

18.14 Reynolds lived in a rented house under a one-year lease. Local laws and state statutes were in conflict as to the responsibility of the tenant or the landlord for the repair of heating and plumbing services. The hot-water system ceased to operate, and Reynolds contended it was the landlord's responsibility to make the repairs. The landlord felt otherwise and threatened suit if Reynolds did not pay rent that he had withheld. What action may Reynolds take in this matter?

Reynolds may place his rent in escrow with a court of proper jurisdiction. The court would make a determination of the rights of the landlord and the tenant. If it is determined that the landlord has the responsibility to make repairs, the court will hold Reynold's payment of rent until repairs have been satisfactorily made. If it is the tenant's responsibility, the rent will be paid over to the landlord by the court without further delay.

Review Problems

18.15 What is a *license?*

18.16 Explain a *tenant by sufferance.*

18.17 What are the landlord's duties to third parties entering rented premises?

18.18 Does the landlord have the right to enter rented premises at any time?

18.19 In a lease, what is meant by *peaceful enjoyment?*

18.20 Is a tenant compensated for voluntary, expensive improvements made to rented premises?

18.21 By common law, may the landlord evict a tenant for failure to pay rent?

18.22 (1) Is a tenant obligated to continue paying rent when a rented building is destroyed? (2) Is your answer the same if the tenant occupied only one apartment in a building with many apartments?

18.23 Under what conditions may a tenant *not* assign a lease?

18.24 What is the legal arrangement between landlord and tenant for furnishings provided in a furnished apartment?

18.25 Does a landlord have a right of lien on the tenant's personal property for unpaid rent?

18.26 Is a real-property lease that is oral enforceable?

18.27 How may one automatically renew a lease for a second year on a *year-to-year tenancy?*

18.28 What is the meaning of the term "ordinary wear and tear" found in many leases?

18.29 Is it the responsibility of a landlord to inform a prospective tenant of zoning laws regulating the use to which rented property may be put?

Answers to Review Problems

18.15 A license is a personal right extended by a landowner giving permission to another to enter his or her lands for some particular purpose. It does not give the licensee a property right.

18.16 A tenant by sufferance is one who, because of failure to give notice of intention to vacate, may be treated either as a trespasser or as a holdover tenant by the landlord.

18.17 The landlord is responsible for third parties' injuries resulting from known hazards or dangerous situations that the landlord should have been aware of.

18.18 A landlord may enter only if permission has been given by the terms of the lease, and then only at reasonable hours and with the permission of the tenant.

18.19 The tenant will not be interrupted in her or his legal rights to exclusive occupancy of the rented premises.

18.20 No.

18.21 No.

18.22 (1) Yes, with exceptions as provided by state statutes. (2) The answer is no when one is a tenant of only a part of a building.

18.23 Assignment is not allowed only when it is prohibited by the terms of the lease agreement.

18.24 An implied mutual-benefit bailment exists.

18.25 Yes, if the property is on the landlord's premises. If the rent is not paid within a reasonable time, the tenant's personal property may be sold by court order to defray charges for unpaid rent.

18.26 Yes, it may be, but not for a period longer than one year.

18.27 A tenant may renew the tenancy by signing a new lease or by tendering rent for the month following expiration if the landlord accepts it.

18.28 It is the gradual depreciation of rented premises resulting from reasonable use.

18.29 No. Zoning restrictions are available for public inspection by persons renting another's property; prospective tenants are responsible themselves for finding out about such restrictions.

Legal Terms

Distress for rent. A landlord's right of lien for unpaid rent on tenant's personal property that is housed in the rented premises.

Eviction. The act of dispossessing a person by process of law from property held or leased.

Holding over. The act of retaining possession of leased property after the term of the lease has expired.

Landlord's right of lien. A landlord's right, granted in many states, allowing him or her to place a lien on the personal property of a tenant who has not paid rents or has caused damage to the rented premises; the lien must be on property still housed in the rented premises.

Lease. An oral or written contract between a landlord and tenant covering the rental of real property; it grants the use of real property for a definite period of time in consideration of the payment of rent.

License. A right granted by the owner of real property to another for the use of real property; it is usually oral, without consideration, and may be terminated by the grantor (licensor) at any time.

Tenancy. The leasehold estate created by a lease between a landlord and tenant.

Tenancy at will. A tenancy not covering any agreed-upon period; may be terminated by either party at any time by giving the required notice—usually thirty days.

Tenant by sufferance. A tenant who fails to notify the landlord of his or her intention to vacate the premises when the lease expires; tenant then becomes a trespasser or a "holdover" tenant.

Chapter 19

Wills and Estates of Decedents

After spending a lifetime working, investing, and building an estate, a majority of persons in this country—as many as 70 percent—leave this life without the benefit of a will. It seems that these people have little or no interest in what will become of their estates after their deaths.

This chapter outlines the various types of wills, the legal capacity necessary to draw a will, and the steps to be taken in actually writing a will. The chapter also reviews what happens to the estates of those who die without leaving a will.

A study of the complexities of will-making suggests that the advice and guidance of a lawyer are essential. The rigid requirements of state statutes and local ordinances, as well as the special legal meanings of words commonly used in wills, make great demands on a person not familiar with the law of wills. This chapter merely touches on the highlights of this subject.

TYPES OF WILLS

19.1 Wills

A *will* is a recognized legal document expressing the manner in which a *testator* directs an *executor* to distribute his or her property to a *beneficiary* after death. A will has no legal validity whatsoever until after the death of the testator. (A will is distinguished from a deed in that a deed takes effect during the grantor's lifetime.) A *bequest* refers to a gift of personal property; a *devise* refers to a gift of real property.

Probate is the legal procedure of establishing the validity of a testator's last will and testament after his or her death. The executor does this by referring all matters relating to the will to a probate court for adjudication. The validity of the will is attested to by the witnesses, who appear before the court at the request of the probate judge. They affirm that they witnessed the testator's signature to the will and one another's signature as witnesses.

EXAMPLE 1. George executed a will in proper form, signed it, and had it witnessed. In it, he left his entire estate to his brother, Carl. Carl was permitted to read the will. Seven days prior to his death, George destroyed the will and wrote a second one, in which he left all of his belongings to Katheryne, a friend. Carl has no rights whatsoever in George's estate.

19.2 Gifts *in Causa Mortis*

A gift made during one's lifetime, but at a time when death is imminent because of a known illness or disease, is called a *gift in causa mortis*. A gift *in causa mortis* that has already passed to the beneficiary must be returned to the donor or the donor's estate if death did not result from the illness or disease feared.

EXAMPLE 2. Hayes, who thought he was close to death because of pneumonia, gave his gold watch and military decorations to Raymond, a close friend. Hayes did die two days later, but the doctor indicated that death was due to causes other than pneumonia. Heirs of Hayes would be permitted to demand the return of the watch and medals from Raymond because a gift *in causa mortis* is nothing more than a *conditional gift*, and the condition had not been met in this case.

19.3 Holographic Wills

A *holographic will* is one written *entirely* in the handwriting of the testator. Some states still recognize holographic wills. Their validity is determined by the requirements of local law. Such a will must be signed by the testator but does not, under most conditions, require witnesses.

EXAMPLE 3. Thorne, in the privacy of her rented room, wrote a letter in which she outlined the disposition of her few belongings after death. She signed the document and placed it among her valuable and confidential papers in a family Bible in her desk. The will could be accepted as a valid document, and her wishes would be carried out. However, if she had typed in even so much as the date and her address, the will would have been void because a holographic will must be *entirely* in the testator's own identifiable handwriting.

19.4 Nuncupative, or Oral, Will

Historically valid in most states, the *nuncupative will* today will be accepted for probate in only a few jurisdictions. A person fearing death may dictate to three or more persons her or his desires in the distribution of property. At their first opportunity, the witnesses should then reduce the deceased's wishes to writing and sign the document as witnesses. Such wills are usually valid only when made under extreme circumstances, such as when death is imminent in battle or in other such urgent situations. Nuncupative wills are today considered a thing of the past.

19.5 Formal Will

A written document that expresses a testator's wishes and is prepared according to the requirements of the resident's state statutes is a *formal will*. All states today recognize the validity of formal wills. Statutes regulating formal wills differ from state to state. A will satisfying the laws of one state may not be accepted in another state where the testator may have owned real property.

EXAMPLE 4. Dukes, a resident of New Jersey, wrote a will that had two witnesses, as required under New Jersey law. The will left a farm to his brother. The farm was situated in New Hampshire, where the law required three witnesses to a will. Dukes's will, valid in New Jersey, would not be accepted for probate in the state of New Hampshire.

REQUIREMENTS OF A FORMAL WILL

19.6 Formal Wills Must Be in Writing

There is no such thing as an oral formal will. A formal will *must* be in writing. It may be handwritten, typewritten, or printed with parts filled in by hand or by typewriter. (The law is not specific in the definition of *writing*.) Copies of the will may be made for reference and distribution to family members, but only the original will is acceptable for probate. Indications of burning, mutilation, or tearing may invalidate the will on an interested party's claim that the testator intended to revoke the instrument.

EXAMPLE 5. Bramble's last will and testament was found in a safe-deposit box after his death. The will had been partially torn, and certain heirs attacked its validity. These heirs claimed that the testator must have intended to revoke the instrument. A court would have to rule on the validity of the instrument.

19.7 Formal Wills Must Be Signed by the Testator

A will must contain the signature of the testator. If the will covers more than one page, it should be signed at the bottom of each page. A testator who does not know how to write may make his or her mark in the presence of witnesses. If the testator is physically unable to do even that, another may sign for the testator in her or his presence and in the presence of witnesses. Under any condition, however, the testator must sign in the presence of witnesses.

EXAMPLE 6. Pennfield signed a will that had been prepared for him by his attorney. No witnesses were present. At a later time, Pennfield acknowledged to two friends that the signature was his. They then signed the will as witnesses. If contested, the will would be held void. The two witnesses would have had to *witness* Pennfield actually sign his name to the document.

19.8 A Formal Will Must Be Witnessed

Unless witnessed, a formal will will not be accepted for probate. The number of witnesses required is different from state to state. (Most states require two witnesses.) Each witness must sign in the presence of the other or others, and in the presence of the testator.

EXAMPLE 7. Krieg and Spahr agreed to witness Homan's will. Homan signed the document as testator, and Krieg signed as a witness. Krieg then left the office, not remaining to witness Spahr add her signature to the document. If contested, the will could be declared void because each witness had not observed the other's signing.

19.9 Use of Correct Terms

A will is a legal document, and its words used must conform to their accepted legal meaning. The use of terms that have more than one meaning results in confusion, and a court will apply the legal meaning rather than the meaning that the testator may have intended. (The court really has no other choice, since it would be impossible to question the testator on the meaning intended.)

EXAMPLE 8. Ehrgood left a will in which he stated that he wished to have his real and personal property divided equally among his *heirs*. Ehrgood had four surviving children. When he had used the word *heirs*, he had believed it to be synonymous with the word *children*. The court had to give the word *heirs* its legal interpretation, resulting in a division of property very different from the one Ehrgood had intended. Consultation with an attorney in the drawing of this will would have avoided this misunderstanding.

19.10 Testamentary Capacity

State laws prescribe the ages at which persons have *testamentary capacity*—the capacity to make a valid will. Differences also exist in the ages required by various states for a bequest of personal property as compared with a devise of real property. Most states originally required a person to be twenty-one years of age to draw a will. Many states have now lowered the required age to eighteen. Persons declared insane are considered incapable of creating a valid will, whatever their age.

EXAMPLE 9. Beuter, while intoxicated and unaware of what he was doing, signed a will that had been prepared for him by persons who wrote themselves into the will so that they would share in the distribution of his estate. Others in the group, who were sober, signed the document as witnesses. Beuter died without knowing anything of this will. When the will was presented for probate, relatives presented proof of Beuter's condition at the time of the signing and witnessing. The will would be declared void, and Beuter's property would be distributed according to state provisions for those dying without a will.

19.11 Restriction against Alterations

A will containing erasures, strikeovers, or other alterations may be declared void on the grounds that such alterations were made without knowledge or permission of the testator. If it can be proved that an alteration was made before the signing and witnessing, the alteration may be accepted. In any event, it is inadvisable to make any alterations in a will because of the danger that it might be contested.

EXAMPLE 10. Marsland's will was completed, signed, and properly witnessed. At a later date, he reread the document and decided to strike out a bequest made to a friend who had turned against him. Marsland drew a line through that part of the will. After Marsland's death, the will was offered for probate. It was pronounced void because of the alteration. It would be impossible to determine whether the alteration had been made by Marsland or by another who might have had possession of the instrument. Marsland's estate will now be distributed as though he had died without a will.

19.12 Undue Influence by Named Beneficiary

Proof that the testator was under the undue influence of a beneficiary will serve to void the instrument. Undue influence, in this case, does not stem from direct threats (duress) but from a party's acts or statements that are construed to have been used to influence the testator's judgment in making bequests.

EXAMPLE 11. Gumpert died, leaving three grown children. Martha, who lived closest to Gumpert, had the opportunity to give more care and attention to her father than did the others, who lived at distant parts of the country. Martha, in the presence of others, seriously criticized the other children for their inattention to their father. Her constant repetition of criticism poisoned her father's mind against the other two, and as a result he changed his will, leaving his entire estate to Martha. When the will was offered for probate, it was contested by the other children on the grounds that Martha had used undue influence on her father.

19.13 Superior Claim of One with Dower or Homestead Right

A surviving wife has the right to demand her *dower right* or *homestead right* in the property of her deceased husband. It is not important in enforcement of this right that the widow is not named in the deed as a joint tenant or a tenant in common. The widow's right is *automatically* superior to rights of other claimants, creditors, and beneficiaries named in the will. A surviving husband also has rights (*curtesy rights*) in the real property of his wife unless she disinherited him in her will and left her estate to others. In community-property states, the husband and the wife are assured of at least one-half of the property owned by the other if the property was secured after marriage.

19.14 Additions and Changes through Codicils to the Will

A valid will that already exists may be changed by additions or alterations incorporated in the will by a *codicil*, sometimes called a *supplement*. This document, added to a will, requires the same formalities required of the will itself. It must be in writing, signed by the testator, and properly witnessed. It is important that the codicil be incorporated into the will by reference to the original document so that no doubt of its validity will exist.

EXAMPLE 12. Valenti had written a will in 1968, the terms of which were satisfactory to him until 1976, when, through good investments, he became quite wealthy. He now decided to leave $25,000 to his church, a bequest that would have been inconceivable under his former financial status. Rather than write a new will, Valenti had his attorney prepare a codicil, which was incorporated and made part of the original document. Valenti, by this action, was relieved of the necessity of preparing an entirely new will.

19.15 Revocation of an Existing Will

A testator writing a new will must be careful to follow local statutes and judicial decisions in revoking a former will. It is sufficient in some states that the new will contain a declaration such as "this being my last will and testament, all former wills are hereby declared revoked." Other states require expression of the specific intention to revoke a former will when two wills are located and are offered for probate. Such an intention is best evidenced by the tearing up or burning of the former will. In some states, lack of such evidence will result in the earlier will being given precedence over the later one.

EXAMPLE 13. When Rutledge died, relatives produced one will written by Rutledge in 1968 and another written in 1977. There was no statement contained in the 1977 will revoking the earlier will, nor had the earlier will been torn or marked in any way that indicated its signer's intent. Under the circumstances, the earlier will was declared by the court to be the valid will. This was, no doubt, in opposition to the testator's last wishes.

EXECUTORS AND ADMINISTRATORS

19.16 Executors Named in a Will

A person or a bank or other institution may be named in the will by the testator to administer the distribution of the deceased's estate. Such a party is called the *executor*. More than one executor may be named. Alternate executors may be named in the event that the one named in the will predeceases the testator, has become incapable of performing the duties necessary, or refuses to accept the responsibility. Executors are permitted to retain an attorney to assist in the settlement of the estate. The attorney's fees come from the estate. The fees are usually set by statute and depend on the value of the estate. The executor, in most cases, is also permitted a fee. Executors are required to furnish a bond, unless excused from doing so by terms of the will. Under certain circumstances, a bond will be required by the state even if the executor is excused from doing so by terms of the will. Major creditors and others with a personal interest in the estate may dispute the appointment of the executor and petition the register of wills (or some other public official) for the appointment of another executor.

EXAMPLE 14. Harrigan was named as executor of Liebert's will. When Liebert died, he was in great debt to the Citizens Bank & Trust Company. The bank knew Harrigan to be an uninformed and undependable person. The bank therefore petitioned the register of wills to replace Harrigan with a more capable and reliable individual to carry out the executor's duties.

19.17 Administrator Appointed by Court

If an executor is not named in the will, has predeceased the testator, has been declared incompetent, or is unwilling to serve, a court or the register of wills may appoint an *administrator*. Parties who have an interest in the estate of the deceased have a right to suggest persons or banks as administrators. The register of wills or a court will review these suggestions and then, using independent judgment, appoint the administrator. The administrator's duties and responsibilities are no different from those of an executor.

19.18 Responsibilities of the Executor or Administrator

With some differences provided for under individual state statutes, the executor or administrator is required to perform the following duties:

1. Present the will for probate to the proper authority, usually the register of wills or a probate court.
2. Retain a lawyer for assistance in the settlement of the estate.
3. Petition the register of wills or some other official, through the attorney, for *letters testamentary*, which give the state's authority to the executor or administrator to act in settling the estate; and, at the same time, subscribe to an oath required of executors and administrators.
4. Take possession of the *decedent's* (deceased's) property.
5. Make a proper accounting of all debts owed by the estate, advertising notice to all creditors to submit claims against the estate. Collect debts owed to the estate.
6. Make an inventory of all real and personal property of the deceased. Prepare an estimate of the value of the property through qualified persons appointed to carry out that task.
7. Protect property from unnecessary depreciation, vandalism, and other damage. Collect rents, mortgage payments, or other claims due the estate during the period of administration. File necessary claims payable to the estate and its beneficiaries.

8. Prepare all income- and inheritance-tax reports due either the state or federal government in connection with the estate; and file similar reports on past earnings of the decedent.

19.19 Intestacy

A person dying without benefit of a will is said to have died *intestate*. Distribution of such a person's estate is determined by the laws of each state. Personal property provides the administrator with funds to be used in the settlement of debts and claims against the estate. Personal property remaining after all proper debts have been paid is distributed among the next of kin, according to state law. Real property is distributed according to the provisions of dower and curtesy rights, community-property rights, and homestead rights. Real property that is free of such claims is distributed to the closest heirs.

EXAMPLE 15. Bartlett died intestate. He left but few debts, which were paid by the administrator out of an available savings account. Bartlett left a wife, two sons, and a grandchild whose father (Bartlett's son) had predeceased Bartlett. After Bartlett's widow received her share of her late husband's real property, the remainder was distributed to the two sons and the grandson, share and share alike. The grandson receives his right *per stirpes*, representing his deceased father's share in Bartlett's estate.

19.20 Trusts

State laws, with certain federal restrictions, permit living persons to establish *trusts*, to which property may be deeded. A person who establishes a trust gives up the right to repossess property in the trust. The trust includes the names of those who will receive income from the trust property following the death of the person who created the trust. Those benefitting from the trust are known as the *cestue que trust*. Trusts are usually created for the preservation of large estates that would otherwise be severely depleted by state and federal estate taxes.

Solved Problems

19.1 Quinlan, who was sixteen years of age, was the owner of Woodward Estates through his late father's will. Quinlan wrote a formal will himself, signed it, and had it properly witnessed. The will was perfect in form. It left the Woodward Estates to a school guidance counselor who had always been helpful to Quinlan. Was this will valid?

Most state laws require one to be of legal age (eighteen or twenty-one) to make a valid will. Quinlan's will would be declared void for want of *testamentary capacity*.

19.2 Suppose Quinlan, of Problem 19.1, had been seventeen and had enlisted in the armed forces. He was sent overseas and was engaged in combat. He left the usual will, prepared under military instructions, and he was killed in combat. Would this will be held valid?

Yes. Exceptions are made for persons who are members of the armed forces and those who, through marriage, are considered to have reached their majority. Under the conditions cited here, Quinlan's will would be held valid.

19.3 Corrozi was hospitalized and close to death. An attorney was called, and Corrozi asked her to prepare a will. Corrozi wanted his entire estate to go to a friend of many years. The will was prepared, signed, and witnessed. Corrozi's heirs contested the will's validity after Corrozi's death by questioning Corrozi's mental capacity to make the will. Will the will be upheld?

If the witnesses to the will testify that Corrozi was capable of understanding his thoughts and actions in making the will, it will not be defeated. (Physical capacity has no definite bearing on the testator's mental ability to create such an instrument.) Attorneys who anticipate such challenges to a will may secure the notarized statement of an attending physician or nurse, who could attest to the patient's mental capacity at the time of signing.

19.4 Kylen signed a will leaving all of his property to his invalid brother. The witnesses to his signature were, at the time, fourteen, fifteen, and seventeen years of age. On Kylen's death, the will was contested because of the ages of the witnesses. Will this defeat the will?

No. It is not essential that the witnesses be adults. It is necessary only that they have the mental capacity to understand that which they witness.

19.5 Harrison, in his will, left all of his property to the Kappa Omega Phi fraternity. When the will was offered for probate, the register of wills noted that it contained only two witnesses to Harrison's signature. Harrison lived in Georgia, where the law required three signatures. Will the fraternity receive title to Harrison's property?

No. Unless statutory formalities are adhered to, a will may not be accepted for probate. One more witness to the will was necessary for the will to be valid. Harrison's property will be distributed as though he had died intestate.

19.6 Steininger, a law student, typed his own will in proper legal form. He alone signed it and put it among his valuable papers for safekeeping. The next week, Steininger was killed while playing football. The will was offered for probate as a holographic will. Is Steininger's will valid?

No. A holographic will, in states that still recognize them, must be entirely in the handwriting of the testator. Steininger's will therefore does not qualify as a holographic will. In addition, it will not be accepted for probate as a formal will because it lacks witnesses to his signature.

19.7 During a skirmish with enemy troops, Armstrong was mortally wounded. He recited to the seven surviving members of his squad his last wishes. When they returned to their base, the seven men set forth in writing the wishes expressed by Armstrong. All then signed their names to the document. Was a valid will created?

The will was a *nuncupative, or oral, will.* In any state that still accepted nuncupative wills for probate, Armstrong's wishes would be carried out.

19.8 Suppose, in Problem 19.7, that Armstrong had made similar statements to his fellow squad members three months earlier, when he had visions of being killed in battle. Nothing was done about the matter until after Armstrong was wounded and killed. Could the squad members still create a valid will?

No. A will created under these circumstances would fail on probate. Unless made *at the time* of imminent death from accident, illness, or battle, it would not qualify as a nuncupative will.

19.9 Joanna, one of three grandchildren, gave much time and effort to assist her grandmother during her last years. Joanna read to her, bought her gifts, and even gave her a color television set. By a legally valid will, the grandmother left Joanna a sizable estate, leaving nothing to the two other grandchildren, Joanna's sisters. They contested the will on the grounds of undue influence. Will they succeed?

There is no law against kindness and generosity. The assistance was not given to the elderly grandmother because of a selfish interest. The other two sisters will fail in their complaint against the will.

19.10 Gentry, a wealthy investor, signed a will in which his entire estate was left to the attorney who assisted Gentry in drawing up the will. He left not one cent to his children, who had always befriended him and aided him in his personal problems. The children contested the will, asking to have the estate distributed as though Gentry had died intestate. What outcome will probably result?

A charge that undue influence was used by the lawyer would no doubt influence a probate court. The court might very well declare the will void. A token bequest to the attorney, with the rest of the estate going to the children, would probably be the result in this case.

19.11 In 1953, Raskin had a will prepared. It was properly signed and witnessed. In the will, he left the bulk of his estate to his sister, Estelle. Five years later, she turned against Raskin, testifying against him in a tort action in which he was an unsuccessful defendant. He wrote another will, leaving everything to the Sunday Breakfast Mission. He included no words in the new will that indicated that he was revoking the former one. After his death, both wills were discovered and offered for probate. How will this matter be decided?

When two wills are offered for probate, the first one written will be given preference in the absence of explicit revocation in the later will. Estelle, the sister, will succeed to Raskin's entire estate.

19.12 Shapiro, a single man, wrote a will that left his entire estate to the American Heart Association. Ten years later, he married but did not change his will. On Shapiro's death, his widow entered a claim against the estate, asking that the will made before marriage be declared void. Will she succeed?

By the laws of most states, wills made prior to a marriage are declared void after the testator's marriage. Under such laws, the estate will be distributed in the same way as it would had the testator died intestate. Shapiro's widow may also claim her dower or community-property rights, whichever applies.

19.13 Grafton, the father of three minor children at the time he prepared his will, provided for the distribution of his property among his surviving wife and the three children. After the will was made, another child was born. Is this fourth child, who was three years old at the time of Grafton's death, entitled to any part of her father's estate?

The laws of most states provide for a minor child not mentioned in a will. The child in this case will probably share in her father's estate as if he had died intestate. All states do not follow the same procedure, but the child would most likely not be excluded from a share of her father's estate.

19.14 Polk left a will in which all of his property was bequeathed to his son Bruce. His wife was not living, and a second son, Darby, contested the will, claiming that he had been overlooked and that he had an equal right with Bruce in the estate. Evidence showed that Darby had left home at an early age, against his father's wishes. Will Darby share in the estate?

Children do not, as a general rule, have a vested right in the property of their parents. A parent may disinherit a child if he or she so desires. In light of the circumstances surrounding this case, Polk undoubtedly intended to disinherit the son who, during his father's life, had broken off all relations with the family.

19.15 Fehr left a will containing a bequest of $10,000 "to my devoted nephew, Robert ________." (An ink smear had made the last name of the nephew illegible.) Fehr had two nephews named Robert. One had been close and attentive to Fehr, the other distant and uncaring. How will this bequest be treated?

Unless contested on other grounds, the bequest will no doubt be granted to the nephew known to have been close and attentive to Fehr. The intent of the court is to carry out the obvious wishes of the testator. Had both nephews been equally attentive or inattentive to their uncle, the decision would be different.

19.16 In his will, Mensch left a savings account of $8,995 to his sister, Margaret Shaw. Hours before his death, Mensch made a gift *in causa mortis* of the savings account to his attending physician, who had made great efforts to cure Mensch of his illness. Mensch assigned the savings account to the physician by executing a form included in the passbook itself. Shaw contested the gift, stating that she had superior rights to the money because of the bequest in the will. Was Shaw correct in her claim?

Shaw will lose out. By a doctrine known as *ademption*, a testator may revoke and withdraw intentions contained in a will by acts that make a bequest or devise impossible. At the time of Mensch's death, there was no longer a savings account to bequeath to Margaret Shaw.

19.17 Dunleavy, by his will, left his miniature helicopter to his daughter Harriet. Several weeks prior to his death, he traded in the helicopter for a much larger one with a turbo-jet engine. On Dunleavy's death, Harriet claimed ownership of the new aircraft. By Dunleavy's will, will she succeed to its ownership?

No. As in Problem 19.16, ademption has denied the one named in the will of the bequest. The helicopter mentioned in the will did not belong to Dunleavy at the time of his death. At the time the will was written, there was no thought of a more modern, more expensive helicopter than the one he owned. The helicopter will be disposed of as though Dunleavy had died intestate.

19.18 Evans died intestate. At the time of his death, he possessed a house and lot and sufficient funds to pay his debts, last medical bills, and funeral expenses. Evans had a wife and one son. How will the property be divided?

The wife will be assured her share of the house and lot, as provided by either her dower right or her community-property right. The son will succeed to the remainder. Under dower right, the widow often receives only a life interest in her spouse's real property (homestead rights), the remainder going to the son after her death.

19.19 Harland died, leaving a will in which he left his entire estate to his wife. Hilgate filed a claim of $5,000 with the executor. He claimed that this money was owed him as the result of a personal loan to Harland one year before. Payment was refused by the executor, and Hilgate sued the estate for $5,000. Will Hilgate succeed?

Under the so-called "dead-man statute," oral claims like this one are denied. Only if the claimant has written proof of the debt will he or she succeed. *Dead-man statutes* are founded on the principle that the deceased is not available to confirm or deny the claim, and it is therefore denied. Hilgate has very little chance of collecting the alleged debt.

19.20 Brandt, executor of the Peco estate, sold two race horses to satisfy debts against the estate. Both horses, by Peco's will, had been left to Peco's breeder and trainer. Brandt had made the sale and paid off the debt without the permission of the estate attorney. What right does Peco's former trainer have in this matter?

The executor did not have the right to sell selected personal property without the approval of the court. Brandt has overreached his rights and may be held personally responsible by the former trainer for his unpermitted act. The trainer would of course be estopped in any attempt to retrieve the horses from an innocent purchaser.

19.21 Rappaport died intestate. The only asset of any consequence was a life-insurance policy for $100,000, with his wife named as beneficiary. His actual estate assets amounted to less than $19,000. Creditors, with claims of more than $60,000, attempted through court action to seek payment out of the $100,000 life-insurance payment. Will this be permitted?

Proceeds from life-insurance policies are not to be confused with other estate assets. They are the sole property of the person named as a beneficiary in the policy. Rappaport's debts will be paid from his estate. General creditors will be paid after the payment of medical bills for his final illness, hospital bills, funeral expenses, taxes, and other preferred claims against him.

Review Problems

19.22 Explain the terms (1) *testate* and (2) *intestate*.

19.23 What is the meaning of (1) *dower rights* and (2) *curtesy rights?*

19.24 Is community property the rule in all states?

19.25 How does a *holographic will* differ from a *nuncupative will?*

19.26 Explain the *dead-man statute*.

19.27 What effect does *ademption* have on bequests contained in a will?

19.28 How important is it to observe local statutes in preparing a will?

19.29 What is the one difference between an *executor* and an *administrator?*

19.30 Is there a difference in meaning in the two words *children* and *heirs?*

19.31 What is the advantage of forming a trust rather than transferring property through a will?

19.32 What is a *codicil?* When is it used?

19.33 How may an existing will be revoked?

19.34 What is meant by *testamentary capacity?*

19.35 Explain a gift *in causa mortis*.

Answers to Review Problems

19.22 (1) Dying with a will; (2) dying without a will.

19.23 (1) It is a widow's one-third life estate, or an estate as otherwise provided by state statute, in the real property of her deceased husband. (2) It is the right of the husband in the wife's real property, dependent on the birth of a living child by the marriage.

19.24 No. It is a new concept, adopted by only a small number of states.

19.25 A holographic will is one written entirely in the handwriting of the testator. A nuncupative will is actually an oral will dictated to others and reduced by them to writing at the first opportune moment.

19.26 It is a state law that requires written evidence of a debt claimed against the estate of a decedent.

19.27 Ademption is an act or promise that invalidates a bequest or devise in an already existing will. Ademption rules out the provision contained in the will.

19.28 It is vitally important. Unless a formal will satisfies the requirements of a state statute, it will not be admitted to probate.

19.29 An executor is one named by the testator in the will. An administrator is a party named by the register of wills or probate court to act in the distribution of the estate and in carrying out the provisions of a will. Otherwise, both parties have the same responsibilities and obligations.

19.30 Yes. Children are the direct descendants of the parents. Heirs can be any blood relatives.

19.31 A trust is usually created for the purpose of preserving a large estate that would otherwise be greatly depleted by the imposition of state and federal estate taxes, as is the case when property is disposed of by will.

19.32 A codicil is an addition to a will, requiring the same formality in its creation as is required of a will. It is used to make additions to or changes in the provisions of an already written, signed, and witnessed will.

19.33 It may be revoked by a statement in a succeeding will or by burning or tearing the will in question. State law and judicial decision determine valid methods of revocation in any one state.

19.34 It is the age and mental capacity needed to execute a valid will.

19.35 It is a gift by a person who expects imminent death from a known illness, disease, or accident. Death from any other cause or survival of the donor will invalidate the gift and require its return to the donor or the donor's estate.

Legal Terms

Administrator. A person named by the court or some other official body to carry out the terms of a will in those cases where an executor has not been named, has been disqualified, or refuses to act; also, a person appointed to settle the estate of one who dies without leaving a will.

Beneficiary. One who is entitled to the proceeds of a life-insurance policy or one who receives a gift under a will.

Bequeath. To give *personal property* to another by will.

Bequest. Personal property left by a will; a legacy.

Decedent. A deceased person.

Devise. To give a gift of *real property* to another by will.

Executor. A person named in the will by a testator to carry out the terms of the will.

Gifts in causa mortis. Gifts given by one who anticipates imminent death from a known cause; the gift is conditional on the donor's death from the feared cause.

Holographic will. A will written entirely in the handwriting of the testator; wills of this type do not follow the requisites of a formal will.

Intestate. The term used to describe one who dies without a will.

Issue. Direct descendants; children.

Legacy. A gift of personal property by a will.

Nuncupative will. A will prepared by witnesses, according to a dying person's last oral wishes; usually occurs during a battle or an equally urgent situation; not valid in most states today.

Post mortem. After death.

Probate. The legal procedure of proving a will.

Testator. The person who writes a will or for whom a will is prepared by another.

Chapter 20

Secured Transactions and Bankruptcy

This chapter is a review of two distinct but related areas of the law: secured transactions and bankruptcy.

Both the sellers and buyers of expensive items—such as real estate, furniture, automobiles, and machinery—take risks when they sign *security agreements*. Such agreements create risks for sellers because they allow buyers to "spread out" payments for goods over a specified period of time. Likewise, buyers who enter into security agreements take risks because if they fail to make the scheduled payments, they are penalized by the terms of the agreement: they may be required to return the merchandise purchased without reimbursement for monies paid or to give up title to collateral (property named as security in the agreement).

Article 9 of the Uniform Commercial Code covers security agreements, or *secured transactions*. This article has been amended often and to this day it is still not recognized by many states. (Some people have called it the "Un-Uniform Commercial Code.") Prior to the writing of the article and its limited acceptance by the states, legal agreements such as the chattel mortgage, the bailment lease, and the conditional sale were in effect in all states. These time-honored legal agreements are still in wide use, and they are thus treated first in this chapter.

One of the problems with secured transactions is that individuals, partnerships, and even corporations may enter into agreements that they cannot really afford. They may thus be forced into (or enter voluntarily into) *bankruptcy*, the second major topic discussed in this chapter. The review here focuses on bankruptcy as relief from indebtedness for the over-spent individual, partnership, or corporation. We have already, in this book, discussed the rights of distressed creditors and debtors. This chapter confines itself to a discussion of the terms of the National Bankruptcy Act, a federal set of regulations that has been adopted, with few modifications, by all fifty states.

SECURED AGREEMENTS BEFORE THE CODE

20.1 Conditional Sale

A *conditional sale*, in most cases, is one that states in the sales contract that title to the goods sold does not pass to the buyer until all conditions of payment have been met. The seller retains the right to retake the goods if the buyer fails to make payments as promised. Conditional sales agreements have been universally accepted in the installment sales of automobiles, home appliances, and other expensive items.

EXAMPLE 1. McDevett purchased a new car for $5,200. Payments were to be made monthly over a period of two years. Boyce Auto Sales sold the car under a conditional sales contract, agreeing to release title to McDevett only after all payments had been made.

20.2 Bailment Lease

A *bailment lease* agreement provides that the buyer who is in possession of goods pays a regular rental for their use over a stipulated period of time. After rental payments equal the sales price of the goods, title will go to the buyer on payment of a nominal final installment. The bailment lease is in use in only a few states today.

20.3 Chattel Mortgage

Under a *chattel mortgage*, the debtor gives creditors the right to take personal property, inventoried in the agreement, as collateral security for money borrowed or for purchases made on credit. The chattel mortgage gives the mortgagee the right to take possession and to sell the debtor's property in the event of the debtor's default on the promise of payment.

EXAMPLE 2. Withers purchased carpeting for her new condominium. Her total indebtedness was $2,900. The Modern Carpet Company accepted a chattel mortgage on all of Withers's furniture and her piano as security for payment of the money owed. A chattel mortgage was a very desirable form of security to Modern Carpet because carpeting removed from the floor, in the event Withers defaulted in payments, would have very little resale value. Withers's furniture and piano, however, could easily be sold for much more money.

20.4 Assignment of Accounts Receivable

Debts between merchants, wholesalers, and the like are often secured by the assignment of the debtor's accounts receivable. Default in payment of a debt gives a creditor the right to collect monies owed the debtor, up to the amount of unpaid debts plus expenses and interest.

20.5 Factor's Lien

A *factor* is an agent who has possession of another party's goods for the purpose of selling such goods. A factor has a property interest in the goods and may sell them in his or her own name. A factor is thus *secured* in the right to sell the goods and to retain the money from the sale.

20.6 Trust Receipts

A *trust receipt* is a document in which a lender has no title to goods on which a lien is given. The goods remain in possession of the borrower. The creditor lends money to the borrower on security of the *sale* of these goods, which the borrower-in-possession has the right to sell clear of any lien. The borrower agrees to pay to the lender all or part of the receipts of the sale. The purchase of automobiles and trucks is often financed by banks for dealers who give trust receipts to the banks for vehicles delivered and paid for out of the money borrowed. Trust receipts are rarely used except in commercial ventures.

EXAMPLE 3. Compton Motors ordered five new ten-ton trucks from a manufacturer. Cash was to be paid on or before delivery of the trucks. Compton Motors issued a trust receipt to the Franklin Savings Bank in return for a check to cover payment due the truck manufacturer. Compton was obliged to report each truck sale immediately and to make a cash payment for each to the Franklin Savings Bank. Buyers of the trucks were innocent purchasers for value, who accepted the trucks free of liens. The liens given the bank by Compton Motors on the trucks were security for the bank's loan until the trucks were sold. The liens did not follow the trucks when Compton sold them because of Compton's agreement to turn over the proceeds of the sale to the bank.

SECURED AGREEMENTS UNDER THE CODE

The security agreements outlined in Sections 20.1 through 20.6 continue to be in general use. However, with the growing acceptance of Article 9 of the Uniform Commercial Code, laws relating to security agreements in various states are coming closer to conforming, providing uniformity of understanding and enforcement.

20.7 Security Interest under the Code

A security interest, as stated in the U.C.C., is: "... (a) any transaction (regardless of its form) which is intended to create a security interest in personal property or fixtures, including goods, documents, instruments, general intangibles, chattel paper or accounts; and also (b) to any sale of accounts or chattel paper."

The security interest is created through a security agreement, which identifies the debtor's collateral that is offered as security. The one in whose favor the agreement is made is called the *secured party.*

EXAMPLE 4. Hinkson purchased a tractor from Riley Brothers. A security agreement was executed in favor of Riley Brothers. The agreement named the tractor and other personal property belonging to Hinkson as collateral that was subject to the agreement.

20.8 Location of Collateral

The personal property offered as collateral in a secured transaction must either be given to the secured party or must be fully described in the security agreement signed by the debtor.

20.9 Attachment and Perfection

To create an effective security interest, there must be an *attachment* of collateral to guarantee the rights of the buyer and seller (creditor and debtor). Attachment is accomplished through the description of the collateral and a statement of the creditor's rights in such collateral.

Perfection is the means of giving protection to the *secured party*. Perfection gives the secured party priority rights over claims that might be later made by third parties. (See Sections 20.10 and 20.11.)

20.10 Perfection by Possession

The secured party may *perfect* her or his security interest by taking possession of collateral. Possession of the debtor's property gives third parties clear notice of the security interest. When this method of perfection is used, a written security agreement may be dispensed with without injury to the secured party. Possession is the only acceptable and safe form of perfection when collateral is in the form of instruments. When there is a written security agreement, there may be perfection *without possession*, but only for a period of twenty-one days.

EXAMPLE 5. Jordan loaned Gerald $300. As security for repayment, Gerald gave Jordan possession of a watch and diamond ring that were valued at $1,000. No written security agreement was needed in this transaction. Jordan's possession of Gerald's collateral satisfied the Code's requirements for perfection.

20.11 Perfection by Filing

Perfecting a security interest may be accomplished by filing the *security agreement* or a more simple *financing statement*. (See Section 20.12.) The financing statement merely describes the collateral, states that the debtor and secured party have entered into a security agreement, and identifies the parties and their addresses. A financing statement is preferred by most parties because it does not disclose confidential matters contained in the security agreement. Filing the financing statement gives constructive notice to all interested parties of the rights of the secured party.

EXAMPLE 6. Harbison Farms borrowed $15,000 from the Kent Central Bank. As security for payment, Harbison signed a security agreement. Both parties filed a financing statement covering all of Harbison's farm machinery and growing crops. A third party buying from Harbison would thus be warned of Kent Central's superior rights in Harbison's property. Kent Central would not be estopped from retrieving the machinery and crops from one who might claim to be an innocent purchaser of them for value.

20.12 Place of Filing Financing Statement

Article 9 of the Code gives the states three options in the location of offices where financing statements are to be filed: (1) a central filing system, usually in the state capital; (2) a local filing system, usually in the county seat; or (3) a combination of the two. Central filing is ordinarily used for inventory and equipment; local filing is often used for fixtures attached to real property, consumer goods, and farm-related collateral. Motor vehicles and other items of personal property that require a government-issued certificate of title are excepted under these rules. In such cases, the secured party's interest is simply noted on the face of the title certificate itself.

EXAMPLE 7. Suppose that the transaction in Example 6 took place in a state requiring that farm tractors used as collateral be so registered on the title certificate from the original purchase. Kent Central Bank would require the state registration office to record on Harbison's title certificate (and probably on moter vehicle records) the existence of Kent Central's security interest.

BANKRUPTCY AND INSOLVENCY

20.13 Bankruptcy

Bankruptcy proceedings, which wipe out the debt of a party considered *insolvent*, have been incorporated into American law as a way of giving financially troubled individuals, partnerships, and corporations the opportunity to again use their talents. Bankruptcy frees a party of a crippling indebtedness that might otherwise terminate the party's service to society.

EXAMPLE 8. Larkin, because of economic reverses and inflationary trends, was reduced to a position where he owed creditors $63,700. He had assets of only $2,375. Through honest work, it would take Larkin the rest of his life to wipe out his indebtedness. With the assistance of an attorney, he asked to be declared a voluntary bankrupt. Within a year, he could be free of creditors' demands and could start a new life of service to his trade and to his community.

20.14 National Bankruptcy Act

In earlier years, each state provided its own bankruptcy laws. Today, however, bankruptcy is regulated by a federal law called the National Bankruptcy Act. (State laws, in some instances, complement the provisions of the National Bankruptcy Act.) The United States District Courts have jurisdiction over bankruptcy cases. (There is at least one U.S. District Court in each state.) There are two basic objectives of the National Bankruptcy Act:

1. To provide debtors with the means of being released from debts that beyond any reasonable doubt they would not be able to meet.
2. To collect the bankrupt's assets and divide their value among the creditors in a fair and equitable manner, prohibiting selected creditors from confiscating the debtor's entire estate at the expense of other creditors.

20.15 Administrative Officers in Bankruptcy

Four officers are appointed by the judge or judges of a U.S. District Court to administer bankruptcy proceedings:

1. *Referee.* The referee is appointed for a period of six years to oversee bankruptcy proceedings. To qualify, a referee must: be a member of the bar of the state in which the court is located; be impartial in rulings; not be related to the judge; and be disassociated from any bankruptcy case in which he or she may have a personal interest. The referee schedules all meetings of creditors and gives notice of such meetings.
2. *Trustee.* A trustee is a person appointed to take physical control of the bankrupt's property, preserve it during the proceedings, collect all debts owed the bankrupt (and in

general administer the estate), keep accurate records, and make final reports to the court on the physical and financial matters concerning the bankrupt's property.

3. *Appraiser*. The court may appoint one to three persons as appraisers, who make a fair and reasonable evaluation of the value of the bankrupt's estate.
4. *Receiver*. A receiver is one appointed by the court to preserve the assets of the estate until a trustee has been qualified by the court to take over these responsibilities. In cases of a going business, the receiver is given authority to continue the business for the benefit of creditors.

20.16 Insolvency

Insolvency, in its general sense, describes a party who cannot meet his or her indebtedness when bills become due. A party's fixed assets may exceed her or his liabilities, but if the assets are not available for immediate use, the party may still be declared insolvent. *Insolvency in bankruptcy*, however, describes only those parties whose liabilities are greater than their total assets.

EXAMPLE 9. Blanchard had overspent her income in the purchase of an expensive car, expensive home appliances, and a four-month trip through Europe. She owed creditors $19,300. Her assets, including savings, furniture, jewelry, and all other property, were worth only $2,160. Blanchard's accounts proved her to be insolvent as defined by the National Bankruptcy Act.

KINDS OF BANKRUPTCY

20.17 Voluntary Bankruptcy

Individuals, partnerships, or corporations may petition the U.S. District Court to be declared bankrupt. This is termed *voluntary bankruptcy*. Excepted from this right are banking institutions, insurance companies, railroads, and municipal corporations.

EXAMPLE 10. Blanchard, of Example 9, got the assistance of an attorney and declared herself a voluntary bankrupt by petition to the United States District Court. Her insolvency and genuine distress could qualify her for this privilege.

20.18 Involuntary Bankruptcy

A debtor may be judged an *involuntary bankrupt* on a motion filed by three or more creditors with evidence of claims amounting to $500 or more. A person with fewer than twelve creditors may be declared a bankrupt on a petition filed by a single creditor. To do this the creditor must have proof that the debtor: (1) owes $1,000 or more; (2) is insolvent; and (3) has committed an *act of bankruptcy*. (See Section 20.19.)

Involuntary bankruptcy is permitted any individual, unincorporated business, financial business, or commercial corporation, with the exception of farmers and wage earners whose salary does not exceed $1,500 per year.

EXAMPLE 11. Cycle Sales, Inc., owed a total $130,000 to twenty different creditors. The annual report, available to creditors, showed that the business had only $55,000 in assets. Fearing that one or more creditors might get judgments against Cycle Sales and confiscate all of its assets, a group of five creditors, through an attorney, petitioned the court to declare the firm bankrupt. If the court granted the petition, each creditor would be treated equally in the prorated distribution of the firm's remaining assets.

20.19 Acts of Bankruptcy

Any debtor who acts in a way that indicates a preference for certain creditors or in a way that shows the intention of defeating other creditors' rights has committed *acts of bankruptcy*. Under the National Bankruptcy Act, the acts of bankruptcy listed on page 252 give a creditor the right to try to have the debtor declared bankrupt:

1. Conveying, transferring, or concealing property with the intent to hinder, delay, or defraud creditors.
2. Transferring a portion of the debtor's property to selected creditors with the intent of preference in payment of accounts owed.
3. Giving preference to one or more creditors over others or permitting any creditor to obtain such preference through legal proceedings.
4. Making a general assignment of property for the benefit of creditors; or, because of insolvency, applying for a trustee or receiver of property.
5. Making a written admission of the inability to meet debts and showing a willingness to be adjudged bankrupt on those grounds with the intent to divide assets among creditors.

20.20 Obligation of Petitioning Creditors

Creditors petitioning the court in an effort to have someone declared an involuntary bankrupt must file, within four months of the date of the debtor's alleged acts, a statement listing the acts of bankruptcy of which the debtor is accused.

20.21 Duties of the Bankrupt and the Creditors

The bankrupt must attend the first meeting of the creditors. It is the duty of each creditor to file a proof of claim with the bankruptcy court within six months of the debtor's adjudication as a bankrupt. Otherwise, the claim will be barred. If proven, the claim will be admitted, and the creditor will share in the division of the bankrupt's property. The bankrupt must prepare and file a schedule of all property and its location and a list of creditors and the amount owed each. It is the bankrupt's responsibility to check the correctness of all creditors' claims and to be cooperative with the administration of the proceedings, responding to questions and attending meetings scheduled in the case.

20.22 Exemption of Bailed Property

Property to which others may prove ownership and which is in the temporary possession of the bankrupt may be reclaimed by its owners. Such property is not to be confused with the bankrupt's own assets, which are available to creditors.

EXAMPLE 12. The Hamilton Company rented a computer from Modern Electronics. Hamilton used the computer in their accounting office. When Hamilton was declared bankrupt, the court permitted Modern Electronics to reclaim the computer.

20.23 Goods Delivered after Declaration of Insolvency

The Uniform Commercial Code permits the owner of goods delivered to a bankrupt after declaration of insolvency to reclaim those goods. Demand for the reclamation must be made within ten days of the date on which the goods were received by the bankrupt.

EXAMPLE 13. Filling an order that had been received several days before, the Climber Company delivered ten twelve-foot extension ladders to the Rainbow Painting Company. Unknown to Climber, Rainbow had already been declared insolvent by the local U.S. District Court. When he learned of Rainbow's insolvency, Climber's president demanded the return of the ladders within the ten-day period. The ladders were returned.

20.24 Property Exempt from Seizure

All states have statutes that exempt certain property belonging to a bankrupt from inclusion in assets taken by a trustee for the benefit of creditors. Under most statutes, the bankrupt is permitted the right to retain household furnishings to a certain appraised value; tools of the bankrupt's trade, also limited as to value; school books, the family Bible, and other items considered necessary to the bankrupt's survival and ability to continue working.

EXAMPLE 14. Molloy, a bankrupt television mechanic, surrendered all of his assets, including personal and real property, to the trustee appointed by the U.S. District Court. Prior to the sale and liquidation of the remaining assets, Molloy was permitted to select a minimal amount of furniture, tools of his trade, and a few other items regarded as necessary to the survival of his family.

20.25 Priorities in Allowance of Claims

When the bankrupt's collected assets are not sufficient to meet all creditor claims, priorities are given, and payment *in full* is made to certain classes of creditors that are named in the National Bankruptcy Act or in state statutes. Debts to be paid in full before the distribution of remaining assets to other creditors are listed below in order of priority:

1. Cost of preserving the estate and expenses of administration and liquidation of the bankrupt's assets.
2. Wages, not to exceed $600 to each claimant, earned within three months of the date of the filing of the petition in bankruptcy.
3. Reasonable costs and expenses filed by creditors and approved by the court related to the refusal, revocation, or setting aside a bankrupt's discharge or in adducing such evidence.
4. Taxes due city, county, state, or the federal government.
5. Debts due anyone entitled to priority under the law (state or federal); also, rent due a landlord if the landlord is entitled to priority by state law.

20.26 Distribution of Assets Remaining after Priorities

The assets remaining after all priority creditors' claims have been satisfied are distributed to general creditors on a prorated basis. Secured claims, represented by liens and other recorded encumbrances, are paid first from money realized from the sale of named collateral. Any remaining balance is paid on a prorated basis to unsecured creditors.

EXAMPLE 15. Hooley's assets, when liquidated, brought only $18,000 against creditors' claims of $35,000 filed with the court. One claim of $3,000 was offered by a secured creditor who had perfected her security interest through the filing of a financing statement that named Hooley's tractor and combine as collateral. The $3,000 thus secured was paid in full, reducing to only $15,000 the amount available to other creditors. Each creditor's claim will be liquidated by payment of only 46.8¢ on the dollar.

20.27 Claims Not Discharged under Bankruptcy

The bankrupt is not discharged from future liabililty on certain claims. Claims not discharged, which the bankrupt remains fully responsible for and which must be paid out of future earnings or other income, include:

1. Any balance of unpaid taxes.
2. Losses resulting from the bankrupt's intentionally fraudulent misconduct and breach of trust.
3. Claims resulting from the bankrupt's willful or malicious acts or torts.
4. Claims allowed wage earners, noted in Section 20.25, and not satisfied in the distribution of bankrupt's assets.
5. Alimony owed and future alimony due a bankrupt's former spouse.

20.28 Executory Contracts of the Bankrupt

Contracts enforceable against a party before bankruptcy are *not* valid and enforceable following petition and adjudication in bankruptcy.

EXAMPLE 16. Center College contracted with the Universal Press for the printing of its adult-education fall catalog. Time was of the essence in the typesetting and printing of the catalog. The Universal Press went into bankruptcy in August, and the catalog was never completed. Center College had no claim that it could bring against the bankrupt printing company. Care must be exercised in placing all such contracts. It is imperative that the solvency of such a promissor be ascertained with reasonable certainty.

20.29 Discharge in Bankruptcy

Upon application, a bankrupt may be discharged from debt within one month and before the expiration of twelve months of having been adjudged a bankrupt. Discharge in bankruptcy will be refused when: (1) the court discovers that the bankrupt had been allowed to plead voluntary bankruptcy within six years of the present petition; (2) the bankrupt has not given a satisfactory explanation of losses; (3) the bankrupt has issued false financial statements; (4) the bankrupt has transferred, concealed, or destroyed property within one year with the intent to harm creditors; (5) the bankrupt has falsified, concealed, or destroyed records; and (6) the bankrupt has not cooperated in supplying information requested by the courts.

20.30 Assets Acquired by Bankrupt after Discharge

Assets of any kind acquired by a bankrupt after discharge are free of confiscation by previous creditors, with the exception of those listed in Section 20.27.

EXAMPLE 17. Weissman was discharged in bankruptcy. Claims against him were paid off by the court on the basis of only 8¢ on the dollar. His total indebtedness had been $250,000. Two weeks after discharge, Weissman received a bequest of $500,000 under the terms of his late uncle's will. Weissman is under no legal obligation to satisfy the former creditors' claims out of his recently acquired wealth.

20.31 Reorganization under Chapter XI

An insolvent business that possesses the ability to work itself out of its insolvent condition may petition the court for a corporate reorganization or rearrangement under Chapter XI of the National Bankruptcy Act. A feasible plan of continuing the business to the benefit of the creditors may be instituted by approval of a majority of the creditors and the court. Successful operation under reorganization may mean that the insolvent party will recoup losses and honor creditors' demands with 100¢ on the dollar.

EXAMPLE 18. The Saigado Shoe Company had become insolvent. The company's financial problems stemmed from the lack of high-quality animal hides that it had used in the manufacture of expensive shoes. New foreign sources for the hides were discovered, however. In such a case, Chapter XI of the National Bankruptcy Act would probably be the best course of action for the benefit of creditors.

Solved Problems

20.1 Bennett bought six tires for his truck. The tires cost him $460. He paid $100 down and promised to pay the remainder within sixty days. At the end of ninety days, Bennett had not yet made an effort to pay any part of the $360 he owed. May the seller repossess the tires?

There had been no security agreement between Bennett and the seller. No financing statement had been filed to protect the seller from claims of any third parties. The seller's only recourse would be a court action against Bennett for the money owed.

20.2 Maguire sold Pash a washing machine for $380. The terms were $80 down and the balance due in ninety days. It was verbally agreed that failure to meet the payments on the debt would give Maguire the right to repossess the washer. Was this security agreement between Maguire and Pash enforceable?

No. Security agreements must be in writing to be enforceable. Maguire has nothing more than a right to sue Pash on his open charge account.

20.3 Suppose that the parties of the previous case had signed a security agreement that gave Maguire the right to repossess the washer if payments were not made on time. Pash was delinquent in his payments. May Maguire enforce their agreement?

Yes. Because it was in writing, the security agreement between Maguire and Pash was valid. Maguire may enforce the agreement and repossess the washer.

20.4 The parties of the previous case reduced their security agreement to writing and signed it. However, Maguire did not file a financing statement in the location provided by state statute. Pash sold the washer to Hopper, an innocent purchaser, for value. May Maguire enforce his security agreement against Hopper?

A financing statement that certifies the fact that a security agreement does exist must be filed in a public office. It thus protects the secured party from the superior rights of an innocent purchaser for value. Maguire has no rights of repossession against Hopper.

20.5 Trammel loaned $2,500 to Gilbert. Gilbert gave Trammel possession of a set of expensive dishes as security for the loan. Gilbert was involved in a tort action with Kieffer. Gilbert lost her case, and a judgment of $1,000 was placed against her. Kieffer attempted to secure possession of the dishes so she could sell them to help satisfy the judgment. Will Kieffer succeed?

No. A secured party may perfect a security interest by taking possession of property of a debtor that is given as collateral. A perfected security interest takes precedence over claims made by other parties. Trammel's right to the dishes are superior to those of Kieffer.

20.6 The Goldman Motor Company sold a new car to Katzman. Goldman filed a financing statement in the state office. The statement evidenced the debt still owed on the car and listed the car as collateral. Katzman sold the car to Hellman, who did not check the state office to ascertain whether a financing statement had been filed. What are Goldman Motor's rights against the innocent purchaser of the car?

Many states require that liens against auto vehicles be registered with the motor vehicle commission and noted on the vehicle's title certificate. In such a state, Goldman Motor would have no rights against Hellman. In states whose laws provide for perfection of a security interest in motor vehicles by filing a financing statement in a state office, Goldman Motor would be protected. Under these conditions, Goldman may repossess the auto even from an innocent purchaser (Hellman) if Katzman did not pay what was still owed on the car.

20.7 Conklin Industries borrowed $30,000 from the Central Trust Company, signing a security agreement giving the bank a security interest in all of Conklin's accounts receivable. Conklin Industries had always been faithful in repayment of its loans, and the bank dispensed with filing a financing statement in the public office. Conklin failed after all accounts receivable had been collected, and no security collateral was any longer available to Central Trust. What are the bank's rights?

Central Trust erred in not filing the required financing statement. The bank's only recourse would be to secure a judgment against Conklin and to wait until Conklin accumulated sufficient assets, which Central Trust might claim in satisfaction of the loan.

20.8 Ratliff's Variety Store borrowed money from Ramsdell. Ratliff gave Ramsdell a signed security agreement that named Ratliff's coin collection as collateral for the loan. Ratliff borrowed additional funds from Meserold, giving a security agreement that described the same collateral and terms of repayment. Meserold filed a financing statement, which Ramsdell had neglected to do. In the event of Ratliff's default, which party has priority over the collateral named in both agreements?

Priority in rights to collateral is given the party who first *files* the security agreement or financing statement in the designated public office. Meserold's rights are thus superior to Ramsdell's in this case.

20.9 Constance repossessed a piece of machinery from Kingston. The machinery was described as collateral in an agreement they had signed. The agreement had been filed as required by law, and Constance, the seller, was thus secured. Kingston had already paid Constance more than half the money owed at the time of repossession. Constance informed Kingston of his intention to merely keep possession of the machine as liquidation of the remaining debt. May Kingston prevent Constance from doing so?

A debtor may disapprove of a secured party's proposal to merely *keep* collateral to liquidate a debt. However, the debtor must express this disapproval in writing and within twenty-one days of receipt of the secured party's intentions. Kingston has the right to demand that the collateral be sold either by public or private sale and at the best price. Any remaining balance, in excess of that owed the secured party, must be returned to the debtor, Kingston.

20.10 Suppose, in the previous illustration, that Kingston had satisfied 70 percent of his debt, which was secured by the machinery. On August 1, Constance repossessed the machinery because of a default in payment by Kingston. What are Constance's obligation to Kingston?

When collateral is repossessed on debts that have been satisfied to within 40 percent of all that is owed, the secured party must dispose of the collateral within a period of ninety days or be subject to a charge of *conversion*. Constance would have been required to sell the machinery by public or private sale within the three-month period, keeping for himself only that which was still owed on the collateral sold.

20.11 Jersey Car Sales filed a financing statement on a truck that had been sold to Craven. $5,780 was owed on the truck, and Craven had missed two of his installment payments. An agent of Jersey Car Sales towed the truck away from where it was parked on the street and returned it to Jersey's lot. Craven threatened to sue the secured party for this action. Does Craven have rights in this matter?

The constitutionality of Jersey's actions may be questioned. If its actions were found to be constitutionally correct, Jersey would be permitted to repossess the truck in this manner as long as it did so without disturbing the peace. (Jersey's agent would have been wrong if he had broken into a garage and removed the truck.)

20.12 Suppose that Jersey Sales, of Problem 20.11, had properly repossessed the truck at a time when Craven's indebtedness had been reduced to $2,500. The truck was sold at public sale and brought $5,000. Jersey Sales made no report of the sale to Craven and pocketed the entire $5,000. Would Craven have any rights against Jersey Sales on learning the facts of this transaction?

Yes. The secured party may keep only an amount equal to the unpaid debt, plus expenses of advertising and conducting the sale, etc. In all probability, Craven would have a claim for the balance remaining after the amount due Jersey Sales had been paid.

20.13 The Citizens Bank & Trust Company became insolvent because of poor real estate investments. Liabilities to depositors and others totalled $4,500,000. Total assets were only $2,195,886. The directors of Citizens Bank voted to petition the court in voluntary bankruptcy. Would this be proper?

No. By regulation of the National Bankruptcy Act, neither banks nor insurance companies may petition the U.S. District Court in voluntary bankruptcy.

20.14 Klair Brothers, farmers, were indebted to more than a dozen creditors to an amount that exceeded the brothers' combined assets. Five of the creditors with substantial claims against the two farm partners filed involuntary bankruptcy against them in the U.S. District Court. Lawyers for Klair Brothers petitioned the court to have the bankruptcy action dropped. Will they succeed?

Farmers are free from having involuntary bankruptcy motions filed against them. The court will dismiss this action.

20.15 Herman Coleman, a laborer, was hopelessly indebted to many creditors. He had no forseeable opportunity of ever rising above his indebtedness. He therefore filed for voluntary bankruptcy. One creditor objected, stating that this was a right available only to insolvent business operations. Did Coleman have this right?

Voluntary bankruptcy petitions may be filed by individuals, partnerships, or corporations (with a few exceptions outlined in the National Bankruptcy Act). Coleman had the right to take this action.

20.16 McKinney, a mechanic who was married and had family responsibilities, was in debt to general creditors to the amount of $7,500. The creditors joined in an action petitioning the court to judge McKinney an involuntary bankrupt. McKinney asked for dismissal of the petition on grounds that he was a wage earner. Did the court accept his agrument?

The National Bankruptcy Act defines wage earners as those who earn no more than $1,500 a year working for someone else. If McKinney could prove that all the wages he earned during the year amounted to less than $1,500, his appeal would be accepted and the bankruptcy charge dismissed.

20.17 Coverdale Company was insolvent and was being watched carefully by creditors who had large claims against the firm. Investigation showed that Fred Coverdale, the president, had secretly sold machinery and inventory during the past two months. The president had placed this money in accounts in foreign banks. Creditors filed for involuntary bankruptcy against the Coverdale Company, claiming an act of bankruptcy. Were they correct?

Yes. Confiscation of an insolvent's assets as a means of defrauding creditors is an act of bankruptcy. The filing will be accepted by the court.

20.18 Suppose, in the previous case, that Coverdale used proceeds from the sale to pay off a $12,000 debt owed to one creditor with whom he had always had friendly dealings. Other creditors now filed for involuntary bankruptcy against Coverdale, claiming another act of bankruptcy. Were the creditors justified?

Yes. Giving preference to one creditor over all others is an act of bankruptcy. The creditors were again justified in filing their petition.

20.19 Harrington Stores were in bankruptcy. The presiding judge named Jacobs as the referee in the company's liquidation. Jacobs appointed a friend, Hilyard, as trustee. Creditors complained of this appointment. Did the creditors have grounds for their complaint?

Yes. Creditors, by the National Bankruptcy Act, nominate and elect the trustee. It is not within the powers of the referee to appoint a trustee. Creditors in the Harrington case may appeal to the judge and seek to remove Hilyard. They would then elect their own trustee.

20.20 Suppose that a relative of the owners of Harrington Stores, of Problem 20.19, had loaned the company $15,000 on a promissory note. This note was included with other claims filed against the bankrupt firm. Could the relative participate in the election of the trustee?

Relatives of the bankrupt are prohibited from voting for the trustee. (If Harrington Stores had been a corporation, no shareholder, officer, or director would be permitted to participate in the voting for the trustee.)

20.21 Stanback Motors sold a car to Tingle for $6,500. Stanback Motors held a perfected security interest on the car in the amount of the $4,500 that had been financed in the purchase. Tingle filed for voluntary bankruptcy, and Stanback Motors filed a claim for $2,700, the balance still remaining at the time Tingle filed for bankruptcy. Will this claim be accepted by the court?

One who has a perfected security interest may not file a claim in bankruptcy proceedings. Stanback Motors has the right, with the permission of the court, to sell the Tingle car and recover any debt still owed by their security agreement. If the secured party received more than $2,700 (the balance due) when the car was sold, the remainder must be turned over to the court.

20.22 Hawthorne, anticipating serious financial difficulties, paid Rogers & King $3,500 on January 15. This money represented income from the sale of a piece of ground adjacent to Hawthorne's property. At the time of the land sale, Rogers & King were aware of Hawthorne's financial difficulites. In August, creditors of Hawthorne brought involuntary bankruptcy proceedings against him. The trustee of Hawthorne's property started legal action to obtain the return of the $3,500 from Rogers & King, claiming that Hawthorne had shown a preference in paying this money to them. Would the trustee succeed in this demand?

The distribution of assets, even to preferred creditors, four months before a bankruptcy petition is filed may not be voided by an action brought by the trustee. (It is presumed that four months prior to the date of petition one would not anticipate bankruptcy.)

20.23 Mr. and Mrs. Howard owned a house and farm as tenants by the entireties. Howard was in financial difficulties. On October 1, he filed a petition for voluntary bankruptcy. Mrs. Howard was not a party to the bankruptcy, and creditors had no claims against her. May the trustee include the house and farm as part of the assets to be used in the satisfaction of Mr. Howard's creditors?

The trustee in the bankruptcy of one spouse may not make a claim upon property held by a husband and wife as tenants by the entireties. Only if Mrs. Howard were a partner in her husband's business or had signed notes and other documents of indebtedness would the house and farm be subject to the creditors' claims.

20.24 Schramm, the sole owner of Schramm's Sporting Goods Store, entered into voluntary bankruptcy. At the first meeting with creditors it was suggested that Schramm had been generous with the firm's funds in giving gifts to his girlfriend. She had, of late, started driving a new car, wearing expensive clothes, and living in an exclusive apartment building. Schramm was asked questions concerning possible gifts to the young woman. He replied, "It's none of your business!" What action may the court take against Schramm?

A bankrupt is required to cooperate with creditors and those in charge of the administration of the bankrupt's property. Schramm may not claim the Fifth Amendment because the questions did not involve him in criminal charges. The court may charge him with contempt of court and at the same time deny him the right of discharge of debts through bankruptcy.

Review Problems

20.25 How does a conditional sale differ from a bailment lease?

20.26 Why is it preferred to file a financing statement rather than the entire security agreement?

20.27 Explain the workings of a chattel mortgage.

20.28 What is meant by a *perfected security agreement?*

20.29 Name two ways in which a security agreement may be perfected.

20.30 Is Article 9 of the Uniform Commercial Code a settled body of law accepted by the majority of the state legislatures?

20.31 Why are persons permitted to file for voluntary bankruptcy in the United States?

20.32 What is the income-from-wages limit set by the National Bankruptcy Act for one claiming to be a wage-earner?

20.33 What is meant by an *act of bankruptcy?*

20.34 Name the four officers involved in the administration of a bankruptcy.

20.35 How does ordinary insolvency differ from insolvency under the National Bankruptcy Act?

20.36 Are bankrupts discharged from *all* financial obligations when their cases are closed and they are discharged?

20.37 What are the two general types of bankruptcy?

20.38 Is any of the bankrupt's property exempt from inclusion in assets taken by the trustee for the benefit of creditors?

20.39 What are the rights of the bankrupt's spouse in property held by both as tenants by the entireties?

20.40 Are all creditors treated alike in the distribution of the bankrupt's estate after the sale and liquidation of personal and real property?

20.41 What is Chapter XI of the National Bankruptcy Act?

Answers to Review Problems

20.25 In a *conditional sale*, the buyer's installment payments are considered payments that reduce the buyer's debt to the seller. In a *bailment lease*, the same payments would be described as rent for the use of the chattel being purchased.

20.26 The financing statement does not make public all of the confidential information contained in the security agreement between the buyer and the secured party.

20.27 A chattel mortgage is a type of security agreement in which the debtor's personal property (all or part of it) is given as security for the debt owed.

20.28 A perfected security agreement is one that has been made public by the filing of the security agreement or financing statement in a state office provided for that purpose.

20.29 It may be perfected (1) by taking actual possession of the debtor's collateral; or (2) by filing a financing statement (or the security agreement) in a public offfice.

20.30 No. (It is sometimes even called the "Un-Uniform Commercial Code.")

20.31 They can thus relieve themselves of indebtedness so great that it would otherwise practically terminate their usefulness to society during the remainder of their lives.

20.32 Persons with wages of not more than $1,500 per year may not be declared bankrupt.

20.33 It is any act of the insolvent party that threatens to result in the unfair or fraudulent distribution of the remaining assets to the disadvantage of certain creditors.

20.34 They are: (1) the referee, (2) the trustee, (3) the appraiser, and (4) the receiver.

20.35 *Ordinary insolvency* is a condition wherein, for any reason, one may not be able to pay his or her bills. Assets may be frozen, temporarily unavailable, or not yet received; however, total assets could be sufficient to clear all indebtedness. *Insolvency under the National Bankruptcy Act* is defined as an excess of one's liabilities over one's total assets.

20.36 No. Taxes, alimony payments, and similar claims against the bankrupt are not discharged.

20.37 (1) Voluntary bankruptcy and (2) involuntary bankruptcy are the two types.

20.38 Yes. Furniture to a certain stated value, tools of the trade to a declared value, school books, the family Bible, and other items are exempted by state law.

20.39 The bankrupt's spouse may retain the real property in which both are tenants by the entireties. Exceptions would be when both husband and wife are partners in the same business or in cases where one party guarantees or accommodates the spouse's creditors by signing commercial papers or other documents that make him or her a co-debtor with the spouse.

20.40 No. Certain types of secured creditors are given preference in the settlement of debts before remaining assets are distributed to general creditors.

20.41 Chapter XI of the National Bankruptcy Act provides for the reorganization of an insolvent business, under the direction of the court, when it appears possible that the business might again prosper and that creditors may be paid in full for all claims against the insolvent party.

Legal Terms

Bailment lease. The sale of personal property whereby the buyer receives only possession of goods for which rentals are paid; upon completion of an agreed-upon number of rental payments, the bailee-buyer is permitted to take title by payment of a token amount, usually $1.

Bankrupt. A person who has done some act that indicates his or her inability to pay debts and has therefore been adjudged bankrupt under federal bankruptcy law.

Chapter XI. A provision of the *National Bankruptcy Act* that permits the reorganization of a bankrupt business that has the possibility of working itself out of its insolvent condition; this right is granted when it is anticipated that the bankrupt will be able to repay creditors without having to terminate the business, liquidate the assets, and divide any balance remaining among creditors.

Chattel mortgage. A security agreement whereby a creditor is given a mortgage on a debtor-buyer's personal property as security for money owed.

Collateral. Property pledged as additional security for a debt.

Composition. An agreement between an insolvent debtor and her or his creditors whereby the creditors are to be paid less than the amount of their individual claims.

Compromise. The settlement of a claim by mutual concessions.

Conditional sale. A sale of personal property containing conditions determining the passing of title and the right to possession.

Discharge. To release from further obligation, as in the discharge of a bankrupt by court order.

Factor. An agent employed by a principal to sell, on a commission basis, merchandise delivered to the agent.

Insolvency. In bankruptcy, proof that a debtor's liabilities exceed his or her total assets.

Involuntary bankruptcy. Bankruptcy petitioned by a group of creditors who act together against a common debtor who is known to be insolvent.

Lien. The right of a creditor against specific property that is named as security for a debt.

National Bankruptcy Act. A federal law regulating bankruptcy and bankruptcy proceedings; under the jurisdiction of the U.S. District Courts.

Perfection. A means of giving protection to the secured party; assures the secured party of priority of claims over others; perfection may be made by taking possession of debtor's property or by filing proper forms in a designated public office.

Referee. A person appointed by a court to hear and decide on a disputed matter.

Security interest. Under the U.C.C., any transaction intended to create a security interest in personal property or fixtures, including goods, documents, instruments, general intangibles, chattel paper, or accounts.

Trustee. A person who holds the legal title to property and who employs it for the benefit of another.

Voluntary bankruptcy. Bankruptcy permitted on petition of the bankrupt.

Examination IV

Property, Secured Transactions

1. Donaldson contracted to purchase "a lot, house, garage, and other real property" located at 2923 Waverly Road, Greensboro. After settlement, Donaldson made an inspection of the property and discovered that the seller had removed shelves from the basement, a doorbell consisting of an expensive installation of Westminster chimes, and a recently planted fruit tree. Donaldson demanded that the seller return these items to the property. Will Donaldson succeed?

   Yes. All of the items removed had been installed as permanent fixtures to the real property. Each item would have been personal property only before installation. A doorbell (of whatever kind), shelves built into the house, and a tree planted on the grounds all denote an intent of permanence. Without any strong argument to overcome these presumptions of permanence, Donaldson will succeed in his demand for the return of his own real property.

2. Freedman rented an apartment for ten months through an oral agreement with the rental manager of Mt. Devon Realty. After only six months occupancy, Freedman became dissatisfied with the location. She informed the manager of her intention to move, basing her right to do so on the absence of any written lease. May the landlord demand rental payments for the full term of the oral agreement?

   Yes. The statute of frauds requires a written agreement for the sale of any interest in real property except in the case of leases for periods of less than one year. Freedman was bound by the oral lease for ten months.

3. Holliday's neighbors used a path across the rear of his five-acre estate. (The path was a convenient shortcut to the local commuter bus station.) Holliday was aware of the neighbors' use of his land, although he had never expressed a willingness to permit such use. After more than twenty years, Holliday began construction of a fence around his entire property. Does he have the right to block access to the long-used path that runs across his property?

   No. Holliday's neighbors have developed an easement over the property through adverse use. They have the right to demand that Holliday provide gates for them in the fence and allow them continued use of an equitable right that is superior to Holliday's legal right of ownership. (If the neighbors did not complain and demand continuance of their right, however, their failure to act would serve as proof of their abandonment of the easement in the future.)

4. Grover wrote a formal will in 1952. It was properly witnessed and signed and in every way satisfied state laws regulating the preparation of wills. Grover's family responsibilities were drastically changed over the next twenty-five years. In 1977, he wrote another will and placed it in his safe-deposit box. He did not remove or destroy the previous will, nor did he explicitly revoke it. Following Grover's death, would-be heirs under the first will complained of their disinheritance under the second will. Will the objections of these claimants receive the consideration of the probate court?

   Yes. When two satisfactory wills are presented for probate, the court will adopt the first will, according to the dates on the two instruments. Had Grover destroyed the first will, his intentions would have been unquestionably clear, and the second will would have been the one that was followed. Unless the second will contained a statement declaring all previous wills to be invalid (as permitted by some states), the first will would have superior right over the second.

5. In a common-law state, Zellman married a young woman whom he had known for several years. During the years of their marriage, he acquired several parcels of real property, the deeds of which showed him to be the sole owner. Would Mrs. Zellman have any vested rights in these properties owned by her husband?

Yes. A wife in a common-law state has a dower right in the real property of her husband. A dower right is equal to a one-third interest unless changed by state statute. Before Zellman could transfer title to any of his properties, Mrs. Zellman would be required to give a quitclaim or release to her dower right. Unless such a release is willingly given, the new owner would have to respect Mrs. Zellman's continued dower right in the properties formerly owned by her husband.

6. Quillan purchased farm machinery from White Brothers Supply. He paid $5,000 at the time of delivery and signed a security agreement for the unpaid balance of $15,500. The security agreement listed the machinery and other personal property belonging to Quillan as collateral for the unpaid debt. The office manager at White Brothers placed the agreement in the office safe. Quillan defaulted on the debt payments, and the seller sought to take back the machinery and secure other collateral listed in the agreement. Much of the collateral had been sold to other parties or pledged as collateral in other security agreements. These other pledges had been filed, with a financing statement, in a proper public office. Does White Brothers have a superior claim to the collateral over these others, who now claim title on a security interest?

No. Failure to file the security agreement and financing statement with a public office designated by state law has restricted White Brothers' right to the collateral. Creditors who filed such required documents in the public office have rights superior to those of White Brothers. Innocent purchasers of part of the collateral also have a better right to the property than do White Brothers, who failed to give notice to innocent third parties of the existence of any security agreements with Quillan.

7. Sears rented a building from Henderson Brothers. Included in the lease was the right to operate a machine shop on the premises. Concurrent with accepting the lease, Sears applied for fire insurance on the building. The insurance was issued. Sears later filed a claim of $960 to cover a fire loss under the policy. The insurer refused payment, stating that Sears did not have an insurable interest in the property. Will Sears collect?

Yes. Sears *did* have an insurable interest in the property. As a tenant, he is responsible for repairs to the rented premises. Sears, as a tenant, has the obligation to return the building to its owner in the same condition in which it was delivered to him, less reasonable wear and tear. He therefore accepted a lease which represented a financial obligation and created an insurable interest.

8. With her own private funds, Mrs. DuVall purchased several houses as a real estate investment. She died intestate and was survived by her husband and two children. Does the husband have any rights in this property (1) in a common-law state? (2) In a community-property state?

(1) Yes. In a common-law state, Mr. DuVall would establish curtesy rights in the real property possessed by the spouse. This right is for the husband's lifetime and depends on the fact that children had been born of the marriage. At the husband's death, the property would descend to the surviving children. (2) Yes. In community-property states, property held by each spouse entitles the other spouse to a one-half interest if the property was acquired after their marriage. This is not, as with curtesy right, a right for one's lifetime; it is an unconditional right.

9. Mallory, Inc., anticipated financial difficulties and insolvency. One month prior to involuntary bankruptcy petitions by its creditors, the firm paid off in full three creditors that the firm had favored for many years. Did this constitute an act of bankruptcy?

Yes. Acts that in some way defraud any of the firm's creditors are acts of bankruptcy. Selecting preferred creditors for payment at the expense of other creditors is one of many acts of bankruptcy.

10. Archino purchased a valuable piece of land adjacent to the Atlantic Ocean. The property was in the resort town of Bethany Beach. Prior to the summer season, he parked a mobile home on the lot, erected a six-foot board fence around all but the beachfront, and installed a high-powered amplification system with outdoor speakers. On this system, he played loud and offensive music from early evening to early morning. Is Archino permitted to enjoy his land without restrictions or consideration of the rights of others?

No. A man's house *is not* his castle. Archino would no doubt be restricted in many ways. Zoning restrictions in the area of his property would probably restrict the parking of a mobile home on the lot. The high board fence would, in most localities, be against local statutes that protect the rights of others to an unobstructed view of the ocean at a seaside resort. Playing the offensive music at all hours, to the discomfort and annoyance of other persons, would soon be declared a private or public nuisance or bring about Archino's summary arrest on a charge of disturbing the peace, a misdemeanor.

Comprehensive Examination

Each of the following cases calls into question more than one legal principle on which the decision may rest. Review the principles that in your judgment relate to the case. Then, on the basis of your evaluation of the facts submitted, determine the rights and obligations of the parties involved.

1. Thornton Radio Stores advertised a portable radio that was priced at \$140 during a special sale period. Danby entered the store and requested one of the sets, tendering the money. Thornton Radio would not accept the money. Instead, a salesman showed Danby another set, which was available for \$229. The salesman told Danby that this set was more powerful than the other and that it had a greater range of both transmission and reception. He also stated that the \$229 set contained more transistors, had a larger speaker unit, and an unbreakable case. Danby agreed to buy the \$229 set. He later learned that much of what the salesman had said was false. Danby tried to return the set, but Thornton Radio refused to discuss the matter. The store argued that without a written agreement, Danby had no legal grounds for a complaint. What will be the outcome of this matter?

Without regard to statutes regulating advertising, the advertisement of the \$140 radio does *not* qualify as an offer to any individual, including Danby. It is merely an invitation to trade. Keeping the argument to strict contract law, Danby's act of tendering the \$140 amounted to an offer which Thornton Radio could therefore either accept or reject. It could be concluded, however, that the Thornton salesman did make false statements on which Danby relied in making his purchase. Thornton's salesman had superior knowledge of the merchandise, and it would probably be assumed that he knowingly took advantage of Danby. This amounted to fraud, which could be the basis for a suit for damages and the return of Danby's \$229. Thornton's argument concerning the necessity of having a written contract is without legal basis. Had the price of the purchased set exceeded \$500, and had no money or merchandise passed between the parties, Thornton's argument might have been valid. Here, however, it has no validity whatsoever. Danby, in an action on the contract, would have his money returned. He could also demand damages for any losses he experienced because of the misrepresentations of Thornton's salesman.

2. The Minneapolis Grain Company sold Western Bakeries 10,000 bushels of wheat. This wheat was stored with other wheat in Elevator 1289, located near a siding on the C.B.Q. Railroad. An elevator receipt containing this information was issued to Western. No written agreement was signed by the parties. A fire caused by lightning destroyed Elevator 1289 and its contents. Minneapolis Grain demanded full payment for the wheat. Western refused to pay. A suit was brought against Western Bakeries for the entire purchase price. What principles are involved in this case, and what do you think was the decision?

First, to whom did the wheat belong at the time of the fire? Cereal grains are fungible goods; they do not need to be separated from the property of others to effect passing of title. Although the elevator held wheat belonging to others, the issuance of the elevator receipt to Western Bakeries was sufficient to pass title to the 10,000 bushels. There were no other conditions of sale that required further action on the part of the seller, who had done all that a seller is required to do. At this point, the only obligation to be fulfilled to complete the agreement would have been payment by the buyer. The buyer had the right of possession at any time it desired. No conditions stood in the way of the passing of title to Western. Usually one would expect a written agreement for the sale of goods valued at more than \$500 (by the statute of frauds). This is not necessary, however, when there has been either full or partial delivery of goods or when a partial payment has been made. In this case, there had been a complete delivery of the 10,000 bushels of wheat in question. Western bakeries is therefore liable to the seller for the full purchase price of the wheat, plus any fees owed for storage of the wheat in the elevator.

3. Rybicki, who was divorced, made alimony payments of $250 per month to his former wife. Rybicki contacted his insurance broker and applied for a $10,000 policy on his former wife's life. Rybicki gave the broker a check in an amount that covered the first six-month premium. The broker issued a binder slip, stating that Rybicki's former wife was fully covered as of that moment. Before Rybicki received a policy, his wife was killed in an accident. Rybicki entered a claim for the $10,000. Is this claim valid? Also, explain the legal principles related to this case.

Initially, Rybicki did *not* have an insurable interest in his former wife's life. He would suffer no loss through her death because he depended on her for nothing. Any policy issued could be declared invalid for this reason alone. If anything, Rybicki stood to gain by the woman's death because alimony payments would cease. Furthermore, Rybicki was issued a binder, but the insurance broker was not an *agent* of the insurer and had no power to issue the binder on his own. (Only the insurance company or one of its *agents* can accept such a risk.) The claim will not be allowed. Rybicki will receive only a refund of the premium he paid to the broker.

4. Heatherton, the daughter of wealthy parents, was a minor and still lived at home. She purchased an expensive fall suit at Society Hill Clothes. She made the purchase in her own name and on her own charge account for $285. When the bill arrived, she returned the suit to the shop on her rights as a minor. The store announced its decision to enforce payment of the $285. What principles of law are involved in this case? What are the rights of the parties?

(1) A minor's contracts are not enforceable except in those instances where the minor has contracted for what would be termed a necessary. Necessaries differ according to one's social position, economic status, and evidence of need. (2) Did the young woman already have a fall suit? Was it in keeping with what would be expected of her according to the social demands of her wealthy family? (3) If the store accepted the return of the suit, could Heatherton be charged a reasonable amount for the use of the suit for the one week during which she had it? (4) In buying the suit, did the daughter act as an agent for her parents and thus make them responsible if she did not pay the $285? These are questions stemming from principles surrounding the minor's contract. Under ordinary circumstances (if she was the daughter of parents of modest income), Heatherton could disclaim responsibility without argument. The question might be answered differently for the daughter of wealthy parents, especially one still living under the roof of parents who have no doubt approved previous purchases and paid for them when the minor failed to do so.

5. Starling gave his personal check, which was written on the Traders' Trust Bank, to Henley Stores. The check, for $25, was in payment of a tennis racket. Starling wrote in the figures in such a way as to make it quite easy for the holder to increase the amount without detection, and the holder did increase the amount to $425. A not-so-neat job was done in changing the amount that was written in words. The alteration left distinctive smears and erasure smudges. A bank teller honored the check by paying the holder $425. Does Starling have any rights against the bank?

A paying bank is not responsible for alterations when such alterations are made possible by the drawer's own gross negligence in writing the check. A bank is liable for any overpayment of an altered instrument, however, when one would suspect alterations after ordinary examination of the instrument. An experienced teller would have immediately recognized the effects of the alteration in the written words as they appeared on Starling's check. The teller had a warning that should have made him or her suspicious. The teller, as an agent of the bank, made the bank liable for Starling's loss, which could have been prevented. The bank would be obligated to reimburse Starling's account in the amount of $400.

6. Parker rented a car from Drive-It-Yourself, Inc. He agreed to the usual requirements, promising to return the car in reasonably the same condition as it was delivered to him. He made a security deposit of $100, which protected the bailor from any damages to the vehicle. While driving through a parking lot, Parker hit the brakes to avoid striking a light standard. The brakes did not work, and the front right fender was damaged. Drive-It-Yourself, Inc., refused to return Parker's $100 deposit, claiming that the damaged fender would cost that much to repair and repaint. Parker questions the right of the bailor to retain his deposit.

Parker had accepted the added responsibility of being an insurer of the bailor's car. Without that promise, Parker would have been free of liability unless it were shown that he had been negligent with the automobile. However, a bailor has the responsibility of providing the bailee with a safe chattel. This, apparently, was not the case, as the defective braking system so well demonstrated. The accident and damage resulted from the failure of the brake system and the bailor's ineptness and negligence in keeping the car in good repair. If a jury accepted his argument and testimony about the cause of the accident, Parker would be reimbursed.

7. Bailey Brothers, machinists, did extensive work for the Acme Manufacturing Company. They installed and tested machine tools in Acme's new factory. Acme owed Bailey $18,000 for services and materials. To secure the debt, a security agreement was prepared. It listed small but very valuable testing equipment as collateral for the debt. The collateral was delivered to Bailey Brothers and kept in their guarded warehouse. Acme later listed the same equipment in another security agreement it gave to another creditor. This agreement was filed in a proper office, as designated by state law. Both creditors later claimed the same collateral on Acme's failure to make promised payments. What are the rights of the two creditors?

A creditor may perfect a security agreement in one of two ways: (1) by taking actual possession of collateral named in the agreement; or (2) by filing the agreement and a financing statement in a public office designated for that purpose. Bailey Brothers and the other creditor had both acted properly in perfecting their respective security agreements. Bailey Brothers, however, had priority in their claim because they entered into an agreement earlier and took possession of the collateral before the date of the second creditor's filing.

8. Hobart, who lived in a common-law state, left a will in which he provided his widow with a lump-sum settlement of $5,000. The $5,000, the will stated, was given "in lieu of dower." Hobart died leaving more than $150,000 in real estate in his own name. He had purchased the property during his married years. What are the rights of the surviving spouse under the will and through her marriage to Hobart?

Mrs. Hobart, if she accepted the $5,000, would give up her dower right in the real property owned by her husband at the time of his death. If she demanded her one-third dower right in the property that had been owned by him, she would not be entitled to the cash bequest of $5,000. Obviously, Mrs. Hobart would be advised to turn down the $5,000 and demand her dower right.

9. Public-spirited citizens banded together to organize what was to become the new Crandell College. They discussed what type of organization should be created in the formation of the new institution. It could not operate as a sole proprietorship or a partnership; neither was it the wish of the organizers to form a corporation and sell stock. What type of business organization would give the new college the power to get started, to gather funds, borrow money, and fulfill its purpose as an educational institution?

The organizers would petition the secretary of state for a charter as a nonprofit corporation. No stock would be issued or sold, and no profits would be generated for the benefit of stockholders. In all other respects, the college would be an operating entity, with its powers set forth in its corporate charter.

10. The manager of the Appliance Sales Stores sought ways of increasing profits through demonstration sales in buyers' homes. Discussions were held as to the type of sales agreement that would best serve the firm and protect it from losses. The advantages of a sale-on-approval sales agreement were presented by one party. Others favored the sale-or-return contract. Which would best fit the purposes of Appliance Sales?

A sale-on-approval agreement assures the seller that title would not pass to the buyer until such time as the buyer expressed satisfaction with the merchandise delivered. This leaves the seller with the responsibilities of ownership of goods in the buyer's possession. The sale-or-return agreement would pass title to the buyer on delivery, with the buyer having the right to return merchandise. The buyer would have both title and possession, with all responsibilities thereto. A better solution would be the sale-on-approval agreement with the added obligation of returning the seller's goods in the same condition as they were received. Thus the buyer, while not having title, would have all of the responsibilities of someone who did have title. This would best fit the needs of Appliance Sales Stores.

11. Taney, in exchange for a loan of $500 from the Security Loan Company, signed the following note, which was accepted by Security's note clerk: "Thirty days from date I promise to pay to Security Loan Company $500, with interest at 8 percent. Signed, Henry Taney, February 16, 19—." The manager of Security Loan criticized the loan clerk, stating that the amount of the loan should have been written out in words as well as being expressed in figures. Would that have qualified the instrument as a negotiable promissory note?

The Uniform Commercial Code does not require that the amount of an instrument be expressed both in figures and in words. This is a custom of the market place that removes uncertainties as to the face amount of a note, but is not legally required. The note was not negotiable, however, due to another reason: it did not contain the words of negotiability, *to the order of* or *to the bearer*. Although not negotiable, the instrument still remains a valid and enforceable contract between Taney and Security Loan; and, although it may not be negotiated, it may be transferred by assignment.

12. Kappa Omega Phi social fraternity engaged the Wailers to furnish music at a dance scheduled for December 14. Contracts were signed with the group, the dance was advertised, and tickets were sold. Other opportunities came up for the Wailers, so they delegated the job to another well-known group after a conversation between the two band managers. The fraternity registered a complaint with the Wailers and refused to accept this new arrangement. Discuss the rights of the parties.

Contracts may usually be assigned. However, the delegation of duties by those who contracted to perform services of a professional or artistic nature may not be made. The Wailers were hired because of their particular style. Another group, although competent, could not possibly duplicate the music of the Wailers. Thus the assignment of the job to the other band would be unsatisfactory and would result in a breach of the original agreement. In addition, the *assignment* (even though it was not legal) should have been in writing, considering the written contract between Kappa Omega Phi and the Wailers, because of the equal-dignities rule.

13. Katz was one of four partners engaged in a real estate venture known as Hi-Point Developers. Thousands of dollars had been spent in the development of the firm's public image. While the other partners were attending a regional real estate convention, Katz entered into a contract with a third party to sell the name and goodwill of the partnership for $150,000. On their return, the other partners started proceedings to block the sale. Did the one partner in this case have the power to act as an agent for the other partners in selling the partnership's name and goodwill?

In the usual course of a partnership business, each partner may act as an agent for the other partners in dealings with third parties. Although such representation may be restricted by provisions of the articles of copartnership, the restrictions do not affect third parties unless they have been made aware of such restrictions. An exception to the above is the lack of authority of any partner, without being joined by all partners, to sell the name and goodwill of the partnership. Thus, Katz's agreement with the third-party buyer will be set aside and not enforced against the partnership.

14. Appleton purchased a five-acre tract and the buildings thereon from Ballenberg. A title search and an engineering survey supported the information contained in the owner's deed and confirmed his right to sell the property with good title. After taking possession, Appleton discovered that there were easements on the property that favored adjoining property owners. Appleton sought to bar these persons from entering his property. He also complained of a faulty deed that did not include information on these easement rights. What are Appleton's rights in this case?

Easement rights may be developed through adverse use, rather than through permission granted and shown in a deed. Easement rights are equitable rights, not legal rights, when they are created by adverse use. Unless ordered to be added to the deed by petition of the ones benefitted by the easements, they would not show up in the title search. Appleton may not terminate the easements except by agreement with the parties who benefiit. (He may try to purchase back these easement rights.) Furthermore, it is very doubtful that Appleton would have any actionable complaint against those who made the title search.

15. Schaefer found an envelope containing $2,000 in cash while he was walking through a residential section of his town. The envelope contained no markings that permitted the identification of the owner. Schaefer pocketed the money, took it home, and watched the lost-and-found column in the local paper, hoping to learn of the real owner. After six weeks of patient waiting without success, he decided that the money belonged to him by virtue of the long-accepted layman's rule of "finders keepers." What rights and obligations did Schaefer have in this matter?

There is no legal authority that supports the old adage "finders keepers." Schaefer would be required to make an effort to find the owner of the money. It is not enough to stand by and wait. Secreting the money to one's own benefit may be classified as an act of larceny or embezzlement. A finder is actually a bailee of another's property, with an obligation of giving care. Schaefer is not the owner of the lost money. Furthermore, he did not carry out his duties to seek out the owner by public advertising or other inquiry. (Even in states that permit a finder to claim title to property after six months or one year, the finder must show that an honest effort was made to locate the real owner during that period of time.)

16. Sheer assisted a neighbor in building a small shed on the rear of her property. Sheer did the work without expectation of reward. It required several weekends of hard work. When they were finished, the neighbor said to Sheer, "Would you be willing to take $100 in consideration of all the time spent on this job?" Sheer immediately accepted the offer. Sheer was never paid, so finally he sought collection of the $100 through legal action. Discuss this transaction and the rights of the parties.

It appears that Sheer and the neighbor entered into a binding agreement: there was an offer and acceptance, both parties were competent to contract, the agreement was concerned with valid subject matter, and there was no indication of fraud, duress, undue influence, or any other element that would defeat the agreement. Furthermore, consideration of $100 was agreed to by the parties. The consideration, however, was not anticipated when the initial agreement of giving service was made. Such past consideration does not support or create an enforceable contract. Sheer would fail in any attempt to force payment of the $100.

17. Tobin bought a diamond ring from an acquaintance for $1,700 and gave it to his fiancée. She was later ordered to give up the ring to detectives, who claimed that it was stolen property. Tobin sought a return of the $1,700. The seller claimed that he did not know the ring was stolen and that he paid $1,500 for it himself. He also claimed that he had guaranteed the ring to be genuine but had never guaranteed its title. Does Tobin have any rights against the seller?

A good contract was made between Tobin and the other party. There was no proof of fraud or dishonesty on the part of the seller, and all elements of a valid agreement were present. The seller, however, denies any guarantee of the title. The law, on the other hand, imposes three implied warranties upon all sellers. A seller always warrants that: (1) he or she has good title to the goods, (2) he or she has the right to sell the goods; and (3) the buyer will not be interrupted in enjoyment of the goods. On the grounds of these three implied warranties, all of which were breached by the seller, Tobin will recover his $1,700. Only the true owner has any rights to the ring itself.

18. Teis sold a house and lot to Lamond. After settlement and exchange of the purchase price, Lamond's attorney took possession of the new deed, which was to be recorded in the county recorder's office. The recording of the deed was delayed for several weeks because of the attorney's negligence. In the meantime, Teis, who was aware of the delay, sold the same property to Helman. Helman's attorney made a title search and recorded Helman's deed shortly after settlement was completed. Lamond discovered this second sale and sought to have Helman's deed declared invalid. Discuss the rights of all parties in this case.

Obviously Teis was a wrongdoer because he was responsible for the two sales. Helman was an innocent purchaser of the property. Neither Helman nor his attorney had any means of knowing that the property had been sold to another. Both Lamond and Helman had performed their responsibilities as required by law, without knowledge of the other's involvement. Lamond's attorney, however, is guilty of negligence in not having the Lamond deed recorded at once, or at least within a day or two. Helman's attorney discovered nothing wrong with Teis's recorded proof of ownership in the county office. Helman's deed was the first one recorded, and he is the rightful owner of the property. Lamond has the right of action against both Teis (for fraud) and his own attorney (for negligence).

19. Stern's brand new car, with only 389 miles showing on the odometer, was wrecked when it was hit by a truck at a busy intersection. Stern was in no way responsible for the accident. Stern entered a claim, asking that the insurer replace the wrecked car with another new one that cost $5,800. The insurance appraiser secured estimates for repairing Stern's wrecked car. This could be done for $3,250. Stern was emphatic in his demand for a new car to replace the wrecked one. Will Stern succeed?

The insurer has the option of either replacing or repairing. It is clear that it will be to the insurer's advantage to have Stern's car returned to its original condition rather than to present him with a replacement. Stern will not have the satisfaction of receiving a new car.

20. Hopkins received in the mail recordings and tapes that she had not ordered. Included with this merchandise was a letter that stated that unless the goods were returned within ten days, the seller would assume that Hopkins had accepted them. The letter also urged Hopkins to send in a check or money order for $12.50. Will Hopkins be liable to the offeror if she delays in responding to this offer?

An offeror may not impose silence as a means of acceptance unless the offeree has previously agreed to such a condition. Hopkins has no obligation to act in any way whatsoever. (She is not obligated to return the merchandise, to send the $12.50, or to mail back the package.)

21. Sparkman, an Olympic weight-lifter, was elected to the board of directors of a corporation that specialized in the manufacture, design, and sale of exercise equipment that was popular with coaches and amateur athletes. Sparkman was a minor and he had no stock in the corporation. A stockholders' suit was brought to have him removed for those two reasons. May Sparkman continue as a member of the board?

The bylaws of a corporation at times define the qualifications that must be met by those who are candidates for election to the board of directors. In the absence of specific requirements, the law permits persons who are minors and those holding no stock in the firm to serve as directors. There is no legal reason why Sparkman may not continue as a board member.

22. A local telephone company erected poles on each side of Hudson's property and strung wires between them. The wires crossed Hudson's yard at a height of thirty feet. Hudson had not given permission for the company to do so. He demanded that the wires be removed from above his property. Does he have this right?

The owner of real property has both air rights and subterranean rights. Air rights extend to a point above the surface over which the owner has reasonable control. This is usually to the height of the highest structure on the property and a reasonable distance above. The telephone company has trespassed into Hudson's property and may be required to remove the unwanted wires. However, quasi-public corporations that serve the public may be granted the right of eminent domain. They are granted this right in cases where, for the public good, it becomes necessary to cross over or go beneath privately owned property. These powers stem from both the common law and local statutes. Thus, Hudson might be required to permit the wires to remain if their use is deemed necessary to the public good.

23. Reitz, who was married and the father of three children, failed to provide food and clothing for his family. Mrs. Reitz visited stores in which her husband had charge accounts. She purchased food and clothing for herself and her children and charged the purchases to her husband's accounts. Among the clothing purchased was an expensive sportswear outfit that Mrs. Reitz selected for herself. Must the husband pay for these purchases? Is the wife the agent of the husband in all matters related to the household?

A wife is the implied agent of her husband in carrying out those duties which are deemed necessary in the maintenance of the health and welfare of the family. This right does not exist when the husband has provided these things himself. The husband, Reitz, is liable for the purchases of necessary food and clothing billed to him. Whether or not the expensive outfit purchased by Mrs. Reitz would qualify as a necessary is another matter. If it was not a necessary, the husband will be excused from paying for it.

24. Collector's Antiques agreed to sell Hawkins an eighteenth-century grandfather clock for $6,100. Hawkins gave his check for $1,000 and received a receipt with the following notation, signed by the seller: "Delivery to be made on August 15, on receipt of balance of $5,100 from Hawkins." Hawkins tendered the balance on August 15, but the seller stated that he had changed his mind and attempted to return the $1,000 already paid. What are Hawkins's rights and options?

The buyer may elect either to sue Collector's Antiques on the contract or to seek a decree of specific performance from a court of equity. Hawkins's decision will depend on whether a judgment in damages for breach or the acquisition of the clock would be more important and satisfying. Clearly, Collector's Antiques will have no real defense to either action by Hawkins.

25. Sullivan selected and bought a used motorcycle from Ambler Cycle Sales. The salesman suggested that Sullivan take the machine out for a run before making up his mind. Sullivan replied, "If you think it is a good deal, that's enough for me." He did not note that oil was dripping from the motor and that the front tire showed excessive wear. Sullivan later returned to the company and complained of the purchase. He then demanded either full reimbursement or the repair of the cycle. Does Sullivan have justifiable grounds for a legal complaint?

The seller made no attempt to take advantage of Sullivan. Sullivan elected not to make an inspection or take a trial run on the motorcycle he selected. The seller would be able to defend his position under the doctrine of *caveat emptor*. A buyer has a responsibility to inspect the merchandise purchased when the opportunity is given. Ambler Cycle concealed nothing from Sullivan. Ordinary examination or a trial run would have clearly disclosed the defects to most buyers.

INDEX

Catalog

If you are interested in a list of SCHAUM'S OUTLINE SERIES send your name and address, requesting your free catalog, to:

SCHAUM'S OUTLINE SERIES, Dept. C
McGRAW-HILL BOOK COMPANY
1221 Avenue of Americas
New York, N.Y. 10020